THE LIFE AND TIMES OF
HANNAH CRAFTS

ALSO BY GREGG HECIMOVICH

Hardy's Tess of the D'Urbervilles: A Reader's Guide

Austen's Emma: A Reader's Guide

Puzzling the Reader: Riddles in Nineteenth-Century British Literature

THE LIFE AND TIMES OF HANNAH CRAFTS

THE TRUE STORY OF THE BONDWOMAN'S NARRATIVE

GREGG HECIMOVICH

ecco
An Imprint of HarperCollins*Publishers*

 For information, address HarperCollins Publishers, 195 Broadway, New York, NY 10007.

HarperCollins books may be purchased for educational, business, or sales promotional use. For information, please email the Special Markets Department at SPsales@harpercollins.com.

A hardcover edition of this book was published in 2023 by Ecco, an imprint of HarperCollins Publishers.

FIRST ECCO PAPERBACK EDITION PUBLISHED 2024

Library of Congress Cataloging-in-Publication Data has been applied for.

ISBN 978-0-06-233474-9 (pbk.)

24 25 26 27 28 LBC 5 4 3 2 1

For the descendant communities of Bertie County and Hertford County, North Carolina, who preserved the stories of women like Hannah Crafts for future generations.

Autobiographies display the triumph of experience, but novels are acts of hope.

—HILARY MANTEL, "The Shape of Absence,"
London Review of Books (August 8, 2002)

CONTENTS

FOREWORD

THE LIFE AND TIMES OF *THE BONDWOMAN'S NARRATIVE*

> Towards noon the clouds blew off, and the sun came out. The young leaves whispered and talked, the birds sang, and the winds laughed among the trees. There was mirth and music around us; there was youth, and love, and joy for all things, but our troubled hearts.
>
> —HANNAH CRAFTS

SO WROTE THE FIRST KNOWN AFRICAN American female novelist in a passage describing her initial attempt to escape bondage, attributed to her self-named protagonist, Hannah. The passage captures at once the optimism, love of nature, and even joy that suffuse her novel and her life, too. For Hannah Crafts, "troubled hearts" will beat against their confinement, but every natural fiber will still reach for freedom. The passage also demonstrates the author's generous, self-taught compositional style, just as the title she chose for her manuscript demonstrates her wit: for as Gregg Hecimovich reveals, the author cleverly placed the secret to this young female author's identity right before her readers' eyes, embedded in a pun in her novel's title: for much of her life, it would seem, Hannah Crafts's slave name was "Hannah Bond," and she, no doubt, had been frequently referred to, in the manner common to plantation slavery, as "the Bonds' woman" before she escaped her enslavement by fleeing to the North shortly after her thirtieth birthday. All along, then, the title of her book was a clever pun, a veiled and cloaked clue to her hidden identity left in plain view for a century and a half for any of her potential readers to see.

As Gregg Hecimovich's biography now establishes, Hannah Crafts began life in 1826 in Bertie County, North Carolina, the mixed-race daughter of her first captor, Lewis Bond, and her enslaved mother, identified only as Hannah Sr. in slave inventories. Crafts shared with her contemporaries Harriet Jacobs, Frederick Douglass, and William Wells Brown both the paternity of her enslaver and the boldness to use her proximity to the household to steal the forbidden fruit of literacy. And steal this fruit she did, to an extent so very sophisticated as to arise in skeptics doubts that an unschooled, untrained enslaved Black female in the middle of the nineteenth century could possibly have penned such a sophisticated novel, one clothed in prose as compelling as the narrative style of her fugitive slave contemporary Frederick Douglass.

I first engaged Crafts's story obliquely through my many conversations with my old friend Dorothy Porter Wesley, the world-renowned librarian, archivist, and bibliographer. After I authenticated the identity of Harriet E. Wilson and published Wilson's novel, *Our Nig* (1859), the earliest novel to later appear in print by a Black woman, Dorothy liked to tease me. "It won't even be close!" she playfully taunted, referring to a work she claimed to have in her possession. She told me that the work she held was rarer and even more valuable than *Our Nig*, but that she had not completed her research on it.

I thought she was signifying, to tell you the truth. But after she mentioned this lost treasure several times, after her teasing had itself become a leitmotif during our visits, I began to wonder to what lost masterpiece she could be referring. When Dorothy's daughter, Coni, settled her mother's estate, she arranged to sell some of her papers at auction. I discovered this fact when I received the Swann Auction Galleries catalogue in 2001. There it was: Lot 30, "Unpublished Original Manuscript." The item was listed as a "301-page handwritten manuscript purportedly written by a female fugitive slave." And most important, it came from the estate of Dorothy Porter Wesley.

In 2002, I published my authentication of this manuscript and its contextual history with the first edition of the novel. There, my work identified Hannah Crafts as the likely former slave of the North Carolina politician John Hill Wheeler and his wife, Ellen Sully Wheeler. Through contextual clues and archival work, I also placed the likely composition dates between 1853 and 1861. After I completed my own efforts researching the manuscript, I donated it to the Beinecke Library, located at my undergraduate alma mater, Yale University, where the work is preserved and available for further scholarship.

Naturally, there were details that I got wrong twenty years ago. For instance, I misidentified the plantation where Hannah Crafts was enslaved and from which she escaped. As Hecimovich discovered, Hannah Crafts escaped not from John Hill Wheeler's "Ellangowan" plantation on the banks of the Catawba River in Lincoln County, North Carolina, but instead from the Wheeler family plantation called Liberty Hall, near Murfreesboro, North Carolina.

It would take two decades of research by a doggedly determined and extremely gifted literary scholar to uncover Hannah Crafts's life story. Gregg Hecimovich has slowly pieced together the sources behind the manuscript. As Hecimovich acknowledges, he draws deeply on the research of a wide range of fellow scholars to make his discoveries. *The Life and Times of Hannah Crafts* is the fruit of this shared labor.

Hecimovich's biography opens with Hannah Crafts safe from her pursuers, at an obscure farmhouse in Central New York. Here, we observe Crafts edit the manuscript and disclose the precise name of her captors, the Wheeler family. Later, the work circles back to the details of the escape and the people and forces that helped shape the stories Crafts smuggled out of slavery.

Then Hecimovich unearths the intergenerational drama of the author's forebears. Purchased by the wealthy North Carolina planter Thomas Pugh Sr., the author's relatives were shipped from Jamaica to

Port Roanoke, Virginia, in 1779 and then marched in chains to Pugh Sr.'s expansive Indian Woods plantation. Here, these captives helped establish a plantation later called Willow Hall, the model for Lindendale in Crafts's novel. To build this property, Pugh Sr. swindled the Tuscarora Nation of nearly 42,000 acres while serving as a land agent for North Carolina. His personal gain was a plantation of over 1,000 acres in Indian Woods that later became the property of his son-in-law Lewis Bond. On this land, Crafts's family toiled. And yet, they also fought back. Hecimovich uncovers the story of James Barefoot, the author's great-uncle, who in 1802 helped plot an insurrection later called the Bertie County Conspiracy. Now long forgotten, the conspiracy helped shape Nat Turner's bloody revolt nearly three decades later in nearby Southampton County, Virginia.

The violence that suffuses the early chapters of Crafts's autobiographical narrative mirrors the violence that predated her birth and formed the circumstances of her childhood in Bertie County. As Hecimovich demonstrates, Crafts's enslaved community knew lynch violence intimately. The Bertie conspirators were hanged from the so-called Gospel Oaks, a well-known Indian Woods crossroads little more than a stone's throw from Crafts's slave cabin. And, as Hecimovich documents, after her sale to Jacob R. Pope, Crafts's grandmother Rosea Pugh was also hanged, on a nearby plantation. The signature scene of Crafts's novel depicts this death, which some critics felt to be too horrific to have actually occurred. In the novel, Sir Clifford De Vincent ties a female domestic slave named Rose to a tree and then, from his front porch, listens sedately to her slow asphyxiation. Hecimovich's early chapters recount the bloody struggles against slavery fought and, mostly, lost by the author's predecessors.

Hecimovich's narrative unfolds like a riveting detective story; accordingly, his *Life and Times* draws in the other enslaved women within Hannah Crafts's immediate circle. These are the women with whom the author served and grew up alongside, and they form a powerful backstory, too, to the narrative arc of Hannah Crafts's life. Milly and Martha Murfree, Mary Burton, Eliza Morgan, along with the well-known fugitive Jane Johnson—all shared the stories of their lives with the author of *The*

Bondwoman's Narrative, and Crafts used these stories to give force to her autobiographical protagonist's journey. The sharing of the recoverable lives of Crafts's "slave sisters" provides the biography with deeper insight both into the context of the author's life and into the sources of her art.

Hecimovich dives deep into extant property records to reconstruct the childhoods of Crafts, her family, and the cohort of domestic servants with whom they served. This work is signaled in the chapter "Property," where he uncovers twenty-eight fellow captives sold by the Wheeler family in 1836, even as the author lost her mother to a different kind of sale: Hannah Sr. was taken from her and given to her enslaver's daughter-in-law as a wedding gift. This forced the mother's separation from her ten-year-old child by thousands of miles. The estrangement Crafts experienced from this rupture, as Hecimovich demonstrates, marked the author more than any other loss in her life. In many ways, it seems reasonable to conclude that the novel Crafts wrote drew from her need to reconcile and compensate for this loss. It is no surprise that, at the end of her novel, the narrator and her mother are happily reunited in freedom, in an act of fictional wish fulfillment that the reality of slavery had rendered impossible.

In real life, Crafts's separation from her mother at the age of ten was part of the exploitative treatment many enslaved females suffered near adolescence. Carefully, Hecimovich documents the sexual manipulation and assault the author endured and how these proved formative to the shapes and themes of *The Bondwoman's Narrative*.

But, again, how did Hannah Crafts become a novelist? Here, Hecimovich expands on his careful recovery of Crafts's labor within the Wheeler household, where she assisted students who attended the adjacent women's college, Chowan Baptist Female Institute. Through truly ingenious archival effort, Hecimovich demonstrates parallels between the writing exercises practiced among the young women Crafts served and the author's prose. Most striking is the expansive use Crafts makes of Charles Dickens's novel *Bleak House* (1852–53), which the author adapted to help shape her novel even as she listened to student boarders recite the very passages she would rewrite, passages from excerpts that Frederick

Douglass, as it turns out, also serialized in his widely read newspaper. Borrowing liberally from the groundbreaking work of Hollis Robbins and a few others, Hecimovich demonstrates how Crafts inscribed herself within Dickens's text, reclaiming it both for herself and for the Black tradition. Or, as Hecimovich also puts it, "If the famous, enslaved, and self-taught Frederick Douglass (1818–1895) found in his treasured *Columbian Orator* a guiding star to develop his literary voice, for Crafts it seems to have been a dog-eared copy of Charles Dickens's *Bleak House* probably acquired from a student boarder."

Life illuminates art, and art illuminates life, and so it is with Hecimovich's biography. His work details Crafts's astute understanding of Harriet Beecher Stowe's *Uncle Tom's Cabin*, both for its power to reach the hearts of its readers and for its potential subversion to serve as blackface theatrical. Crafts's command of such literary works explains the surprising and ingenious intertextuality of her novel. But this brilliance also flummoxed readers who, two decades before, were not ready to accept Crafts's artistic sophistication. Hecimovich is unapologetic in recognizing the depth of the accomplishment of the author's work, aligning *The Bondwoman's Narrative* as a founding document—along with *Our Nig*, by Hannah Crafts's contemporary Harriet Wilson—that forms the foundation of the Black female tradition of the novel stretching forward to Toni Morrison and beyond.

The last third of *Life and Times* unspools evidence tracing the author's escape route to Craft Farm in Central New York. Here, we learn of the close friendship Crafts formed with fellow captives Eliza Morgan and Jane Johnson, whose contacts with the leading Underground leaders of Black Washington began in D.C.'s Black churches—like the First Colored Baptist Church, where Morgan, Johnson, and Crafts were all members.

Diligently, Hecimovich pieces together the escape route and the participants who helped the author make her way, first, to Craft Farm near McGrawville, New York, and, later, to Burlington, New Jersey, where she established her new life under her married name of "Hannah Vincent." Drawing from what Crafts shares in her autobiographical novel and what years of archival work uncovered, he helps note the extraordinary but mostly undocumented work of Black activists and their white supporters in freeing hundreds from bondage. At long last, Hecimovich's two decades of exhaustive research, personal interviews, and reconstructive genealogy have brought Hannah Bond Crafts back to us as fully as possible given the gaps in the archival record.

Hecimovich's conclusion that Crafts married in 1858 and took the name "Hannah Vincent" is convincing based on circumstantial evidence, a claim that matches my own conjectures in 2002. But although supported further by Hecimovich's work, even this new research is not yet ironclad. As he notes, until further records like birth, marriage, and death certificates can be unearthed, some aspects of this biography will remain necessarily speculative. Accordingly, I hope other scholars will take up the search as doggedly as Hecimovich has done.

The writer who called herself Hannah Crafts was, in fact, who she claimed to be: a formerly enslaved Black woman who somehow managed to transform the raw materials of her suffering in bondage into a novel whose authenticity can no longer be questioned. A century and a half after this young Black woman embarked on a most audacious goal of becoming a novelist, and two decades after I published the first edition of her handwritten and self-edited text, Hannah Crafts's life and work, for so very long lost, now are found.

—HENRY LOUIS GATES JR.

THE LIFE AND TIMES OF
HANNAH CRAFTS

INTRODUCTION

I

ON A SWELTERING DAY IN AUGUST 1857, a light-skinned woman arrived in the small town of McGrawville, New York. She had traced a route along the Tioughnioga Valley, where few slave catchers operated. Her hair was cropped short, and she wore men's clothing: a dark jacket, a vest, and trousers. A broad-brimmed hat lined with dust and sweat partially sheltered her face. She called at 19 West Academy Street, the "Farm House," on the grounds of New York Central College, where a caretaker took her travel case, a gentleman's valise, and ushered her out of the heat. At the back of the house, he opened a door to expose a hole in the wall. Five narrow steps led down a cool, dim tunnel. The root cellar, constructed with dry masonry and lined with heavy stones, stretched some fifty yards before opening onto Smith Creek. Crouched in semidarkness, smelling the baked earth above, the woman ate radishes and waited for her next move.[1]

After nightfall, the door opened, and boots appeared. A Black man stepped down, bringing food, water, and light. The two shared a meal by candlelight. Then he related the bad news: bounty hunters had picked up her trail. Her enslaver, John Hill Wheeler (1806–1882), was in New York City, personally directing the search for her return. The usual passage—through Auburn, Rochester, and then into Canada—was deemed unsafe. She would have to disappear into the countryside to wait out her pursuers. Conveyed in a wagon, she reached Horace Craft's farm just before midnight.[2]

Two days later, concealed in Craft's attic, she removed a manuscript from her valise. Her sweat mixed with ink as she returned her attention to her work. With a dash of her pen, she struck out the name she had been disguising as "Wh—r." She dipped her pen, drew up fresh ink, and took a risk: beside the marked-out passage, she wrote, "Wheeler" (MS 190). The ink still fresh on her quill, she backtracked through the manuscript. In every place where she had written "Wh—r," she returned and identified her enslavers (see Figure 1). "Their names are Wheeler" (MS 159), she wrote, darkening the missing letters over the dash so there would be no mistake: "Mrs. Wheeler informs . . ." (MS 159), "Mrs. Wheeler came . . ." (MS 184), "Mrs. Wheeler complained . . ." (MS 184), "Mrs. Wheeler sent for . . ." (MS 185). She refreshed her ink, touched her pen to her wipe, and continued revising the pages of her work.[3]

For an enslaved person, the fact that she could read and write was extraordinary. That she had escaped with a manuscript in her suitcase is astonishing. Hidden at Horace Craft's farmhouse, using materials smuggled to her from New York Central College, she continued work on the narrative she would complete months later in New Jersey. Only after she had finished the work did she include a title page: "The Bondwoman's Narrative by Hannah Crafts, a Fugitive Slave Recently Escaped from North Carolina." This is the closest she came to identifying herself. Like the

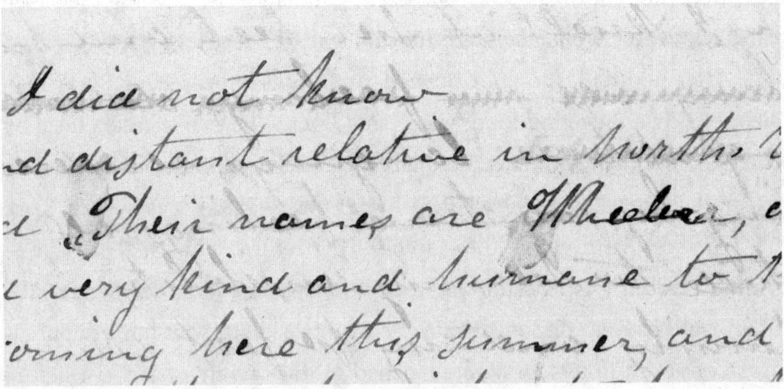
I did not know
distant relative in
"Their names are Wheeler,
very kind and humane to
here this summer, and

FIGURE 1: Detail of "The Bondwoman's Narrative," MS 159

first male novelist of African descent writing in the United States, William Wells Brown (c. 1814–1884), she adopted the name of the Quaker family who sheltered her: she called herself "Crafts."[4]

For nearly 150 years, this manuscript remained lost to history. Someone, probably the author, affixed hard covers to it with glue and cardboard and then stitched a homemade binding. If the pages were read by anyone beyond its author and the work's first collectors, no record exists of this. All that is known for certain of the work is that Emily Driscoll, an autograph and book dealer who kept a shop in New York City, acquired the manuscript in 1948 and listed it in her sales catalogue as "a fictionalized biography, written in an effusive style, purporting to be the story of the early life and escape of one Hannah Crafts, a mulatto." Driscoll also noted, "From internal evidence it is apparent that the work is that of a Negro who had a narrative gift. Interesting for its content and implications. Believed to be unpublished." In 1951, Driscoll sold the hand-bound papers to Dorothy Porter (1905–1995), a leading African American librarian and bibliophile, for eighty-five dollars. Driscoll told Porter that she had "bought it from a scout in the trade" and that all she had gathered of its prior history was "[the scout] came upon it in Jersey!" After some initial research, Porter typed a short note that was later appended to the work. It reads:

> The most important thing about this fictionalized personal narrative is that, from internal evidence, it appears to be the work of a Negro and the time of composition was before the Civil War in the late forties and fifties. There is no doubt that she was a Negro because her approach to other Negroes is that they are people first of all. Only as the story unfolds, in most instances, does it become apparent that they are Negroes.

The manuscript and note went into Porter's file drawer.[5]

The work and Porter's notes about it did not come to light again until 2001, when the celebrated scholar and historian Henry Louis Gates Jr.

purchased the manuscript at auction, authenticated it, and then published it in 2002 to great fanfare. *The Bondwoman's Narrative* appeared on the *New York Times*'s Best Sellers list in April of that year and sold nearly two hundred thousand copies. Almost overnight, Hannah Crafts had earned a rare literary celebrity. But while Gates was certain that the author's captor was John Hill Wheeler, he could not locate the mixed-race fugitive author who called herself Hannah Crafts.

Who was this extraordinary writer? Why did she tell her story as a novel that (mostly) hid her identity? And why did her story remain unpublished in her lifetime? Because of the lack of official records, it is not surprising that the life of the author has gone untold. The identities of the enslaved during the period when Hannah Crafts lived were obscured by a system that regarded captives as nonpersons, not worthy of distinct record keeping except as property. And even then, as property, the enslaved were uniformly anonymous. Commerce involving human chattel required no gathering and registering of information about captives as individuals. Federal census data, the only standardized documentation, limited a bondperson's "official" legal existence to age, race, gender, and number, with few other distinguishing identity markers.

In September 2013, after more than a decade of archival research and work among private papers, I identified the author. Hannah Crafts was Hannah Bond, born in the household of Lewis Bond (1788–1851) and Catherine Pugh Bond (1792–1828) in Bertie County, North Carolina, in 1826. Light-skinned and highly prized, the author—like the near-white "Hannah" in her novel—was brought up to be a house slave. In the spring of 1857, Bond escaped north with part of the manuscript hidden among her belongings. As the *New York Times* first reported in front-page coverage in 2013, I discovered the writer through faint traces preserved in diaries, account books, law cases, and probate and census records. By disclosing and piecing together new source materials, I uncovered not only primary documents revealing her life and times but also historical records giving voice to dozens of enslaved people intimately connected to her narrative.[6]

This book is a chronicle of my quest to bring to light the identity of the author and to reclaim the events upon which the autobiographical novel is based. The design is deliberately procedural. As in a detective story, you can always page forward to learn the specific details of Hannah Crafts's life, but to do so would be to miss the point. The writer chose to tell her life story as literary fiction, a move that was motivated by more than the need to shelter herself from the psychic trauma of her past. Like her male counterpart, novelist William Wells Brown, Hannah Crafts assumed a literary persona. As Hannah Crafts, she assembled stories of those she encountered in slavery: Milly and Martha Murfree, Mary Burton, Eliza Morgan, Kitty Bell, and Jane Johnson. Then, with great skill, she refined these stories and oral tales into a composite text that did justice to the fragmented experience of enslaved life as she understood it. Similar to Brown, who was "a many-handed, all-purpose collector of stories," Crafts reproduced the representative lives of her peers and mixed them into her personal saga.[7]

II

The clues to the writer's identity lie in the manuscript itself. Do thimble marks impressed on correction slips confirm that the writer is female? What can be made of stationer's embossments, the crestlike designs in the upper-left corner of the stationery sheets used to produce the manuscript? Do punctuation irregularities, handwriting style, and literary "thefts" from earlier authors point to an autodidact, someone who possessed the courage to steal literacy and learning? Or do these signal the work of a crafty abolitionist, or both? Is the direct mention of Wheeler's captive Jane Johnson a distinguishing clue? What about the reference to Clark Mills's equestrian statue of Andrew Jackson installed in Lafayette Square in Washington, D.C., on January 8, 1853? In this study, I weigh a wide range of forensic evidence and historical circumstance and pair these with authorial sources.

Milly and Martha Murfree's presence in locations given in the novel (Wheeler's plantation in Eastern North Carolina, the Wheelers' temporary residence in the District of Columbia, and even the household of Wheeler's relatives in rural Virginia) suggests that parts of the novel may be based on their lives. I first uncovered their names scribbled in the margins of John Hill Wheeler's almanac in a neglected file at the Library of Congress.[8] Or, perhaps Mary Burton served as a source for the author? I unearthed her presence by locating her deed of sale executed by Wheeler in the Lincoln County Courthouse in Lincolnton, North Carolina. On July 28, 1849, Wheeler sold Burton to former U.S. congressman James Graham for six hundred dollars, when she was sixteen, because Wheeler's second wife, Ellen, suspected Wheeler of having a sexual relationship with the captive. The strident critique of sexual predation that runs throughout *The Bondwoman's Narrative* may be partially inspired by Burton's experiences.[9]

Other evidence points to a collaboration between Eliza Morgan and Kitty Bell as joint authors. Morgan and Bell's stories align with what we know of the Wheeler household and of important details disclosed in the manuscript. The author's escape route follows a path first marked by Morgan and Bell a decade earlier. And Bell's experiences in Charles County, Virginia, match parts of the narrative.

Another theory, which many scholars believe, supports Jane Johnson as the author. On New Year's Day 1854, John Hill Wheeler purchased Johnson and her two children from Cornelius Crew near Richmond, Virginia, and Johnson appears as a character in Crafts's narrative. My research confirms her status as an inspirational model.[10]

To disclose the full story behind *The Bondwoman's Narrative*, I establish the case for authorship of the novel by telling the stories of Hannah Crafts's friends and subjects, the six Wheeler-related captives who are potential rivals for production of the work. By discovering their life stories, I was able to build the evidentiary profile necessary to establish the origins of the manuscript and to mark the experiences of its author. For this reason, this book is an investigative encounter into the events behind the novel and a real-life recording of the experiences that shaped *The Bondwoman's Narrative*. Through the power of imaginative art and the alchemy of fact and fiction, Hannah Crafts's astonishing novel comes to represent the story not only of her own life but also of the lives and times of those she knew in slavery.

III

There is a good reason that Hannah Crafts wrote her personal narrative as autobiographical fiction: much of her life had already been stolen from her. By the time of her escape, the author had rejected the familial claims of her original enslaver, Lewis Bond (1788–1851), even though Bond was almost certainly her estranged father. Denied a kinship group to help shape her story, the author instead forged a new identity, as Hannah Crafts, to make meaning out of a life fractured by slavery.

The discoverable facts of Hannah Crafts's life can be stated here, although many details probably remained unknown to the author. As Hannah Bond, she began life in Indian Woods, North Carolina, at Willow Hall, the model for Lindendale in the novel. Nearly fifty years earlier, her family became forced migrants brought to North Carolina from Jamaica by Col. Thomas Pugh Sr. (1726–1806) on his trading sloop, the *Carolina*. Pugh purchased the author's grandmother Rosea from his mother's Trelawney plantation in Jamaica in 1779. Crafts's mother, called Hannah Sr., was born on the Pugh property near Quitsna, North Carolina, in 1794. Light-skinned and protected as property, Hannah Sr. likely held some familial connection to the Pugh family.[11]

In *The Bondwoman's Narrative*, Crafts emphasizes her journey to literacy, beginning while she was enslaved at Willow Hall: "[W]hile the other children of the house were amusing themselves I would quietly steal away from their company to ponder over the pages of some old book or newspaper that chance had thrown in [my] way. . . . I loved to look at them and think that some day I should probably understand them all" (*TBN* 7). Crafts's stealthy means of learning to read testifies to the author's theft not only of the art of literacy but also of the very tools of writing, likely purloined from her enslavers. At the age of twenty-four, Crafts became the property of Esther Bond, a daughter of Lewis and Catherine's, and in 1852, she was forced into the role of maidservant to another daughter, Lucinda Bond Wheeler (1814–1879), wife of Samuel Jordan Wheeler (1810–1879) of Murfreesboro, North Carolina.

Hannah Crafts and other captives in the Wheeler family household enjoyed unique access to literary texts in part because they served numerous student boarders who lived in the Wheeler home while attending Chowan Baptist Female Institute, a prominent college located in Murfreesboro. One of the texts students commonly studied in this community was Charles Dickens's *Bleak House* (1853). If the famous, enslaved, and self-taught Frederick Douglass (1818–1895) found in his treasured *Columbian Orator* a guiding star to develop his literary voice, for Crafts it seems to have been a dog-eared copy of *Bleak House* probably acquired from a student boarder. This may account for Crafts's surprising familiarity with and reliance on *Bleak House* in developing her autobiographical novel.

In the early summer of 1856, because of debts that Samuel owed his brother John Hill Wheeler, Hannah became the domestic captive of John's second wife, Ellen Sully Wheeler (1816–1896), identified in *The Bondwoman's Narrative* as "Mrs. Wheeler," the vain and shallow mistress prime for satirical attack in the novel. Like the novel's Hannah, Crafts lived with the Wheelers in Washington, D.C., in 1856 and 1857, while her enslaver, a former U.S. minister to Nicaragua, hunted for a government appointment. In the spring of 1857, Hannah Crafts escaped from the Wheeler family's plantation outside Murfreesboro. Disguised as a man and hiding a manuscript she had already begun, Crafts, like Hannah in her novel, made her way north.

Using a tapestry of stories gained directly from those she knew in slavery, Hannah Crafts then resumed her autobiographical narrative. If, as Hannah Crafts, the author knits together the stories of Wheeler-related bondwomen, she also frames their shared experiences through the lens of sentimental fiction. Produced shortly after the extraordinary success of Harriet Beecher Stowe's *Uncle Tom's Cabin* (1852), *The Bondwoman's Narrative* (1858) is Hannah Crafts's attempt to portray slavery in the same dramatic fashion as Stowe—only, this time, with the genuine knowledge gained "from a sphere so humble." Indeed, *The Bondwoman's Narrative* can be read as a kind of roman à clef, or "novel with a key," a story about real life overlaid with the fictional devices of gothic and sentimental literature. Just as Stowe underscored the truth behind her *Uncle Tom's Cabin* by publishing *A Key to Uncle Tom's Cabin* (1853) to "show out of what real warp and woof [the novel] is woven, and with what real colouring dyed," so the search for Hannah Crafts untangles the real-life stories behind the writer's extraordinary art.

IV

I was drawn into the story in 2003 by scholar Hollis Robbins, who was seeking potential sources for the novel in Eastern North Carolina. Robbins had spent months digging into obscure archives that led her to believe the author of *The Bondwoman's Narrative* could be discoverable among Wheeler family members in that region. She engaged me as a scholar living in the region who could do boots-on-the-ground research. I began by knocking on doors in Bertie County, North Carolina, following one of Robbins's leads that placed the author in the family of John Hill Wheeler's brother Samuel Jordan Wheeler. At the time, Hollis and I considered it possible that the book's author was a family member with a grudge against Mrs. Wheeler, perhaps her nieces Kate (1837–1912) or Julia Wheeler (1843–1898), both of whom were frequently in their aunt's company and who were known to be literary. Our preliminary research discovered a record of friction between the two Wheeler families. I hoped to link the handwriting of one of these nieces to Crafts's manuscript.

The idea that the novel was written by a formerly enslaved fugitive appeared to me too good to be true. I found my muse among the skeptics: Nina Baym, Richard J. Ellis, and Thomas C. Parramore.[12] These critics maintained that no antebellum enslaved person "recently escaped from North Carolina" could have possessed the literary skill to write a novel so notable for its studied allusiveness.[13] Baym, a leading authority on nineteenth-century American literature, sums up and shares this skepticism: "It is . . . not just difficult to imagine a slave Hannah who could read, but it is very difficult to imagine such a Hannah could write and just about impossible (for me, at least) to imagine a Hannah with access to the necessary tools for producing a weighty manuscript full of literary allusions like *Bondwoman*."[14] Such reasonable doubt and scrutiny helped direct my search. I felt confident that I would discover the author among the family of Samuel Jordan Wheeler.

What I uncovered instead was direct evidence that the Wheeler family and their relatives prized literacy as a trait among at least some of their domestic captives. Research among private papers and an extensive array of archival materials quickly disabused me of the literacy limits I had imagined for an enslaved person in the Wheeler circle. I discovered that Samuel Jordan Wheeler, the occupant of the Wheeler family residence in Murfreesboro, kept a domestic body servant named Moses who also served as his secretary. Not only was Moses literate but he was also a correspondent of the Wheeler children.[15] As I would later learn, Moses was likely a relative of the author, born at Willow Hall plantation in Indian Woods.

Literacy was not an aberration for the enslaved in the extended Wheeler family, either. In 1849, for example, John Wheeler Moore, John Hill Wheeler's nephew, brought his body servant, Harvey, to the University of North Carolina at Chapel Hill to assist him with his studies. Harvey, like Moses, was an enslaved man who served as Moore's personal secretary.[16] Even the Wheelers' children at times dictated their letters to captive servants. Julia Wheeler, daughter of Samuel Jordan Wheeler and Lucinda Bond Wheeler, employed an enslaved "amanuensis," or dictation assistant, while attending Chowan Baptist Female Institute (the future Chowan University) in 1860.[17] It would appear that the fictional Ellen Wheeler, in assigning Hannah to take dictation of her letters in *The Bondwoman's Narrative* (157), is only exercising what was, at least occasionally, a literal occurrence in the Wheeler and Moore families: the enslaved performed their literacy as part of their service. In these highly literate homes, a captive's value could depend, in part, on their literary skill.

I was wrong in my assumption that the author was a member of the Wheeler family. Although I continued to examine carefully the candidacy of the Wheeler nieces and other white members of the extended household, I found my work gravitating toward authorship by a former captive and Gates's original conclusions—conclusions that would prove astonishingly prescient. For the next eight years, I traced every scrap of paper passing in and out of the Wheeler family. I audited the public and private papers of extended family members, seeking to match the unique traits embodied in the manuscript: paper type, ink and pen evidence, the author's eccentric punctuation, even thimble and thread marks showing how the author stitched together folios as the narrative progressed.

In 2011, I made two important discoveries. First, in an obscure archive in rural North Carolina, I uncovered evidence that the paper on which the writer had produced the manuscript was traceable to the Wheeler household in 1856 and 1857.[18] In those years, John Hill Wheeler composed letters on two specific types of paper that match precisely the stationer's marks, cotton and fiber composition, and size dimensions of the folio paper used by the author of *The Bondwoman's Narrative*. The way paper was manufactured and distributed in the 1850s suggests that this is more than a surprising coincidence. Indeed, it is reasonable to conclude that the author of the novel procured the paper from the same stock used by John Hill Wheeler for his correspondence during those years.[19]

Second, after being led by Wheeler family papers to a file at the Library of Congress, I went through an old almanac that John Hill Wheeler kept in 1831–32. In Wheeler's rarely accessed "Miscellaneous" boxes, I discovered notations in the almanac detailing the Wheeler family's role in putting down Nat Turner's insurrection in August 1831. Fallout from that revolt must have profoundly shaped the lives of authorial candidates. In the back pages, Wheeler left behind the strongest clue yet: the names and ages of five enslaved "servants," the only known slave inventory extant among records kept by the family. Under the listing "Age of Servants

1832," Wheeler claimed his human property: "Milly aged about 35 years, Martha aged about 6 years, Tecumseh born about 1st Sept 1831, Elizabeth born April 1818, Jack aged about 15 years" (see Figure 2). Could Milly or Martha be the author? Or possibly Elizabeth (Eliza)? And what became of Tecumseh and Jack? I was determined to find out.

V

Why spend nearly twenty years researching and writing a biography of Hannah Crafts? This book has always been a passion project for me. In 2002, I moved to take a new teaching position in the English department at East Carolina University. That same year, Gates published *The Bondwoman's Narrative*. When I read the work that spring, I was hooked. Here were the many strands of my devoted interests: archival research, literary mysteries, the African American tradition, and the most fascinating historical puzzle of all—who was Hannah Crafts? Then came the surprising

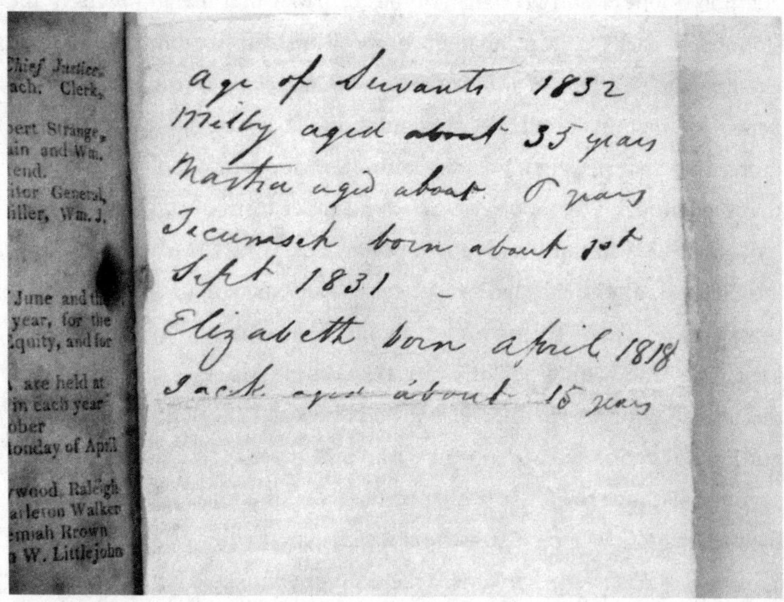

age of Servants 1832
Milly aged about 35 years
Martha aged about 6 years
Tecumseh born about 1st
Sept 1831
Elizabeth born April 1818
Jack aged about 15 years

FIGURE 2: Detail of John Hill Wheeler's 1832 almanac

revelation, first noted by scholar Hollis Robbins, that Crafts had shaped part of her narrative by reworking specific passages from Dickens's *Bleak House*. This further fueled speculation over the origins of the novel. When Robbins contacted me asking for assistance doing archival work, I jumped at the chance.

In the fall of 2003, I began investigating the Kate Wheeler Cooper Papers, housed in the manuscript collection of the J. Y. Joyner Library at East Carolina University. I was looking to see if there were any materials there that might illuminate Crafts's history and the reason her novel draws so heavily on Dickens. As literary scholars who work with source materials know, there is something palpably exciting about sorting through unread manuscripts, letters, receipt books, and school records on an original quest. In this case, I found myself entering the day-to-day world of the Wheeler, Bond, and Moore families in Bertie and Hertford Counties, the very families identified by Gates and Robbins as those with the strongest ties to the manuscript. My initial work in family archives uncovered important errors of fact connecting the manuscript to the Wheeler family; it also opened up exciting new leads for discovering the author. At the urging of both Robbins and Gates, I took up the project as my own.[20]

In the early days of this research. I arranged to give talks at small community centers in Eastern North Carolina. From these meetings, I began to collect source materials detailing the stories and contexts of Hannah Crafts's life, sources out of the reach of most other scholars. At one of my talks in Windsor, North Carolina, in 2004, I made the acquaintance of Mack and Clara Bell. Every Saturday morning that March and April, the Bells invited me into their home to discuss Bertie County history, including what they knew of their ancestors, the descendants of the Wheelers, Pughs, Bonds, and Rascoes—all families connected to Crafts's narrative. On my very first visit, Mack brought down from the attic a family tree with meticulous notes detailing the interrelated marriages and property arrangements of his planter family forebears. On a subsequent visit, the Bells kindly arranged for copies of their family tree and other genealogy records to be made for me. Even years later, with the advent of online databases like Ancestry.com, Mack and Clara's personal records proved superior as a tool for tracing many of the genealogies behind *The Bondwoman's Narrative*. Further, on one Saturday morning in April, Mack drove me out to property he identified as "Willow Hall," the plantation I later discovered as the site of the author's origins.

Mack died in 2008, and Clara in 2014, but even years later, I drew on their expertise, especially in writing the Bertie County chapters of this book. The early experiences and details they provided were essential in making my later research focused and productive. It would still be another decade before I identified the author, but I am indebted to Mack and Clara Bell for helping to launch this project. Only as I worked on revisions of this book did I realize that the Bells, along with being husband and wife, were also distant cousins. They both descended directly from the early Bertie County planter and politician Lewis Bond. They were each, in fact, immediate kin to Hannah Crafts. How I wish I could have shared this truth with them.

VI

A word about nomenclature. Through every iteration of the writer's journey, Hannah Crafts held on tightly to the identity bestowed by her mother. The author cherished the name "Hannah" as part of a matriarchal tradition stretching back to her mother's native West African culture: Crafts was named "Hannah" just like her mother, as the mother's name passed to her firstborn daughter, carrying forward the matrilineal thread. In the following pages, I will use "Hannah Crafts" and "Crafts" to signify the author (as the writer herself does); I will use "Hannah" when discussing the autobiographical protagonist of *The Bondwoman's Narrative*; and I will use "Hannah Bond" and "Hannah Jr." for the author when she was a child, before she could renounce her association with the Bond family. Crafts's identity as "Hannah" in art, in history, and in fiction preserves a truth that even 150 years of violent assault and forced separation could not obscure: she was her mother's daughter.

Why does identifying the author matter? And why reclaim the lives of enslaved people connected to the manuscript? The answer is simple: *The Bondwoman's Narrative* is an unprecedented document, yet the voices that shaped its production remain unheard. Hidden within the records that disclose the life and times of Hannah Crafts rests a counternarrative, "the half [that] has never been told," as the former captive Lorenzo Ivy described it in 1937.[21] The forensic sleuthing necessary to uncover Crafts's identity excavates a history of American slavery only now being brought to the surface by scholars. In her novel, Crafts reclaims scores of the pioneering voices that helped emancipate a nation even while their lives went unrecorded and ignored by those seeking to perpetuate a narrative of white supremacy.

There are forerunners to this kind of scholarship. Despite several decades of intensive literary and historical study, the biographical portraits of many of our most celebrated African Americans are based on sparsely documented historical records: William Wells Brown, Frances Ellen Watkins Harper, Sally Hemings, Harriet Jacobs, Ona Judge, Sojourner Truth, Harriet Tubman, and Harriet Wilson. Inferences, circumstantial evidence, materials appropriated from white enslavers, hidden tokens of purpose—these are the signals and signposts upon which most early African American biography depends.[22]

Every scholar of pre–Civil War Black history confronts the problem of the archive. As the historian Jill Lepore has encapsulated the difficulty: the "archive of the past . . . is maddingly uneven, asymmetrical, and unfair."[23] Researchers who explore Black lives in pre-twentieth-century America are left with a fragmentary record, one in which Black people are only dimly legible in what has been preserved and maintained. Local, state, and federal archives hold only the scraps and shards of lives broken by design. Endeavoring to reconstruct early Black history, then, requires tools beyond traditional historiography (reconstructive genealogy, oral history, and communal memory) and a piecing together of the fractured record of Black lives preserved in traditional archives.[24] The following pages feature more than a decade of intensive work gathering fragments and scraps of lives otherwise consigned to oblivion.

One of the reasons Hannah Crafts's novel *The Bondwoman's Narrative* is so important is that it is one of the only narratives of the Black experience to survive slavery's holocaust intact and unaltered. To disclose the life and times of Hannah Crafts is to sound out the personalities and passions of a network of enslaved people bound by the art, ink, and thread of the earliest known novel written by an African American woman. From the Bertie County Conspiracy and Nat Turner's rebellion (Milly and Martha Murfree) to the sexual conflicts faced by female slaves (Mary Burton); from the attempted escape of seventy-seven fugitives on the schooner *Pearl* (Eliza Morgan and Paul Jennings) to the activities of the Underground Railroad and African American community in the North (Hannah Bond and Jane Johnson)—the search for "Hannah Crafts" provides a portrait of the lives and times of a generation of enslaved people whose literary record the author marks, uncovers, and vividly brings back to life. At once a detective story, a literary chase, and a cultural history, this book discovers a Dickensian tale of love, friendship, betrayal, and interracial violence set against the backdrop of the United States' slide into civil war. As Hannah Crafts herself noted in *The Bondwoman's Narrative*, "to those who regard truth as stranger than fiction it can be no less interesting" (MS Preface). Her words prove prophetic.

CHAPTER 1

BEGINNINGS

I

IN JULY 1779, HANNAH CRAFTS'S family became forced migrants carried to the United States by Col. Thomas Pugh Sr. (1726–1806) on his trading sloop, the *Carolina*. A largely unknown family saga was unfolding. Born in 1777, the author's grandmother Rosea Pugh was two years old when she was abducted from Jamaica and removed to Indian Woods, North Carolina, with other family members. As human cargo, Crafts's relatives arrived at Port Roanoke, Virginia, crammed into the ship's hold. Nineteen additional stolen captives are named in the shipping manifest for the vessel.[1]

As the twenty-three forced refugees disembarked, they were organized into coffles. In such cases, the women were linked together by a rope tied to cord halters encircling their necks. Rosea, a toddler, probably went unsecured. The practice was to bind the men with a more durable cord. And so, the author's great-grandfather Achilles and great-uncle James Barefoot would have been outfitted with iron collars, manacles, and chains. The collar was fitted around the neck, the hasp of an open brass padlock locking the latch in front. Then a heavy chain was passed inside the curve of metal, the hasp, and the body of the padlock, creating a heavy iron stringer that trapped the men like fish strung through the gills. The manacle on the wrist of each captive was linked by a short chain to the manacle of the next man. This compelled each row of men to walk in step, two by two, next to each other. Gigged on lines of iron and chain, rope and halter, these men, women, and children must have staggered the ninety-five miles from Roanoke Port, across the alien swamps of southeastern Virginia and northeastern North Carolina, and into Indian Woods.[2]

In 1779, at the time of their abduction, there was a growing need for slave labor in North Carolina, especially in the areas where no prominent trade circuit reached. By 1770, the colony had amassed an enslaved population of about forty thousand captives—fifth among British North American colonies. But most of these captives came overland from neighboring colonies in Virginia and South Carolina, where trade routes had been established with slave ships extracting captives from Africa and the West Indies in exchange for Virginian and South Carolinian plantation goods (tobacco, wheat, rice, indigo, and, eventually, cotton). North Carolina, however, lacked the wealthy merchant syndicates of its neighbors, networks that were willing to speculate on captives from Africa or to execute the kinds of Middle Passage trading attractive to British merchants. Further, the famously challenging North Carolina coastline made navigation difficult and portage for large vessels risky, to say nothing of the pirate crews plying the area of the coastal Outer Banks.

Hannah Crafts's ancestors, then, became forced migrants brought to the United States as a part of an informal circuit. The Roanoke port that fed Col. Thomas Pugh Sr.'s plantation supported only smaller shipping interests, and the majority of merchant vessels that traded there followed similar routes. Passage among New England, North Carolina, and Jamaica offered one of the few mini-circuits serving Pugh Sr.'s region. Centered on Port Roanoke, the circuit provided access to international markets. Pugh Sr. seems to have followed what others, such as John Hill Wheeler's own father, did. Wealthy planter-merchants in Eastern North Carolina financed their trade ventures to the Caribbean in commissioned sloops or ships they had built. The founding families of North Carolina—like the Pughs, Bonds, Morgans, Burtons, and Wheelers—knew that their success and power depended on importing West Indies captives into the state. Enslaved labor and its increase determined a family's fortune. These same forces shaped the author's origins.

II

Born in 1826, Hannah Crafts began life at Willow Hall in Bertie County, North Carolina. No definitive documentation detailing the circumstances of her birth is available, but property records and early census schedules sketch her childhood. From what can be reconstructed, Crafts's early experiences match those of her namesake in the novel: "I was not brought up by any body in particular that I know of. I had no training, no cultivation. . . . No one ever spoke of my father or mother" (*TBN* 5). Her words echo those of her near contemporary, the famous African American writer and escaped captive Frederick Douglass: "[Of my father] I know nothing; the means of knowing was withheld from me. . . . My mother and I were separated when I was but an infant—before I knew her as my mother."[3]

Like Douglass, Crafts was aware of her mother, even if the two appear to have been separated for long stretches of the author's childhood. Douglass explained the practice in 1845: "Frequently, before the child has reached its twelfth month, its mother is taken from it, and hired out on some farm a considerable distance off, and the child is placed under the care of an old woman, too old for field labor. For what this separation is done, I do not know, unless it be to hinder the development of the child's affection toward its mother, and to blunt and destroy the natural affection of the mother for the child."[4] Crafts was likely conceived in rape, so her paternity, like the paternity of Frederick Douglass, remains a mystery—though most signs point to the author's first enslaver, Lewis Bond, as her father.

Crafts's mother, Hannah Sr., was born in 1794 on Thomas Pugh Sr.'s property near Quitsna, North Carolina. In 1807, when she reached sexual maturity, Hannah Sr. became the personal servant of Pugh Sr.'s granddaughter Catherine Pugh. Four years later, Hannah Sr. was bestowed as part of Catherine's dowry upon the occasion of her marriage to Lewis Bond in 1811. The arrangement was common: enslaved domestic servants were frequently trafficked as part of a young bride's property transfer. Born around the same time as Catherine, Hannah Sr. seems to have been groomed to be her waiting maid and may well have been her half sister. Lewis Bond held possession of the author's mother from the time she was seventeen until she was forty-one, when she was trafficked to family members in another state.

Crafts grew up largely separated from her mother. The author's longing to forge an intimate and lasting bond with her seems to be replicated in the quest undertaken by the protagonist of her novel. In *The Bondwoman's Narrative*, Hannah seeks to align herself with older female characters in the text: the Quaker woman who teaches her to read, her new "mistress" at Lindendale, Mrs. Wright in jail, Mrs. Henry ("I could not lightly sacrafise [*sic*] the good opinion of Mrs. Henry"), and even, to some degree, Mrs. Wheeler. In each case, the protagonist's enslavement places an unbreachable barrier to the maternal intimacy she craves.

If Hannah's quest to forge maternal bonds is recorded in Crafts's novel, it was no less present in the author's lived experiences. When Lewis Bond's oldest son, Judge William Pugh Bond (1812–1894), married in 1835, the author experienced a more complete rupture as her mother became a gift to Lewis Bond's new daughter-in-law, Lucy Rascoe. With the marriage, Crafts's mother was forced to move nearly eight hundred miles away to help settle a new household in Haywood County, Tennessee, where Judge Bond established his law practice. Just nine years old at the time, Crafts wrote about this seeming permanent estrangement from her mother years later in her narrative: "I had no mother, no friend," she writes. "How it augments the importance of any little success to them that some one probably a mother will receive the intelligence with a show of delight and interest."

Something of Crafts's motherless years can be gained from estate records. Crafts notes in her novel, "Of my relatives I knew nothing." She observes that, as a child, she "soon learned what a curse was attached to my race, soon learned that the African blood in my veins would forever exclude me from the higher walks of life" (*TBN* 5–6). Probate records show that Rosea, Hannah Sr., and, later, Hannah Crafts occupied a unique place among enslaved people in the Pugh and Bond families. They are specifically exempted from sale outside the family, probably because they held blood ties to their owners. There are painful hints, however, that they were also trafficked sexually among family members.

Crafts's young adult years, without a mother to protect her, seem to have featured separation, sexual exploitation, and, possibly, concubinage or a forced polygamous relationship with a white man. The racial passing narrative that is central to her autobiographical novel may relate to Hannah Bond's experiences as a trafficked captive. As Crafts puts it in the novel, "my lot and portion . . . seemed the harder to be borne, because my complexion was almost white" (*TBN* 6). When she was a teenager, Hannah Jr. was transferred to the household of Lewis Bond's nephew Thomas Bond Jr. to escape a property claim. At Thomas Jr.'s plantation in Indian Woods, she seems to have been forced to serve as Thomas Jr.'s sexual partner, an arrangement she would have understood from her mother's experiences. When she came to develop her narrative, Crafts disguises much of her suffering among Bond family members, attributing what were likely her experiences of concubinage to her protagonist's foil, Lizzy, in the story: "She suffered the extremes of a master's fondness, a mistress's jealousy and their daughter's hate" (*TBN* 34).

Crafts's apparent sexual abuse at the hands of Thomas Bond Jr. matches the experiences of other mixed-race captives in the region, including fellow novelist Harriet Jacobs. At the age of fifteen, Jacobs, like Crafts, became prey to white men, including her possessor, Dr. James Norcom, who planned to remove her to a remote property where he could imprison and rape her. In Jacobs's case, she accepted the sexual designs of a different powerful white man in the community to help shield her from the plans of her owner. Crafts's sexual suffering is more deeply disguised in her novel and less traceable in the historical record, but she, too, seems to have been forced into a sexual relationship with a powerful white enslaver. Like Jacobs, Crafts turned to autobiographical fiction to share the mental and physical torment. Likely there was no other way she could productively reach and convey her suffering.

Significantly, Hannah Crafts's experiences of sexual trauma became the source of her novel's primary mystery: the racial identity of the narrator's unnamed "mistress." In the work, Crafts pairs her autobiographical narrator with the anonymous "mistress" who passes for white in the text. The two then serve as doppelgängers for each other, probably reflecting the complicated double life the author suffered as a sexual captive for the years she lived in bondage in the possession of Thomas Bond Jr. Scholars have long puzzled over the strange symbiotic relationship between the protagonist Hannah and the mysterious and indistinct "mistress" in the novel. The author's personal life suggests that both appear as complex projections of the author based on Hannah Crafts's own physical and psychic torment as a sexually trafficked captive. The darkest parts of the author's life are balanced against the shielded piety of the author's narrator.

By 1851, Hannah Jr. is recorded as back at Willow Hall and in the possession of Lewis Bond. That same year, her mother, too, reappears in Bond's inventory of captives. Possibly, Hannah Sr. returned after the death of Lucy Rascoe Bond in 1844—to whom she had originally been bequeathed. In *The Bondwoman's Narrative*, Crafts is unusually open about discussing sexual relations between enslavers and their female captives. As the work's editor, Henry Louis Gates Jr., notes, "Crafts repeatedly stresses the sexual vulnerability of all female slaves, but especially that of house servants and mulattos" (*TBN* 247). It is no exaggeration to say that Crafts was born into a cradle of distrust, rebellion, and sexual assault. Like Jacobs, she found not only refuge but also resistance in her narrative exposing a system that sought to make her a permanent victim.

But, like Harriet Jacobs, Crafts had other plans. Escape and artistic expression became weapons with which to fully reclaim the integrity of her life. Without the realistic potential of physical violence that was open to some of her male relatives, Crafts, like Jacobs, had to find other tools to mark and punish her abusers. History would prove the power of Crafts's and Jacobs's aims. If their captors are remembered at all today, it is not for the prominent roles they played in white society; rather, they are known for their racism, bigotry, and predation as vividly depicted and memorialized in Crafts's and Jacobs's narratives.

The success of Hannah Crafts's rebellion should be of no surprise. Crafts was born into a family of proud resistance. Probably without fully realizing it, the author was directly related to at least two potential insurgents, Rosea Pugh/Pope and James Barefoot (1774–unknown). Evidence suggests that these family members may have helped plan a slave revolt that directly prefigured Nat Turner's insurrection a generation later. Indeed, the 1802 Bertie County Conspiracy, as it came to be called, drew on many of the same sources of religious awakening and social justice that formed Nat Turner's revolt in 1831 and the author's own reach for freedom in 1857. Inspired rebellion seems to have been in the author's blood. As a writer, Hannah Crafts would transmute blood into ink years later, but the blood would come first—in the failed Bertie Conspiracy of her forebears and, later, in the bloody aftermath of Turner's revolt. From their earliest days as enslaved subjects, Crafts's family seems to have understood the formula for reaching liberty: religion, resistance, and rebellion marked the path to freedom.

III

Former North Carolina governor William R. Davie raised the initial alarm in February 1802. Writing from his Halifax plantation, Davie alerted his successor that plans for a slave revolt were forming in Southampton County, Virginia, and being seeded in communities extending along the Roanoke River Valley into North Carolina. An unidentified literate "Negro" in Southampton County was suspected of being the organizer and had allegedly written an intercepted letter addressed to the "Representative of the Roanoke Company." In language steeped in America's political struggle for freedom, the letter stated that once the "conflagration" began, whites would "acknowledge liberty & equality" and be "glad to purchase their lives at any price." Whites must learn that "the breath of liberty is as free for us as for themselves." The letter was signed a "true friend in liberty or death." Davie compared the situation with that in the French colony of Saint-Domingue (present-day Haiti), where Toussaint Louverture had led a successful slave revolt in 1791. The Saint-Domingue revolt brought the murder of several thousand whites, "staining the whole Colony," according to Davie.[5]

The organizers of the 1802 Bertie County Conspiracy stated the object of their revolt clearly: "[to] fight against the white people to obtain their liberty." "They were to kill all the white people to burn houses and blow them up," testimony later revealed: "Kill the people and do all they could to furnish themselves with arms from those who were first killed."[6] The plan was remarkably similar to the one Nat Turner would hatch nearly thirty years later. The interconnected waterways of southeastern Virginia and northeastern North Carolina served as the conduit. The conspirators consisted largely of "confidential" captives—that is, those whose service provided them access to mobility, tools, and the regional networks that linked trade.[7] Among the fourteen brought to trial, there were at least two carpenters, two blacksmiths, a tavern cook, a mill supervisor, an agricultural worker, and probably two watermen. As trial records indicate, a surprising number of these "confidential" bondpeople were also literate.[8]

Freedom of movement and literacy enabled the network to mobilize and sow insurrectionary plans along the tributaries of the Roanoke River. The conspirators included Hannah Crafts's great-uncle James Barefoot and, possibly, Rosea Pugh, her maternal grandmother. Barefoot's occupation is not revealed, but his birth in Jamaica and his high value reflected in property records suggest that he, too, probably served in a "confidential" capacity. Around the time of the conspiracy, Barefoot appears alongside Hannah Sr. in probate records as property to be spared from sale for family debts. According to the case, three additional Pugh enslaved men were named as co-conspirators in the planned attack: "Lohle, Ambrose, and Jim."[9]

Barefoot's deposition places part of the organizing activities in the very Indian Woods fields where the author passed the earliest days of her childhood: "there was to be a meeting at Mr. George Outlaw's old field . . . to concert a plan that they would rise up and kill the whites at Windsor first, get into the houses and kill the people as they come out of the houses."[10] That "old field"—then in the control of George Outlaw I—was a neighboring plantation to the Pugh and Bond possessions and one notable for its Gospel Oaks, a set of trees that marked a prominent crossroad stretching back to the Tuscarora Nation. The shade of those remote trees provided a gathering point for the enslaved in the area, as it had for early Native Americans and rural traders.

At the beginning of the nineteenth century—a time of religious awakening—the Gospel Oaks also served as a place for enslaved religious gatherings. The site eventually came to the attention of white authorities, who at first supported religious instruction for local captives as part of the region's wider "Great Awakening." But as liberation theology became mixed with the other elements of spiritual revival, planter families and local governments grew anxious about participation by enslaved people. In late 1801, as giant camp meetings moved eastward from Kentucky to North Carolina, enslavers began to see the Great Revival as a potential threat to the social order.

In 1802, one of the Bertie County Conspiracy's organizers was a local enslaved preacher known as Dr. Joe. It is impossible to say if James Barefoot knew Dr. Joe, or if Dr. Joe preached revolt under the Gospel Oaks of Indian Woods, but suspicions about his activities and those of other enslaved preachers seem to have been well founded. Records confirm that Dr. Joe and other Black co-conspirators used religious meetings to plot revolts in the region. One enslaver, a Baptist elder from Bertie County, provided his bondwoman permission "to hold a night Meeting on Monday Night," but later learned that the service involved "plans for a revolt."

In April of that year, Dr. Joe was accused of fomenting rebellion among slaves in neighboring Pasquotank County. In May, the Pasquotank County court indicted Dr. Joe for conspiring "to Rebel and make insurrections."[11] That same month, Cashie Baptist Church pastor Aaron Spivey unwittingly authorized a camp revival under the Gospel Oaks in George Outlaw's "old field," scheduled for the night of June 10. Spivey did not know that the revival had been arranged by organizers—possibly James Barefoot—who planned to assemble recruits and then march them to "seize the arms & etc deposited at Mr. Pin's" before robbing "gunpowder at Mr. Hunter's store" in Windsor. The next act was to be a surprise attack on the leading white men assembling to attend the Kehukee Baptist Association's quarterly meeting just east of Windsor, at the "Freeman's Chappelle, in Bertie." Ingeniously, it appears the plan was to assassinate as many of the local slaveholders as possible while they were unarmed and gathered to organize their religious affairs. One insurgent stated succinctly that "they were to begin at the Quarterly Meeting."

Before these plans could reach fruition, however, the trial of Dr. Joe heightened attention and enhanced slave patrols. On June 1, as the Bertie plot moved toward execution, Fed Fitt, a Bertie County bondman, encountered several enslaved men on a road near Colerain. (They go unnamed in his testimony.) Fitt was asked to carry a letter to one of the leaders of the Bertie plot, King Brown, a literate blacksmith who worked jobs for his enslaver in both Hertford and Bertie Counties. Fitt obviously knew of the conspiracy, for he was informed upon receiving the letter that "the 10th June they were agoing to make a Start & come down to the Ferry [and] then come to Mr. Hunters Store & Break it open & get what powder was there." But when Fitt reached the slave cabin of Judy Rayner, who may have been his wife, he gave the letter to her "little Girl [and] told her to give it to her mother."[12]

The next day, slave patrollers forced their way into the cabin. There they found a small piece of paper that listed the names of fourteen enslaved men from the community. The communication began, "Captain Frank Sumner will command," and then identified the conspirators, including Fitt, King Brown, James Barefoot, and the Pugh-related captives Lohle, Ambrose, and Jim (see Figure 3). The rebels appear to have chosen June 10 to initiate the attack to provide them unique access to the region's slaveholders: "we wil ris as 1," the author of the intercepted missive wrote.[13]

Slave patrols immediately rounded up those named in the plot. In 1802, John Bond, the brother of the author's first enslaver, Lewis Bond, served as sheriff and probably helped apprehend the conspirators. The suspects were held in the Windsor jail and questioned separately over the course of the next two weeks. Each suspect was shown the intercepted letter and told that it "implicated him, on the evidence of others, so as to convict him fully." If he "fairly and honestly declared all that he knew, he should be forgiven"; but if he "denied what he perfectly knew," none could protect him, and "he would surely be hanged."[14] The ploy worked. Although clemency was not seriously considered, many of the suspects provided testimony that independently and consistently disclosed the plot.

FIGURE 3: June 1, 1802, letter addressed to King Brown regarding Bertie County Slave Conspiracy, North Carolina State Archives, Raleigh.

When James Barefoot was questioned by planters and local magistrates, he "deni[ed] having any knowledge of or connection with the conspiracy—he heard last Monday evening from a Negroe [*sic*] boy of his mistress which boy said an old woman about the house informed him—there was to be a meeting at Mr. George Outlaw's old field." Further, he noted that he "understood that Mrs. Turner's Gain was the head man in calling the meeting."[15] Other court records show there was bad blood between Barefoot and "Gain," so it is interesting that Barefoot used the opportunity to betray a rival. Gain, for his part, denied any involvement and said nothing else in his deposition.

Property records show that whatever else went unrecorded, Barefoot's life was spared. Eleven of the fourteen were sentenced to hang, including King Brown, Frank Sumner, Fed Fitt, Gain Turner, Lohle, Ambrose, and Jim Pugh. Although no records state the precise setting for these lynchings, local custom holds that the punishments—probably arranged by Sheriff John Bond—took place at the Gospel Oaks as a warning to area captives. If so, Frank Sumner, Fed Fitt, Gain Turner, Lohle, Ambrose, and Jim Pugh were hanged from the same grove of trees where the co-conspirators had planned to commence their attacks. King Brown was remanded to Hertford County for punishment, the same county where his enslaver resided. There, he, too, was lynched as an example, bringing to a close the Bertie Conspiracy.

Why did James Barefoot not share this same fate? It could be the influence of Francis Pugh, one of the planters who served on the three-person panel adjudicating the case. Barefoot, like his sister Rosea and the child Hannah Sr., were the property of Pugh's extended family. Special mention of James Barefoot along with Rosea and Hannah Sr. suggests some distinction that spared him from the fate of his fellow conspirators, including other Pugh captives who paid with their lives. That distinction may well have been blood ties to his enslavers.[16]

In her novel, Crafts uses the real-life stories surrounding the Gospel Oaks to create "the legend of the Linden," a set piece for the early part of her novel condemning enslavers and promising divine retribution and the avenging justice of future generations. In the novel, the spirit of revenge is embodied in the matrilineal figure of Rose—homage paid to the author's stolen grandmother, Rosea Pugh. Pugh was twenty-two years old at the time of the Bertie Conspiracy and was likely swept up in the religious and revolutionary fervor that had touched her brother James Barefoot.

Early in her life, Crafts developed the same religious and revolutionary fervor that years before had given rise to the Bertie Conspiracy. She would choose a different path from Dr. Joe's and, perhaps, her grandmother's, but she would carry the same righteous critique of slavery and faith in God's deliverance. Like Dr. Joe, the author would sermonize and use her gifts with language to call for the abolition of slavery. And like James Barefoot, she would organize and demonstrate the courage to resist. In the spirit of her forebears James Barefoot and Rosea Pugh, Crafts would come to mount her own rebellion. Fifty-four years after the 1802 Bertie Conspiracy, she stole pen and paper from her enslaver, John Hill Wheeler, and began writing her autobiographical novel, one she would complete in freedom. The people she carried to freedom in those pages would include Rosea Pugh, James Barefoot, Dr. Joe, and the enslaved women she met in service to the Wheeler family: Milly and Martha Murfree, Eliza Morgan, Mary Burton, and Jane Johnson. Crafts would become a different kind of Dr. Joe, a new version of her ancestor James Barefoot, and yet her identity would remain mostly a mystery to her. It is uncertain how much of the history of her ancestors she could have known. The true story of Hannah Crafts is a crime story that begins with the theft of the author's identity and ends with the reintegration of her family, real and imagined, in freedom and in fiction. Like that letter of hope carried by Fed Fitt to Judy Rayner, Crafts's novel carries the revolutionary news of her forebears: "we wil ris as 1."

CHAPTER 2

THE SEARCH

I

THE AUTHOR WHO IDENTIFIED HERSELF as Hannah Crafts made corrections on slips of paper prepared with a cutting instrument (probably sewing scissors). Then she pasted her edits over her manuscript's original text. "It was necessary to make an example of them," the author wrote on a change slip, revising an early scene in the narrative where a Quaker couple is punished for teaching the protagonist to read. "Years passed, however, before I learned their fate," she continued: "The cruel overseer would not tell me whither he had removed them, but to all my inquiries he simply answered that he would take good care I never saw them again." From the sewing kit, the author took a wafer paste (a flour-based adhesive used as sealing wax), moistened it, and affixed the correction slip to her manuscript (see Figure 4).

Forensic evidence tells a story. The direction of the wipe erasure marks (wet ink removed with a finger) suggests that the author was right-handed. Ultraviolet analysis demonstrates that Crafts made use of rejected portions of the manuscript, recycling every bit of paper that held blank space. Ultraviolet and microscopic evidence strongly suggests that major revisions were mounted only after the author had escaped to freedom.[1] We know an extraordinary amount about the composition of "The Bondwoman's Narrative" manuscript because of the scientific analysis conducted by two leading pen and ink experts: Kenneth W. Rendell and Dr. Joe Nickell. Rendell is a world-renowned dealer in historical documents, and Dr. Nickell, a trained expert in forensic document analysis. In 2001, Henry Louis Gates Jr. and his Warner Books publishers hired Rendell and Nickell to perform forensic tests on the manuscript. Both experts had been involved in exposing false claims about discovered documents, including the case of Jack the Ripper's diaries. In 1993, Warner Books stopped publication of *Jack the Ripper Diaries* just weeks before its debut when Rendell and Nickell determined the work to be a fraud.

Gates began with Rendell, who had developed a simple process for determining ink type and dating its adherence to paper. At Rendell's home in South Natick, Massachusetts, Gates waited anxiously as Rendell peered into the lens of a microscope. "What you are looking at," Rendell told Gates, "is iron-gall ink." Iron-gall ink is made from iron salts and tannic acids, widely in use until 1860. Next, Rendell conducted an ion migration analysis to determine potential disparities between the age of the ink and the age of the paper. In the *Jack the Ripper Diaries* case, for instance,

FIGURE 4: Detail of "The Bondwoman's Narrative" MS, p. 168

Rendell's analysis uncovered a mismatch of twelve years between the age of the ink and the age of the diary notebook. The dates the diarist claimed did not match the ink and paper evidence. By this method and others, the *Diaries* were exposed as forgeries. In the case of "The Bondwoman's Narrative" manuscript, however, Rendell's initial analysis showed concurrence between ink and paper. His testing placed the manuscript, ink, and paper as dating to the mid- to late 1850s. As Rendell told Gates at parting, "Now the manuscript has to undergo the intense scrutiny of Dr. Joe Nickell."

Nickell describes himself as "an investigator and historical document examiner." In April 2001, Gates sent the manuscript by hand courier to Nickell at the Center for Inquiry in Amherst, New York, for him to conduct a battery of chemical tests and forensic examinations. As Gates later observed, "[N]othing . . . had prepared me for the depth of detail of the results of Nickell's examination, nor for the sheer beauty of the rigors of his procedures and the subtleties of his conclusions" (*TBN* lxiii).

For six weeks, Nickell subjected the ink, paper, and other manuscript artifacts to stereomicroscopic, chemical, and ultraviolet tests. At night, he read a typescript of the novel, looking for clues in the text. Nickell's analysis of the origins of the manuscript supported Rendell's initial assessment that the work was authentic. As Nickell notes, if the known provenance of the novel was incomplete, it was not suspicious, given that the manuscript could be traced back half a century to a time when the work was not so valued and, therefore, not a likely target for forgery. The manuscript was traceable, first, back to Dorothy Porter (now Wesley) of Howard University; then back to autograph and book dealer Emily Driscoll of New York; and, before that, to a book scout in New Jersey in 1948. Because Wesley and her estate possessed the manuscript from 1951 until 2001, there was little opportunity for the work to have been subject to tampering.

Wesley's records describe the work as a "Manuscript Novel" and a "fictionalized personal narrative" that had been "written in a worn copy book."[2] In fact, the work was penned on folio sheets (sheets of paper folded in half and thus having two leaves and four pages) and subsequently bound. The manuscript consists of four different types of stationery sheets, two of which bear embossed stationers' crests, designs impressed in the upper-left corner of letter folios. The crests in Crafts's manuscript were from the Southworth paper manufacturing company, one of which is traceable to paper first produced in 1856 (see Figure 5).

Significantly, examination with ultraviolet light revealed that there were numerous instances of "ghost writing"—that is, mirror image fluorescing traces of writing caused by ink corrosion from a facing page. Its presence in Crafts's manuscript was in marked contrast to its absence in the fake Jack the Ripper diaries. The ghosting of ink further demonstrated signs of age in the manuscript. Ample evidence showed that "The Bondwoman's Narrative" had been written with a dip pen, exhibited by sequences of writing that became progressively lighter and then abruptly dark again as Crafts reinked her pen. Nickell notes in his analysis that sometimes the pen strokes become finer, indicating a shift from a blunt to a sharp nib, characteristic of use of a quill pen. As Nickell notes,

FIGURE 5: "The Bondwoman's Narrative" MS with Southworth Manufacturing Company stationer's crest

stereomicroscopic inspection showed an absence of the kinds of markings common to mechanical nib pens. Quill writing instruments were largely abandoned by the end of the Civil War. Further, Nickell determined that standard goose quills had been used, rather than the crow quills employed to produce the tiny script sometimes affected by upper-class women of the period as an expression of femininity and social position.[3]

Nickell's expertise as a handwriting specialist yielded further results. He observes in the report, "Because the writing materials of the manuscript indicated it had been written in the 1850s, the absence of archaic forms (such as the long *s*) suggested to me that the writer was relatively young." Nickell continues: "The penmanship was of a quality I described as 'serviceable' (neither elegant or [*sic*] untutored), and though it was natural, genuine handwriting, it had been penned relatively slowly, as if to render it legible."[4]

No periods appear at the ends of sentences, just one of many unconventional details related to the work's punctuation. In eccentric fashion, where compound words straddle two lines, the hyphen appears not at the end of the first line but at the beginning of the next; occasionally, a hyphen is placed in both spots. Quotation marks and apostrophes are placed not as they should be, in the superior spot aligned with capital letters, but rather at the inferior, or baseline, of sentences, like commas (see Figure 6). The uniqueness of these composing traits signals the hand of a writer for whom literacy was earned by unconventional means.

If evidence of the author's reach for literacy was important, so, too, was Nickell's determination that the manuscript was a "composing copy," or holograph. Holograph manuscripts, or the working "fair copy" of published works, are exceedingly rare in the nineteenth century for African American literary works, a surprising fact given that hundreds of belletristic writings by African Americans were published before the Civil War. But for all these many literary efforts—slave narratives, autobiographies, religious tracts, novels, books of poems, antislavery political tracts, scientific works, etc.—only two other holographic manuscripts written by former captives survive, having been handed down by friends and family. In 2009, the prizewinning historian David W. Blight brought to light John

18

-sion to one of wrath and gloom, that the calm brow
should become wrinkled with passion, the lips turgid
with malevolence— yet thus it was
Though filled with superstitious awe I was in no has-
-te to leave the room; for there surrounded by mysteri-
-ous associations I seemed suddenly to have grown old,
to have entered a new world of thoughts and feel-
-ings and sentiments I was not a slave with these
pictured memorials of the past They could not en-
-force drudgery, or condemn me on account of my color
to a life of servitude As their companion I could
think and speculate In their presence my mind seem-
-ed to run riotous and exult in its freedom as a rat-
-ional being, and one destined for something higher and
better than this world can afford
I closed the windows, for the night air had become shar-
-p and piercing, and the linden creaked and swayed
its branches to the fitful gusts, Then, there was a sha-
-rp voice at the door It said, "child what are you do-
-ing" I turned round and answered "Looking at the
pictures,"
Mrs Bry alarmed at my prolonged absence had ac-
-tually dragged her unwieldly person thither to ascer-
-tain the cause
"Looking at the pictures" she repeated, "as if such an
ignorant thing as you are would know any thing
about them"
Ignorance, forsooth Can ignorance quench the immo

FIGURE 6: "The Bondwoman's Narrative" MS, p. 18 (detail)

Washington's and Wallace Turnage's holographic slave narratives detailing their escapes to serve in the Union Army. But even these works, first published together by Blight as *A Slave No More* (2007), were composed after the Civil War.[5]

Why is this so important? With the exception of a few poems by Phillis Wheatley (1753–1784), no Black-authored holographic manuscript written before the Civil War is known to exist, except for Hannah Crafts's novel. Even for towering figures like Frederick Douglass, his pre–Civil War writings come down to us in published form reproduced only through the agency of the white editors and abolitionists who shepherded the works into print. No working drafts or literary manuscripts in Douglass's hand remain. And this is the case for every single other Black author in the antebellum literary canon: Solomon Northup, William Wells Brown, Harriet Wilson, Harriet Jacobs, and so forth. As Gates eloquently observes, for this reason, Crafts's narrative holds special importance: "[T]o be able to study a manuscript written by a Black woman or man, unedited, unaffected, un-glossed, unaided by even the most well intentioned or unobtrusive editorial hand, would help a new generation of scholars to gain access to the mind of a slave in an unmediated fashion heretofore not possible." He continues: "Between us and them, between a twenty-first-century readership and the pre-edited consciousness of even one fugitive slave, often stands an editorial apparatus reflective of an abolitionist ideology, to some degree or other." He concludes: "[N]ever before have we been absolutely certain that we have enjoyed the pleasure of reading a text in the *exact* order of wording in which a fugitive slave constructed it" (*TBN* lxvii).

The science only confirmed what Gates felt in his bones: he had acquired the earliest known novel written by an African American woman. As he describes in his introduction to *The Bondwoman's Narrative*, he noticed precisely what the librarian and collector Dorothy Porter had intuited: the work reads like a Black-authored text. Porter observed the transparent and color-blind way the author treats her Black characters: "Only as the story unfolds, in most instances, does it become apparent that [Black characters] are Negroes." White writers of the 1850s and well beyond tend to introduce Black characters by immediately signaling their "blackness." This is true even of well-meaning authors writing in support of the abolitionist cause. Take, for example, Harriet Beecher Stowe's *Uncle Tom's Cabin*. The reader first glimpses Uncle Tom by witnessing him as "a full glossy black" with "a face [with] truly African features." Aunt Chloe surfaces into view with a "round black shining face." Meanwhile, Tom and Chloe's sons, Mose and Pete, appear in the text as "a couple of wooly headed boys." When white characters are introduced, however, no racial identity is signaled, because whiteness is the default lens for the author. Again, witness Stowe's Mr. Haley, who comes into sight as "a short, thick-set man"; and Solomon, "a man in a leather apron"; and Tom Loker, "a muscular man" (*TBN* lii).

As Gates observes, the exact opposite is true for *The Bondwoman's Narrative* and other Black-authored texts. Hannah Crafts's Black characters are consistently described without racial markers as they enter the narrative. Only later—usually because of the contexts of their position—are their racial identities marked. If Crafts tends to treat the Blackness of her characters as the default, she also occasionally signals the whiteness of her characters by bringing into view their unexpected paleness—such as Mr. Trappe's "large white fingers" parting window curtains and Anna's "white arms" (*TBN* 64, 133).

When the author does engage in racial colorism, it is usually in the service of her sense of class distinction among the enslaved. Domestic captives, like the author and her heroine, stand apart from those enslaved in the huts and cabins. Gates's introduction to the novel argues that one of the reasons the work is so arresting and rings so true is that Crafts's narrative provides a nuanced and candid portrait of class distinctions among African Americans—precisely a truth that was neither interesting to abolitionist white authors nor helpful for them to address.

Gates felt certain that he had acquired from Dorothy Porter Wesley's estate the very document Wesley had hinted at for the many years of their friendship. Whenever Gates talked with Wesley about his own discovery of what many considered the first known novel written by an African American woman, *Our Nig* (1859), by Harriet Wilson, a work Gates published to acclaim in 1984, Wesley would tell him "that she had a treasure that was even more rare and valuable than *Our Nig* tucked away in a file cabinet, but that she was too busy to undertake any thorough research about it or the author." As Gates explains, he originally thought Wesley "was playing the dozens with me—that is, until I read the Swann Gallery [auction] catalog" (*TBN* xii).

II

In 2002, when Henry Louis Gates Jr. published *The Bondwoman's Narrative*, he proposed a set of potential authors for the work based on the intersection of names used in the manuscript, census data, and geographic location. The list of potential writers included Hannah Vincent, a white New Jersey schoolteacher; Hannah Kraft, a candidate Gates himself ruled out; another woman named Hannah Vincent, this time listed as "mulatto" in 1870 and 1880 census records; and another potential author, explored later in this book, Jane Johnson. Subsequent scholarship could not corroborate any of these as the author. Further candidates offered by other scholars also foundered.

If Gates's work did not immediately identify the writer, Gates did authenticate the text and place the manuscript in its immediate historical context. As his research demonstrates, the autobiographical novel must have been composed between 1853 and 1861. Gates gathered expert testimony to set a factual baseline for mounting a search for the work's author: (1) The work was most likely written by an African American woman with a composition date between 1853 and 1861; (2) the "serviceable," but relatively inelegant, script (classified as "American round hand") suggests a self-taught writer based in the United States who worked hard to overcome poor spelling and eccentric punctuation; and (3) the writer appears to have been intimately connected to the family of John Hill Wheeler or at least acquired sufficient private information about the family to provide a convincing depiction of real-life details privy only to those closest to the Wheelers.

In 2004, Mack and Clara Bell first helped me build on this powerful base. Beyond the records they provided, they also put me in touch with a relative, Margaret Worthington, a descendant of the Wheelers who also held family papers. In 2005, I drove to Margaret's home in Wilmington, North Carolina, to conduct a series of interviews and to review private papers that she and her family had preserved for the Wheeler, Bond, and Rascoe/Outlaw families. Among unique works in Margaret's possession: the only known portrait of Lewis Bond and the unarchived papers of

Margaret's great-great-grandfather Samuel Jordan Wheeler of Murfreesboro. Further, Margaret's father, Sam Worthington, an amateur historian, had kept meticulous records detailing family properties in Bertie and Hertford Counties. Less auspicious to my eye were the many old almanacs Margaret possessed of Samuel Jordan Wheeler. But Margaret drew my attention to these almanacs as being especially noteworthy: Samuel Jordan Wheeler, she told me, had a habit of writing memoranda into their pages. That is, his almanacs served as a quasi-diary, detailing weather, daily activities, and occasional observations. All these items would come to serve the search for the author.

But, more immediately, Margaret's insight into Samuel Jordan Wheeler's almanacs invited further scrutiny of similar records kept by his brother John Hill Wheeler, Hannah Crafts's enslaver at the time of her escape. Like Gates before me, I spent hours in the Library of Congress in Washington, D.C., taking notes drawn from Wheeler's diaries preserved in the John Hill Wheelers Papers there. But what I had overlooked, probably like most other scholars, was the "Miscellaneous" boxes that were a part of Wheeler's records. As with Margaret's private papers, these seemed unimportant to me, as they contained only "almanacs." I now had good reason to return to Washington and comb through those records.

Indeed, upon my return to the Library of Congress, I found that John Hill Wheeler kept personal notes in his almanacs, just like his brother. And, significantly, his memoranda for 1831 and 1832 demonstrated that, at the age of twenty-five, he served in the Murfreesboro militia sent out to put down Nat Turner's rebellion. The margins of Wheeler's 1831 almanac provided unrecorded details about his and the Murfreesboro militia's responses to Turner's uprising. Further, noted on a blank page at the back of his 1832 almanac, Wheeler recorded the presence and names of his household "servants": "Milly," "Martha," "Tecumseh," "Elizabeth," and "Jack." John Hill Wheeler's almanacs opened a window onto Wheeler's central role in putting down America's bloodiest slave revolt and also provided the first threads for uncovering the lives and times of Wheeler family captives, including Hannah Crafts.

CHAPTER 3

NAT TURNER, THE WHEELERS, AND *THE BONDWOMAN'S NARRATIVE*

I

CLUSTERED IN PINK STALKS, THE flowers whitened and then ripened. By midsummer, these simple plants burst into fruit, black-purple berries that broke and bled. Enslaved people knew the pokeberry plant well, as boiled poke leaves provided an important source of protein not readily supplied by slaveholders. Other parts of the plant were useful, too. With powerful hands, Nat Turner crushed the frothy poison from the root and stem and distributed it to his co-conspirators to ward off mosquitoes. Then he extracted the blood-red juice and gathered it into an impromptu inkwell on the banks of Cabin Pond. In rural Southampton County, Virginia, on a hot summer night in June 1831, Turner charted the deadliest slave rebellion ever conducted on North American soil. With pokeberry juice, he helped shape the course of American history.

The map Turner drew marked their intended path. The white households that possessed the wives, mothers, children, brothers, and sisters of the conspirators—these would be first. Nat Turner and his band of four men planned to attack families from the neighborhood who held slaves and avoid those who did not, a pattern they would follow to the end. The first four attacks—and six of the first nine—traced a route through farms and plantations where at least one of the insurgents had been enslaved in the past or remained so that day.[1]

The life and times of Hannah Crafts also passed through Turner's hands. From the North Carolina planting communities of Princeton, Murfreesboro, Powellsville, and Indian Woods to rural Lincolnton, North Carolina, and Caroline County, Virginia—Turner's revolt remapped the experiences of an entire generation of Black people. Unlike the unsuccessful plot of the Bertie Conspiracy, defused weeks before the attack, Turner's revolt caught the region by surprise. The ferocity and violence shocked enslavers and led to a new campaign of terror directed against free Blacks and captives. This proved especially true for the enslaved people directly affected by the attacks. Each potential author—Milly, Martha, Mary, Eliza, Hannah, and Jane—harvested the bitterest fruit of the plot. The childhoods of all six were written in the blood of the Virginia pokeweed.

The region in which these six enslaved women came of age was haunted by the racial hatred and fear exposed by the revolt (see Figure 7). Rumors of fresh rebellions circulated every few years in the white communities where each potential author of *The Bondwoman's Narrative* suffered. In 1832, 1833, 1838, 1842, 1846, 1849, and 1850, local militias violently attacked enslaved and free Blacks to reestablish authority over imagined threats. As late as the spring of 1857, just before Hannah Crafts fled north, armed whites again terrorized Murfreesboro, searching for Turner-inspired insurgents.[2]

Just as the land had formed the world of Fed Fitt, King Brown, Judy Rayner, and James Barefoot, the author of *The Bondwoman's Narrative* found her world knitted by the same geography of soil, rivers, and waterways of Nat Turner and his insurgents. The tools Turner handled,

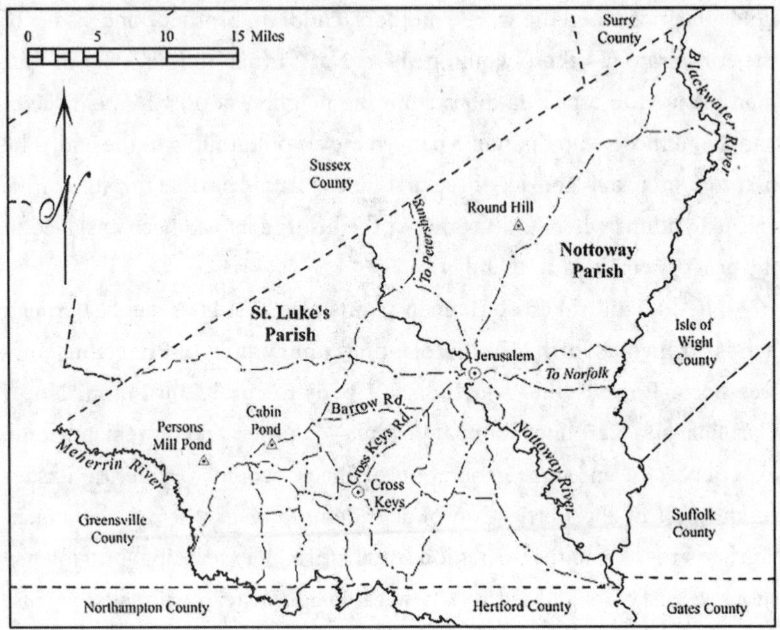

FIGURE 7: Map of Turner and Crafts territory

the local markets he frequented, the customs and kinship networks that formed his shadow community—these the author had in common with her older neighbor, even as a toddler. To track the course of Nat Turner is to trace the faint trail of America's first known Black female novelist.

II

"It was quickly agreed we should commence at home," Nat Turner explained.[3] Starting on Sunday night, August 21, and continuing all day on Monday, Nat Turner and his men followed a winding route across St. Luke's Parish, stopping at sixteen targeted houses. The zigzag course they followed was not the thoughtless and barbaric march toward Jerusalem remembered and constructed by whites but, rather, a targeted blow against a specific institution and its representatives, one sanctioned by Turner's sense of religious mission. The original conspirators—Nat Turner, Hark

Moore, Henry Porter, Nelson Edwards, and Will Francis—began at the source—the syndicate of families who owned them.[4]

At 3 a.m., in the moonlight, Hark Moore touched the ladder against the second-floor window of the Travis home. The sound was meant to be discreet, like the rebellion, and to build from there. No loud firearm reports, only a silent ascent to the bedroom, the seat of power, where the fate of the enslaved and the lives of their families became entangled in the sexual arrangements and property designs of slaveowners. As Turner related later, he held "no cause to complain of [Joseph Travis's] treatment to me." Travis was "a kind master, and placed the greatest confidence in me." As for Turner's mistress, Sally Francis Travis, the feeling bordered on friendship. Turner had assumed the role of foreman during her brief widowhood, a period when his mistress even cooked for him. But these fatalities, like others, were divinely sanctioned: "[A]rmed with a hatchet, and accompanied by Will, I entered my master's chamber, it being dark, I could not give a death blow, the hatchet glanced from his head . . . Will laid him dead with a blow of his axe, and Mrs. Travis shared the same fate, as she lay in bed."

The assailants chose their weapons carefully, especially for these early attacks, favoring Will Francis's strong arm and broad axe, which could dispatch lives quickly and quietly. The same arm and axe strengthened and sharpened by clearing trees from the fields of Travis family members—these were the tools brought to bear against the institution and people that owned them. "The murder of [the] family, five in number, was the work of a moment, not one of them awoke," Turner later reported. Thomas R. Gray noted the physical evidence at the home a day after the murders: "A little infant with its head cut off," he observed, "was forced to exchange its cradle for the fireplace." That child was Putnam Moore, Nat Turner's legal owner. This gruesome theater heralded a truth: slaveholding was a capital crime that corrupted the blood of generations. There could be no plea of innocence.[5]

Shadows danced across corpses. In the bedroom, they flitted over the featherbed with its dead contents, past the bed curtains, the carpet, and a rocking chair. At the dressing table and looking glass, the shadows paused and gathered as a pair of men searched for valuables. In the parlor/dining room, the shadows moved again, beyond the chairs and a dining table to the privacy screen at the far end of the room. Behind this screen, the rebels ransacked the apprentice's wardrobe before exiting with money, clothes, and the victims' boots.[6]

The swiftness of the attacks is suggested by the value of the unbroken china and dinnerware: six dessert plates, ten dining plates, a set of china, a salt cellar, two glass pitchers, five glass cans, a sugar dish, and cup plates went undamaged. The family hymn book and Bible, a small parcel of books, a set of silver teaspoons, a second looking glass, picture frames, and even a bottle of castor oil, an umbrella, and a snuff bottle—all outlasted the household's human occupants.[7]

III

The immediate aim of Turner's rebellion was to paralyze the white population with fear, gain recruits and arms, and then seize Jerusalem, where the growing army would find a foothold in a town named for the biblical cradle of Christendom. Turner understood the killing of women and children to be a necessary but temporary tactic. As he explained later to Thomas R. Gray, the militia member and lawyer who famously recorded and interpreted Turner's "Confessions" in *The Confessions of Nat Turner* (1831), "until we had armed and equipped ourselves, and gathered sufficient force, neither age nor sex was to be spared." As Turner also explained to William C. Parker, a magistrate and a leader of the responding Jerusalem militia, who examined him, "He says that indiscriminate massacre was not their intention after they obtained a foothold, and was resorted to in the first instance to strike terror and alarm. Women and children would afterwards have been spared, and men too who ceased to resist." And in many ways, the plan worked. A steady trickle of militia conscripts fled service after witnessing the dead remains of those assassinated by Turner's force. Terror and alarm slowed the white response.

The object was not to "massacre" inhabitants of Southampton County or even to occupy Jerusalem, as the whites believed, but, rather, Turner's goal was to gain liberty for his people, "as the white people did in the revolution." As Turner made clear, he sought "revolution"—not merely "insurrection, as you call it," he told Gray at the outset of their interview. But Turner's practical intent, like the pokeberry juice map he drew up before the attack, became buried in the response, lost in pro-slavery violence and the deep-seated racial hatred that could see only riot, disorder, and bloodlust in the actions of the rebels.

"As the black spot passed over the sun," Turner told them, "so shall the blacks pass over the earth." He referred to an unusual atmospheric condition observed a week earlier in the southeastern United States. Decades later, scientists attributed the strange occurrence to volcanic dust caused by proximate volcanic eruptions in the Mediterranean, West Indies, and Pacific Rim. This atmospheric dust coincided with a solar eclipse positioned over much of the Eastern Hemisphere, vividly on display in Turner's Southampton County and at the Wheeler plantation.[8]

For Nat Turner, it was a sign: "The great day of judgement was at hand." In some books of the Old Testament, the Spirit kindles not forgiveness but the uncompromising fire of holy warriors like Samson and Saul, commanding them to slay all the Lord's enemies down to the last man, woman, and child. "I had too much sense to be raised in bondage, and if I was, I would never be of any service to any one as a slave," Turner explained. We know that four men joined them at Elizabeth Turner II's plantation, including agricultural workers Sam and Jordan Turner and two others unidentified in sources. A fifth, named Davy, required conscription: "If he did not join them," Turner instructed the twenty-one-year-old, "he should die there." The enslaved man complied.[9]

As with Dr. Joe before him, Turner's religion was as practical as it was potent. The guns the insurgents carried included small traces of sand mixed by Turner to extend gunpowder stores. The ink and paper charting their course were the products of Turner's earlier experiments developing writing materials. To Turner, God was signaling that the time was now.

His great object and purpose had come. As he rose up in the saddle of his master's horse, he must have appeared radiant in the light. His powers of religious vision and scientific experiment were now on full display. Eight hours into the revolt, and the insurrection began to catch fire.

IV

In the early morning heat, a man on horseback charged into the small Eastern North Carolina town of Murfreesboro shouting that the slaves were in rebellion sixteen miles away in Southampton County. Thomas Weston, an elderly resident, came out on his porch, heard the news, and dropped dead of fright. To the north, Nat Turner's band of men were "butchering" slave owners and their families—or so contemporary accounts produced by whites described the events. Two such victims were the wife and child of John "Choctaw" Williams, the very man who, maddened by shock, carried the alarm to Murfreesboro. Williams, who had earned the nickname "Choctaw" because of his olive skin and because he wore his hair long, like a native, could only keep repeating, in a hoarse and unworldly voice, that the slaves had "killed his wife and cut his child's head off." Shortly after, another Southampton enslaver arrived to corroborate Williams's story. Levi Waller's tale was even more gruesome: his nursing infant had been snatched away from its mother and dismembered. Then, all ten of his children and his wife had been "hacked to pieces."[10]

By this time, hours into the insurrection, Nat Turner's men had claimed the lives of some two dozen slave owners and their family members. The rebels followed instructions Turner himself claimed to have received six years earlier from the Holy Spirit, to "arise and prepare myself, and slay my enemies with their own weapons . . . for the time was fast approaching when the first should be last and the last should be first."[11] As panic gripped Murfreesboro and other nearby communities, Turner spurred his men on their way toward Jerusalem, the county seat of Southampton, Virginia.[12]

In Murfreesboro the same day, "a well-dressed and sober" man rode into town at great speed announcing that the rebels were advancing from Boon's Bridge, on the Meherrin River, a mile and a half away. According to Dr. Thomas Borland, "Frantic distress was depicted in every face" as men and women cried out "what they should do." Even as this threat abated, fresh alarms were sounded. Murfreesboro was inundated with families from outlying areas rushing to town seeking security in numbers as the rumors swirled. Whites in more remote areas sought protection at the larger farmhouses or the plantation homes of their neighbors. At a farm a few miles west of Murfreesboro, in Northampton's Gumberry section, a witness told of women and children "put into the largest room in the house. The door was securely fastened by putting chairs against the lock on the inside. The gun I loaded myself putting in a double charge of powder and shot so as to kill several at one fire. . . . Besides this we had an axe in the room. None but the children slept any that night."[13]

The author of *The Bondwoman's Narrative* was just a kid as these events unfolded near her community. She would not have been able to understand the scope of the violence as it began to circle back and tighten its grip on her world. Other African Americans quickly saw the long-term threat brought by the rebellion—not only in the stories of scrambling militias and dismembered whites but also in the surveillance, suspicion, and violence that shadowed enslaved people's every move. The mask was off, and the savage barbarity of America's founding institution stared forth.

V

John Hill Wheeler, Hannah Crafts's enslaver, raced on horseback to his plantation near Princeton, North Carolina. He should have been attending the court session in Winton, but news of the uprising had called him away. He entered his house to secure the safety of his wife and child. In the bedroom, he must have encountered a very pregnant Milly and her daughter, Martha, both tending to Mrs. Wheeler and their infant son, Richard Mentor Johnson Wheeler, named for the famous Kentucky senator, a close friend and political ally of Mr. Wheeler's. Milly's late-term pregnancy positioned her perfectly to serve as wet nurse to little Richard, even if breastfeeding him could hurry her pregnancy along. In the South, a mother's milk could be robbed even before childbirth, as Milly probably knew. Wheeler likely took his son from Milly's bosom when he ordered her out. The enslaved nursemaid would deliver her boy a week later.[14]

Milly, Martha, Mary, Eliza, Hannah, and Jane—any one of these enslaved people could have written the account of suffering and transcendence that comprises *The Bondwoman's Narrative*. At thirteen years old, Eliza Morgan could hold only a dim sense of the horror unfolding. Too young to be a waiting maid, she bided her time doing chores at Wheeler House in town. She must have been caught up in the reprisal violence that was rife in Murfreesboro, at least in those first hours and days. Later, as vigilante crimes continued in town, Morgan was placed into the custody of the Wheelers' overseer seven miles outside town, near Liberty Hall, where neighboring planters understood the value of slave property.

Huddled in a slave cabin in nearby Indian Woods during the violence, Hannah Bond was equally poised to receive the racial hatred that was her inheritance. Just five years old, she sought refuge with some ninety other captives in the quarters provided by her enslaver, Lewis Bond, sheriff for his district. Lewis Bond patrolled Bertie County with a posse of volunteers, reasserting white supremacy, as their many slaves had cause to know. The author of *The Bondwoman's Narrative* captures a similar experience: "No one seemed to care for me till I was able to work, and then it was Hannah do this and Hannah do that. That toil unremitted unpaid toil must be my lot and portion, without even the hope or expectation of any thing better" (*TBN* 5–6).

While Mary Burton, the youngest figure connected to the novel, was not yet born, the events of 1831 helped form the environment of racial hatred that swaddled her tighter than any blanket. The same held true for Jane Johnson. Bought in the nation's capital at the age of six, Johnson also experienced the painful separation common to enslaved families. Forever parted from her family in 1828, she now served among strangers in Caroline County, Virginia. When the violence surrounding Turner's revolt first erupted, she could not look to family members for comfort and protection. Burton's and Johnson's experiences match Crafts's words: "Of my relatives I knew nothing. No one ever spoke of my father or mother. . . . I had much to make me miserable and discontented" (*TBN* 6, 11).

VI

John Hill Wheeler scribbled notes in his almanac detailing his reaction to the revolt: "22nd Most alarming intelligence reached us at our County Court of an Insurrection among the negroes in Southampton at the Cross Keys about 18 miles from the 'boro—Court after ordering the militia out immediately adjourned." At the time of the attack, Wheeler was twenty-five years old, recently married, and a father busy establishing his legal and political career. Like others, he scrambled back to his family's plantation to secure the safety of his wife and child and the loyalty of his slaves before assembling in militia ranks. As shocking as the news proved to be, Wheeler and the other members of Murfreesboro's "Governor's Guards" had trained for racial unrest. They understood the power of violence as a measure of justice from their work on slave patrol.

Wheeler was one of nearly a hundred Hertford County troops, both volunteer and commissioned, dispatched to Cross Keys near the scenes of carnage. A home guard of another 150 protected Murfreesboro from possible attack. Retribution killings began almost immediately. In nearby Maneys Neck, farmer Benjamin Britt killed a slave for disobeying a command. At the intersection of the Barrow Road and the Jerusalem–Cross Keys Highway, the Governor's Guards, just taking the field after securing the town, seized nine black prisoners and summarily executed them: "The heads of three negroes were stuck up on poles, and for weeks their grinning skulls remained, a warning to all who should undertake a similar plot." Until February 2021, when it was renamed, the site was still known as Blackhead Signpost Road.

On Thursday, August 25, a free colored man from Ahoskie, to the east, bent his course toward Southampton, attempting to pass through Murfreesboro. The home guard immediately emptied their guns into him: "[A]t Mr. Maney's office, there was about 8 or 10 Guns fired at him by the [militia], they then cut off his head and stuck it on a pole, and planted the pole at the cross streets near old Wm [William] Rea's Store house [Fourth and William]; his body was thrown in the bottom not far from where the [Broad Street] bridge was." The same afternoon, "A lady from the country going in Town . . . with her children in her carriage, and her driver behaved imprudently, so as to alarm her almost to death, and he was cut to death after the lady got to town."[15]

During their six-day engagement, Murfreesboro's Governor's Guard gained a reputation for cruelty. Near Cross Keys, the New England tutor and militia recruit Oliver M. Smith wrote his family a grisly description of the violence he witnessed: "It has been nothing, but kill, kill! Murder, murder!" he wrote, "I never supposed human beings could be capable of such barbarity, much less did I ever expect to be in the midst of, and witness to such scenes!" Smith reported seeing as many as twelve Black prisoners "tantalized [tortured] to death in try[ing] to make them disclose the plot . . . nearly 120 people [Black and white] have been slaughtered."[16]

VII

In the opening pages of her novel, begun twenty-five years after Nat Turner's rebellion, the author who adopted the name "Hannah Crafts" omits direct representation of the violence surrounding the Bertie and Southampton uprisings. Instead, Crafts relates a story passed down about an old house slave named Rose and her beloved dog, the favorite of a daughter who had been sold into slavery in Alabama. When her cruel master orders Rose to kill the dog, she refuses, and as punishment, woman and dog are suspended horrifically from a linden tree. Crafts frames the story as one that "we had heard . . . told in the dim duskiness of the summer twilight or by the roaring fires of wintry nights" (*TBN* 25):

> "Now take this old witch, and her whelp and gibbet them alive on the Linden" [Sir Clifford De Vincent] said his features distorted and his whole frame seeming to dilate with intensity and passion. . . . An iron hoop being fastened around the body of Rose she was drawn to the tree, and with great labor elevated and secured to one of the largest limbs. And then with a refinement of cruelty the innocent and helpless little animal, with a broad iron belt around its delicate body was suspended within her sight, but beyond her reach.
>
> And thus suspended between heaven and earth in a posture the [*sic*] most unimaginably painful both hung through the long long days and the longer nights. Not a particle of food, not a drop of water was allowed to either, but the master walking each morning would fix his cold cruel eyes with appalling indifference on her agonised countenance, and call to inquire whether or not she was ready to be the minister of his vengeance on the dog. For three consecutive days she retained the strength to answer that she was not.

Early critics, searching the text for authentic detail, found Rose's death unconvincing. If this was truly an autobiographical novel, they asked, why all the creaking gothic machinery? A ghostly power "loosen[s]" the portrait of her master "from its fastings in the wall." The "decayed branches of [the linden tree]" clatter at the master's window ("Whence is that frightful noise?") (*TBN* 29–30). The spectral presence of the murdered slave haunts the text. But what else could an enslaved person who had grown up in the shadow of the Gospel Oaks and Nat Turner have written? The scene is, indeed, based on a true story, as we will see in the next chapter.

There is a reason the earliest African American writers, including Harriet Jacobs and Harriet Wilson, identified with and wrote in the vernacular of the gothic. As victims of caprice, these authors could not look to reason or justice to save them. Rather, with its panoply of forced separations, haunted enclosures, instruments of torture, and gruesome violence, the associative logic of the gothic fit the emotional and situational truths of their lives. Forced separation, torture, rape, death—extremes of psychic and physical violence—this was the everyday stuff of their existence. In the gothic, these authors found the terms of a life they recognized and one, as writers, they could imaginatively control and make meaningful by appropriating its terms.[17]

These principles are likely what propelled rebels as diverse as Nat Turner and Hannah Crafts to command the same materials.[18] Crafts, too, designed her graphic revenge by putting her hand, as Turner did, in the hand of the Almighty. In her preface, she asks, "Have I succeeded in portraying any of the peculiar features of that institution whose curse rests over the fairest land the sun shines upon?" And she answers, "[P]ious and discerning minds can scarcely fail to recognise the hand of Providence in giving to the righteous the reward of their works, and to the wicked the fruit of their doings" (*TBN* 3). Crafts divined justice with her pen, just as Turner hewed it with an axe.

The author's world exploded with violence just as she began to form an understanding of her environment. These events would help determine the mistrust, abuse, sexual violence, and hatred that suffocated her early years and adolescence. Even in her genteel plantation home, even as she played alongside her master's children, she saw the skull behind the master's smile. As Crafts would discover, slowly, and with inspired passion, only the bold swing of her pen and the swift motion of her feet could free her from this snare. Like Nat Turner, she, too, was called to "slay [her] enemies with their own weapons." But it would be some two and a half decades before she was prepared to make her strike and to glimpse, and even experience, what Nat Turner had prophesied. She, like Turner, would be in the prime of life when her vision took hold and she struck out for freedom. She, too, would make darkness visible, but this time, the weapon would be her quill pen, a sewing box, and paper stolen from her enslaver.

CHAPTER 4

THE REVOLT

IN AUGUST 1857, IN HIDING at Horace Craft's farm, Hannah Crafts revised her manuscript. On recycled paper, she wrote, "What strange ways the wind has and how particularly anxious it seemed to enter the drawing-room in the southern wing, rattling the shutters and shrieking like a maniac, and breathing out a low gurgling laugh like the voice of childhood." She continued on a second slip, "Then the linden lost its huge branches and swayed and creaked distractedly, and we all know that was said to forbode [*sic*] calamity to the family" (MS 20). From the sewing kit, she took a sealing wax adhesive, broke it in half, moistened the halves, and affixed the changes to her narrative with her thimble.

Crafts was editing the scene near the beginning of her narrative where Sir Clifford De Vincent tortures Rose for refusing to kill the dog she cherishes because it was a gift from her daughter. For the author, the scene is emblematic: a woman who nursed and raised her enslavers' offspring is lynched for maintaining a link to her own kidnapped child. The curse Rose delivers in the novel is generational: "'I will brood over this tree . . . and when death, or sickness, or misfortune is to befall the family ye may listen for ye will assuredly hear the creaking of its limbs'" (*TBN* 25).

If the prose rasps with irony, it also documents real life. In 1822, in nearby Halifax, North Carolina, Jacob R. Pope tortured and murdered Crafts's grandmother, Rosea Pugh/Pope. On property first deeded to the family in the early eighteenth century, Pope tied up Rosea for an offense that has gone unrecorded. With her clothes tied "about her head," Pope "suspended" Rosea with "her legs lapped around the trunk of the tree some inches above the ground." He then commenced "beat[ing] her with a cowskin to the extent of more than 250 lashes." Left suspended to the tree, Rosea Pope died a death as gruesome as that attributed to the hand of Sir Clifford De Vincent in Crafts's novel. For years, the story circulated widely among the enslaved communities connected to *The Bondwoman's Narrative*.[1]

Rosea's "half-hanging" was not unique to Halifax, North Carolina, or to Crafts's narrative. Blacks were increasingly punished and tortured in precisely this way, especially in the wake of Turner's revolt. The former captive Henry "Box" Brown, who lived in Richmond, Virginia, describes the practice: "[M]any were 'half hung,' as it was termed; that is they were suspended to some limb of a tree, with a rope about their necks, so adjusted as not to quite strangle them. . . . This half-hanging is a refined species of cruelty, peculiar to slavery, I believe."[2]

The author of *The Bondwoman's Narrative* grew up in sight of these practices and the bloody history of trees like the Gospel Oaks. If well-known stories of the Gospel Oaks informed Crafts's narrative of Rose's death on the "Linden tree," she may also have drawn on the death of Nat Turner in nearby Jerusalem (later renamed Boykins), Virginia.

According to African American folk tradition, the tree upon which Nat Turner's body was hoisted and then shot became strengthened with his blood, eventually flourishing for the next seventy-five years. The limb to which the hanging rope was fastened, however, proved cursed. Louis Lee Jones, "a black conjure man" from Boykins, explained to F. Roy Johnson, the Murfreesboro-based folklorist, "They hung him up there and shot him; they tell me that limb died on that tree . . . and broke slam off where the rope was tied." From that place to the trunk, the limb remained as "healthy as ever, and ain't nary bit of it fell off" (see Figure 8).[3] Turner's last actions would be as defiant as those attributed to Rose in

The Bondwoman's Narrative. "He betrayed no emotion but appeared to be utterly reckless of the fate that awaited him," according to one observer, "and even hurried the executioner in the performance of his duty!"[4]

The conflation of Rose with her dog further echoes the legends of Turner. In the oral tradition, many in the region envisioned Turner's spirit returning to stalk backcountry roads and lanes in the guise of a dog. One oral tale descended that Turner returned as a "dog [with] a hyena-like head," and "people say they won't walk [the Blackhead Post] road at night for nothing." In another telling, Turner appeared as a "big Shepherd dog." If a traveler cracked their horsewhip at the dog, "his eyes turned red as fire." Crafts would likely have heard stories of "Old Nat" at "Blackhead Post" pacing "as a headless dog." In the spirit tales of the region, the insurrectionists continued to prosecute their rebellion, fleeing their pursuers in the form of dogs, bulls, and other wild animals.

The primary source behind the scene in the novel, however, seems to be the real-life death of Rosea Pugh/Pope. Crafts's character "Rose" reflects the experiences of the author's grandmother Rosea Pugh, who became the property of the Pope family before the author was born. The Pughs knew the Popes intimately from the early Colonial period, when both families emigrated together from England. The Pughs and Popes first settled in what was then Nansemond County, Virginia, and later moved onto Tuscarora land in North Carolina in the mid-eighteenth century. Hannah Crafts seems to tell this story through the figure of Sir Clifford De Vincent in the novel. Like the De Vincent family in the novel, the Pughs and Popes developed their wealth over many generations: "[G]eneration had succeeded generation, and a long line of De Vincents occupied the family residence" (*TBN* 16).[5] By acquiring land and slaves and profiting from the booming tobacco economy that characterized Virginia's Tidewater region, these families consolidated and extended their wealth and stature. When Virginia soil became exhausted from over-farming, the Pughs, Popes, and later the Bonds moved their operations to North Carolina.

In what became Bertie County, North Carolina, all three families leveraged their influence and wealth to procure land grants. For the Popes that meant nearly 500 acres near Halifax (300 acres in 1742 and 161 additional acres in 1749).[6] Resettled on two plantations centered on the banks of Deep Creek, a tributary of the Roanoke River, the Pope family flourished. Jacob R. Pope (one model for Crafts's slave speculator Mr. Trappe) purchased an additional 203 acres in 1804, bringing his North Carolina

FIGURE 8: "The Nat Turner hanging tree," *Godey's Magazine*, March 1898

holdings to nearly 700 acres. By the time Jacob R. Pope tied Crafts's grandmother to his tree, he was "an extensive land owner . . . prosperously employed in agricultural pursuits . . . carrying on his large plantations with the help of his slaves."[7]

Like Rose in the novel, Rosea Pope served as a nursemaid to her murderer's offspring. At the time of her death, she cared for six of her enslaver's children: Sally Anne (age ten), Priscilla (nine), Mary Susan (seven), Bithena Winefred (five), Elijah (two), and Joseph (one). The historical record first notes Rosea's presence in the 1790 U.S. federal census record of Thomas Pugh Sr. She appears again in the 1810 and 1820 federal census record of Jacob R. Pope, enumerated only by gender, her status as property, and recorded as between the ages twenty-six and forty-four (the metric for data collection in 1820). By squaring earlier census data listing age and gender, Rosea can be reasonably traced from the Pughs to the Pope family through Jacob R. Pope. She is depicted as an "elderly servant" in Crafts's novel, but she was probably in her late forties when she was murdered.[8]

Did the author really know the minute details of her ancestor's life? Probably not. But the scandal of Rosea Pope's death in nearby Halifax was a story that was passed down to Crafts's own enslaved community. By pressing quill to paper and reimagining Rosea's life, Crafts immortalized a woman with whom she held kinship. In Crafts's novel, she reimagines and records the site of Rosea's torture: "The servants all knew the history of that tree. It had not been concealed from them that a wild and weird influence was supposed to belong to it." She continues: "Calmly and resolutely the old woman arose with something of the martyr spirit burning in her eye. To his inquiries she answered plainly that she should not and could not obey his orders," Crafts wrote (*TBN* 22).

In telling the story of Rose's lynching in the novel, Crafts thus kept alive the real-life story of Rosea Pope, demonstrating the communal death inherent in such a brutal act—a deadening experience not only for captives, but also for the enslavers and their families forced to witness human depravity. ("[S]lumber entirely fled the household of Sir Clifford.

His Lady heretofore one of the gayest of women was never seen to smile afterwards") (*TBN* 24). The scene parallels the first-person account of similar violence recorded by Frederick Douglass. In his 1845 *Narrative of the Life of Frederick Douglass*, Douglass famously recounts witnessing the whipping of his aunt Hester: "[Colonel Lloyd] commenced to lay on the heavy cowskin, and soon the warm, red blood (amid heartrending shrieks from her, and horrid oaths from him) came dripping to the floor." He continues: "He was a cruel man, hardened by a long life of slaveholding." From a closet in which he is sequestered, Douglass describes experiencing the scene as his "entrance to the hell of slavery. . . . The louder she screamed, the harder he whipped; and where the blood ran fastest, there he whipped longest."[9]

For Crafts, the cruelty of her character Rose's torture is compounded by the fact that Rose is also forced to witness the torment of her dog, the living token of her kidnapped daughter. In the novel, Sir Clifford is heedless to the entreaties of his wife and son to pardon Rose and the dog: "Sir Clifford made it a boast that he never retracted, that his commands and decisions like the laws of the Medes and Persians were unalterable" (*TBN* 22). His wife asks that he at least end their torture with death, as "the sight of their agonies and the noise of their groans would haunt her to her dying day" (*TBN* 24). But Sir Clifford refuses. Only after discovering the dead body of the dog in the morning does he propose to take the servant down from the tree.

That is when Rose places her curse:

> At the sound of his voice she opened her blood-shotten lack-lustre eyes,—and her voice as she spoke had a deep sepulchral tone. "No" she said "it shall not be. I will hang here till I die as a curse to this house, and I will come here after I am dead to prove its bane. In sunshine and shadow, by day and by night I will brood over this tree, and weigh down its branches, and when death, or sickness, or misfortune is to befall the family ye may listen for ye will assuredly hear the creaking of its limbs." (*TBN* 25)

When Crafts composed these words, she likely drew on the fate of Jacob R. Pope. The author was seventeen years old at the time of Pope's death, and the event seems to have made a deep impression. Like Sir Clifford in her novel, Pope was found in a pool of his own blood in 1843. First thought to be an act of suicide (again, like Sir Clifford), Pope's death was later determined to be the work of assassins. Newspaper accounts note that "he had scarcely reached the door when he was shot with a large squirrel shot, which entered his abdomen making an orifice about two inches in diameter—he continued in his senses until his death, which occurred about eighteen hours thereafter." The story of Pope's demise was widely circulated and must have passed by word of mouth from slave quarter to slave quarter. Crafts reserves a similar death for the chief villain of her novel, the slave speculator Mr. Trappe. While a newspaper account wrote that Pope was shadowed by "some persons in the old field opposite his house trying to shoot him," Crafts describes a similar kind of justice condoned by captives: "Mr. Trappe's man-servant caught a glimpse once or twice of [enslaved] fellows answering their description, who seemed to be lurking, as he thought and as it proved, for evil purposes around the habitation of the former."[10]

The pages the author conveyed to freedom carry Rosea Pope's avenging spirit. In Crafts's story, Nat Turner's ghost finds its proxy in the figure of Rose. Robbed of her daughter, her body an object used to nourish her enslaver's children, Rose is crucified alongside her dog, her only link to a stolen child. Like Turner, she arranges her death to be a defiant promise of vengeance: "No. It shall not be. I will hang here till I die as a curse to this house, and I will come here after I am dead to prove its bane." This is a very different message from the one Harriet Beecher Stowe's Uncle Tom offers just before he is tortured to death in *Uncle Tom's Cabin* (1852): "[A]s to my raising my hand agin any one here, I never shall" (196). As with Turner, Hannah Crafts's ghostly Rose offers harm for harm in the service of an avenging deity. The haunting truths that first alarmed Bertie and then Southampton County helped bind the novelist's art.

CHAPTER 5

THE CANDIDATES

I

ALL NAT TURNER'S ENSLAVERS DERIVED from the same syndicate of families who touched the lives of authorial candidates. The best candidates for authorship—Milly, Martha, Mary, Eliza, Hannah, and Jane—all became property in neighboring communities. The first alliance, a marriage in 1807, connected the Turner and Francis families, longtime neighbors. In 1818, a nearby branch of the Reese family joined, as did the Moores and the Whiteheads in 1819. Joseph Travis married into these families two years before Nat Turner's revolt.[1] Among this loose network of associate families were the enslavers most directly connected to *The Bondwoman's Narrative*: the Wheelers, Turners, Moores, Grahams, Bonds, and Pughs.

The interests of the planting and merchant elite commingled. Sons and daughters of the leading Southampton families—including the children of the Francis, Moore, and Whitehead clans—resided in Murfreesboro while attending the Hertford Academy and, later, Mrs. Banks's "Female Academy," boarding schools designed to serve affluent families in the region. The two-story brick building that housed operations for both schools stood on grounds owned by the patriarch John Wheeler Sr., an original trustee and founder of these academies, located adjacent to Wheeler House on Broad Street in town. As we will see, the author of *The*

Bondwoman's Narrative practiced a literary style consonant with the lessons, books, and composition exercises taught in these academies.[2]

The day after Turner's revolt, the academies' main building was being fortified by militia members, who were stationed outside it. Inside, Harriet Banks and her staff worked to calm neighbors seeking shelter at the school. A security detail was assigned to the business district, including the academies' building and Wheeler's merchant store, as local leaders sought to create safe zones for those pouring in from the countryside. But the circle of protection could reach only so far. By late afternoon, Margaret Whitehead, a beloved graduate and former teacher at the "Female Academy," would be found murdered, her head split open on a fence rail near her home in Southampton County. This is significant because Whitehead, like her sisters and brother (also victims that day), was a close friend of the Wheelers, perhaps even boarding with the family when she attended school in Murfreesboro.

II

Milly and Martha Murfree began their lives in Murfreesboro, born into the household of William Hardy Murfree, son of Murfreesboro's founder Hardy Murfree. John Hill Wheeler recorded their presence in his almanac book. At the time of the revolt, Milly was "aged about 35 years," and Martha, "about 6 years." County records of "Inventories & Sales of Estates" show that on July 8, 1830, John Hill Wheeler purchased "Milly & Child Martha" from the estate of neighbor George Cryer for $143.[3] George's mother, Sally, was the daughter of Hardy Murfree. Milly and Martha can be traced back to a network of light-skinned domestic captives serving in the households of the town's leading families.

Census records for Sally Murfree Cryer indicate that Milly (1820 census) and then also Martha (1830 census) resided on the Murfree-Cryer family holdings in Northampton County, not far from the Wheeler plantation. During those years, Milly served as domestic help for Sally Murfree Cryer and her husband, Samuel Cryer, and, later, for the widowed

Sally and her son, George. After Sally's death in the early 1820s, mother and daughter continued on as domestic servants to George Cryer, who by this time suffered from blindness. When George died, unmarried, in 1830, John Hill Wheeler purchased the mother and daughter pair as part of Cryer's estate settlement.

A glimpse of their life serving on the Cryer-Murfree holding can be gathered from the same court records that establish Wheeler's purchase. The Cryer property was modest, consisting of only four enslaved people serving both domestically and in the fields. Before their deaths, the Cryers resided in a house similar to the one where Milly and Martha now served as Wheeler's domestic servants. Records suggest that the relative wealth of the Cryer-Murfree household came through the slave dowry that Sally Murfree brought to her Cryer marriage, including Milly Murfree and two enslaved youths, "Bill" and "Jim."[4]

Wheeler purchased Milly and Martha two weeks after his marriage to Mary Brown in April 1830. Clearly, he was seeking an experienced waiting maid and house servant for his well-born, educated wife. More than ten years her junior, Wheeler would have known Milly first as a domestic servant in the prominent home of William Hardy Murfree, son of Hardy Murfree, and later, he would have encountered Milly's service for the nearby Cryer family.[5]

For Wheeler, the Cryer sale could not have been more fortuitous. The fact that Milly had a six-year-old daughter satisfied Wheeler's need to establish future domestic service; furthermore, little Martha's presence proved Milly's suitability for bearing other children. Indeed, Milly became pregnant shortly after joining the Wheeler household. It is even possible Wheeler arranged her pregnancy. If he did so, he would have been practicing control over her reproductive capability in a fashion not uncommon for the period and region. Arranged insemination of a bondwoman—or rape—provided both a potential nursemaid and a possible playmate and, later, a bondservant for a slaveowner's offspring.

There is no way to know for certain if Milly was compelled to conceive a child after Mary Brown Wheeler's pregnancy became apparent, but the fact remains that she gave birth just months after the birth of Wheeler's son Richard Mentor Johnson Wheeler. The names of the two children—Mary's and Milly's—confirm John Hill Wheeler's controlling stake in both: his son was named for Wheeler's political mentor Kentucky senator Richard Mentor Johnson, and Tecumseh, Milly's child, was named for the Shawnee chief and rebel warrior who worked to unite Native American tribes. The pair of names is peculiar and clearly the work of Wheeler: In 1813, at the Battle of the Thames, Richard Mentor Johnson shot Tecumseh to death in a cavalry charge. The legend of Johnson's supposed assassination of the Shawnee leader greatly aided his subsequent political career. The implied threat to Milly's son, Tecumseh, born just after Nat Turner's failed rebellion, could not go unnoticed.

Wheeler's friendship with the future vice president even led Wheeler to name Johnson the godfather of his firstborn, Richard. Although Johnson could not attend the christening, he did send a baby carriage, a valuable gift for his political understudy and for his namesake. Johnson's intimacy with the married couple is less surprising when you realize that he boarded with Mary Brown Wheeler's father, the Rev. Obadiah Brown, in Washington, D.C., at precisely the time that the young Wheeler was courting Mary Brown. Because a number of important senators and congressmen boarded with the Browns during congressional sessions, their hearth and table became an unofficial site of political power. Indeed, during President Andrew Jackson's administration, the circle became known as Jackson's "Kitchen Cabinet." The Rev. Obadiah Brown helped craft policy in his parlor, including coauthoring with Johnson a long-standing theory of the separation of church and state. Reverend Brown was a founder and trustee of Columbian College, now George Washington University. As a student at Columbian, young John Hill Wheeler became friends with Brown's son William Van Horne Brown. This friendship allowed Wheeler to become an intimate of the Brown household, where the ambitious Wheeler not only sought his entry into politics but also gained Mary Brown's hand in marriage.[6]

"About the 1st of this month Milly had a little son—Tecumseh," Wheeler wrote in his almanac book in September 1831. Tecumseh was a powerful name to bestow upon the first captive born into his newly established household, especially in light of Turner's rebellion. The Shawnee rebel Tecumseh, like Nat Turner, envisioned a race war against the white man to secure the liberty of his people. Like Nat Turner, he was killed in the attempt, and his movement ended with his death. Wheeler, a man who spent a lifetime studying and preserving American history, understood these details. He also records in his almanac the gift from his son's namesake: "[April] 6th His little basket carriage the present of his namesake Hon. R. M. Johnson arrived from New York." Tecumseh's future white enslaver Richard Mentor Johnson Wheeler would come to fall asleep cradled in a "basket carriage," a gift of Chief Tecumseh's killer. Or, so the revisionist historian John Hill Wheeler had devised.

As a close friend of Johnson's, Wheeler would have been well apprised of Johnson's unconventional domestic arrangements. The lifelong bachelor's sexual relationships with enslaved women were well known in his native Kentucky and among his friends. Most prominently, there was Julia Chinn, whom Johnson acquired in the division of his father's estate. Chinn served as head of Johnson's household at "Great Crossing," the Johnson plantation in Kentucky, where she managed Johnson's affairs in his absence. Chinn bore Johnson two nearly white daughters, Imogene and Adaline, whom Johnson educated, positioned to be accepted into white society, and quietly married off to prominent white men. The passing plot that figures so prominently in *The Bondwoman's Narrative* is not simply an invention of the author; it is also traceable to the stories Wheeler's captives heard about the Kentucky household so intimately tied to their own. Hannah Crafts's own forced sexual captivity was not unique, and it is not surprising that the plot of Crafts's novel turns on enslaved women navigating a world of sexual control.

III

For planter families, the conception of a child necessitated the planning and reordering of domestic service. Another enslaved female who became a part of John Hill Wheeler's domestic circle around this time was Eliza Morgan. Eliza was the daughter of an enslaved woman called Molly Morgan, who served as waiting maid to Wheeler's stepmother, Sarah Clifton Wheeler. The light-skinned Eliza, just thirteen years old, was marked early for domestic service. Her family's long experience as respected, lighter-skinned "servants" in Murfreesboro may be reflected in *The Bondwoman's Narrative*. The Morgan children, like Eliza Morgan, carried the rare distinction of being accorded a surname, like their mother. Crafts captures the latitude accorded special "servants" even as young children: "By and by as I grew older, and was enabled to manifest my good intentions, not so much by words, as by a manner of sympathy, I was quite astonished to see how much I was trusted and confided in" (*TBN* 9).

For the early part of her life, Eliza assisted her mother in tending to Sarah Clifton Wheeler and the many Wheeler children living at Wheeler House in Murfreesboro. Her bearing and speech developed through the influence of the household where she served through her proximity to her mother. But even under the relative safety of her mother's eye, Eliza still had to encounter the unsettling chaos and violence that swept Murfreesboro in the wake of Turner's revolt.

There is no direct record, beyond elements in *The Bondwoman's Narrative*, of the Black experience during this time in Murfreesboro, but we do have an account by Harriet Jacobs, in nearby Edenton, North Carolina. In *Incidents in the Life of a Slave Girl* (1861), Jacobs describes the reprisals: "It was a grand opportunity for the low whites, who had no negroes of their own to scourge. They exulted in such a chance to exercise a little brief authority, and show their subservience to the slaveholders." As in Murfreesboro, the Edenton militia were called to muster: "When the slaves were told there was to be another muster, they were surprised and rejoiced. Poor creatures! They thought it was going to be a holiday." Jacobs goes on to write, "Those who never witnessed such scenes can hardly believe what I know was inflicted at this time on innocent men, women, and children, against whom there was not the slightest ground for suspicion. Colored people and slaves who lived in remote parts of the town suffered in an especial manner. In some cases, the searchers scattered powder and shot among their clothes, and then sent other parties to find them and bring them forward as proof that they were plotting insurrection."

In developing her manuscript, Jacobs originally omitted all mention of Turner's insurrection. To the white imagination, she knew, Turner only conjured fear and prejudice. But at the request of her white editor, Lydia Maria Child, she recounted the violence: "Every where men, women, and children were whipped till the blood stood in puddles at their feet. Some received five hundred lashes; others were tied hands and feet, and tortured with a bucking paddle, which blisters the skin terribly." Terror touched all, free and enslaved: "The dwellings of the colored people, unless they happened to be protected by some influential white person, who was nigh at hand, were robbed of clothing and every thing else the marauders thought worth carrying away." Jacobs continues: "All day long these unfeeling wretches went round, like a troop of demons, terrifying and tormenting the helpless. At night, they formed themselves into patrol bands, and went wherever they chose among the colored people, acting out their brutal will." Rape was one of the tools used by whites as reprisal: "Many women hid themselves in woods and swamps, to keep out of their way. If any of the husbands or fathers told of these outrages, they were tied up to the public whipping post, and cruelly scourged for telling lies about white men." In such an environment, Eliza Morgan came to understand the violent claim whites could make over her body. Enslaved women like Morgan were eventually consigned to safekeeping at remote plantation homes, away from marauding bands of militia centered in towns like Murfreesboro and Edenton.

IV

In 1811, Hannah Sr. followed Catherine Pugh into the household of Lewis Bond as part of Catherine's wedding dower. In her teenage years, Hannah Sr. came to occupy an important role assisting her mistress in maintaining the Bond household. In 1826, Hannah Sr. bore a "quadroon" daughter, also named Hannah. By the time of Turner's revolt, when Hannah Bond was a young child, mother and daughter resided at Lewis Bond's house in Windsor, North Carolina, eleven miles to the east of the Bond plantation in Indian Woods. Five-year-old Hannah's value, and her kinship with the Pugh and Bond families, are suggested by a series of lawsuits contested by the Bertie County planter Lewis and his brother John.

The neighboring Turner family brought a property suit, seeking to possess Hannah Sr. as a captive claimed by Catherine Turner, the mother of Thomas Turner, whom she had married in 1810. Turner died just days after the marriage, but that did not keep the mother-in-law from claiming Hannah Sr., whose light skin and dignified bearing must have attracted John and Lewis Bond. Together the brothers contested Catherine Turner's legal maneuvers. The reason for the Bond family's extraordinary legal and extralegal treatment of Hannah Sr. and, later, her daughter appears to be consanguinity. Hannah Sr. was most likely a half sister to Catherine Pugh, born, like Catherine, on the Pugh family's extensive property holdings in Quitsna, North Carolina. The even lighter-skinned "Little Hannah" probably owed her paternity to a Bond relation.[7] Whatever the bloodlines, Nat Turner's insurrection upset Lewis Bond's arrangements in Windsor. Like others, Bond felt compelled to move his enslaved property out of town and to the more secure control of his overseer, while Bond, as sheriff for the region, helped organize and deploy the county's militia to protect the area.

Significantly, Bond's keeping Hannah Sr. and "Little Hannah" in a separate Windsor residence bears a striking resemblance to scenes in *The Bondwoman's Narrative*. In the novel, Crafts tells the story of slave owner Mr. Cosgrove, who places his enslaved victim, Evelyn, miles away from the plantation domain of his wife. Like Mrs. Cosgrove in the novel, Catherine Pugh Bond may not have been aware of the extent of her husband's relationship to Hannah Sr. until shortly before Catherine's death in 1828. In Hannah Crafts's novel, Mr. Cosgrove's relationship with Evelyn demonstrates not only the system of rape perpetrated in slavery but also the damage such evil inflicts on the enslavers themselves. In the novel, the Cosgroves' marriage declines into physical abuse that hastens the death of Mrs. Cosgrove. Whether the depiction of the Cosgroves' marriage is based on Lewis and Catherine Bond must remain wholly speculative.

In August 1831, amid terror and violence, the young Hannah must have realized afresh—like Hannah Crafts in the novel—the disdain those in the slave huts felt for her: "[T]hey regarded me curiously as I entered, grinned with malicious satisfaction that I had been brought down to their level" (*TBN* 215). At Bond's Windsor home, "Little Hannah" had experienced the privileges accorded to her mother. Suddenly, at the plantation, the five-year-old found herself facing the ill will of those in Willow Hall's slave huts. The dramatic, if temporary, demotion of circumstance may account for the sharp class consciousness that pervades *The Bondwoman's Narrative*. Hannah in the novel frequently objects to "association with the vile, foul, filthy inhabitants of the huts" (*TBN* 211).

V

Jane Johnson—considered by many scholars as the most likely author of the manuscript—found herself sold away from her family, an orphan in Caroline County, Virginia. Very few records remain extant from which to draw a picture of Johnson's childhood. She passed those early years on the plantations of the Chesapeake before becoming enslaved by the Wheelers. Born around 1814 in Washington, D.C., Johnson was the daughter of an enslaved man named John Williams and his wife, Jane. In Jane Johnson's early teens, she became a captive to the Johnson family based in Caroline County, probably in the household of James A. Johnson. Her earliest confirmed owner was Cornelius Crew of Richmond, Henrico County, Virginia, who sold Jane and two of her children to John Hill Wheeler around New Year's Day 1854.

Jane Johnson's life serving the Wheeler family in Washington, D.C., between 1854 and 1855 parallels details in *The Bondwoman's Narrative*. Her dramatic escape from Wheeler on Wednesday, July 18, 1855, became one of the first challenges to the 1850 Fugitive Slave Act, and the records maintained from the court case, known as the *Case of Passmore Williamson*, provide some of the only factual details available to reconstruct her life. Fortunately, William Still, the important Underground Railroad leader, recorded an account of Johnson before and after her escape in his seminal book *The Underground Railroad* (1872).

In August 1831, however, Johnson could not know the history-shaping experiences that awaited her. Instead, she faced the terror and reprisal violence sweeping Virginia and North Carolina in response to Turner's revolt. Henry "Box" Brown records what Johnson may well have witnessed:

> I did not then know precisely what was the cause of these scenes, for I could not get any very satisfactory information concerning the matter from my master, only that some slaves had undertaken to kill their owners; but I have since learned that it was the famous Nat Turner's insurrection that caused all the excitement I witnessed. Slaves were whipped, hung, and cut down with swords in the streets, if found away from their quarters after dark.[8]

In all likelihood, Johnson, too, observed similar scenes of trauma, before and after Nat Turner's revolt.

VI

John Hill Wheeler and the Guard did not return to Murfreesboro until midday August 29, 1831, after "having scoured every foot of [the insurrection area] and apprehended every black going at large who submitted, and shot all who fled and could not be taken alive."[9] The next day, Wheeler merely noted in his almanac that the revolt had been quelled: "About 78 persons killed," he wrote. But he recorded only the projected tally of whites. He did not count the "negroes" killed as "persons" in this, his personal mortality roll. The same day he marked his almanac, Wheeler prepared a report for the influential Washington, D.C., newspaper *The*

Globe, where he held personal connections to the paper's editor, Francis Preston Blair: "There have been about 50 to 100 negroes killed," he admitted. But he buried these deaths in a self-serving narrative that discounted the loss of Black lives.

Instead, anonymously, Wheeler assured Northern readers and, especially, Washington, D.C., policy makers, that slavery remained safe and viable—an institution that affectionate slaves would fight to preserve: "We still keep up an active watch," he wrote. "We fear that there was some concert in the disturbance, but, from the vigilant measures which have been pursued, they must be convinced of the utter hopelessness of their undertaking. The slaves in this place [Murfreesboro, North Carolina] with few exceptions, have manifested the greatest affection for their masters; and I verily believe that had we been attacked here . . . they would have aided us in exterminating the rebellious negroes."

Wheeler's report of the insurrection, one of the first eyewitness accounts to be published outside the South, held enormous influence in shaping the way Turner's insurrection would be viewed not just at the time, but for generations. In Wheeler's account, and in the countless "official" records of the events that would follow, the only "barbarous murders" to be seen were those perpetuated upon whites, whose deaths served as emblems of Black savagery. Wheeler writes, "I write to you under the same emotions as a mariner would, who had long been tossed on the troubled ocean, after he arrived in a safe and quiet harbor."

Conspicuously absent in Wheeler's account are details of the retributive killings in which Wheeler, his brother Samuel Jordan Wheeler, and others took part. The Black men who were beheaded and whose skulls were staked at Blackhead Post are simply "nine negroes, who had been engaged in the work of death . . . immediately executed." Rather, Wheeler's account tracks with the white records by which Nat Turner's rebellion initially would be remembered and passed down through history. Animalized brutes ("panthers") thirsty for blood and discord were thwarted by courageous whites, like the Wheeler brothers. Affectionate slaves fought side by side with their white masters to preserve the safety of the community. Here, like a kind of African safari, Wheeler and other members of the Governor's Guard encounter "the panther of the desert, [whose] . . . savage nature once tasted blood, it thirsted for more." Meanwhile, "animated by plunder, they proceeded in their fell work of desolation and death, sparing neither decrepit age, or helpless infancy, until they laid waste a whole neighborhood of about eighty persons." The "disturbance" of these "blood-thirsty" "wretches" met with "vigilant measures," and Wheeler and the other forces quickly reestablished order.

In private letters, Capt. Solon Borland, Wheeler's friend and classmate, stated more bluntly the reason for the retaliatory slayings conducted by the Governor's Guards. "It seems necessary," he wrote his brother Roscius, "that very decisive and severe means should be resorted to by us, as the murders in Southampton are of such a kind as to plainly show the horrible nature and temper of our internal enemy—old women—girls—boys—infants of the smallest size butchered and mangled in a manner that, as we would believe, the Cruelest nature would shudder at it. It is nearly requisite for some time yet to show in full force, that the blacks may have view of the power which can be speedily used against [them]. The impression must be made on their fears through the medium of their eyes and bodily feelings."[10] As he related to one Raleigh acquaintance, "[N]ot one black was Spared that fell into [our] hands."[11]

If Nat Turner's insurrection became a journey—as if by sea, to a savage land—that is only because John Hill Wheeler and other enslavers had constructed a world to make it so. Unknown to Wheeler, a captive from his very household would finish and preserve a counternarrative to the one that Wheeler and men like Borland sought for the South. It would take decades for the balance to shift, more than a century and a half from the time of Nat Turner's rising, but a little girl caught up in the confusion and chaos of this slave insurrection would come to forge a new personal view of history, one that ultimately displaced the public, "official" history Wheeler made it his life's mission to secure and establish. Hannah Crafts's literary effort would be designed to demonstrate what the white masters refused to see, the results of their own unholy work: "mangled" slave lives—"Old women—girls—boys—infants of the smallest size." If Wheeler, the future historian and diplomat, staked his life on a world where white planters conquered and exploited other races, Hannah Crafts, like Nat Turner, disrupted this story. Her life and her autobiographical novel told a "truth stranger than fiction," and she aimed that story directly at a slave master and his claims of writing true "history" for an expanding American republic. Crafts's novel would outlive Wheeler's warped history.

CHAPTER 6

CHILDHOOD

I

IN THE BONDWOMAN'S NARRATIVE, *THE* author emphasizes her protagonist's alien experience of childhood. "When a child they used to scold and find fault with me because they said I was dull and stupid," she notes. "Perhaps under other circumstances and with more encouragement I might have appeared better." Crafts continues, noting her narrator's attentive nature: "I had . . . a silent unobtrusive way of observing things and events, and wishing to understand them better than I could." Although her "complexion was almost white," her racial identity was set: "the African blood in my veins would forever exclude me from the higher walks of life" (*TBN* 5). Yet, despite these challenges, the author channels the lowborn character Esther Summerson in Charles Dickens's *Bleak House*. Drawing partially from the despised Summerson, Crafts writes of Hannah: "'I am a slave' thus my thoughts would run. 'I can never be great, nor rich; I cannot hold an elevated position in society, but I can do my duty, and be kind in the sure and certain hope of an eternal reward['"] (*TBN* 11). The childhood experiences of all six potential authors featured similar estrangement, and Crafts built her autobiographical narrative by drawing on the lives of those she knew in slavery.

Milly and Martha Murfree began their lives in Murfreesboro, North Carolina. Located at the head of navigation on the Meherrin River, Milly and Martha's natal community was founded in the middle of the eighteenth century at Murfree's Landing, on ninety-seven acres that Hardy Murfree deeded to the state in 1787. The site was the highest point on the waterway accessible to seagoing vessels. Positioned just so, Murfreesboro captured most of the land trade of the surrounding countryside.

In the early eighteenth century, growth was rapid. Murfreesboro saw a steady stream of vessels arriving by way of Albemarle Sound and the Chowan River to disgorge or pick up cargo. Coastal shipping grew, and a flourishing trade with the West Indies developed. The town became a river port for export commodities: staves for barrel making, tar, turpentine, bacon, lard, corn, wheat, cotton, and tobacco. Merchants arrived attracted to Murfreesboro's active shipping exchange, including the Rea brothers of Boston, the Gordons and Warrings of New York, and, eventually, the Wheeler family via New Jersey and Bertie County, North Carolina. These emerging merchant families established warehouses and stores and, in the process, developed distribution and retail businesses selling textiles, tools, farm implements, paints, drugs, tableware, stationery, and books.

In nearby Indian Woods, the Pugh and Bond families built extensive plantations on lands taken from the Tuscarora Nation. Like their neighbors to the west in Murfreesboro, Windsor and the Indian Woods community helped fuel trade in the region by capitalizing on access to water—namely, with vessels arriving via the Cashie River from Albemarle Sound and smaller craft plying the Roanoke River. Because Windsor held the deepest channel leading inland, it, like Murfreesboro, became a successful tributary port where shipbuilding and trade prospered. By 1833, Windsor supported its own newspaper, the *Windsor Herald*. Its pages show a vibrant town with professional classes already established: lawyers, doctors, carpenters, tailors, blacksmiths. Businesses operating in the early 1830s included icehouses, cotton merchants, turpentine stills, printing offices, and twenty other proprietorships serving the expanding community. Social life centered on churches and religion.[1]

The economies of the region depended upon enslaved labor to

cultivate fields, process goods, and transport produce and other area products to near and distant markets. The domestic sphere, too, relied on enslaved "servants" to maintain the luxuries of enslavers' homes and the grand properties of the merchant class. In Murfreesboro, Milly and Martha Murfree were two such captives. Milly was born on the Murfree family plantation around 1797, more than a decade before Hardy Murfree moved the majority of the Murfree clan to Tennessee in 1809. When she reached her midteens, she became the property of the recently married son William Hardy Murfree, an attorney, who carried forward the Murfree family business and merchant holdings in North Carolina. With William Hardy's marriage to Elizabeth Maney in 1807, the new household needed a waiting maid. Milly suited. Her childhood and early womanhood, then, coincided with Murfreesboro's early growth and increasing wealth. Milly's training and then forced employment as a house servant correlated with the success of the town and the growing need for skilled domestic work in the wealthy households of its leading families.[2]

When William Hardy Murfree also immigrated to Tennessee, in 1825, Milly, then just twenty-eight years old and pregnant with Martha, joined the household of one of the few Murfree family members who had stayed in North Carolina, Sally Murfree Cryer. Probably Milly's advanced pregnancy with Martha saved her from the grueling journey to Central Tennessee with her enslaver and his wife. William Hardy Murfree set off to assume his patriarchal role within the larger family, establishing a second town called Murfreesboro, on the west fork of the Stones River just southeast of Nashville.

What were Milly's and then Martha's childhoods like? Milly's early years, as depicted in Crafts's novel, would have been tied up with a "great house with its bustle, confusion, and troops of servants of all ages and colors" (*TBN* 7–8). As an infant and toddler, Milly probably accompanied her mother, most likely a domestic bondwoman serving at Melrose, the Murfree family's primary property and the crown jewel of the emerging town's Broad Street homes (see Figure 9). Here, Milly's mother may have been a waiting maid to the Murfree matriarch, Sally Brickell Murfree,

FIGURE 9: Melrose House, Murfreesboro, North Carolina, 1933

before the latter's death in 1802. Milly probably accompanied her mother in tending to the six Murfree children before the balance of the family immigrated to Tennessee. In 1813, when Milly was sixteen years old, her enslaver William Hardy Murfree, no longer requiring the opulence of Melrose, sold the house to a relative, Brig. Gen. Joseph F. Dickinson, and moved the remaining household a block away, to a property (still standing) known today as the Murfree-Williams House (see Figure 10).

Milly, then, lived most of her enslaved childhood assisting her enslaver Elizabeth Maney Murfree (1796–1860), wife of William Hardy Murfree. In 1825, pregnant with Martha, Milly became the property of widow Sally Murfree Cryer and moved seven miles outside Murfreesboro to the small farming operations of Sally's unmarried son, George Cryer, who suffered from blindness and needed assistance. After Sally Cryer's death in 1826, Milly and Martha served George.

The Cryer farm was a small operation that depended largely on two captives, Bill and Jim. An inventory of this household appears in Hertford County records for 1830–31. For five years, from age twenty-eight to thirty-two, Milly cooked with the frying pan, kettle, iron pot, and Dutch oven later sold in June 1830 at the Cryer estate sale. In 1830, John Hill

FIGURE 10: Murfree-Williams House, Murfreesboro, North Carolina, 2014

Wheeler would purchase a pair of fire irons from the Cryer auction—the same implements Milly likely used to press and iron George Cryer's shirts and pants. At the same sale, Samuel Jordan Wheeler bought a lot of Cryer's "old books," and Dr. Thomas O'Dwyer, a family friend, bought a "negro bed," likely the very bed Milly and Martha shared on the floor of Cryer's kitchen dependency.[3]

The Cryer household was unusually literary, judging from the estate sale, suggesting that, before his loss of sight, George Cryer was an avid reader and writer, possibly a lawyer or clergyman. The fact that Milly and Martha became his primary caregivers after he lost his sight, and shortly after the death of their mistress, Sally Murfree Cryer, suggests the potential for Milly to access the tools of literacy. In turn, she may have been able to impart early literacy to her daughter, Martha. In the novel, Crafts describes what this may have been like: "Though I knew not the meaning of a single letter, and had not the means of finding out[,] I loved to look at them and think that some day I should probably understand them all" (*TBN* 7).

Hannah Crafts's protagonist shares praise from her mistress that resembles Milly and Martha's experiences with the Cryer family: "You are of a great use here. What will the old people, and the children as well as the helpless ones do without you" (*TBN* 52). The phrasing rings true with what Milly and Martha could have heard from Sally Murfree Cryer. Milly and Martha provided essential domestic care for Mrs. Cryer in her old age, for the many Murfree offspring and the children of the enslaved, and for those facing disability, like George Cryer.

In June 1830, at the same time that he procured the fire irons, John Hill Wheeler purchased both Milly and Martha for $143.[4] The fact that Milly and her daughter remained together as property from the Murfrees to the Cryers to the Wheelers matches an economic imperative for their possessors: an enslaved woman's value increased in proportion to the number of children she bore and then nurtured through infancy as she grew older. That is, Milly's value increased for John Hill Wheeler when Wheeler also purchased Martha from the Cryer estate—proof, should Wheeler decide to sell Milly later, of her childbearing and rearing success. Milly's value then increased further in 1831, with the birth of her son, Tecumseh. Milly and Martha's bond as a mother-daughter pair through multiple purchases fits with data compiled from some estate records: in some regions, daughters were less likely than sons to be separated from their mother. In one study, over 60 percent of enslaved women ages twenty to twenty-four remained with their mothers when the estate was divided, as did 90 percent of those ages twenty-five to twenty-nine.[5]

In the novel, Hannah Crafts signals an ambiguous relationship with her mother, and her friendship in later years with Milly and Martha may reflect a yearning to hold an intimate bond with her missing mother, a situation she saw rectified in the bond between Milly and Martha. Hannah's imagined reunion with her mother in Crafts's novel could represent the warmth from that relationship. In chapter 1, the author describes a childhood absent a mother. But by the end of her novel, the protagonist, Hannah, is reunited with her mother in freedom in circumstances that appear miraculous:

> Can you guess who lives with me? You never could—my own dear mother, aged and venerable, yet so smart and lively and active, and Oh: so fond of me. There was a hand of Providence in our meeting

> as we did. I am sure of it. Her history is most affecting and eventful. During my infancy she was transferred from Lindendale to the owner of a plantation in Mississippi, yet she never forgot me nor certain marks on my body, by which I might be identified in after years. (*TBN* 244)

In real life, Crafts's mother, Hannah Sr., disappears from property records by 1858. Her poor health is signaled in the declining valuation she carries in the last years of her life, as reflected in slave inventories. In November 1852, after the death of her captor, Lewis Bond, she is listed as "Old Hannah," with a value of "$95" (she was fifty-eight years old then). In late 1857, the last time Hannah Sr. appears in a Bond family slave inventory, she is listed at "$00." After that point, she disappears. She likely died the same year that Hannah Crafts wrote of their imaginary reunion in freedom.[6]

In her novel, Hannah Crafts imagines emancipation for her mother. Crafts describes the protagonist's mother being transferred to a household in Maryland, where "she became acquainted with a free mulatto from New Jersey, who persuaded her to escape to his native state with him, where they might be married and live in freedom and happiness" (*TBN* 244–45). As elsewhere in her novel, Crafts assumes a fictional alternative to realize an experience she could only imagine because slavery had stolen her own mother away. Still, the joyful picture of her protagonist's mother-daughter bond may draw on the lifelong relationship Hannah Crafts witnessed in Milly and Martha, one she resurrects in her novel to adopt as her own.

II

Eliza Morgan, too, grew up in the Murfreesboro community. Her mother was Molly Morgan, an important enslaved woman whose role in the Wheeler household commanded special mention in the 1833 will of John Hill Wheeler's stepmother, Sarah Clifton Wheeler: "I also leave the two above dear children [Anna Slaughter Wheeler and Junius Wheeler] to my negro woman Molly called Molly Morgan until the 1st of June 1841. I also wish that the said Molly shall be kept in the family so long as she live."[7] It is possible a white Morgan family member was Eliza's father. Per the will, Molly Morgan does seem to have remained with the Wheeler family as a primary caregiver to the many children growing up at Wheeler House in Murfreesboro.

Enslaved people who commanded surnames—like Molly Morgan, Milly Murfree, and Hannah Bond—carried a class marker. Often the surname denoted some tacit bond (potentially a blood tie) to the associated family. For instance, Molly Morgan seems to have held an intimate tie to the family of James Morgan, an early business associate of John Wheeler Sr., the Wheeler patriarch. James Morgan was a wealthy trader and early merchant in Murfreesboro. In the 1810s, on the strength of his successful trading and wholesale businesses inherited from his father, the junior James Morgan built a prominent two-story brick mansion on Broad Street in Murfreesboro that still stands, now called the Morgan-Myrick House (see Figure 11).

Evidence suggests that Eliza Morgan was born at Morgan's Broad Street property in April 1819. Here, Eliza's mother, Molly, served James Morgan's family, including his wife, Celia Harrell Morgan, and their two daughters and two sons. At some point, before Morgan moved his entire household to the Texas territory in 1830, he sold Molly and Eliza to the Wheeler family. By the 1830 federal census record, Eliza Morgan, eleven years old, is enumerated as the possession of John Wheeler Sr. This matches the birth date of April 1819 as noted in John Hill Wheeler's 1832 almanac book.

The light-skinned Eliza holds a curious connection to a legend surrounding another enslaved woman tied to James Morgan, who may have been Eliza's sister, Emily Morgan. According to an Englishman, William Bollaert, a chance conversation in 1842 on a steamer from Galveston to Houston uncovered Emily Morgan as the inspiration for the folk song and legend of "The Yellow Rose of Texas." In Bollaert's telling, the decisive battle for Texas in 1836 turned on the captive Emily's detaining Mexican

FIGURE 11: Morgan-Myrick House, Murfreesboro, North Carolina, 2022

president Gen. Antonio Lopez de Santa Anna in his tent when the Texans charged the Mexican camp on April 21. Bollaert writes, "The battle of San Jacinto was probably lost to the Mexicans, owing to the influence of a Mulatta Girl (Emily) belonging to Col. Morgan who was closeted in the tent with G'l Santana." If any of these details was true, Emily could not have known of Sam Houston's plans to feign retreat and then attack. Unlike the figure in the folk song, Emily was an unwilling victim, not a champion of her original captors.[8]

Still, the story was told in barrooms and around campfires celebrating "The Yellow Rose of Texas," transforming Emily and her rape into a sentimental tale of patriotism and white supremacy. That same spring, however, Emily seems to have escaped Texas and her forced connection to Morgan. According to traceable sources, she found refuge with Isaac N. Moreland, an artillery officer, who provided her with a passport to New York under the name "Emily D. West," an identity Emily Morgan could reasonably assume: Emily D. West was a free woman of color from New York whom Morgan had worked with in Galveston and whose passage to New York would not draw suspicion. The switch may even have been with West's blessing. Such an interpretation of sources requires creative construction of scant materials, but the passport does remain as potential evidence.[9] In any case, the story of Emily Morgan's escape from Texas is much more convincing than the mythologizing racism behind the legendary song.[10]

Eliza Morgan's experiences must have been more mundane, although her journey would also involve travel and enslavement among powerful and influential families. Eliza's childhood consisted of service as domestic help to James Morgan and, later, providing household labor to the Wheeler family. While her mother, Molly Morgan, continued to be the primary caregiver for Sarah Clifton Wheeler's infant children, Junius and Anna, Eliza found herself paired in service to John Hill Wheeler's only daughter, Elizabeth Wheeler, born in 1832. Eliza's childhood, then, included a strong attachment to her future enslaver, Elizabeth, for whom she grew to become a constant presence. As waiting maid, Eliza became Elizabeth Wheeler's most reliable female companion, and this proved especially true upon the death of Mary Brown Wheeler in 1836, when Elizabeth Wheeler was only four years old. At the age of seventeen, then, Eliza Morgan became a nearly full-time caregiver to her young mistress, forming a bond that was probably complicated two years later when John Hill Wheeler married a second time, to Ellen Sully Wheeler (the "Mrs. Wheeler" depicted in Crafts's novel).

Crafts remarks upon the close relationship waiting maids held with their captors: "Those who suppose that southern ladies keep their attendants at a distance, scarcely speaking to them, or only to give commands have a very erroneous impression. Between the mistress and her slave a freedom exists probably not found elsewhere." Crafts continues: "A northern woman would have recoiled at the idea of communicating a private history to one of my race, and in my condition, whereas such as thought never occurred to Mrs. Wheeler. I was near her" (*TBN* 154).

The power dynamics must have been complicated. Young white Southerners, by virtue of being white, were empowered by law and custom to exercise authority over any enslaved person in their control. This would have created a challenging tug and pull for Eliza as Elizabeth's primary caregiver for so many years—required as she was to perform servility even to a child thirteen years her junior. One narrative passed down relates how an enslaved young woman named Ellen Thomas was taught to serve in her new household. Her training involved "being blindfolded and then [being] told to go through the motions of serving" so that she could "learn to do so without disturbing anything on the table."[11] It is possible that Eliza Morgan experienced similar training in her service.

Frederick Law Olmsted, the landscape architect and observer of Southern customs, published a record of an encounter he witnessed between a Southern white girl and an elderly enslaved man:

> I have seen a girl, twelve years old in a district where, in ten miles, the slave population was fifty to one of the free, stop an old man on the public road, demand to know where he was going, and by what authority, order him to face about and return to his plantation, and enforce her command with turbulent anger, when he hesitated, by threatening that she would have him well whipped if he did not instantly obey. The man quailed like a spaniel, and she instantly resumed the manner of a lovely child with me, no more apprehending that she had acted unbecomingly, than that her character had been influenced by the slave's submission to her caprice of supremacy.[12]

Enslaved domestic servants like Eliza would already have learned and reckoned with the bonds of their unfree status from the painful separations so frequently entailed in enslaved communities when enslavers moved west—as James Morgan did in removing to the Texas territory in 1830. Eliza must have witnessed with her mother, firsthand, the painful wreckage of the kinship networks they had fostered among the sixteen other enslaved men and women serving in the Morgan household, now forever sundered. Seven years later—only five years after Turner's insurrection—the last kinship bond was broken: Molly Morgan and her daughter, Eliza, were separated when, in 1837, John Hill Wheeler moved his family to Charlotte, North Carolina, after Wheeler was appointed superintendent of the Charlotte branch of the U.S. Mint. In 1842, Eliza followed her enslavers to Beatties Ford, North Carolina, where Wheeler had established a second plantation, Ellangowan, on the banks of the Catawba River. Molly Morgan remained behind.

Eliza's childhood, as for most enslaved domestics, was short-lived, and she, too, would have been subject to humiliating training and physical and mental hardships. She would have witnessed sexual abuse, one of the most pervasive and damaging forms of violence faced by enslaved women and girls, as Crafts so graphically depicts in her novel. Even as a twelve-year-old serving at Liberty Hall before Turner's rebellion, Eliza Morgan must have understood the transactional nature of Milly's arranged pregnancy—designed to provide a wet nurse and companion to John Hill Wheeler's first child, Richard Mentor Johnson Wheeler. Later, Eliza observed the trauma that played out for Mary Burton on John Hill Wheeler's plantation in Lincoln County in 1842. That was certainly when Mary Burton's childhood ended.

III

In 1832, Mary Burton was born on the plantation of Robert H. Burton (1781–1842) at Beatties Ford. Her enslaver was the son of Revolutionary War officer and Continental Congress delegate Col. Robert Burton. Robert H. Burton followed his father into law and plantation management, settling at Beatties Ford, where he bought and inherited land upon his marriage to Mary Fulenwider in 1813, shortly after his graduation from the University of North Carolina at Chapel Hill. Burton distinguished himself at law, serving at different periods as judge of North Carolina's Supreme Court and as treasurer of the state, along with elected office in the state. The Beatties Ford property was his base of operations for the legal and political pursuits that occupied his life as an elite planter born into wealth and privilege.

The historical record is particularly limited for the enslaved Mary Burton, but some reasonable conclusions can be drawn. Likely, her mother was an enslaved woman named Cresy, whom Burton inherited upon the settlement of his father's Granville County estate in 1828. Probate records show that Cresy was robbed of the earlier child she gave birth to between the time of her enslaver's death in May 1825 and the settlement of his estate in April 1828. Because the birth came after the death of Cresy's enslaver, the infant passed into the possession of Burton Sr.'s widow, Agatha Williams Burton, to meet the terms of Burton Sr.'s will. Burton Jr.'s brother Horace, the executor of their father's estate, signified the stolen infant in a sales paper among the probate records simply as "Child-X born after Death of Testator" (see Figure 12). The child is then tallied into the account of the widow. Such cruelty must have haunted Cresy, making her, perhaps, cling even more tightly to Mary when she was born on the Beatties Ford plantation four to seven years later.[13]

Crafts may have heard of Cresy's story from Eliza Morgan when their paths crossed again in 1856 and 1857, in Washington, D.C., when Crafts was conceiving and secretly starting to write her novel. Such injustices would have inspired a budding novelist hoping to tell an insider's account of the "peculiar institution." Indeed, Crafts depicts vividly the horrors experienced by women like Cresy, who had children stolen from them. For effect, the novelist tells one story from the perspective of the slave trader "Mr. Saddler." "But heavens, how they did carry on, and one, Louise by name, and the freshest and fairest in the gang, actually jumped into

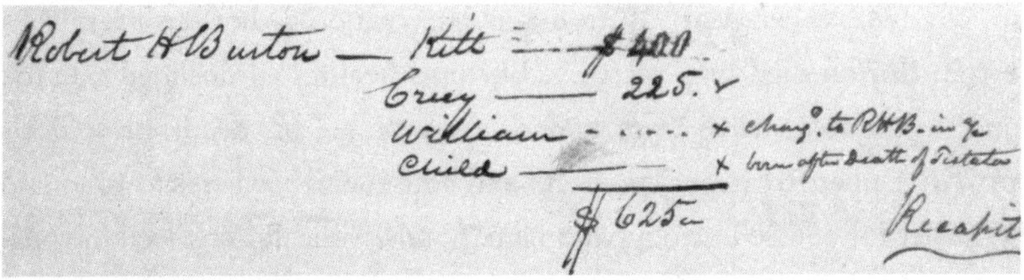
Robert H Burton — Kitt — $400
Cresy — 225.
William — x
Child — x born after death of Testator
$625
Recapit

FIGURE 12: "Col Burton's negroes—as valued," Robert Burton Estate Papers (detail)

the river when she found that her child was irretrievably gone." Saddler continues: "Another one escaped and ran off the place where she supposed her boy to have been carried. The overseer was the first to discover her, and knowing her to be a stranger, he lugged her off with the bloodhounds. They were real devils fierce, eager, and fiery—they tore he dreadfully, spoiled all her beauty, rendering her utterly unfit for my traffic; and I sold her for a song" (*TBN* 108). In the novel, Crafts frames family theft through the eyes of a man who traffics in human flesh, but Cresy would have experienced an evil just as cruel and one probably much more common: a lawyer's mundane math squaring property accounts with the legal stipulations of a testator's will.

An enslaved man named Kitt, also noted in the 1828 slave inventory, may well have been the father of Cresy's stolen child and quite possibly Mary's father, too. In the 1840 census, Robert H. Burton possesses two large plantations in Lincoln County, North Carolina, with forty-three enslaved people working one agricultural site in the "Upper Regiment" of the county and a second "Upper Regiment" site where Burton lived with his wife and large family and where he also enslaved nineteen people. The focus at this second property was manufacture and trade (eight enslaved occupied with those jobs), with only two enslaved members at this location engaged in agriculture. There was a third property, too, in the "Lower Regiment," with five enslaved people under the overseer, Wesley Pryor, who lived on the site. Confirmed in later property records, Kitt, Cresy, and Mary Burton are enumerated as part of the same Upper Regiment property as Robert H. Burton, which strongly suggests that Mary Burton, like Cresy, served in a domestic capacity.[14]

In 1842, when Mary Burton was ten years old, her enslaver Robert H. Burton died unexpectedly. Burton's health had declined rapidly, and he knew his debts were extensive, so, before his death, he sold his prized "Upper Regiment" property and house with 556 acres to John Hill Wheeler for $56,000. Along with bank bonds, Wheeler financed the purchase with a large bill he held on credit from his political guide, Richard Mentor Johnson, then the vice president of the United States, promising

Johnson's repayment of two bonds of $5,000 apiece that Johnson owed Wheeler. Stipulated and included in the sale were "Kitt, Mingo, Bill, Henderson, Billy, Jim, and Stephen for the sum of four thousand three hundred and 25 dollars." Mary Burton was also transferred in the sale, and presumably Cresy, too. Here, at Upper Regiment, in 1842, Wheeler established Ellangowan, the plantation most scholars link directly to Crafts's novel.[15] In 1938, before the area was flooded to create Lake Norman, Frances Benjamin Johnson photographed the site as part of a survey of vanishing Southern architecture (see Figure 13).

The abuse came sometime after Mary Burton reached puberty. If John Hill Wheeler did not force a sexual arrangement on his teenage captive, at least his then wife, Ellen Sully Wheeler, seems to have believed there was impropriety in Mr. Wheeler's bearing to the enslaved Mary. Something of Ellen Sully Wheeler's jealousy is captured in her portrait

FIGURE 13: Burton House/Ellangowan, Beatties Ford Plantation, Lincoln County, North Carolina, 1938

in Crafts's novel. When Mr. Wheeler defends Hannah in the novel, Mrs. Wheeler "vent[s] her spleen" and retorts, "Slaves generally are far preferable to wives in husband's eyes." At that, Mr. Wheeler's "face flushed with anger" (*TBN* 172). The scene may recall aspects of the Wheeler household at Ellangowan when Ellen Wheeler became suspicious of her husband's interest in Mary Burton. In 1845, Wheeler's ward and half brother, Junius Brutus Wheeler, who was living at Ellangowan at the time, wrote his sister about the oppressive atmosphere in the household and the jealous rages of his half sibling's wife, the same Mrs. Wheeler depicted in Crafts's narrative:

> My Dear Sister Amie, You and Sister Julia are the only ones in NC that care for me. It is only to you, that I unburden what is contained in my heart. . . . Mrs. Wheeler, wife of Col. J. H. Wheeler but ought not to bear the name, has not spoken to me since, and she is as snappish as an old bear cutting his wisdom teeth. I will expect it of you not to let no one know anything about this matter and show no one this letter until I am by and looking which you may expect soon as she has wished me at home two or three times & called me more names than the devil can think of himself and she will listen to no explanation from me.[16]

Mary Burton was thirteen years old at the time of Junius's letter. Two years later, in 1847, Junius Brutus Wheeler ran away from the household and enlisted as a private in the Twelfth Infantry Regiment during the Mexican-American War (1846–48). He was "appointed Lieut. By the President for bravery in the field" during the same year. Distinguishing himself, Junius Wheeler began what would be a stellar military career, including appointment to the United States Military Academy at West Point in 1851. He would fight to preserve the Union during the Civil War, declaring, "I am a Union Man." And he would have very little further contact with John Hill Wheeler, repelled, likely, by the deep unhappiness he experienced at Ellangowan.

In July 1849, probably at the bidding of his wife, John Hill Wheeler sold Mary Burton to his friend James Graham (1793–1851), a lifelong bachelor and former U.S. congressman, for $450 (see Figure 14). The sale must have been devastating to Mary, who was now lost to Cresy and Kitt and who found herself removed sixty miles away, to Graham's remote plantation near Rutherfordton, North Carolina. Wheeler's sale of the captive Mary calls to mind the words of the villain in Crafts's novel, Mr. Trappe:

> "My conscience never troubles me" he repeated. "The circumstances in which I find people are not of my making. Neither are the laws that give me an advantage over them. If a beautiful women [*sic*] is to be sold it is rather the fault of the law that permits it than of me who profits by it. If she sells cheap my right to purchase is clear; and if I choose to keep her awhile, give her advantages, or otherwise increase her attractions and then dispose of her again my right is equally unquestionable. Whatever the law permits, and public opinion encourages I do, when that says stop I go no further." (*TBN* 102)

This would not be the first time John Hill Wheeler bought and sold enslaved people without regard to breaking up Black families. Indeed, he would be the source of division for each potential author of Crafts's narrative: Milly and Martha Murfree, Eliza Morgan, Mary Burton, Jane Johnson, and Hannah Bond/Crafts. The figure of Mr. Trappe in Crafts's novel is not simply a fictional bad guy; he is also an embodiment of the enslaver John Hill Wheeler, the ultimate target of Crafts's text.

As stated earlier, Hannah Crafts built her autobiographical narrative out of the composite lives of those she knew in slavery. Three of her earliest acquaintances, Milly and Martha Murfree and Eliza Morgan, played important roles. As early as the late 1830s and '40s, Hannah Bond became acquainted with the three during family visits at Liberty Hall, Wheeler House, Willow Hall, and the Bond mansion in Windsor. Lewis Bond, her enslaver during that period, would come to Murfreesboro to visit his

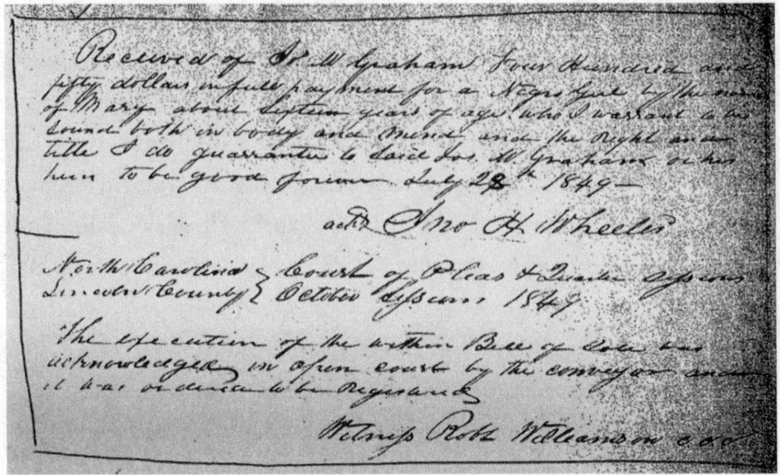
Received of Jos. W. Graham Four Hundred and fifty dollars in full payment for a Negro Girl by the name of Mary about sixteen years of age who I warrant to be sound both in body and mind and the right and title I do guarantee to said Jos. W. Graham or his heirs to be good forever July 28th 1849—

Jno H. Wheeler

North Carolina } Court of Pleas & Quarter Sessions
Lincoln County } October Sessions 1849

The execution of the within Bill of Sale was acknowledged in open court by the conveyor and it was ordered to be Registered

Witness Robt Williamson c.c.

FIGURE 14: Receipt of the sale of Mary Burton, July 28, 1849

daughter Lucinda Bond Wheeler, and the Wheeler family made trips to spend time in Indian Woods and Windsor to see Lewis Bond. During these visits, Hannah Jr. and Martha shared similar tasks in support of their respective mothers, Hannah Sr. and Milly, who served as primary waiting maids to the Wheeler and Bond families. Eliza Morgan, too, would have been on hand whenever young Elizabeth Wheeler attended.

Crafts devotes very little to childhood in her novel. As for Milly and Martha Murfree, Eliza Morgan, and Mary Burton, much of Hannah Bond's childhood would be lost to the coercive demands of male enslavers, sometimes involving sexual torment and subjugation. This seems to have formed the most painful part of Hannah Crafts's life and would help shape the most dramatically insistent assertions of her novel: sexual violence was a crime equal to or worse than slavery. There had to be a reckoning. Hannah Crafts would signal that reckoning by seeking rebellion through art.

CHAPTER 7

PROPERTY

I

ONLY AN ACCIDENT OF HISTORY saved the property records that help sketch the author's life. In 1862, Union forces burned down the Hertford County Courthouse in Winton, North Carolina, where the *Hertford County Record of Accounts* ledger and other legal papers were stored.[1] This was the second devastating fire. A fire in 1830 had destroyed most Colonial and early nineteenth-century records for the county. But one volume survived both fires, the volume containing the Wheeler family's property inventories. Hours before the 1862 fire, a clerk carried the volume home, along with others, as a precaution after two Union war boats were repelled by local troops on the Chowan River. The next day, Union forces attacked the town from the river, and much of Winton was burned. The clerk and the records escaped. Thanks to the clerk's foresight, we are able not only to reconstruct the physical details of Wheeler House and Liberty Hall, near Murfreesboro, North Carolina, but also to gain valuable insight into what it must have been like to be enslaved within the Wheeler circle.

The Wheeler inventory begins in the east room of Wheeler House, identifiable as the primary living space by fireplace tools and furnishings. Here the person taking the inventory in 1832 recorded an expensive "Brussels Carpet & hearth rug," a fire fender, and a "large mantel Looking Glass." Further, here, too, were the family's "1 Sett Mahogany Tables," a "dozen hair bottom chairs" [seats of hair cloth], and the "Sophia," or mahogany sofa with haircloth upholstery. A "settee and lamp" signal the last items of the family's sitting area. The room was large, spanning the whole of the first floor, and it served as the formal dining space, too. Light was plentiful here, and so, "4 Callico [*sic*] Window Curtains" adorned the four windows. The china, glass, and silver enumerated were drawn from the cupboard of this room, described in the inventory as a "beaufat" [*sic*], or buffet/sideboard furnishing.

Other accent furnishings adorned the room, including "2 fancy flour [flower] pots" and two engraved landscape portraits. One "house Bell" is also enumerated, the "servant bell" used by Wheeler family members to call for domestic service. This bell probably sat on the "small Mahogany Table" listed just below it in the inventory. At one time or another, Milly and Martha Murfree, Eliza Morgan, Hannah Bond, and Jane Johnson must have answered this bell or its replacement. Indeed, Crafts writes such a scene into her novel: "A little bell stood on a table by her side, and its ting a ring ding reminded me of my servitude a hundred times a day" (*TBN* 165).

High-quality furnishings also equipped Liberty Hall, the Wheeler plantation house outside Murfreesboro. Liberty Hall formed part of a network of family properties settled originally by John Hill Wheeler's grandfather in an area then known as Wheelerville. Local historian É. Frank Stephenson Jr. helped me pinpoint the location during one of my many visits to Murfreesboro. Stephenson alerted me to the existence of a hand-drawn sketch of the Wheeler property prepared by historian, newspaper publisher, and writer F. Roy Johnson in the 1960s. The drawing is in the collection of the Murfreesboro Historical Association.

Items from the plantation house appear in the rescued inventories alongside items for Wheeler House and other Wheeler properties. These can be reasonably separated by location. For instance, enumerated items for the Wheeler mercantile business can be distinguished from the domestic furnishings of both Wheeler House and Liberty Hall. Further, by comparing the property records for the nearby Whitehead plantation, one can isolate the items associated with the Liberty Hall plantation. Because the Whitehead house survived into the late twentieth century (though in decay), its plan can be more precisely reconstructed to provide a stronger understanding of how a similar home, Liberty Hall—where the author of *The Bondwoman's Narrative* served at least a portion of her servitude—was likely structured.

At both Liberty Hall and the Whitehead house, more than eight rooms were devoted to specific functions: hall, parlor, dining room, kitchen, workroom, storage room, with at least two bedrooms, including sleeping areas on the second floor shared by extended family relations. According to both the Wheeler and Whitehead inventories, there were andirons for four fireplaces in the houses. Pianos furnished the parlors of both properties, a rare sign of these families' wealth. Plentiful bed linens, carpets, curtains, and other textiles adorned the rooms; the inventories of such goods demonstrate multiple sets of windows to allow in light. Looking glasses and an extensive library of books and writing desks are signs of the cultivated nature of these households. Buffets, sideboards, sets of china, large numbers of wineglasses, decanters, and significant stores of wine and brandy point to the sociality these families engaged in within their communities.

Dependencies, or outbuildings, included exterior kitchens, slave huts, and stables that contained multiple horses, counting valuable steeds that hint at the occupants' participation in the area's fascination with thoroughbred racing at well-regarded area race tracks. Livestock was plentiful on both plantations, with scores of cattle, hogs, sows, pigs, and goats. The chief crop at both holdings appears to have been cotton, with smaller production of corn, bacon, potatoes, wheat, and brandy. Both properties included double gig carriages, a cotton gin, and ample tools for dozens of enslaved workers to maximize cultivation of modest-size acreage (roughly three hundred acres).

Eleven Wheeler captives are named in an 1832 family probate inventory, but these represent only those associated with John Wheeler Sr.'s stake in the family plantation outside town: Will, Patsy, Jacob, Isaac,

Dick, Sam, Chunk, Britt, and "2 small Negroes bill & luiza." As we will see, this young boy, Bill, could well be "Bill the field hand" whom the overseer assigns as Hannah's mate in 1857, shortly before her escape in *The Bondwoman's Narrative* (*TBN* 210–11). In 1831, John Hill Wheeler owned four other captives who tended the Liberty Hall household: "Milly, Elizabeth, Martha, and Jack."[2] Like the unfree people serving the Francis-Moore-Travis syndicate, an extended network of familial ties placed numerous captive networks within the Wheeler circle. Surviving records suggest that Wheeler Sr.'s enslaved subjects occupied the slave huts, while John Hill Wheeler's four servants probably slept in the kitchen dependency.

Wheeler House in Murfreesboro still stands, restored after a careful reconstruction of the inventories I have just noted (see Figure 15). The consistency of the Wheeler household is attested to in family letters. Emily Bland Southall, a cousin to the Wheeler brothers, visited Wheeler House in 1861 and described it then as matching the detailed remembrances of her mother from before 1837: "I can't describe that quaint old brick house

FIGURE 15: John Wheeler House, Murfreesboro, North Carolina, May 2022

better than she [mother] has often done. It stands just as she left it, with the exception of a new gallery in front. The furniture is the same, even to the carpets. In the stories she has often related connected with the house, I recognize rooms, closets, and pieces of furniture. It is such a pleasure walking over it and remembering these things."

The restored property—now called the John Wheeler House—is protected, registered with the National Park Service and maintained by the Murfreesboro Historical Association. The inventories that survived the 1862 Winton fire guided the restoration during its initial restitution in the 1980s. If you visit the property today, however, what you will not hear about is the lives of the enslaved; nor will you learn anything about Hannah Crafts or the other Wheeler captives. The same care that scholars and local boosters put into lovingly refurnishing and restoring the physical property of John Wheeler House was not extended to recovering the lives of the enslaved people who enriched the Wheelers. One aim of this biography is to change that.

II

The lives of enslaved people in the region reflected geographic circumstances. A set of interlocking rivers shaped the district. The Meherrin and Cashie run south toward the Chowan River and Albemarle Sound, rather than north to the more robust, Chesapeake-related economies of Richmond and Norfolk. These rivers provided only marginal navigability, making transportation too inconvenient and costly for the development of large-scale plantation economies. Instead, these counties were dotted with small farms and modest plantations producing cotton, corn, hogs, sweet potatoes, peas, a regionally renowned apple and peach brandy, and, in some sections, rice. At the time of Nat Turner's revolt, the Wheeler family held a mix of cotton, corn, meat, leather, and dairy production.

The extent of operations at Wheeler House and the Wheeler plantations has been misunderstood by historians. This was no minor farm, as it has been portrayed, but rather, an extensive and expanding syndicate of businesses controlled by the Wheeler family. In 1832, the Wheeler family owned 267 acres of land, a tanyard, stables, multiple slave huts, a four-wheel carriage with two dray horses, scores of hogs, three dairy cows, and several houses and properties in Murfreesboro and Winton. Seventeen captives labored on plantation fields north of the town, with the usual assortment of agricultural tools and coopering instruments: cotton, grub, weed hoes, picking bags, lathes, and field axes. Each of our six authorial candidates would have been familiar with the items stocking the kitchen dependency: four large washing tubs; two tin milk buckets; shovels, tongs, and andirons; waffle and wafer irons; a brass kettle heater; a bathing tub; a butter churn; and a Dutch oven.[3] With these tools, at different times, Milly, Martha, Eliza, and Hannah labored: they laundered and darned clothing, oversaw dairy production, prepared meals, maintained fires, pressed clothing, and assisted in the fields to supply the kitchen. These enslaved women also provided child care for their enslavers, took charge of enslaved children too young to work, and, in some cases, served as wet nurses.

Records suggest that the Wheeler family's wealth was substantial. In 1832, the Wheeler estate was valued at nearly $43,400 (more than $16 million in 2023). Such sums represented generational wealth for Wheeler family members. Still, that wealth was not shared by their captives. The lived experience of Wheeler family slaves mirrored closely conditions familiar to Nat Turner and the other insurgents in the region. Not only did material and environmental factors correspond, but living arrangements also matched. Slave cabins in the region were uniform, consisting of untreated logs arranged and braced according to a peg construction. No more than four hundred square feet in total size, they featured earthen floors and shingled roofs. The chimneys, usually four to five feet wide at the hearth, were built of mud and sticks. A few had "slop" brick bases and mud-and-stick stacks (Figure 16). Natives from Southampton County remembered area slave huts as leaky and squalid structures, the only insulation provided by a coat of mud known as daub.[4] Some of these repurposed log hovels dated back to the Revolutionary War. Crafts describes them in detail in her autobiographical novel: "These huts were old and ruinous with decay . . . many [were] even older than the nation, and had been occupied by successive generations of slaves" (*TBN* 205). It was only after she was consigned to live permanently in one of these hovels that the author made her escape.

III

Economic logic ensured the dissolution of Hannah Crafts's family. As early as 1819, the Pugh family moved assets, including the author's great-uncle James Barefoot and her great-grandfather Achilles, south to Louisiana. In 1836, the author's mother, Hannah Sr., joined the westward expansion of slavery, although her migration would bring her to western Tennessee—not the Deep South, as for so many others. Milly and Martha had already lost relatives to the Murfree family's resettlement in Central

FIGURE 16: Slave houses, Broad Street near Wheeler House, n.d.

Tennessee in the 1820s. That same decade, Eliza Morgan lost relatives to the Morgan family's removal to the Texas territory. Nat Turner's revolt was a strike against an unacceptable future: a forced second migration that would break up families and enforce further trauma on people already held in bondage.

The historic dimensions of these ruptures meant that nearly one million African Americans were torn from their families and sold south from 1820 to 1860. Families like the Pughs, Bonds, and Wheelers followed the exodus of capital reinvested in lands bought or stolen from native populations and with lands gained in the Louisiana Purchase (1803), the acquisition of Florida (1819), and the Mexican-American War (1846–48). So, the enslaved charted what historians have called the "Second Middle Passage," a period during which Black families that had reconstituted themselves in the United States after suffering their original displacement from Africa or the West Indies now faced a new threat to their cohesion. Enslavers began to acquire new lands appropriated from native populations in Alabama, Mississippi, Louisiana, and other areas. They then established new plantations there, resettling their able-bodied younger captives to work the new lands. The result was a changed map of North America. In less than a generation, the forced migration of nearly a million Black captives forever splintered families and sundered kinship networks: 155,000 enslaved people were separated and pushed west in the 1820s; 288,000 in the 1830s; 189,000 in the 1840s; 250,000 in the 1850s. Historians estimate that the interstate trade destroyed 25 percent of Black marriages and fully 50 percent of Black nuclear families, and that one out of every two enslaved children lost one or both parents to such trafficking.[5] It is no wonder that the author of *The Bondwoman's Narrative* grew up an orphan.

The human exchanges that fueled this wholesale redistribution of Black Americans were brokered by an increasingly sophisticated network of capitalists, traders, and speculators who manipulated price differentials to deliver human beings and profits. In her novel, Hannah Crafts depicts such men in the figures of Mr. Saddler, a slave trader, and Mr. Trappe, a slave speculator. Crafts describes a transaction in the novel quite possibly drawn from her own experience:

> Both men came in, while I shrunk into a distant corner.
>
> "Nay: Hannah, that won't do" said Trappe. "Come out here and show yourself. I don't think Mr[.] Saddler ever saw a better looking wench. Come out I say.["]
>
> I obeyed reluctantly.
>
> "Now I'll tell you what" said Trappe. "You won't find a nicer bit of woman's flesh to be bought for that money in old Virginia. Don't you see what a foot she has, so dainty and delicate, and what an ankle. I don't see how in conscience you can expect me to take any less. Why you'd make a small fortune of her at that rate."

In the scene, Mr. Trappe has brought Mr. Saddler to view Hannah with the object of buying her "to fill [an order] at New Orleans and all for young and beautiful women without children." Explicitly, Trappe and Saddler are conspiring to profit from a subset of human trafficking, namely sexual enslavement. Trappe explains the high-end nature of his trade: "Now a woman of eighteen or twenty without a child, and a slave, is not so easy to find, to say nothing of looking for fifty or a hundred" (*TBN* 106–7).

The trade "in the line of good-looking wenches," as Saddler puts it in the novel, flourished in the same high-end, high-volume markets where the author and her fellow captives lost so many relatives: Memphis, Natchez, El Paso, and New Orleans. Traders and speculators worked in tandem to extract fresh captives from communities like Indian Woods and Murfreesboro, canvassing door-to-door by promising "Cash for Negroes" and enticing enslavers to cut losses, clear debts, and capture rising values. Kinship ties that had formerly kept human property close to home ceased when profit margins rose in distant markets. Such human trafficking became the norm.

The story that Jacob Stroyer carried out of slavery in South Carolina was probably familiar to the author, as similar scenes played out in her community. Stroyer records that his sisters were purchased by a "Mr. Manning, known as one of the greatest slave traders in the South," when their previous enslaver faced financial hardship due to spring flooding near Columbia, South Carolina. J. L. Manning, the former governor of South Carolina, sought to move Stroyer's sisters and other captives to Louisiana, where they were far more valuable. Louisiana, as Jacob Stroyer observes, was "considered by the slaves a place of slaughter, so those who were going did not expect to see their friends again."[6]

Stroyer describes the experience of watching his sisters and the others on the day of their departure compelled to walk to the train depot by Manning's overseer. When the day came for them to leave, some refused and were "handcuffed together and guarded on their way to the cars by white men." Stroyer recounts how his sisters and other "women and children were driven to the [train] depot . . . like so many cattle" and that their appearance caused "great excitement" among the other enslaved people in the region. "Imagine a mass of uneducated people shedding tears and yelling at the top of their voices in anguish."[7]

As Stroyer notes, "The victims were to take the cars at a station called Clarkson turnout. . . . The excitement was so great that the overseer and driver could not control the relatives and friends of those that were going away, as a large crowd of both old and young went down to the depot to see them off." Stroyer records that while they were passing along, "many of the negroes left their masters' fields and joined us as we marched to the cars; some were yelling and wringing their hands, while others were singing little hymns." The hymns, Stroyer observes, were those the enslaved had become "accustomed" to singing for the consolation of those being taken away, such as:

> When we all meet in heaven,
> There is no parting there;
> When we all meet in heaven,
> There is parting no more.

Stroyer concludes: "As the cars moved away we heard the weeping and wailing from the slaves as far as human voice could be heard; and from that time to the present I have neither seen nor heard from my two sisters, nor any of those who left Clarkson depot on that memorable day."[8]

IV

In 1836, John Hill Wheeler forced a similar trauma upon Wheeler family captives. His sale of twenty-eight captives that year never appears in the history of North Carolina that he wrote and published in 1851, nor in the expanded second edition published in 1884. Nor do details about the Wheeler family selling human beings appear in the history of North Carolina written by John Hill Wheeler's nephew John Wheeler Moore, whose study became the standard historical textbook for generations of public school students in North Carolina. In his history, John Wheeler Moore credits the Wheeler family with freeing their slaves by repatriating them to Liberia upon John Wheeler Sr.'s death in 1832. But this is a lie. There is no record of such a repatriation traceable in the family's property records, despite John Wheeler Sr.'s active membership in the American Colonization Society, which promoted the migration of freeborn and emancipated captives to Africa.

Rather, historical evidence shows that the Wheelers continued to buy and sell enslaved people, extending their holdings of human beings and selling them as their own financial needs dictated. In 1836, as John Hill Wheeler was closing out the accounts of his father and stepmother, it made sense for the family to sell off nearly half the enslaved people possessed by the extended family. No record of this sale appears in family papers or recoverable county papers, but I did discover shipping records stored at the National Archives in Fort Worth, Texas, detailing Wheeler's sale of more than two dozen men, women, and children to slave traders for the New Orleans market on February 26, 1836.

In the early 1800s, federal law required masters of sailing vessels to submit a list, or manifest, of the Africans and African Americans they carried in and out of U.S. seaports and their legal status. One purpose of these manifests was to monitor compliance with the Act Prohibiting Importation of Slaves of 1807. That law forbade the shipment of slaves into the United States from other nations but allowed the slave trade to continue between seaports in U.S. states and territories.[9] The stories of these distant events are known only because white people cherished and recorded the property exchanges involved in this human trafficking.

The slave manifest detailing Wheeler's sale enumerates sixteen males ranging in age from fifty to four years old, eleven females from ages forty to six, and one infant, gender unidentified. All twenty-eight human beings who had labored for the Wheeler family on their plantations, in their merchant house, and at the family's tannery for one or two generations—all were coerced onto Robert Benthall's nineteen-ton schooner *Hunter* in the February cold at Port Norfolk, Virginia, nearly a hundred miles from their former home and where they must have left behind family members and other loved ones. Locked in chains like those first forced to come to North Carolina, they joined ninety others wearing manacles and compelled to duck into the unsanitary hold of the ship for a monthlong journey by sea to a location they considered, as Stroyer noted, "a place of slaughter." Their names, sex, ages, size, and color are listed in the manifest. Jacob (age twenty-five) and Dick (twenty-seven), mentioned in John Wheeler Sr.'s 1832 property records, were among the twenty-eight sold. Spared from sale were Molly Morgan, Isaac, Sam, Chunk, Britt, Bill, and Luiza, probably because at least some of these people were necessary to maintain the family's plantation and house in Murfreesboro. John Hill Wheeler's domestic "servants" noted in his almanac—Milly and Martha Murfree, Eliza Morgan, Jack, and Tecumseh—also escaped transport. Those who were chained and forced to walk to Norfolk to board the ship to New Orleans were the male Wheeler captives: Reuben (age twenty-one), Spence (twenty-nine), Dave (thirty-seven), Kelly (thirty-seven), Jim (twenty-seven), Henry (fifty), Justin (sixteen), Charles (sixteen), Jacob, Dennis (twenty-seven), Dick, Hercules (thirty), John (seventeen), Moses (four), George (nineteen), and Hannibal (seventeen). And the enslaved women, girls, and children: Amanda (fourteen), Eady (eleven), Hester (twenty-four), Rachel (twenty) and child (three months), Celia (forty), Affey (twenty-five), Philbis (twenty-eight), Phillis (thirty-five), Tanner (ten months old), Nancy (ten), and Ever (five) (see Figure 17).

Like many other Virginia and North Carolina planters, the Wheelers were ready to liquidate. Why? Their captives have become extraordinarily valuable because of the explosion of cotton cultivation in the Deep South made possible by the genocide and displacement of Native Americans. The labor the Wheeler captives could contribute to the expanding plantations near Louisiana encouraged their sale. Suddenly, Wheeler captives became appreciated assets, and separation at whatever cost to the people themselves proved extraordinarily profitable for the Wheelers.

"The announcement fell upon the little circle in that rude-log cabin like a thunderbolt," the captive Elizabeth Keckley would remember when her father was placed in a similar coffle for his forced migration from North Carolina. "The shadow eclipsed the sunshine, and love brought despair. The parting was eternal. . . . We who are crushed to earth with

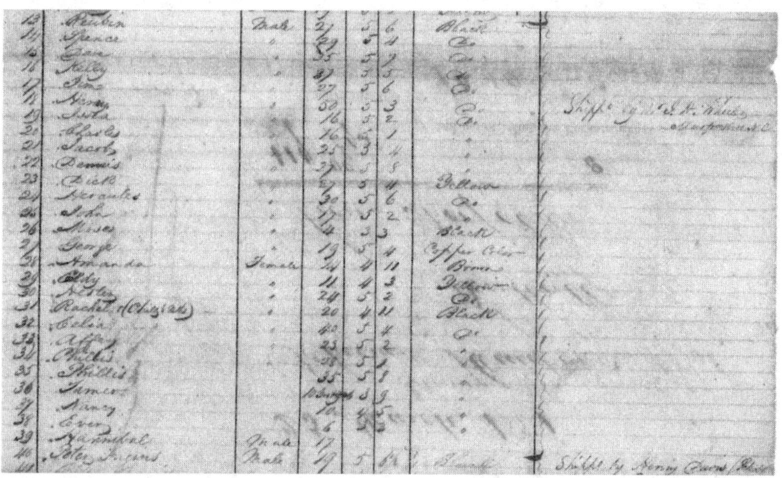

FIGURE 17: Inventory listing the twenty-eight captives John Hill Wheeler shipped to New Orleans to sell on the schooner *Hunter*, departing Norfolk, Virginia, on February 25, 1836 (detail)

heavy chains, who travel a weary, rugged, thorny road, groping through midnight darkness on earth, earn our right to enjoy the sunshine in the great hereafter."[10]

Less than a month after the *Hunter* landed in New Orleans and the twenty-eight Wheeler captives were lost to the city's slave markets, Samuel Jordan Wheeler married Lucinda Pugh Bond at a ceremony at Willow Hall, where the young Hannah Crafts was almost certainly in attendance. In April 1836, Samuel and Lucinda settled into Wheeler House, retaining some of the former captives, but adding those who came as part of Lucinda's dowry. Six months later, John Hill Wheeler lost his wife, Mary Brown, to illness. He left the Wheeler plantation and Liberty Hall in the hands of an overseer and moved back to Washington, D.C., with his sole surviving child, Elizabeth Wheeler, and her servant, Eliza Morgan, for a political appointment in the nation's capital.

CHAPTER 8

ROSEA PUGH AND HANNAH SR.

I

"GENEALOGICAL TREES DO NOT FLOURISH among slaves," Frederick Douglass aptly noted. The fact that Hannah Crafts's family tree is so difficult to cobble together from scattered property records demonstrates how extraordinary it is that her novel survives. Life among the Pugh and Bond families in Indian Woods can be partially reconstructed from property records and from Crafts's novel. Like Sir Clifford De Vincent in her novel, Col. Thomas Pugh Sr. held an enormous amount of property and vast numbers of enslaved people. Much of his property passed on to Lewis Bond and the Bond family, who intermarried with the Pughs to dominate the region. No detailed records of Thomas Pugh Sr.'s plantation house, Quirocky, remain, but there is good reason to believe Quirocky and Willow Hall were the same property and that both are depicted as "Lindendale" in Crafts's novel.

Crafts describes Lindendale as "a great house with its bustle, confusion, and troops of servants of all ages and colors" (*TBN* 8). She observes, "[W]e saw on all sides the appearance of wealth and splendor, and the appliances to every luxury. What a variety of beautiful rooms, all splendid yet so different, and seemingly inhabited by marble images of art, or human forms pictured on the walls." Recounting the labor of housekeeping, she notes the "floors . . . undergoing the process of being rubbed bright, carpets . . . being spread, curtains shaken out, beds puffed and covered [and] furniture dusted and polished, and all things prepared as beseemed the dignity of the family" (*TBN* 14).

Crafts and her mother and grandmother likely played a significant role in child care. The author provides her protagonist with a similar experience. She writes of her first-person narrator, "Then the little slave children were almost entirely confided to my care. I hope that I was good and gentle to them; for I pitied their hard and cruel fate very much." Crafts details with pride Hannah's success: "[I] used to think that, notwithstanding all the labor and trouble they gave me, if I could so discharge my duty by them that in after years their memories would hover over this as the sunshiny period of their lives, I should be amply repaid" (*TBN* 11). She continues: "I was employed about the house, consequently my labors were much easier than those of the field servants, and I enjoyed intervals of repose and rest unknown to them. Then, too, I was a mere child and some hours of each day were allotted to play." Crafts, like her Hannah in the novel, yearned for literacy. "On such occasions, and while the other children of the house were amusing themselves, I would quietly steal away from their company to ponder over the pages of some old book or newspaper that chance had thrown in [my] way" (*TBN* 6–7).

In 1834, when the author was eight years old, Lewis Bond's nephew Thomas Bond Jr. married Sawyer P. Rascoe at Willow Hall. Crafts seems to reimagine the event in her novel, describing the arrival of the new bride and the attendance of Lewis Bond, now described as the author's unnamed enslaver: "Thither he conducted the glittering train across the hall, and along the passages, and through the rooms, and up the staircase to the illustrious presence of ancestral greatness." She continues: "Though not permitted to mingle with the grand company we, the servants, blockaded the halls and passages. We cared not, why should we?

If the fires went out, the chambers were neglected and the remnants of the feast remained on the table. It was our priveledge [*sic*] to look and listen. We loved the music, we loved the show and splendor, we loved to watch the twinkling feet and the graceful motions of the dancers, but beyond them and over them, and through the mingled sounds of joyous music and rain and wind I saw the haughty countenance of Sir Clifford's pictured semblance, and heard the ominous creaking of the linden" (*TBN* 29).

Crafts writes of the experience, viewing the inner world of her enslavers. She records the "oaken staircase" and then the entrance to the bedroom suite, "a door carved and paneled in the quaint old style." In the novel, she writes of observing the newly married mistress assessing her new quarters: "Slaves are proverbially curious, and while she surveyed with haughty eyes the furniture and dimensions of the rooms or opened and shut bureau-drawers, or plunged into caskets and jewel-cases, I was studying her" (*TBN* 27). She may also be relating her own experiences when she became a forced sexual partner to Thomas Bond Jr. and entered the master's quarters.

For men like Rosea's brother James Barefoot and her father, Achilles, life as a field servant was grueling and demeaning. Crafts notes in her novel, "The greatest curse of slavery is it's [*sic*] hereditary character." She continues: "The father leaves to his son an inheritance of toil and misery, and his place on the fetid straw in the miserable corner, with no hope or possibility of anything better. And the son in his turn transmits the same to his offspring and thus forever" (*TBN* 205). It is a world her male ancestors would have known well on both the Pugh and Bond plantations. Many acres of Thomas Pugh Sr.'s land required clearing after he acquired Crafts's male relatives from Jamaica in 1779, and they likely faced months if not years of felling trees and plowing earth to help make Pugh Sr.'s full Indian Woods property suitable for crop cultivation. Their success is recorded in Pugh Sr.'s tax records and in the later tax records of Lewis Bond, which show an extensive and growing cotton operation on the property as more and more land stolen from Tuscarora natives became gainfully farmed.

Meanwhile, Pugh Sr.'s plantations continued to excel at producing wood staves, pitch, and tar for the family's barrel-making business. Another branch of Pugh's plantation expanded: Pugh Sr.'s financial records also show a significant increase in seine (or net-fishing) operations. James Barefoot's later role in the Bertie Conspiracy seems to place him among his enslaver's extensive fishing enterprise, where he would have been in a position to communicate and coordinate with others beyond his enslaver's holdings. Like Crafts two generations later, Barefoot must have leveraged his opportunities beyond the immediate boundaries of his enslaver's property to plot revenge and escape. Like his great-niece, he seems to have had as his weapons a strong sense of justice and, probably, literacy. His sister Rosea Pugh may have also contributed by providing domestic intelligence from within the household. Without knowing it, Crafts's forebears set the foundations of liberty that the author herself carried in her art.

II

The first record we have of the author's maternal grandmother, Rosea Pugh, appears in the ship manifest for Thomas Pugh Sr.'s return voyage from Jamaica in late summer 1779. The trading voyage matches other early commerce records for Eastern North Carolina. The coastal plains of North Carolina were rich in naval stores: tar, pitch, staves, and other barrel-making materials. Other prominent products included herring and shad, two fish abundantly drawn from the Roanoke River and its tributaries. Barrels of pickled herring and shad joined naval stores packed tightly onto Thomas Pugh Sr.'s trading sloop when the *Carolina* set off on its initial journey to Jamaica.

By the time the *Carolina* reached Kingston Port early that summer, sugar production was in full swing. The journey was timed to maximize the value of Pugh Sr.'s cargo. Naval stores were needed to build the thousands of barrels necessary for storing and shipping Jamaican rum, molasses, and sugar. Furthermore, salted herring and shad provided an easily preserved food source for the hundreds of Jamaican captives forced to spend their time on cane cultivation, not on producing self-sustaining crops. And so, Pugh Sr. found a successful market for the yield of his own plantations and, in return, restocked his ship with items in high demand on the coastal plains: rum, molasses, sugar, and, especially, enslaved humans.[1]

Pugh Sr.'s need for labor at the time of his sloop's voyage in 1779 was particularly acute. By 1777, he had over fifteen hundred acres of land, an astonishing size, ready for clearing and cultivation. With the help of enslaved labor, the cost of clearing the land was minimal, and Pugh Sr. had brokered the deal by using his position of power in negotiating a 150-year land lease for half of all Indian Woods Reservation land from the Tuscarora Nation, gaining for the colony of North Carolina a purported eight thousand acres. Pugh was one of three planters to assume control of the property located along the north side of the Roanoke River, between Quitsna Swamp and Deep Creek, in what is now southwestern Bertie County. Ratified in 1766 in North Carolina's Colonial capital of New Bern, the treaty confirmed the state's swindle of the Tuscarora people.[2] Left with about half the land allotted to them by the law of 1748, the remaining Tuscarora sought the protection of Governor William Tryon from further encroachment.

Protection was not forthcoming. The prominent Pope family of Eastern North Carolina, like the Pughs, Bonds, and Wheelers, benefited from the newly opened land when they migrated into the area. Like other pioneering North Carolina families, the Pope family moved south from Virginia seeking more fertile soil. They found it on Deep Creek, on land taken from the Tuscarora. By 1766, the lease became permanent when the Tuscarora exchanged the originally leased property of the 1748 treaty. As an 1803 North Carolina commission noted after the purchase, the Colonial government of North Carolina misrepresented the size of the land purchased as 16,000 acres when it actually amounted to more than 58,000. The margin of error (42,000 acres) was quickly forgotten as families like the Popes, Bonds, and Wheelers acquired this stolen property while contributing to the state's coffers. And so, Tuscarora land became seed money for capital accumulation in Eastern North Carolina. Families like the Pughs, Popes, Bonds, and Wheelers benefited only to further traffic in enslaved laborers to maximize the value of property taken from the Tuscarora. Something of the sources of this wealth is noted by Hannah Crafts writing a century later: "We thought our master must be a very great man to have so much wealth at this command, but it never occurred to us to inquire whose sweat and blood and unpaid labor had contributed to produce it" (*TBN* 14).

Crafts never saw Thomas Pugh Sr.'s 1779 tax documents, but she intuited the truth behind its accounting: Thomas Pugh Sr.'s wealth depended upon appropriated goods, including her family. In the documents, Crafts's family members appear listed under the columns "Negroes," "Land," and "Horses." In 1779, when Hannah Crafts's ancestors were first brought to North Carolina, Pugh Sr. possessed 1,555 acres. That number would increase to more than 5,752 acres by the time of his death in 1806. On this vast property, Rosea's daughter, Hannah Sr., was born, and this was where she would pass most of the first two decades of her life. Crafts's mother (Hannah Sr.), grandmother (Rosea), and great-uncle (James Barefoot) appear together in February 1807 as they are dispensed in Pugh Sr.'s estate records (see Figure 18). The three became the property of Pugh Sr.'s granddaughter Catherine Pugh, with Hannah Sr. likely assuming the role of her maidservant; Catherine was then fifteen. Property records show that Rosea, or Rose, disappears from the Pugh family's traceable records sometime after 1808. She seems to have been sold to or in some other way acquired by the nearby Pope family.

In her novel, Crafts sketches Col. Thomas Pugh Sr. as the patriarch Sir Clifford De Vincent: "It was said that Sir Clifford De Vincent, a nobleman of power and influence in the old world, having incurred the wrath of his sovereign, fled for safety to the shores of the Old Dominion, and became the founder of my Master's paternal estate" (*TBN* 16). The characterization, although not directly true for Col. Thomas Pugh Sr.,

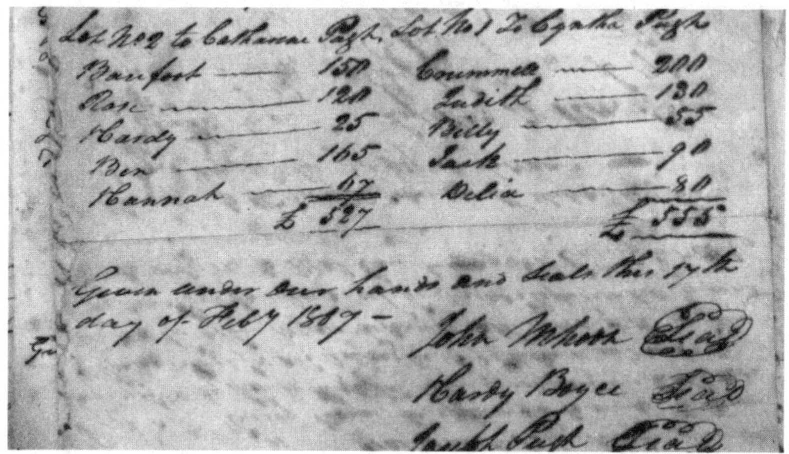

Lot No 2 to Catharine Pugh		Lot No 1 To Cyntha Pugh	
Barefoot	150	Cummee	200
Rose	120	Judith	130
Hardy	25	Billy	55
Ben	165	Jack	90
Hannah	67	Delia	80
	£527		£555

Given under our hands and seals this 17th day of Feby 1807 — John Mhoon Seal
Hardy Boyce Seal
Joseph Pugh Seal

FIGURE 18: Slave dispersal, February 1807, for the property of Thomas Pugh Sr., allotting Barefoot, Rosea, and Hannah to Catherine Pugh (detail)

does capture the essence of his bearing and the family's proud bloodlines stretching back to their noble Welsh roots.

Thomas Sr.'s father, Francis Pugh (1692–1736), was the son of a Welsh squire who lived at "Glendower Hall," matching Crafts's portrayal of Sir Clifford De Vincent as descending from English aristocracy and "flee[ing] for safety to the shores Virginia" after "incur[ing] the wrath" of "his sovereign." The family's claims to nobility stretch all the way back to the Welsh national leader Owen Glendower (c. 1359–c. 1415).[3]

For Crafts, the memory of the Pugh family is marked in her fiction by the pretentions of Sir Clifford De Vincent and his proud claims to noble lineage, including the ceremonial hanging of portraits to memorialize family bloodlines: "Generation had succeeded generation, yet each inheritor had contributed to the adornments of the drawing room a faithful transcript of his person and lineaments, side by side with that of his Lady. The ceremonial of hanging up these portraits was usually made the occasion of a great festivity, in which hundreds of the neighboring gentry participated" (*TBN* 16). In the novel, Crafts conflates the extensive plantation home of Col. Thomas Pugh Sr., called Quirocky, in Indian

Woods, North Carolina, with that of his father, called Jericho, built in Nansemond County, Virginia. The portraiture tradition depicted in the novel appears to have been a Pugh family practice carried forward by Pugh Sr.'s grandson and namesake, Thomas Pugh III (1796–1852), who established sugar and cotton plantations on Bayou Lafourche, in Louisiana, with other relatives as early as 1818. By 1848, Thomas Pugh III had completed Madewood, his plantation house, including the south drawing room where the Pugh family portraits hung.

In her novel, Crafts writes of her protagonist, Hannah, encountering the drawing room portraiture of Lindendale: "I was not a slave with these pictured memorials of the past. They could not enforce drudgery, or condemn me on account of my color to a life of servitude. As their companion I could think and speculate. In their presence my mind seemed to run riotous and exult in its freedom as a rational being, and one destined for something higher and better than this world can afford." Significantly, she describes the moment as one of empowerment, one calling her to be an artist: "I was in no haste to leave the room; for there surrounded by mysterious associations I seemed suddenly to have grown old, to have entered a new world of thoughts, and feelings and sentiments" (*TBN* 17). She continues: "And why was it that as I mused the portrait of my master seemed to change from its usually kind and placid expression to one of wrath and gloom, that the calm brow should become wrinkled with passion, the lips turgid with malevolence—yet thus it was." Hannah finds freedom in the encounter just as the writer Crafts did in her art: "Can ignorance quench the immortal mind or prevent its feeling at times the indications of its heavenly origin. Can it destroy that deep abiding appreciation of the beautiful that seems inherent to the human soul? Can it seal up the fountains of truth and all intuitive perception of life, death and eternity? I think not" (*TBN* 18).

In 2016, the popular artist Beyoncé scripted a similar scene, albeit quite unconsciously. In a moment of artistic convergence, she filmed the portrait scene for her "Formation" video in the Pugh family's drawing room at Madewood, part of her multimedia audiovisual work *Lemonade*.

In Beyoncé's rendering, the drawing room is now hung with French Renaissance–style portraits of Black subjects. As the director of the video, Melina Matsoukas, notes, the portraiture scene was devised to empower Black people: "[F]ilms about slavery traditionally feature white people in these roles of power and position. I wanted to turn those images on their head."[4] Crafts had already made the same audacious move 160 years earlier, inverting the history of white portraiture and power in the first chapter of her novel.

III

Hannah Sr. was born on the Pugh plantation at Quitsna, North Carolina. She is identified as "mulatto" in some of the property records where she is traceable, and her mother is noted as "Rosea Pugh." Rosea was seventeen years old when she gave birth to the author's mother. Like Hannah Crafts herself, Hannah Sr. was likely conceived through rape by a white man, most likely by a Pugh family member. The early part of Hannah Sr.'s life centered on Thomas Pugh Sr.'s extensive holdings in Indian Woods and her consignment to serve as Catherine Pugh's domestic servant beginning in 1807.

Hannah Sr.'s presence in the household of her enslavers paved the way for a lifetime of domestic service to the Pugh, Rascoe, and Bond families. She was thirteen at the time she became Catherine's waiting maid, and much of her childhood seems to have passed among the more privileged accommodations of the Pugh family's plantation home, then called Quirocky. Her favorable circumstances compared to nondomestic captives was likely due to blood ties to her enslaver's family.

Hannah Sr. was part of the sudden expansion of Thomas Pugh Sr.'s property in the late eighteenth and early nineteenth centuries. Details of life for people brought to Pugh Sr.'s plantations can be partially reconstructed thanks to property records. In 1816, Thomas Bond Sr. married into the Pugh family. This is significant because, shortly after his marriage, he filed a lawsuit seeking the restitution of slave property he claimed for his wife, Mary Pugh, on behalf of his father-in-law's estate. The details involve a half dozen enslaved people whom Mary possessed as a minor, their upkeep, and the potential unauthorized sale of one of them. The specifics bear on Hannah Sr.'s experience because the depositions in the case provide information about the diet and care of Pugh Sr.'s captives, including domestic servants such as Hannah Sr. and her mother, Rosea Pugh.

According to these records, for the years 1803–16, between 100,000 and 130,000 herrings were provided annually to feed Mary Pugh's domestic servant Jenny, her children, and four field laborers. A bushel of corn was provided each spring, too. That means roughly two cups of corn and a herring per captive, per day, with Jenny supplying her children from her own portion. Field laborers appear to have been accorded the same measure. Most likely, the overseer distributed the food long after sundown, after the harvest had been brought in, weighed, and recorded. Punishments were administered either at this time or in the morning. Enslaved people who did not meet their quotas for the day were disciplined and, frequently, whipped.

The South Carolina captive and memoirist Charles Ball describes arrangements consistent with these: "After it was quite dark, the slaves came in from the cotton-field, and taking little notice of us, went into the kitchen, and each taking thence a pint of corn, proceeded to a little mill, which was nailed to a post in the yard." Using the mill by turns, each enslaved person "commenced the operation of grinding meal for their suppers, which were afterwards to be prepared by baking the meal into cakes at the fire." Ball describes the process in detail: "After the corn was converted into meal, each one kneaded it up with cold water into a thick dough, and raking away the ashes from a small space on the kitchen hearth, placed the dough, rolled up in green leaves, in the hollow, and covering it with hot embers, left it to be baked into bread, which was done in about half an hour." Sometimes food portions for a domestic captive could include scraps from their enslaver's table, but this was not always the case. As Ball notes, "I observed that the two women who had waited at the table, after the supper of the white people was disposed of, also came with their corn to the mill on the post and ground their allowance like the others. They had not been permitted to taste even the fragments of the meal that they had cooked for their masters and mistresses."[5]

For the enslaved on the Pugh Sr. property, punishments were probably administered before food was distributed. Again, Charles Ball provides details as he experienced them picking cotton on a South Carolina plantation: "On all estates, the standard of a day's work is fixed by the overseer, according to the quality of the cotton." He continues: "In the evening, if it is found that the standard quantity has not been picked, the delinquent picker is sure to receive a whipping. On some estates, settlements are made every evening, and the whipping follows immediately; on others, the whipping does not occur until the next morning, whilst on a few plantations, the accounts are closed twice, or three times a week."[6] Years after she learned to pick cotton in Alabama in the 1850s, an elderly woman named Adeline still couldn't stand to watch clerks weighing the meat she bought at the grocery store: "Cause I remembers so well each day that the slaves was given a certain number of pounds to pick. When weighing up time come and you didn't have the number of pounds set aside, you may be sure that you was going to be whipped."[7]

Herring was the key protein distributed after daily accounts were closed on the Pugh holdings. The earliest herring fisheries began near Quirocky in the 1740s, following the practices of Native Americans like the Tuscarora, who applied the original seine, or net-fishing, technique that became standard for generations. Hannah Crafts does not write about such practices in her novel, but she must have been aware of fishing methods, given that they permeated enslaved life in the region and that she, like other enslaved women in Indian Woods, would have helped darn and maintain the netting in the off-season. Likely, her great-uncle James Barefoot escaped execution at the time of the Bertie Conspiracy because of his skill and value in rigging, weighting, and preparing nets and then directing the haul.

The practice as Barefoot would have known it involved preparing weirs, bow nets, stake nets, drift nets, seines, and slides. Netting used for creating a trap, called a pound, sometimes required tarred rope half a mile long. For the larger operations, the netting remained stationary in the river, held in place by wooden stakes embedded in the bottom. The stakes and net acted as the pound and a long branch of net in the current, called a slide, drew fish into the trap. The pound was then emptied throughout the day, with the use of bow nets, as fish became caught in the trap. The key was placement and timing for the spawning season. In late winter and early spring, great schools of shad, herring, and rockfish (striped bass) left the sea, passed through Outer Banks inlets, swam across Albemarle Sound, and moved up the Roanoke to their spawning grounds. The numbers were astounding, making these waters some of the most productive in the world during the antebellum period.[8]

For Pugh Sr. and, later, Lewis Bond, the rivers and tributaries adjacent to their plantations supplied more than enough food to feed the captives engaged in agricultural pursuits. Indeed, the surplus herring, shad, and rockfish became commodities to be packaged and carried to markets as far away as the West Indies. Like the Tuscarora before them, white people mined value from land and water. The difference was the exploitive nature of the extraction. In Bertie County in 1850, of the fifty-four businesses that annually sold a minimum of five hundred dollars' worth of goods, thirty-four manufactured staves, shingles, or plank; six produced tar and turpentine; and of the remaining, six were mills and eight were fisheries.[9] And these businesses competed with the plantations in harvesting the area's resources. By the end of the nineteenth century, old-growth lumber and marine life had been tapped out for at least a generation.

For Hannah Sr. and Hannah Jr., the bounty of the Roanoke and its fertile soil meant the concentrated wealth of the Pughs and Bonds and demand for domestic service. Crafts describes the luxury of "the great house," with its "conviviality of appearance and manner that seemed almost unbecoming in a mansion so ancient and respectable." In the run-up to the wedding depicted in her novel, Crafts writes, "[M]orning to night and night to morning [the great house] was thronged with guests. Carriages came and went incessantly up and down the long avenue of oaks. Gentlemen on horseback crossed and recrossed the lawn. The windows shutters were all thrown back, for not a room was tenantless, not a mirror blank." In language she later edited out of her novel, Crafts's continues: "We the servants liked it. We liked the fun and frolic, the show the novelties and the nights of revelry though ever and when the mirth was we would hear the doleful creakings [*sic*] of the Linden tree" (*TBN* 31). The creaking of the linden tree is the not-so-subtle reminder of Rose's murder earlier in the novel; that creaking abruptly sounds the alarm of the genocidal exploitation that fueled such "revelry."

In the end, Crafts revised the passage to reflect more evenly the coexistence of splendor and exploitation. Still, either way, the passage reflects personal knowledge. Historical records show the same theme. We do not have accounts specifically detailing the expenses for the author's mother or for Hannah Crafts, but we do have details for Pugh Sr.'s domestic servant Jenny and her children. From depositions and ledger accounts, we can trace with precision Jenny and her children's medical bills, food allotment, and clothing expenses between 1803 and 1816. It is reasonable to assume that Hannah Sr. and Hannah Jr. received similar treatment. Because Pugh Sr.'s granddaughter Mary Pugh was assigned a guardian when she was orphaned, there is a record of Mary's provisions, too.

The contrast is striking. While Mary is accorded extraordinary material advantages—tuition, books, muslin, calico, ribbons, ink, paper, and the service of her waiting maid and other support—her domestic servant, Jenny, and Jenny's two children are provided a meager ration: besides a daily allotment of herring and corn, there is, annually, a length of cloth and one pair of "negro shoes." The shoes were for Jenny; her boys went barefoot, probably because they were already intended for the field. Even as Mary's support regularly tallies six hundred dollars or more each year, not including food, horse, and stable provisions, Jenny and her children receive two dollars and twenty cents' worth of annual support. In this environment, the only path to improving one's material circumstances depended upon proximity to and intimacy with the family of one's enslaver.

Hannah Sr., Hannah Jr., and their family experienced those advantages. And they suffered them, too. At some point, Rosea Pugh became pregnant with Hannah Sr., and the resulting dispute reflects the singular way the author's family was managed as property. Consistently, they are shielded from sale as the Pugh and Bond families seek to maintain Rosea, Hannah Sr., and, later, Hannah Bond as possessions. For instance, in 1809, as a minor, Catherine Pugh married her first husband, Thomas Turner, who was from a prominent neighboring family. Rosea and Hannah Sr. followed Catherine into the household as part of her legacy. But Turner died within the first weeks of their marriage, and there were debts the Turner estate needed to settle. Catherine placed Rosea Pugh and Hannah Sr. beyond control of the estate and off-limits for sale. Then, more than a year later, the captives followed her again, into the household of a new husband, Lewis Bond.

Lewis Bond took up the case for maintaining Catherine's property based on Thomas Pugh Sr.'s will, as the will was still in probate before Turner's demise. Throughout the legal wrangling—the file for the case is lengthy—Lewis Bond and Catherine Pugh sought to protect Rosea, Hannah Sr., and, later, Hannah Bond from sale. Indeed, Hannah Sr. and Hannah Bond would remain the property of the Pughs and Bonds until the author's escape from the Wheelers in 1857. Even later in life, when Hannah Crafts was serving John Hill Wheeler in Washington, D.C., she was legally the property of Lucinda Bond Wheeler through the estate of Lucinda's parents, not the property of the Wheelers. This may account for why there is no written record of John Hill Wheeler trying to obtain Crafts after her escape: he had no legal claim. Crafts's mother, too, would remain in the possession of Lewis Bond's estate, even until her death in 1858. The most reasonable conclusion for the strident protection of Crafts and her mother is kinship.

IV

What was motherhood like for Hannah Sr.? This is impossible to fully determine from direct sources, but records from the period do sketch a view of the experience. The Virginia law of *partus sequitur ventrem* rendered the children of any enslaved woman slaves themselves, and similar legislation spread across the Southern colonies, including North Carolina, whereby, by the time of statehood, the practice was well established in custom and law. Because of legal precedent, slaveholders in North Carolina and elsewhere came to regard female captives as both laborers and potential reproducers for future economic enterprises. By 1808, the abolition of the international slave trade in the United States meant reproduction became even more profitable, as it became illegal to import enslaved people from abroad. As a result, the dual exploitation of enslaved mothers grew more entrenched over time.

The antebellum period was shaped by a growing stratification of gendered spaces separating "public work" from "private home." As such, the "private home" became the domain of a woman's allegedly innate role as caregiver and nurturer, while men were left to the "public work" of earning a living and engaging in economic enterprises. Such stratification saw the increasing elevation of biological motherhood as the natural role for women. But such imaginary spaces and roles proved incoherent, to a degree, when they were applied to enslaved people. Power dynamics of gender and race crossed and became multivalent for Black women. If an enslaved woman sought to transcend her place as property through motherhood, she also found her legal status as property superseding her "natural" right to be the primary caregiver to her children.

Enslavers' exploitation of *partus sequitur ventrem* placed the chattel status of Black female bodies as the guiding force for policing Black mothering practices. This resulted in the custom of separating mothers from their offspring and forcing enslaved women to provide the labor of "other mothering" to children who were not their biological offspring:

enslaved women often became caretakers for the Black children in the slave quarters and, in a separate space, nurturers for white people's children. Commonly, child care was assigned to enslaved girls too young to perform other arduous tasks or to older women unsuited for field work.[10]

Hannah Sr. and Hannah Jr. experienced this kind of "other mothering" even as they were denied the full presence of their own mothers. Slaveholding women used enslaved mothers as surrogates to raise their white children, including nourishing them through breastfeeding. Formerly enslaved in Mississippi, Mattie Logan, a participant in a Works Progress Administration Slave Narratives project, described her mother's wet-nursing: "Mother nursed all Miss Jennie's children. . . . They say I nursed on one breast while that white child, Jennie, pulled away at the other! That was a pretty good idea for the mistress, for it didn't keep her tied to the place and she could visit around with her friends most any time she wanted."[11]

Logan's mother endured the physical toll of simultaneously feeding two babies (her own and her slaveholder's), while her mistress did not face the difficulties and challenges of nursing. This was a practice Milly Murfree likely suffered in the household of John Hill Wheeler by nourishing Richard Mentor Johnson Wheeler and her own infant, Tecumseh, concurrently. As noted earlier, Milly's pregnancy may have been partially forced on her to ensure a surrogate mother for Wheeler's child. The power inherent in slaveholding meant the complete subservience of an enslaved woman's body for the purposes of advancing the interests and comfort of her captors, at least insofar as slaveholders could surveil and control Black mothering practices.

In her novel, Hannah Crafts writes of the unique pressures that made motherhood and enslaved unions unattractive: "[P]ractical common sense must teach every observer of mankind that any situation involving such responsibilities as marriage can only be filled with profit, and honor, and advantage by the free" (*TBN* 135). For the character Charlotte in the novel, performing child care is a burden even if one's enslavers are benevolent: "Her mistress was kind and indulgent, she was not required to do any menial service, but only to attend on the children. What multitudes of people, white and black, might have envied the situations in which she was miserable?" But then, Crafts continues: "Alas; those that view slavery only as it relates to physical suffering or the want of nature, can have no conception of its greatest evils" (*TBN* 134).

Crafts may be reflecting on what she knew of her mother's position, and her own, in the Pugh and Bond families. Both women knew well the "greatest evils" facing domestic captives, sexual control and abuse, and Crafts's novel is full of stories drawn from real life about captive women suffering sexual abuse. Her mother's life and her own must have been minefields of forced alliances and enemies—or, as Crafts puts it in her novel, "alternate cruelty and kindness" (*TBN* 34).

V

In 1836, Hannah Sr. was separated from her daughter and forced to move to lands newly stolen from Native Americans, this time land taken from the Chickasaw as part of the treaty of 1818 that delivered to families like the Bonds soil in West Tennessee. Located between the Tennessee and Mississippi Rivers, the land was rich in clay and sand and ripe for growing cotton and grains. Judge William Pugh Bond, the oldest son of Lewis Bond, brought Hannah Sr. with him shortly after his marriage to Lucy Rascoe, as the pair joined William's uncle Thomas Bond Sr., who had relocated from Bertie County a decade earlier and established successful slave plantations and a steamboat enterprise in the region.

Well before Hannah Sr. arrived, the land acquired from the Chickasaw spurred interest from speculators, especially those from North Carolina like Thomas Bond Sr., who arrived in Haywood County ready to purchase property. But Thomas Sr.'s relocation in 1826 had less to do with speculative investment than with the need to escape the law. The 1809 legal battle with the neighboring Turner family over possession of Rosea and Hannah Sr. had escalated into a feud between the Bond and Turner families in Indian Woods. For more than a decade, the Turner family sought the return of Rosea and Hannah Sr. through litigation. But for this period, the Bond family had stayed one step ahead, successfully manipulating the Sheriff's Office and the local courts to maintain possession of the author's family. The feud reached its height in the spring of 1826, when one of Thomas Sr.'s hound dogs wandered onto Simon Turner's plantation and killed some chickens. Turner responded by capturing the dog and hanging it from a tree in his front yard. Generations of Indian Woods people would remember what happened next.

On Sunday morning, as Thomas Bond Sr. rode to church, he saw his favorite dog gibbeted to his neighbor's tree. He reached for his rifle, called at the front door, and shot Simon Turner dead. By Monday morning, Thomas Sr. was packed and traveling to Haywood County, Tennessee, to establish new plantations in an area already developed by a relative. At the time, his brother, Sheriff Lewis Bond, to aid Thomas Sr.'s escape, assisted in delaying the response. It helped that Simon Turner lived alone and was disliked intensely by local captives because of his cruelty as a slaveholder. Even though Bond's escape occurred the year of her birth, Hannah Crafts seems to have used elements of the story of the hanged dog in her novel, now reimagined as the catalyst for Rose's punishment in the narrative.

In 1826, Thomas Bond Sr.'s thriving plantations in Indian Woods passed to his adopted nephew, called Thomas Jr., and the elder Bond began new operations in Tennessee, building up his slave labor force slowly from twenty-six captives in 1830 to thirty-six in 1840, and so forth—until, by the Civil War, he held as many as five hundred captives. Thomas Sr.'s Tennessee holdings came to be among the largest and most profitable of all the Bond family holdings, making him one of the richest men in Tennessee. The captive Jenny and her two boys, who likely immigrated to Tennessee with Bond Sr. in 1826, are lost as traceable property at this point. They now became illegible among the more generalized accounting records that Thomas Sr. kept as his Tennessee slaveholdings grew.

A decade later, when Judge William Pugh Bond brought Hannah Sr. to the region, along with his wife, Lucy, and his cousin James West Bond,

Brownsville was booming as an agricultural hub and transportation center. At the time, Thomas Bond Sr.'s property in Tennessee included a port on the Hatchie River, a steamboat, and plantations along the Forked Deer River connecting his various cotton fields to Memphis and the Mississippi River. Judge Bond and James first joined and then expanded these operations, and the larger Bond family enterprise thrived. In 1840, Judge Bond held six captives; forty by 1850; and seventy-five by 1860. James, too, found fortune by exploiting enslaved labor and by procuring fertile West Tennessee soil. He amassed more than 17,000 acres and approximately 220 slaves within the two decades of his arrival. In 1859, James West Bond's five plantations yielded more than 1,000 bales of cotton and nearly 22,000 bushels of corn. The federal census for 1860 estimated his total wealth at just under $800,000. By comparison, the total value of all farmland, buildings, and other improvements in the entire county of Johnson—situated in the mountainous region in the northeastern part of the state—was just under $790,000.

The household where Hannah Sr. served as a primary domestic servant was consequently part of a wealthy syndicate of Bond family members in Brownsville and Haywood County. Judge Bond's legal practice included managing the complicated economic endeavors of family members: mercantile establishments, railroad stock, and the family's steamboat enterprise. During Hannah Sr.'s life in Tennessee, all three heads of household, Thomas Pugh Bond Sr., James West Bond, and Judge William Pugh Bond, also held state political office at different times. Along with the family's political work, Judge Bond helped administer commissions at the Bonds' Hatchie River port, which served as a conduit for moving cotton and other produce to Memphis.

It is hard to know precisely what life for Hannah Sr. was like serving in the home of Judge Bond and Lucy Rascoe Bond. As a house servant, she must have helped direct the Bond family's businesses, as Judge Bond likely ran his law practice and accounting work out of his home, built around 1829 or 1830 and located in the commercial district near his uncle's property. Judge Bond's house no longer stands, but Thomas Bond

Sr.'s house is maintained today as the "Bond-Livingston-Tripp House." Likely, Judge Bond's house was built in the same Greek Revival manner as the Bond-Livingston-Tripp House, and probably by some of the same enslaved laborers.

What is clear is that Hannah Sr.'s captor, Lucy Rascoe Bond, gave birth to two surviving children, named Lucy (born 1836) and Lewis (born 1839). In the 1840 census, Hannah Sr. looked after a household that included her enslavers, their two children, and two other children, orphaned family members of prominent Episcopal leader the Rev. John Chilton and his wife, who were early victims of the yellow fever that plagued the region. In 1844, Lucy Rascoe died of the same disease, and Judge Bond married Jane Wood in 1850.

Hannah Sr.'s service in Judge Bond's home would have included raising the infants Lucy and Lewis while also establishing two adopted children into the household. When yellow fever struck Brownsville again in 1844, Hannah Sr. must have tended to Lucy Rascoe in illness and loss. By late 1851, Hannah Sr. (then fifty-seven) is listed back in Bertie County and again in the possession of Lewis Bond. Likely, Jane Wood brought her own waiting maid to her marriage to Judge Bond in 1850, making Hannah Sr. dispensable after the union. The record is sparse for navigating Hannah Sr.'s life, but she appears in Lewis Bond's slave inventory again in 1851, apparently ill, judging from her valuation in Bond family records. It is possible she was sent back to Indian Woods that year, her health permanently damaged after she attended at the death of Lucy Rascoe. Hannah Sr. disappears from all slave accounts by 1858. In her novel, Crafts would resurrect her mother, depicting her as healthy and free in the North. By that point, both daughter and mother, so frequently separated by slavery, were forever free and ready to be united in Hannah Crafts's art.

CHAPTER 9

THE EARLY LIFE OF HANNAH CRAFTS

I

AT THE TIME OF HANNAH Bond's birth, her mother, Hannah Sr., was thirty-two years old, and Lewis Bond was thirty-nine. Lewis Bond kept a house in Windsor, North Carolina, near his mercantile holdings. Here, Hannah Sr. came to serve as the family's in-town housekeeper. Possibly, she gave birth to Hannah Jr. in the kitchen dependency of the Windsor property, where she remained largely out of view of Catherine Pugh Bond, her original mistress. Perhaps an enslaved midwife from the town assisted with the birth. As with many mixed-race captives, the identity of Hannah Jr.'s father was withheld from her. The author's earliest years would have been ones of wonder and searching as she tried to figure out her place in the world.

Hannah Jr. seems to have been separated from her mother and nursed among the slave huts of Willow Hall by a surrogate. Later, the author came to know her mother, although how openly remains unclear. With a refined bearing, Hannah Sr. cut a formidable figure among the enslaved. Light-skinned, she seems to have secured benefits by trading on her blood ties to the Pughs and Bonds. As a trusted mixed-race ally, she established herself as a capable manager in the Pugh and Bond households. The author may have memorialized some facet of her mother in the figure of Lizzy in the novel: "She would assume an air of consequential dignity, and assert that on the contrary it was a very great thing and very important even to a slave to be well connected—that good blood was an inheritance to them." Crafts continues: "when they heard the name of some honorable gentleman mentioned with applause, or saw some great lady flaunt by in jewels and satins the privilege of thinking he or she is a near relative of mine was a very great privilege indeed." The retort Hannah provides in the novel is telling: "And then I said 'Of course' which mollified her rumpled vanity" (*TBN* 33–34).

If Crafts did draw on Hannah Sr. for the figure of Lizzy, she must have been acknowledging some element of pain at her own forced separation from her mother for most of her life. Lizzy's fate may signal what Crafts knew of her estranged mother's bargain: "[N]otwithstanding her good family, education, and great beauty, [she] had . . . passed through many hands, and experienced all the vicissitudes attendant on the life of a slave. She had been the pet of a rich family and the degraded drudge of another. . . . She could tell tales of slavery that made the blood run cold to hear" (*TBN* 34).

Hannah Jr. seems to have been reunited temporarily with her mother at the Windsor house, where she would have begun acquiring the language, habits, and domestic training necessary for her future as a waiting maid to Lewis Bond's daughters, Esther and Lucinda. For five years, then, Hannah Jr. shadowed her mother at the Windsor property and, later, at Willow Hall: emptying chamber pots; fetching water, wood, and coal; and preparing fires, along with assisting her mother with laundry and kitchen work. Likely, Hannah Sr. and Hannah Jr. became domestic servants at Willow Hall after they were recalled at the time of Nat Turner's rebellion. This was when Esther reached marriageable age and required waiting service. Lucinda was not far behind.

By 1836, at the age of ten, Hannah Jr. lost her mother to migration when Hannah Sr. was forced to follow Judge Bond and his new wife to Tennessee. It is unclear whether the author gained literacy before or after her mother's departure, but Hannah Jr. clearly yearned for the advantages that her white contemporaries Esther and Lucinda enjoyed, especially their access to books. In her novel, the author makes clear Hannah's early drive to achieve an education. Crafts narrates how Hannah seeks the help of a local Quaker woman:

> One day while sitting on a little bank, beneath the shade of some large trees, at a short distance from my playmates, an aged woman approached me. She was white, and looked venerable with her grey hair smoothly put back beneath a plain sun bonnet, and I recollected having seen her once or twice at my master's house whither she came to sell salves and ointments, and hearing it remarked that she was the wife of a sand-digger and very poor.

"I desired knowledge," Crafts writes. When the gray-haired woman asks about the book Hannah is concealing "with child-like artlessness," she explains: "I told her all . . . how our Master interdicted it, and how I was trying to teach myself" (*TBN* 7).

Hannah's wish is answered by the stranger, who says, "'Child . . . I was thinking of our Saviour's words to Peter where he commands the latter to 'feed his lambs.' I will dispense to you such knowledge as I possess. Come to me each day. I will teach you to read in the hope and trust that you will thereby be made better in this world and that to come.['"] Crafts describes the moment vividly: "Pleased, delighted, overwhelmed with my good fortune in prospective I felt like a being to whom a new world with all its mysteries and marvels was opening, and could scarcely repress my tears of joy and thankfulness" (*TBN* 7–8).

In the novel, Crafts has Hannah begin her lessons in the small cottage that is home to Aunt Hetty and Uncle Siah, two characters possibly based on real-life neighbors in Indian Woods. The moment seems to have been a turning point for the author, as it was for other fugitives who gained literacy. Crafts writes, "It must not be supposed that learning to read was all they taught me, or that my visits to them were made with regularity.

They gave me an insight to many things. They cultivated my moral nature. They led me to the foot of the Cross." She continues: "Sometimes in the evening while the other slaves were enjoying the banjo and the dance I would steal away to hold sweet converse with them. Sometimes a morning walk with the other children, or an errand to a neighbors would furnish the desired opportunity, and sometimes an interval of many days elapsed between my calls to their house." Crafts describes the growth of Hannah from these encounters: "I tried to remember the good things they had taught me, and to improve myself by gathering up such crumbs of knowledge as I could, and adding little by little to my stock of information" (*TBN* 10–11).

As Crafts writes, after approximately two years of instruction, Hannah's lessons are discovered. "The door suddenly opened without warning, and the overseer of my master's estate walked into the house. My horror, and grief, and astonishment were indescribable." If Crafts is basing Hannah's experience on her own—which is likely—the overseer was almost certainly John Thomas Bond, Lewis Bond's youngest son at the time, whom Lewis had placed as his overseer when Crafts was still a child. Family history holds that John Thomas was the mixed-race son of Lewis Bond, but he passed for white most of his life.[1]

In the novel, Hannah goes unpunished: "My Master was absent at the time, the overseer could find no precedent for my case, and so I escaped punishment I should otherwise have suffered" (*TBN* 13). This seems strange in the context of Crafts's novel, but perfectly understandable based on the conditions reflected outside the narrative. John Thomas held a position that was common in the neighborhood: in Indian Woods, at least, white enslavers sometimes raised a mixed-race son to serve as overseer on their plantations. Wright Cherry, an enslaved boy on a plantation adjacent to Willow Hall, passed down the story of being taught to read by his mixed-race overseer, George Outlaw II. Like John Thomas at Willow Hall, Wright Cherry and George Outlaw were groomed to serve as overseers.

John Thomas and the other mixed-race overseers of Indian Woods used their education daily to direct work on area plantations. Record keeping, crop and livestock management, provisioning and handling enslaved people—these were duties that required reading and writing. Mixed-race female captives, too, sometimes acquired literacy in order to help with domestic service: managing kitchen and domestic inventories, directing household affairs, and sometimes even writing letters and taking dictation. As John Thomas and even Lewis Bond must have known, Hannah Jr.'s reach for literacy could make her even more valuable to the household.

If the author went unpunished, her teachers were not so lucky. In the novel, Aunt Hetty and Uncle Siah are forced out of the community. Crafts explains that they were punished so "that others might be deterred from the like attempt." She continues: "The cruel overseer would not tell me whither he had removed them, but to all my inquiries he simply answered that he would take good care I never saw them again." And Crafts describes the result: "Their cottage of home remained uninhabited for a time, and then strangers came and took possession of it" (*TBN* 13). This scene, too, may be based on real life. There is a newspaper account from Norfolk, Virginia, of a white woman, Margaret Douglass, being jailed for teaching "colored children" to read.[2]

After slavery, John Thomas Bond would live partially with his common-law wife, Mary Hassell, a mixed-race former captive from the Bond plantation. John Thomas would never marry Mary, but he would provide for her and their children, who followed the condition of their mother, even after slavery, and carried the name "Hassell." Because John Thomas's children faced discrimination in Bertie County, the grandchildren migrated elsewhere and passed for white, like their grandfather. They, too, came to claim the patronym of "Bond" and passed over the color line. Hannah Crafts would choose a very different path in freedom.

II

To reconstruct further details about life at Willow Hall during Hannah Crafts's early life, we must rely on Lewis Bond's probate and property records. From 1830 to 1851, according to federal census and slave schedules, Bond enslaved around one hundred captives. During these two decades, he held more than sixteen hundred acres of land, built through family alliance and inheritance. Sales from the estate chronicle the tools used to extract productivity from captives: plows, cultivators, spades, axes, grubbing, and weeding hoes. From the barnyard, the auctioneer's receipts include wagons, harnesses, whips, and ox chains. An expansive number of livestock appear in the sales ledger: forty-three sheep, sixty-three hogs, sixteen sows, nine cattle, and multiple oxen. In the dairy barn, Bond possessed fourteen cows and fourteen calves. And the Willow Hall property also held a full stable of horses: more than two dozen steeds and yearlings and twenty mules. An oak stave–making business operated in Windsor, as noted in tax records. Here, Lewis Bond had eight enslaved captives who produced oak barrels from lumber harvests on his acreage, likely for the herring catch from area fishing operations, including Bond's own.

The produce generated appears in the settlement of accounts. In 1851, Lewis Bond's enslaved people produced two hundred barrels of corn and more than a hundred bushels of peas, fifty stacks of fodder (likely excess herring from the fishing camps), and an impressive haul of cotton bundled and packaged for sale. On February 10, 1852, the estate received $1,685 for the previous year's cotton harvest sold to the factors Biggs and Cherry of Norfolk. This high sum helps demonstrate the scale of cotton cultivation on Bond's holdings. In short, Willow Hall was a large and grand labor complex during Crafts's childhood and young adulthood, like Lindendale depicted in her novel (see Figure 19).[3]

Crafts has Hannah describe the primary house, the great house at Willow Hall: "Heretofore all except certain apartments had been interdicted to us, but now that the chambers were opened to be aired and renovated no one could prevent us making good use of our eyes." As was common, even a domestic captive like Hannah Jr. could access only a limited number of spaces in the mansion house. She describes as much, but on the occasion of Thomas Bond Jr.'s wedding at Willow Hall, Crafts seems to have gained access to forbidden "white" areas, too. She notes: "[W]hat an array of costly furniture adorned the rich saloons and gorgeous halls" (*TBN* 14).

Although Hannah Jr. likely resided in the kitchen dependency near the main house, she provided child care in the slave huts while the parents of younger children worked in the fields. Nineteen slave huts are enumerated on the property. The author's labor in support of enslaved people seems to have sparked a lifelong passion for instructing children, judging from Crafts's later career as a teacher in New Jersey. The author observes of Hannah in the novel, "What a blessing it is that faith, and hope, and love are universal in their nature and operation—that poor as well as rich, bond as well as free are susceptible to their pleasing influences, and contain within themselves a treasure of consolation for all the ills of life." She continues, celebrating the mutual affection she received from the little ones in the huts. "These little children, slaves though they were, and doomed to a life of toil and drudgery, ignorant, and untutored, assimilated thus to the highest and proudest in the land—thus evinced their equal origin, and immortal destiny" (*TBN* 11–12). Here, too, love could reach despite slavery (see Figure 20).

For a period after her mother left for Tennessee, Hannah Jr. served at the neighboring plantation of Thomas Bond Jr. and Sawyer P. Rascoe. The growing family of Thomas Jr.—six children under the age of ten—needed domestic help and child care. Further, in the 1840s, the Turner family again prosecuted the case claiming Hannah Jr. and her mother as property. As a precaution, the author became a permanent fixture in Thomas Jr.'s household in the late 1840s. Here, she seems to have suffered sexual coercion.

Crafts writes the experience into her narrative by introducing a light-skinned, unnamed bride into the novel. She describes the passing bride as a small woman "with a profusion of wavy curly hair, large bright eyes, and delicate features with the exception of her lips which

FIGURE 19: Liberty Hall, built on the property of the Willow Hall plantation near the original Willow Hall, in 1856, shortly after the death of Lewis Bond. Earliest known photograph, n.d.

FIGURE 20: The last remaining buildings on the Willow Hall labor compound, as they stand today (May 2022). During Hannah Crafts's life at Willow Hall, these buildings were the home of Lewis Bond's widowed sister, Mary Bond Ashburn (1791–1868). After the Civil War, Crafts's enslavers Samuel Jordan Wheeler and Catherine Bond Wheeler lived here.

were too large, full, and red." Crafts continues, quite possibly providing a description of herself when she was coerced into serving Thomas Jr.: "She dressed in very good taste and her manner seemed perfect but for an uncomfortable habit she had of seeming to watch everybody as though she feared them." In the novel, Hannah becomes the shadow self to this unnamed mistress as the two plot to free themselves from bondage: "I fancied then that she was haunted by a shadow or phantom apparent only to herself, and perhaps even the more dreadful for that" (*TBN* 27).

John Thomas Bond's example of passing for white may have inspired Crafts to imagine a life in which she, too, could attain security and privilege. It is even possible that while coercing Hannah Jr., Thomas Jr. promised some kind of liberty or advancement. The main plot device of Crafts's novel invokes the figure of an unnamed mistress who was switched at birth, unknown to her white father, who then raised the child as white all the way to her marriage into the planter class. In the novel, Hannah serves this woman until she is betrayed by the slave speculator Mr. Trappe. In reality, Hannah Crafts seems to have experienced the role of both captive and mistress: she was a light-skinned woman who could have passed for white, but instead, she became a trafficked daughter. Her betrayer, probably her father, never acknowledged his bond to her and even allowed her to be sexually abused by a nephew. These traumatizing experiences seem to be at the heart of Crafts's novel.

Crafts explains her views of her enslaver through the protagonist Hannah: "Slaves were slaves to him, and nothing more. Practically he regarded them not as men and women, but in the same light as horses or other domestic animals." Crafts continues: "He supplied their necessities of food and clothing from motives of policy, but [di]scounted the ideas of equality and fraternity as preposterous and absurd" (*TBN* 6). Strangely, just as the identity of the mistress is never disclosed in the novel, neither is a name provided for Hannah's original enslaver in the narrative; rather, the character is presented only as an unnamed male presence. Perhaps both are obscured, like Crafts's personal experience, as a way to convert painful memories into art. Hannah the heroine is allowed to escape what Crafts herself bore.

The Bondwoman's Narrative is rife with the lament of enslaved women suffering the birth and loss of mixed-race children. In Crafts's novel, the characters Lizzy, Evelyn, and Ellen all lose the children forced on them. Like the real lives of those she encountered—Milly and Martha Murfree, Eliza Morgan, Mary Burton, and Jane Johnson—Crafts memorialized a trauma mostly ignored in American literature: mothering and then losing children conceived by rape.

The evidence is scant, but property records and Crafts's autobiographical novel point to Hannah Jr. suffering sexual abuse similar to that ascribed to other domestic captives in the novel. In the 1840s, Crafts gave birth to a child—the sex is not recorded—while in the possession of Thomas Jr. That child appears in Bond family records only once, as "Hannah & child," in a December 1851 inventory of captives hired out after Lewis Bond's death. Very young children and babies are listed in the same inventory as "infants," further placing the birth of Hannah's "child" while she served in the household of Thomas Jr. in the late 1840s.

As we have seen, a mixed-race child would have been considered a prized asset and preserved in family accounts, but the presence of the author's child is recorded only that one time. Indeed, this specific child is not traceable again when family inventories and relevant slave schedules are scoured. And no record of a child follows Crafts into the household of Lucinda Bond Wheeler in 1852. The most likely scenario is that Crafts's child died of typhoid fever in the early months of 1852. That winter, the illness swept through Indian Woods, claiming Lewis Bond's youngest daughter, Esther, and Thomas Bond Jr.'s infant, Hewitt. With Hannah Jr. hired out that winter to serve Esther, it seems reasonable to guess that Crafts lost her own child to the illness, possibly with Esther as a vector for the disease.

Four years after these deaths, Crafts began writing her autobiographical novel, probably in part as a response to the trauma and grief of her loss, including the betrayal and violence behind the conception of her child. In the novel, Hannah explains why she remained single and unconnected in bondage: "I have always thought that in a state of servitude marriage must be at best of doubtful advantage. It necessarily complicates and involves the relation of master and slave, adds new ties to those already formed, and is at the bottom of many troubles and afflictions that might otherwise be escaped." She continues: "The slave, if he or she desires to be content, should ~~never think of~~ always remain in celibacy" (*TBN* 135). The strikethrough text is preserved in the manuscript.

Clearly, Crafts herself was forced from strict "celibacy," but her heroine, Hannah, lives out these principles in the novel. In revising her sentence, Crafts replaces a stricture on "marriage" with one on "celibacy." But, as her novel demonstrates, celibacy is not within an enslaved woman's control, except for an integrity of mind beyond the power of an enslaver's violence. Possibly, the character Hannah controls celibacy in the novel as a projection of the mental control Crafts herself maintained in real life. Indeed, Crafts fashions a plot to dramatize the point.

Hannah is paired with the unnamed light-skinned bride who passes for white in the text until her racial identity is revealed. At that point, she is threatened with being trafficked into sexual slavery. Immediately, the bride dies: "[T]he next moment I discovered that the sofa pillows were tinged with blood that bubbled from her lips." Crafts continues: "Her excessive agitation had ruptured a blood-vessel, and she was fast approaching that bourne where the wicked cease from troubling and the weary are at rest" (*TBN* 103). Hannah lives on as celibate in the text, but only after her shadow self is sacrificed. It is almost as if Crafts had to kill off an image of herself as a passing bride to reconstitute the integrity of the novel's heroine, Hannah. The plot demonstrates the impossibility of a woman choosing her own sexual alliances once she is deemed Black. The enslaved bride's last words—"The Lord bless and sustain you" (*TBN* 103)—serve as a kind of benediction to Crafts's surviving heroine. The passing bride dies before the survivor is whole again.

The novel allows its author to manage difficult truths by exercising narrative control of a life partially stolen from her. In the author's telling,

Hannah Crafts bears a name, one that Crafts chooses, in part, to honor her mother (Hannah) and to celebrate her own agency (Crafts). Meanwhile, her enslaver (Lewis Bond) and abuser (Thomas Bond Jr.) are both effaced in the text; they go unnamed, banished to exist only as ghostly presences in the novel, exposed but ultimately vanquished by Crafts's narrative. The child Crafts seems to have lost in early 1852 is remembered and redeemed in the story of the real-life children the author would come to mentor when she, like her heroine, reached freedom. As Crafts makes clear throughout her novel, *The Bondwoman's Narrative* is a celebration of a survivor's escape, not the story of enslavers' power.

III

How did stolen literacy by the young Hannah Jr. lead to her becoming a novelist? Estate records and family history maintain that Lewis Bond was a very bookish man. An inventory of the library at Willow Hall is unavailable, but surviving records and oral history maintain that Bond's library was expansive. Crafts would also come to serve in the literary homes of brothers Samuel Jordan Wheeler and John Hill Wheeler. An inventory was twice taken of the volumes possessed by John Hill Wheeler, once in 1850 and again in 1882. As Henry Louis Gates Jr. first noted, *The Bondwoman's Narrative* appears to draw heavily on specific books in John Hill Wheeler's collection. It is reasonable to assume that Samuel Jordan also kept an extensive personal library, serving, as he did, as a physician, professor, historian, and publisher. There is a record of the important public library Samuel Jordan Wheeler helped provide to the Murfreesboro community, and this, too, may have helped shape Crafts's novel.

In the 1830s, Samuel Jordan Wheeler collected more than two hundred volumes with the Murfreesboro Baptist leader the Rev. George Thompson, pastor of the local Meherrin Baptist Church. Together, the two developed this library further in the 1840s as a community resource, keeping the works as a circulating collection for the town and housing them in the old academy building in Murfreesboro that was originally donated by the Wheeler family. This library expanded to meet the needs of Mrs. Banks's Female Academy boarding school when that institution occupied the former campus of the Hertford Academy. Because of the popularity of novels among Mrs. Banks's students, the library grew to feature novels, too. By the time Hannah Crafts began her captivity in the Murfreesboro community in 1852, the library had expanded still further, now forming the centerpiece of the new Chowan Baptist Female Institute, the college that opened its doors in 1848 on the former property of Mrs. Banks's Female Academy boarding school.[4]

Perhaps the author's move to Murfreesboro in 1852 was the most influential change that set her on the path to becoming a novelist. Now, outside Lewis Bond's control, her literacy seems to have been warmly accepted, even encouraged, in the Wheeler family, and this matched new circumstances in which Hannah Jr. must have come into contact with the writing instruction and the creative efforts of the young students she served while they boarded at Wheeler House and took classes at Chowan Baptist Female Institute. Serving college students with ready access to an extensive library less than a block away seems to have fed the innate passion Hannah Jr. held for literature and learning. That enthusiasm carried forward into Crafts's later service to John Hill Wheeler's family, where, again, she found herself within reach of an extensive library that scholars have argued may have helped shape *The Bondwoman's Narrative*.

Crafts's arrival and tenure in Murfreesboro from 1852 to 1856 happened to coincide with the town's sudden rise as one of the nation's premier sites for female higher education. For a self-taught captive who gained literacy furtively, the opportunity to interact daily with women pursuing a college education must have been thrilling. Launched four years before Crafts's service to the Wheelers, Chowan Baptist Female Institute was modeled on the rigorous male education at Wake Forest College, founded as the Wake Forest Manual Labor Institute in 1834 and rechartered in 1838, by North Carolina Baptist leaders, including Samuel Jordan Wheeler. Chowan's trustees, again including Wheeler, envisioned a Baptist female college rivaling the male college. The curriculum was to be ambitious, including subjects not traditionally taught to women, like the sciences and classical languages, while bolstering female training in music, written composition, and the domestic arts.

The rapid rise of Chowan Baptist Female Institute's reputation owed much to President Martin R. Fory's efforts. In 1849, after an initial launch under local Baptist leader the Rev. Amos Battle, Chowan's trustees hired Fory to direct the institute, drawing to Murfreesboro a nationally recognized leader of the sciences. The local community warmly accepted the New York transplant, and Fory won a public following for his exhibitions in which he provided "public lectures and demonstrations with philosophical apparatus." In a typical performance, he spoke on "electromagnetic telegraphy, the phenomenology of earth and moon, the tides and seasons, an exhibition and explanation of transmitted telegraph messages, [and an] explanation of Colt's submarine battery." Fory also exploded a mine by "means of the magnetic fluid." His illustrations included "a large number of moving phantasmagorical diagrams, and an eight-foot reflecting telescope."[5] A hungry mind, like Hannah Jr.'s, must have cherished every opportunity to attend such talks in the company of student boarders.

As a part of this new community, Hannah Jr. no doubt found her religious nature strengthened, too, even if she continued to be consigned to service roles. Reverend Battle vividly describes a gathering of Chowan students accepting their rebirth in Christ: "When we arrived at the place (an old fishery on the north side of the Meherrin) the young ladies sat down on a bed of wild flowers to rest. We were on a low sand beach covered with green grass and yellow flowers, interspersed with tall pine and cypress." Battle continues, waxing poetic: "On the opposite side were towering bluffs covered with beech-tree and dogwood, unfolding their deep green leaves and large with blossoms, with here and there the sweet-scented honeysuckle." Then he describes the "company of ladies and gentlemen" that "formed on the Murfreesboro side to witness the event." Here, Hannah Jr. would have been assisting Lucinda Bond Wheeler and Samuel Jordan Wheeler, on hand to celebrate the baptism of friends and student boarders. Likely, Crafts was responsible for transporting picnic items and blankets for the gathering and attending to her captor. "Now behold," Battle observes, "six beautiful young ladies step out . . . all dressed in their deep blue uniforms, with hair neatly bound up with white ribbons." After marching to the bank, "down, down they go . . . Now one is gently laid to the liquid grave, and arises a living Christian. Another and another . . . We regard them as the first fruits unto the Lord from our Institute."[6]

Crafts, older than the students she tended, was, likely, still grieving for the child she had lost and perhaps eager for change. Her servitude in Murfreesboro, now a bustling college town, must have felt like a cosmopolitan life compared to her domestic services at Willow Hall. Around this time, her mother's enslaver, Judge Bond, noted in a letter to his sister Lucinda, "[Y]ou have a house full of boarders I expect, and are as busy as a bee, from 'crack of day' to bed time."[7] In fact, Crafts herself was likely the one relied on most from "'crack of day' to bed time" in assisting the students living at Wheeler House. One benefit of this seems to have been ample opportunity to engage with young college women and the lessons they practiced while she cleaned and cooked for and served the students.

In November 1852, Chowan added a major building, "The Columns," to the site of a new campus being constructed on twenty-eight acres of land the college had procured at the southern edge of town to expand its operations. The Columns represented an ambitious statement about God's plans for female higher education and the Baptists' faith in their daughters. Albert G. Jones of Warren County was contracted to build the structure with his crew of enslaved laborers. A three-story Greek Revival–style stuccoed brick building was raised, featuring a low hip roof and octagonal belvedere. The building stands today, its massive portico and eight iconic Doric columns still at once imposing and inviting. The building became the centerpiece of the college when it fully moved operations to the site in 1856.[8]

Immediately to the west of the new Chowan campus, the Methodists began to erect their own female college, then called the Wesleyan Female Institute, designed by architect Thomas L. Fentress. The new Wesleyan

Female Institute began construction in the summer of 1853 amid Masonic and military pomp, employing the same enslaved crew and foreman who had built The Columns. Wesleyan opened in 1855, with President James H. Davis presiding. The Wesleyan primary building was a steam-heated, cupola-topped brick structure of four stories with an observatory on its tin roof and a row of eleven Corinthian columns across the front. Students lived on the third and fourth floors, which also contained a studio for art and four music rooms. Together, Chowan and Wesleyan maintained similar enrollments of around one hundred students each during the period Hannah Crafts lived in the community.

Chowan and Wesleyan drew women from widely dispersed places. A sense of the geographical range can be gathered from Samuel Jordan Wheeler's account book, in which he records the billing addresses and receipts for those residing at Wheeler House. The accounts show students from as far away as Alabama, Mississippi, and Louisiana. Other students hailed from North Carolina counties Wayne, Columbus, Duplin, Sampson, and Chowan, and from prominent Eastern North Carolina communities like New Bern, Kinston, and Greenville. Southeastern Virginia communities also sent their daughters to Murfreesboro.

William D. Valentine, a prominent lawyer from Bertie and Hertford Counties, kept a diary from 1837 through 1855, and in those pages, he records his first impression of Chowan Baptist Female Institute. After attending the institute's public examination—where female students demonstrated their knowledge and artistic skills—he writes, "[T]he college to this part of state" offered "a thorough collegiate education" in a large and "very credible" building, soon to be enlarged. The examinations he attended were in French, mathematics, botany, composition, and music. During intermissions, the public audience was treated to "splendid music on piano, also guitar, the female voice, and the organ." Valentine was duly impressed by the proceedings. "There is not," he confided, "an institution of education of the first order comparable with anything of the kind in the state or anywhere else. It is destined to be hailed everywhere in this country as a great college of female learning."[9]

The literature department at Chowan was led by Miss Mary Wombrell, who formerly taught English at nearby Elm Grove School. Wombrell believed in recitation exercises, in which students would memorize and recite passages from contemporary works of literature.[10] These and the latest literature of the day thus became subjects of conversation, filling the living spaces where Hannah Jr. served. Shortly after Hannah Jr.'s arrival, Harriet Beecher Stowe's *Uncle Tom's Cabin* became a national sensation, the book everyone was reading and talking about in 1852, and the work must have become a favorite for conversation, if not for recitation, at the pro-slavery Chowan Institute.

Fragments of recitation practice appear in the school records of one student from this period, Julia Munro Southall (1838–1928). Southall was a niece of Samuel Jordan Wheeler and, in 1861, became the music teacher at the Wesleyan Female Institute. In her English composition book, Southall copied out passages from Charles Dickens's *Bleak House* to practice for her recital exercises. In fact, she writes out a passage that Crafts herself would later rework in her novel as she borrowed and reimagined parts of Dickens's novel:

> The town awakes; the great tee-totum is set up for its daily spin and whirl; all that unaccountable reading and writing, which has been suspended for a few hours, recommences. Jo and the other lower animals get on in the unintelligible mess as they can.

The passage is preceded by:

> It must be a strange state to be like Jo! To shuffle through the streets, unfamiliar with the shapes, and in utter darkness as to the meaning, of those mysterious symbols, so abundant over the shops, and at the corners of streets, and on the doors, and in the windows! To see people read, and to see people write, and to see the postmen deliver letters, and not to have the least idea of all that language—to be, to every scrap of it, stone blind and dumb! It must be very puzzling to

> see the good company going to the churches on Sundays, with their books in their hands, and to think (for perhaps Jo DOES think at odd times) what does it all mean, and if it means anything to anybody, how comes it that it means nothing to me?[11]

Southall records the important final lines from the passage attributed to the crossing (street) sweep, Jo: "I don't know nothink about nothink." She observes in her recitation notes, "Poor Jo's reply when questioned."

Crafts would refashion these lines and this sequence to portray the lives of the "lower animals" compelled to live in the "utter darkness" of the Wheelers' "slave huts." She reworks the passage thus in her manuscript:

> Degradation, neglect, and ill treatment had wrought on them its legitimate effects. All day they toil beneath the burning sun, scarcely conscious that any link exists between themselves and other portions of the human race. Their mental condition is briefly summed up in the phrase that they know nothing. They know indeed that it is hard to toil unceasingly for a scanty pittance of food, and coarse garments; nature instructed them thus far. (*TBN* 206)

Crafts seems to have been struck by the same passage that formed a part of Southall's recitation exercise. But she brings to Dickens's art a particularly powerful vision as an enslaved woman. As we will see in chapter 16 of this book, one of the strangest and most powerful aspects of *The Bondwoman's Narrative* is how intimately it engages *Bleak House*. The importance of Dickens's novel to Crafts's narrative cannot be overstated, and it seems likely that Crafts was first introduced to the novel while tending to student boarders at Wheeler House. Later, likely, she procured her own copy, which seems to have been a treasured intellectual companion. Indeed, Crafts must have kept *Bleak House* close as a cherished guide when she developed her personal narrative. A copy almost certainly escaped north with her in May 1857.

IV

Evidence suggests that other composition exercises assigned to young college students served to shape aspects of Crafts's manuscript. Samuel Jordan Wheeler's daughter Kate preserved her English composition notebook from this period. In 1854, she composed various exercises for her English classes. The exercises required students to reflect on common aphorisms, or proverbs, and to expound on these according to personal observation. Among the documents preserved in the Kate Wheeler Cooper Papers are compositions based on poetic verses and reflections such as "How blessings brighten as they take their flight" (September 15, 1854), "Know Thyself" (September 22, 1854), "Novel Reading" (September 29, 1854), "When is the time to die" (October 6, 1854), and "The value of knowledge" (October 18, 1854). Young Kate Wheeler observes in her "value of knowledge" composition:

> How inestimable is knowledge! Its value is infinitely greater than other earthly treasures, yea: "nothing of this earth that can be desired is to be compared to it." Only by hard study & perseverance can we become the possessors of it. "Wealth may take not unto itself wings & fly as an eagle aloft towards heaven." Comfort is but temporary and friends may forsake, but this is a durable treasure, for as it cannot be given by an earthly hand so it cannot be taken by one & it will not forsake us until God think best to dispossess us of it. Then seeing its priceless value we should seek more earnestly for it & avail ourselves of every opportunity afforded us for acquiring it.[12]

If there is a distinctly forced quality to such exercises, they also develop a habit of mind. When Crafts came to write her novel, she seems to have knitted together similar kinds of expressions as part of her narrative.

Take, for instance, an early passage in *The Bondwoman's Narrative* where Crafts describes the power of nature to overcome ignorance. The framing and reflection match composition lessons Kate Wheeler practiced in her school notebook, like the ones also preserved by Julia Munro Southall. Crafts writes early in her narrative from the perspective of her heroine, Hannah:

> Can ignorance quench the immortal mind or prevent its feeling at times the indications of its heavenly origin[?] Can it destroy that deep abiding appreciation of the beautiful that seems inherent to the human soul? Can it seal up the fountains of truth and all intuitive perception of life, death and eternity? I think not. Those to whom man teaches little, nature like a wise and prudent mother teaches much. (*TBN* 18)

Further, Crafts observes:

> It sometimes seems that we require sympathy more in joy than sorrow; for the heart exultant, and overflowing with good nature longs to impart a portion of its happiness. Especial[l]y is this the case with children. How it augments the importance of any little success to them that some one probably a mother will receive the intelligence with a show of delight and interest. But I had no mother, nor friend.

The tone, scope, and length of these passages resemble those of the exercises Kate Wheeler recorded a few years earlier. But Crafts punctures the convention: "But I had no mother, nor friend" (*TBN* 8). Aphoristic comfort breaks down in the face of human cruelty.

Another example is a lengthy description of the house "Forget me not." Here, Crafts describes the Henrys' home where the heroine, Hannah, recovers after the fatal carriage accident that kills the slave trader Mr. Hayes. She writes, "Every house with its surroundings possesses an air of individuality. In some it is more strongly developed than in others, yet it appertains to all in a greater or less degree. 'Forget me not' as this dwelling had been beautifully and not inappropriately named was one of those dear old houses rich in panel work and fresco, and whose construction from first to last bespeaks an association with the past." Crafts continues: "Who does not find a charm about these ancient houses, with their delightfully irregular apartments, embellished with quaint carvings and mouldings, brown with age, and awaking in the mind a thousand reminiscen[c]es of olden times and fashions. Such houses were built rather for solid utility than for show, consequently the materials are durable and the timbers massy, but there is likewise a great deal of variety, taste, and elaborate ornamenting" (*TBN* 125–26).

In the first edition of the novel, Gates annotates this passage with "Whereas plot and character would seem to take a priority over setting in the slave narratives, in her novel Crafts seems to luxuriate in making observations such as these, observations that are broad and general rather than specific to the politics of slavery and race" (*TBN* 256). Likely, Crafts's autobiographical manuscript is recording aspects of the author's stolen training, her instruction gathered during the years she tended to the college boarders practicing their composition exercises. The claim by some modern critics that the author must have been white depends on such passages as evidence of her whiteness. But in Crafts's novel, "the charm about these ancient houses," with "their delightfully irregular apartments," only throws into relief the fact that they are charnel houses for the enslaved, especially female domestics. Such moments appear generic and culturally scripted not because the author accepted their forms but because she appropriated them. Critics have confused the tool for the practitioner.

V

It seems likely that Crafts encountered a specific volume that further influenced the way she formed her novel. Generally, one would expect proslavery schools, like Chowan Baptist Female Institute, to steer clear of the controversy surrounding slavery. But this would be to ignore the intellectual frisson experienced by the educated sons and daughters of enslavers. The extraordinary success of Stowe's *Uncle Tom's Cabin*, even in the

South, demonstrates the pull the subject held in slaveholding communities as well as in the strongholds of abolitionist sympathizers. An examination of John Hill Wheeler's library holdings and the early library records of Chowan Baptist Female Institute show a surprising openness to antislavery works as well as pro-slavery volumes.

Debates around the question of slavery at college literary societies, like the ones John Hill Wheeler and his brother Samuel Jordan participated in as students at Columbian College in Washington, D.C. (later George Washington University), regularly served as fodder for vigorous contests among students. In 1824, for instance, John Hill Wheeler debated the question "Would the immediate and unconditional manumission of slaves in the United State ameliorate their condition?" Not surprisingly, his Enosinian Society team won the debate by arguing the question "[i]n the negative."[13] Intellectual strength then as now depended on engaging multiple perspectives on the most telling questions of the day. As a result, library collections on the subject of slavery were surprisingly robust, even in pro-slavery regions.

The practice persisted into the next generation. Early college libraries, like the one at Columbian, started with collections developed by literary societies like the Enosinian. Past members and graduates of the institution would maintain a subscription to fund and preserve books for new members. Among Columbian's earliest papers are the library records of Enosinian Society members. From these early pages, we know that Samuel Jordan Wheeler's son, John, followed his father and uncle into the same literary society when he matriculated at Columbian College (1856–60). He and his cousin James Moore borrowed both pro-slavery and antislavery books in 1856, along with novels by Walter Scott, the poetry of Byron and Keats, John Hill Wheeler's *Historical Sketches of North Carolina (1851)*, and many other volumes.[14]

Chowan students, too, developed literary societies. Women at the school formed the Philomathean Society as early as 1849. An attendant at the public examination that year notes, "I heard also of a Literary Society, composed of members of the Institute exclusively, and a semimonthly periodical sustained by the young ladies, which gives promise of being ably conducted."[15] Another attendant witnessed the local program and observed, "During the exercises of the examination, occasional extracts were publicly read from *The Casket*, a periodical by the young ladies connected with the Philomathean Society." The witness continues: "The extracts that I heard, both prose and poetry, were really of a superior character."[16]

Chowan's Philomathean Society did not maintain a library. There was no need, not with the large and growing book collection already bequeathed to the school by Samuel Jordan Wheeler and Reverend Thompson. The *Chowan Baptist Female Institute Catalogue* for 1851 observes of this collection, "The Institute has a Library of choice works, which together with the Reading Room, containing periodicals from different sections of the country, furnishes, at present sufficient reading matter."[17] When the Rev. William Arthur Shaw paid an initial visit to the institute in October 1851, he reported, "The library consists of 300 well selected volumes. . . . The Reading Room contains, I observe, 30 periodicals from New York to Alabama. *The Christian Review*, the *American Journal of Science*, and Professor Deems' *Methodist Magazine*."[18]

The relatively few records preserved for Chowan's Philomathean Society show the society engaged in public lectures and literary readings, much like contemporary literary societies. Debates came into practice at Chowan only after Crafts's escape. During her tenure in Murfreesboro, Philomathean Society members composed, edited, and produced a magazine: "The members of the society met regularly and read essays which they composed themselves, and for several years [1849–55] they published a monthly periodical entitled *The Casket*."[19] Judging by the few compositions that have been preserved, the subject of slavery found its way into *The Casket*.

Ann Ward, who boarded at Wheeler House (1849–53) and later married John Wheeler Moore, composed an essay, "American Aristocracy," for the literary society in 1852. In the work, Ward argues that "members of America's Aristocracy" held a sacred duty to "bring Christianity to the

African slave," including making provision to teach Christ and the Bible to "all slaves." Hannah Jr. served Ann Ward for two years while she boarded at Wheeler House, including the period when Ward composed her essay. Perhaps Crafts engaged Ward on the subject. If so, Hannah Jr. may have influenced the emphasis on instruction and Christianity. Horace Mann's volume *Slavery: Letters and Speeches* (1851) became part of Chowan's library around this time, and Ward may have encountered this famous passage from Mann's collection:

> I would give to every human being the best opportunity I could to develop and cultivate the faculties which God has bestowed upon him, and which, therefore, he holds under a divine charter. I would take from his neck the hell that has trodden him down; I would dispel from his mind the cloud that has shrouded him in moral night; I would remove the obstructions that have forbidden his soul to aspire; and having done this, I would leave him, as I would leave every other man, to find his level,—to occupy the position to which he should be entitled by his intelligence and his virtues.[20]

To be sure, Ann Ward's "American Aristocracy" did not set out a vision shared by Mann or, likely, Hannah Jr., but perspectives like those maintained by Mann and Crafts may have helped temper "American Aristocracy." Ward's advocacy for "educating all slaves," even if only for religious reasons, marked an advance in sentiment compared to other calls for upholding "American aristocracy." Often such calls for preserving the planter elite forbade teaching literacy to the enslaved, citing the need for a "mudsill" class to undergird a supposedly "natural" social hierarchy.[21] Likely, Crafts was on hand when Ward read her composition aloud at Chowan's commencement exercises launching the new school year in 1853, the year Ward graduated as Chowan's first valedictorian.[22]

The volume that seems to have held the most influence on Crafts's planning for her autobiographical novel was Lord Denman's collection *"Uncle Tom's Cabin," "Bleak House," Slavery and the Slave Trade: Seven*

Articles (1853).[23] At some point, perhaps as early as 1854, the Chowan library obtained the volume. In 1853, Lord Denman (Baron Thomas Denman, 1779–1854) published his collection addressing the reception and literary merit of two of the era's most successful novels, *Uncle Tom's Cabin* and *Bleak House*. The articles in Denman's volume include an in-depth discussion of slavery and the slave trade, British and American attitudes toward slavery, and the place of literature in addressing the evils of slavery. It is hard to think of a book that would have caught Hannah Jr.'s eye more quickly. With students reciting Dickens's *Bleak House* and fascinated by Stowe's *Uncle Tom's Cabin*, circulation of Denman's work makes sense, with the book perhaps coming to the attention of new Philomathean Society members boarding at Wheeler House.[24]

Of particular note to Denman is Charles Dickens's failure to write an abolitionist novel in the manner of *Uncle Tom's Cabin*, and Denman takes issue with Dickens's view of reforming slavery in the United States in his weekly magazine, *Household Words*. In 1854, a second edition of Denman's book was published in both the United States and England, shortly after the initial successful release of the first volume. A copy of this 1854 edition appears in the rare book collection of Chowan University (formerly Chowan Baptist Female Institute). It is impossible now to say when the copy was acquired—accession records for the library's holdings were not maintained until later—but it is very possible the volume entered alongside *Uncle Tom's Cabin* (1852) and *Bleak House* (1853) in the earliest days of the college.[25] If so, it would have been accessible to the Chowan students boarding at Wheeler House and, perhaps, to Crafts, too. Because of the nature of the novel Hannah Jr. came to write—mixing elements of *Uncle Tom's Cabin* and *Bleak House*—it seems quite possible that Crafts arranged her narrative as a partial response to Denman's work.

The balm of imaginative engagement that Crafts encountered as part of the Wheeler household seems to have nourished her soul and encouraged her to record her inner life, including exercising the freedom of imagining and creating an autobiographical novel ambitious enough to engage works like Stowe's *Uncle Tom's Cabin* and Dickens's *Bleak House*.

It is not impossible to imagine Hannah Jr. listening to student boarders discussing Stowe and reciting Dickens; nor does it strain credulity to envision Crafts's coming into possession of copies of *Uncle Tom's Cabin*, *Bleak House*, and even Denman's work of literary criticism. Echoes of all three seem to reverberate in her stunning production.

Whether she read Denman's call to write an authentic antislavery novel in the style of both Stowe and Dickens is unknown. But, no matter. Crafts's life and her art were on a crash course to do just that. She could have written to Denman precisely the same words that Stowe did in a letter acknowledging his work: "I wrote what I did because as a woman, as a mother, I was oppressed and brokenhearted with the sorrows and injustice I saw, because as a Christian I felt the dishonor to Christianity—because as a lover of my country, I trembled at the coming day of wrath."[26] Crafts wrote as much in her novel published 150 years later.

CHAPTER 10

THE BONDWOMAN'S NARRATIVE AND UNCLE TOM'S CABIN

I

THE JOURNEY OF ROSEA PUGH, Hannah Sr., and Hannah Bond bears surprising similarities to that of the famous author Harriet Beecher Stowe—only, from the other side of the color line.[1] Stowe's maternal grandfather, Eli Foote, like Hannah Bond's maternal enslaver, Thomas Pugh Sr., bought and sold captives as part of his trading ventures based in the Albemarle region of North Carolina between 1789 and 1792. During that period, Eli Foote and his brother Justin built a schooner in Murfreesboro, which they then used to trade naval stores from the banks of the Chowan River to the West Indies as part of the same slaving circuit plied by Thomas Pugh Sr. The wealth drawn from this circuit—Albemarle Sound, the Caribbean, and New England—at once drew Hannah Crafts's family into slavery in North Carolina, while it also established the class status, relative wealth, and educational advantages of Stowe's matrilineal line. Of course, neither author understood the terrible symmetry of their shared history.[2]

Such biographical parallels are not what made Hannah Crafts look to *Uncle Tom's Cabin* for inspiration, but the ghostly parallels remain. For instance, on the morning of Nat Turner's revolt, when Crafts's enslaver, John Hill Wheeler, raced away from the Hertford County Courthouse in Winton on horseback, he galloped past Eli Foote's grave in the small cemetery near the front lawn. Foote had died of a fever he contracted in Murfreesboro in the summer of 1792. First buried on the property of fellow early trader and merchant James Morgan—Molly Morgan and Eliza Morgan's early enslaver—Foote was disinterred and reburied in the courthouse cemetery at Winton in 1822. Before his death, Foote had carried into slavery "black Dinah" and "Harry the bound boy." In her old age, Stowe remembered encountering Dinah and Harry as "servants" in the Connecticut home of her aunt Harriet (Eli Foote's widow), but only as other children whom she outranked, not as stolen property from her grandfather's slaving operations.

After the death of her mother, Roxana Beecher, in 1816, Stowe lived with her aunt Harriet until her father remarried in late 1817. The early intimacy Stowe experienced occupying the same household as Dinah and Harry is never directly disclosed in the thousands of pages Stowe left behind, public or private. Instead, the two captives remain ghostly figures marked only by a passing reference in the biography Stowe's son Charles published of his mother in 1889. Otherwise, Stowe left no trace of her direct links to slavery. Even in the twilight of her career, Stowe avoided reckoning with the fact that her maternal grandfather was a slave trader and that her family possessed enslaved "servants." Perhaps the omission should not be a surprise. Stowe's literary success as the great novelist of the abolitionist movement always depended on her skill at exhuming lives she could not fully comprehend. For Stowe, fiction was a safe medium to avow and claim a history she could not reach in any other way. Considering their inverted origins, perhaps it is natural that Crafts would borrow from Stowe and provide an account of life from the other side of the same ledger sheet.

II

Hannah Crafts, like so many other readers, was moved by Harriet Beecher Stowe's use of generic conventions to undermine America's peculiar institution. Stowe's gift was pairing slavery with sentimental and gothic forms and using both to advance her own passionate style of Christianity. For many, the result was thrilling. When the fugitive captive Eliza Harris carried her child across the ice floes of the Ohio River, readers yearned for their freedom and prayed for their safety. They cheered when George Harris fought off slave catchers at a rocky pass. They cried over the death of the angelic little Eva and were horrified by the fatal lashing of Uncle Tom, the sanctified, if compliant, Christ figure of the text. Topsy's minstrelsy made readers laugh, and still they shed thankful tears when she embraced Christianity. Stowe's readers scorned the selfish, hypochondriac Marie St. Clare and loathed the cruel slaveholder Simon Legree.[3] In gothic fashion, Legree is haunted by his guilty conscience and driven to madness and then death by his own cruelty.

Stowe was not the first to mix sentimental and gothic literary forms, but she was one of the first to explore the question of slavery with both narrative tools. The sentimental novel emphasized emotion and feeling as intrinsic moral strengths—and so, such works feature scenes of distress and tenderness, fine-tuning the reader's capacity to feel moral empathy. The gothic novel usually centered on the forces of the irrational and their power to destroy but also their ability to draw the reader into a sublime awareness of the limits of human consciousness. Characteristics of the form include death and decay, a haunted home or castle, family curses, madness, ghosts or monsters, and powerful love or romance.

Stowe made explicit the Christian vision behind her novel: "There is a ladder to heaven, whose base God has placed in human affections, tender instincts, symbolic feelings, sacraments of love, through which the soul rises higher and higher, refining as she goes . . . and changes, as she rises, into the image of the divine."[4] In *Uncle Tom's Cabin*, each of her characters occupies a different rung of the ladder, with Black characters like

Topsy and Tom at the bottom. In Stowe, the haunted home or gothic castle became the plantations of Kentucky; the curse is bondage; the monster, the perversion slavery entailed on enslavers and their captives. Stowe's novel, then, records the characters' ascent or fall on her fictional stairway to heaven. For Stowe, the sentimental and gothic combined to tell a tale of Christian redemption.

Although the literary gothic was already well established in American literature by authors like Edgar Allan Poe, Stowe was instrumental in popularizing the link to portrayals of slavery. She herself likely found inspiration from slave narratives like Frederick Douglass's groundbreaking *Narrative of the Life of Frederick Douglass* (1845). Authors like Douglass demonstrated the natural fit between gothic convention and the subject position of enslaved men and women. Through the literary tradition of the gothic, Douglass had turned the experience of captivity into a disturbing tale resembling the strange, uncanny, and terrifying world of gothic literature. In telling their life stories, however, former captives had to negotiate the blurring of their horrifying history with gothic fiction and gothic's discourse of racial demonization. This obviously proved more of a challenge for Douglass and, later, Crafts than for Stowe, who could and did traffic in the racial debasement of African Americans, even with her abolitionist sentiments. Still, Stowe's work was important in aligning sentimental and gothic conventions as powerful vehicles for exploring the darker side of American history.

After its appearance in 1852, Stowe's best-selling novel enjoyed unheard-of popularity. Henry James noted that Stowe's novel was, "for an immense number of people, much less a book than a state of vision, of feeling and of consciousness in which they didn't sit and read and appraise and pass the time, but walked and talked and laughed and cried." The Boston preacher Theodore Parker declared that it was "more an event than a book, and has excited more attention than any book since the invention of printing."[5] Publishers who had shunned slavery as a subject for fear of losing "the southern market" eagerly published and marketed at least nineteen fictional responses. With *The Bondwoman's*

Narrative, Crafts joined a multitude of others, both Black and white, who wrote works that responded to or were partially inspired by *Uncle Tom's Cabin*.

Crafts is unique for beginning to develop her response while in bondage. Among the efforts published before hers were the pro-slavery *Life at the South, or Uncle Tom's Cabin As It Is* (1852), *Uncle Robin, in His Cabin in Virginia, and Tom Without One in Boston* (1853), and *The Planter's Northern Bride* (1854). All three of these titles were in the library of John Hill Wheeler, where Crafts likely encountered them in 1856. And, quite likely, she encountered at least a few of these books earlier, as they were part of the circulating library that became the core holdings of Chowan Baptist Female Institute between 1852 and 1856.[6]

Of course, long before Crafts and Stowe began developing their narratives, there was already a lively distribution of antislavery literature, and these works, too, found their way into the hands of enslavers, as Wheeler's book inventories prove. These antislavery works set the foundation for such efforts as *Uncle Tom's Cabin* and *The Bondwoman's Narrative*. Prominent antislavery literature included pamphlets like David Walker's inflammatory *Appeal . . . to the Coloured Citizens of the World* (1829). Walker's pamphlet was said to have partially motivated Nat Turner to mount his insurrection. Other antislavery works also appeared in enslavers' libraries, like the newspaper of white abolitionist William Lloyd Garrison, *The Liberator*; Maria W. Stewart's speeches, which were widely circulated in periodicals; and the first-person testimonies shaped into narratives by former captives, including Frederick Douglass, Josiah Henson, and Lewis and Milton Clarke. The slave narratives of Douglass, Henson, and the Clarke brothers are documented as part of Wheeler's library collection.

There were also antislavery anthologies that Crafts may have encountered. Commonly, these collections featured Richard Hildreth's *The Slave: Or, Memoirs of Archy Moore* (1836); and "The Quadroons" (1842), a short story by Lydia Maria Child, the author who would later help Harriet Jacobs edit and publish her novel, *Incidents in the Life of a Slave*

Girl (1861).[7] The extraordinary success of *Uncle Tom's Cabin*, however, opened the door to the subject of slavery in popular fiction.

In Stowe, Crafts must have seen the promise of artistic license. For an aspiring author like her, this was no doubt necessary. There were no other literary avenues for sharing the intimate violence that was the motivating force behind her work. The kinds of memoirs popular today, exploring trauma and abuse, were not known in Crafts's day, and a writer, Black or white, could not imagine an audience for such direct revelations of private suffering. The likeliest path was the slave narrative genre established by Douglass and other formerly enslaved writers. But there was no place, even in captivity narratives, for an enslaved woman trying to tell the story of sexual abuse. As physically abused captives, Harriet Jacobs and Harriet Wilson would follow Crafts in turning to autobiographical fiction. The stories Crafts knew from a lifetime of enslavement suited the vehicle Stowe had already fashioned in fiction, even if Stowe's innate racism and inability to convey the interior life of her Black characters weakened her art.

In *The Bondwoman's Narrative*, Crafts pictures the ownership of human beings as a gallery of horrors, probably drawing from the portraiture tradition she encountered with her family's first enslavers, the Pughs of Indian Woods. In her early chapters, she reimagines Willow Hall as the haunted Lindendale, built by generations of captives, and the local Gospel Oaks as its cursed linden tree, where old Rose (Rosea Pope) and her faithful dog are tortured and murdered (*TBN* 14, 20–22). In these haunting passages, Crafts echoes the depiction of Simon Legree's plantation on the Red River in *Uncle Tom's Cabin*, with its "black, blasted tree, and the ground all covered with black ashes." Crafts, like Stowe's Cassy, suggests that such trees mark a history that no one dares voice (*UTC* 384).[8]

Significantly, when Hannah Crafts served at both Wheeler House and, later, John Hill Wheeler's residence in Washington, D.C., she had access to Stowe's novel and many of the works it influenced. Wheeler's collection in Washington included Stowe's *A Key to Uncle Tom's Cabin* (1853) and three discussions of Stowe's novel: A. Woodward's *A Review of Uncle Tom's Cabin* (1853); Rev. E. J. Stearns's *Notes on Uncle Tom's Cabin: Being a Logical Answer to Its Allegations, etc.* (1853); and Nassau W. Senior's *American Slavery: A Reprint of an Article on "Uncle Tom's Cabin"* (1856).[9]

The influence of Stowe's narrative is deep in the way Crafts seems to have shaped her autobiographical novel. Crafts's careful references to Stowe's model include Stowe's killing of George Harris's little dog, Carlo. Similarly, in her later chapters, Crafts's description of the madness of her doppelgänger mistress, who is driven insane when reduced to slavery, calls to mind the anguish of Stowe's Cassy, with her "wild, long laugh" and "convulsive sobbings and struggles" (*UTC* 376).[10]

The Bondwoman's Narrative further calls to mind the use of the gothic in *Uncle Tom's Cabin* in the section centering on Charlotte and her husband, William. Like Stowe's Eliza, who is "married in her mistress' great parlor . . . [with] no lack of white gloves, and cake and wine," Charlotte is held by a kind mistress who allows a wedding celebration for her favorite captive: "Cakes, confectionary and wine" were "abundantly provided, and all the servants old and young big and little were invited to be present" (*UTC* 19; *TBN* 122).[11]

The Bondwoman's Narrative recalls *Uncle Tom's Cabin* in portraying the abuse used to control enslaved women. When Hannah's jailer counsels that "If a woman is stubborn or obstinate ask her as a favor, coax her, flatter her and my word for it she'll be pliable as wax in your hands," the trader Hayes observes, "They must mind me either way" (*TBN* 92). Stowe's Loker, too, discloses his savage methods to fellow slave catcher Marks: "Why, I buys a gal, and if she's got a young 'un to be sold, I jest walks up and puts my fist to her face, and says, 'Look here, no, if you give me one word out of your head, I'll smash yer face in.' . . . I tell ye, they sees it aint no play, when I gets hold" (*UTC* 70–71). Hannah's captor explains sexual slavery in the New Orleans market by noting, "[G]ood-looking wenches . . . are a deal sight worse to manage than men—every way more skittish and skeery. Then it don't do to cross them much; or if you do they'll cut up the devil, and like as anyhow break their necks or pine themselves to skeletons" (*TBN* 107). Explaining further to Trappe, he tells the story of Louise, "the freshen and fairest in the gang, [who] actually jumped into the river when she found that her child was irretrievably gone" (*TBN* 108). The scene recalls the death of Stowe's Lucy, who, discovering that her baby has been sold, responds by drowning herself (*UTC* 135–37). Such fictional characters reflect many unrecorded captive suicides, while at the same time portending the historic 1856 case in which Margaret Garner murdered her daughter to save her from a life in slavery. A century later, Toni Morrison's *Beloved* would immortalize this tragic mother.[12]

III

To write a story, an author necessarily looks to other written works as models. The autodidact Hannah Crafts must have made the most of her limited access to reading materials. The deep influence of *Uncle Tom's Cabin* helped shape the narrative design of Crafts's autobiographical story. Crafts echoes Stowe in representing variations on the stock character of the tragic mixed-race figure (frequently called "tragic mulatto"), a wretched light-skinned figure earlier portrayed in Lydia Maria Child's widely read short fiction "The Quadroons." In Child's tale, the mixed-race woman adores her white male betrayer. An immediate stereotype, the tragic mulatto generated many variants, including Stowe's Cassy, who is purchased after the death of her master-father by the white man she loves, who then forsakes her (*UTC* 371).[13]

It seems only natural that a writer like Crafts would have been interested in a figure like Cassy. After all, Crafts occupied a similar position. As the probable daughter of Lewis Bond and the forced sexual partner of Thomas Bond Jr., the author experienced the real violence and betrayal that Stowe can only imagine for Cassy. In white-authored texts, the tragic mulatto is a mixed-race character striving to enter white society, but she dies before that wish can be achieved. Crafts alters the story dramatically.

In *The Bondwoman's Narrative*, the tragic mulatto figure goes unnamed. She enters the story by becoming the bride of the master of Lindendale. As Crafts renders the story, the mixed-race mistress is already accepted in white society but is on a journey, instead, to escape it. The figure seems to draw on Crafts's experiences of being forced to serve as a sexual partner to the real-life Thomas Bond Jr. The protagonist of Crafts's story, Hannah, becomes the helpmate of her work's tragic mulatto. In *The Bondwoman's Narrative*, the tragedy lies not with the mistress's failure to enter white society, but rather, with her difficulty in exiting it. Ultimately, the heroine, Hannah, becomes this mistress's shadow self, a protector of sorts, one who advises her mistress to escape from Lindendale and who agrees to run with her—not as her servant but as "a very dear sister" (*TBN* 49). The protagonist's allegiance to her mistress ("since even my strong desire for freedom, now become the object of my life, could not have induced me to abandon her") matches language common to captives in plantation fiction. But Hannah Craft's real-life circumstances flip the script. The tragic mulatto here is, after all, both mistress and captive. The novel depends upon the death of the mistress as a means of the protagonist's freeing herself from sexual bondage. This is not the affinity of gender bridging the gulf of "race" but, instead, the sisterhood of two halves of one woman, the same Hannah Crafts who is forced to be both nominally "Black" and a sexual victim.[14]

The unnamed mistress in Crafts's novel is just one of several mixed-race figures in the work. Indeed, Crafts seems also to channel the real-life experiences of Mary Burton and Ellen Sully Wheeler in 1849. In chapter 14 of the novel, the author interrupts the narrative and inserts a story that Lizzy recounts to Hannah, describing the sexual exploitation of a light-skinned teenage captive named Evelyn, similar to the historical Mary Burton: "No Turk in his haram ever luxuriated in deeper sensual enjoyments than did the master of Lindendale" (*TBN* 177). Like the circumstances that led to Mary's sale in Lincolnton, North Carolina, the Cosgrove harem scene in *The Bondwoman's Narrative* dramatizes a jealous wife who resents her husband's enslaved favorites. When Cosgrove's imperious wife discovers her husband's progeny with Evelyn and another unnamed captive, she demands that the women and their children be sold. The unnamed woman then kills her baby and herself. The psychic trauma of recasting Mary Burton's life story calls forth from Hannah Crafts a record of self-harm that is historically accurate.

Still later, Mrs. Cosgrove pursues Evelyn, "a beautiful woman . . . with two children, twins, and as near alike as two cherries at her breast," whom her husband sends away and shelters (*TBN* 186).[15] Again, the historical correlations are tenuous and lightly noted in existing sources, but there may be an echo to John Hill Wheeler's personal history. When Hannah Crafts was in Wheeler's possession between 1856 and 1857, Wheeler, like Mr. Cosgrove in the story, maintained and visited a property near Washington, D.C., where he enslaved at least one woman. It is wholly possible that he kept these details from his wife. In the novel, the location is identified as "Rock Glen." The property Wheeler maintained in Prince George's County, Maryland, was situated on Rock Creek, quite possibly known as Rock Glen, although there is no record of Wheeler referring to the property by that term in the few diary records where this property is traceable.[16]

When Wheeler sold the Rock Creek property in 1857, he recorded among his accounts that he received $485.92 for an enslaved woman. He likewise received $360.00 and $400.98, respectively, for two males. He neglects to mark in his ledger account the ages or names of these people, some of the last traceable captives he held.[17] With no further recoverable information available yet about these sales, it does not strain credulity to wonder if Lizzy's strange interpolated story, coming right before Crafts describes her protagonist's escape, might have been based partially on fact. Could Wheeler have been maintaining an enslaved woman and her children secretly, away from his wife? Whatever whispers Hannah Crafts may have heard, she seems to have made powerful use of them in her novel.

The most important mixed-race figure in Crafts's novel is, of course, the narrator, Hannah. But Crafts does not write Hannah as a tragic mulatto. Although she is bought by Saddler and threatened with sale as a sexual slave, like other tragic mixed-race figures in the novel, Crafts's protagonist defies the usual plight of the tragic mulatto. *The Bondwoman's Narrative* provides an early example in fiction of "passing" in which the "Black" protagonist rejects the possibility of becoming "white." In Crafts's narrative, Hannah uses her nearly white skin to escape, first together with the unnamed light-skinned mistress and, later, with the assistance of two fellow freedom seekers, Jacob and his sister. Like Crafts the author, once Hannah is safely in the North, she rejects whiteness, asserts her African heritage, and makes her home in a prospering Black community—an ending that would have been impossible coming from a white writer then, even the most well-intentioned abolitionist. Instead, Crafts is fictionalizing her very path to freedom and to completing the work of her novel.[18]

Crafts also shows enslaved people who are not ethical, but corrupt. Her fellow enslaved people at the Wheelers' North Carolina plantation claimed that Hannah Jr. had betrayed Mrs. Wheeler's secret, and they delighted in witnessing her degradation. Crafts writes that when Hannah was sent to the slave quarter, "[O]ne of the women arose, seized me by the hair, and without ceremony dragged me to the ground, gave me a furious kick and made use of highly improper and indecent language" (*TBN* 215). Stowe describes a similar scene for her character Cassy. When she is sent to do field work, "there was much looking and turning of heads, and a smothered yet apparent exultation among the miserable, ragged, half-starved creatures by whom she was surrounded" (*UTC* 360).[19] Again, Crafts's real-life experiences provided her special insight into the fictive world of Cassy.

As Jean Fagan Yellin's work makes clear, for all the ways that *The Bondwoman's Narrative* is in dialogue with *Uncle Tom's Cabin*, it is essentially a very different work of art. Crafts's novel refutes the extended discussions of "race" that Stowe's narrative frequently entertains. If Crafts notes Mrs. Henry's "hands white and soft and beautiful" and the "white beautiful arms" of little Anna, she never engages in the overtly racist description of Black characters common to Stowe (*TBN* 129, 133). Indeed, Crafts refutes a rigid color scheme where Black people follow racist theories of inferiority. Stowe, for her part, emphasizes racial difference: "There stood the two children, representatives of the two extremes of society. The fair, high-bred child, with her golden head, her deep eyes, her spiritual, noble brow, and prince-like movements; and her black, keen, subtle, cringing, yet acute neighbor. They stood the representatives of their races. The Saxon, born of ages of cultivation, command, education, physical and moral eminence; the Afric, born of ages of oppression, submission, ignorance, toil, and vice!" (*UTC* 254).[20]

As critics have long noted, Stowe's work, for all its antislavery fervor, still portrays Black people as innately inferior. If Stowe's Black characters are simple, docile, and ready to accept white superiority, Crafts's characters refuse such distinctions. The protagonist, Hannah, champions Black motherhood and the kinship strength of friendship as sources of power and defiance. Drawing from her own knowledge of women like Milly and Martha Murfree, Mary Burton, Eliza Morgan, and Jane Johnson, Crafts makes Hannah smart, inventive, and a formidable adversary, despite her forced position of servitude. She is precisely the kind of character Stowe could not have imagined.

IV

Crafts developed her narrative in the tradition of the nineteenth-century sentimental novel, like Stowe's *Uncle Toms Cabin*. As the critic Nina Baym explains of the genre, such works "are written by women, are addressed to women, and tell one particular story about women."[21] *The Bondwoman's Narrative* also follows in the tradition of the sentimental novel by celebrating motherhood. But Crafts's experience of motherhood, as both a child and a mother, complicates and sets her novel in opposition to works like *Uncle Tom's Cabin*. As Crafts shows over and over in the book, the institution of slavery represents a profound attack on motherhood. If Stowe's novel is, as the critic Jane Tomkins observes, "the *summa theologica* of nineteenth-century America's religion of domesticity, a brilliant redaction of the culture's favorite story about itself—salvation through motherly love"—Crafts autobiographical narrative demonstrates the impossibility of such a religion for the enslaved.[22]

Like Nat Turner, Frederick Douglass, and the Bertie Conspiracy's Dr. Joe, Crafts, too, points to the contradiction between America as the land of the free and America as a slavocracy. When the evil Mr. Trappe advises Hannah that, as a captive, "submission and obedience must be the Alpha and Omega of all your actions," Hannah brushes off the counsel. She notes that the "advice was probably well adapted to one in my condition, that is if I could have forgotten God, truth, honor and my own soul" (*TBN* 111). Similar to Turner, Douglass, Dr. Joe, and other contemporaries, Crafts links resistance to tyranny as obedience to God. In this way, her protagonist follows a very different gospel from that preached in *Uncle Tom's Cabin.* The namesake of Stowe's novel, Uncle Tom, faces tyranny by practicing Christian resignation and, so, dies a martyr—a portrayal that prompted Black activists and their white allies to criticize the novel from the beginning.[23] If, ultimately, Stowe crucifies Uncle Tom to try to absolve the sins of her white readers, Crafts marks her white characters as dark souls in need of more than Christian grace to be redeemed. Her Black characters seek the freedom that the author herself seizes.

Stowe concludes her novel by suggesting the expatriation of African Americans to Africa and an appeal to the "Church of Christ" to lead the nation and to avoid God's righteous wrath through "repentance, justice and mercy" (*UTC* 456). Again, *The Bondwoman's Narrative* could not be more different. Crafts echoes neither Stowe's call to ship Black people to Africa nor her bid for religious renewal, but, instead, closes with the practical work of teaching reading to Black children in New Jersey. Hannah, like her creator, rolls up her sleeves to teach to the next generation the tools of freedom. Although the sensation created by *Uncle Tom's Cabin* certainly helped inspire Crafts's novel, and Crafts's narrative drew upon literary devices and motifs Stowe popularized, *The Bondwoman's Narrative* holds a very different vision for the future. By bringing forward from the shadows "black Dinah" and "Harry the bound boy," neglected in Stowe's work and life, Crafts put such figures at the center of her work's consciousness. Together, Crafts's narrative proclaims a very different gospel: the secular story of the God-given right to liberty.

CHAPTER 11

THE NOTEBOOK

I

IN THE SPRING OF 2004, while searching for valuables, vagrants in Bertie County, North Carolina, discarded a notebook they carried outside an unoccupied rural farmhouse. In the brush among items of trash, about eight hundred feet from the house, the notebook was discovered before the next rain. Only good fortune saved these documents. When Dr. Harold E. Mitchell and Walter R. Cray arranged to visit their aunt's property to clean the family cemetery, they were surprised to see a black-and-white composition book lying in a pile of brush near some rubbish. Inside it, in the fluent hand of their aunt, a schoolteacher of more than fifty years, they encountered the title page: "Some Recollections of the Late Wright Cherry and His Beloved Wife Malinda Gilliam Cherry of Bertie County, North Carolina. By Maria Cherry Newsome 1956."[1]

No one in the family had been aware of the notebook's existence before its discovery in 2004. Maria Cherry Newsome was seventy-four years old in 1956, when she recorded her family's history. A retired educator and grandmother of fourteen, she preserved her memories while she was still in good health. By the time of her death twenty years later, the notebook had been lost. When Newsome died in 1976, the composition book went undiscovered among her effects. In 2004, the vagrants who disturbed Newsome's property brought the records to light again. Inside it was a treasure. On lined paper, in her flowing script, Newsome reprised the stories of Judy Outlaw and Wright Cherry, her paternal grandmother and her father, and what their experiences were like in slavery in Indian Woods and Bertie County, North Carolina. In the final pages of the notebook, the nephews Mitchell and Cray found their aunt's request to "remember our forefathers and the sacrifices that have been made for you to be here."[2] I came into possession of a copy of this notebook from Newsome's relative Elbert Bishop, after I gave a talk near Windsor, North Carolina, in 2012.

The author, Maria Cherry Newsome, was the daughter of an enslaved man, Wright Cherry, whose mother, Judy (Judah/Judia) Outlaw, served as a domestic "servant" on the Outlaw plantation immediately adjacent to Willow Hall in the 1820s and '30s. Born in 1810, Judy was a contemporary of both Hannah Sr. and Hannah Bond and lived in the same neighborhood as they until 1838. Her childhood, much like Hannah Sr.'s, unfolded in the shadow of the Gospel Oaks and in the aftermath of the Bertie County Conspiracy. Like Hannah Sr., Judy seems to have advanced to the role of housekeeper and also to have been forced into a sexual relationship with her enslaver. For this period, Newsome records that Judy "lived in a small one-room house in the back of the yard so as to serve her Mistress and her family."[3] Here, on the property adjacent to Hannah Bond's Willow Hall, she birthed seven light-skinned children, two boys and five girls: "Wright, Madison, Harriet, Caroline, Sarah, Esther, and Mariah" (See Figure 21). Newsome observes that "the father was unknown," but she also explains, delicately, that Judy was forced to provide sex: "What usually happened," her granddaughter writes circumspectly, "the master of the plantation was King of the plantation and no laws to prevent it, no criticism, so long as the servant was humble and obedient to him."[4]

The congruent experiences of Judy Outlaw and Wright Cherry provide further insight into the life and times of Hannah Sr. and Hannah Jr. Judy Outlaw suffered the same fate the author's captors designed for her. Crafts lost one child in early 1852, but likely Thomas Bond Jr.'s claims on her would have persisted had not the author's legal possessor also died around the same time. Lewis Bond's will placed Hannah Jr. into the estate

FIGURE 21: Wright Cherry and Malinda Cherry and family, c. 1910s or '20s

of his daughters, and with Esther's death following her father's so quickly, Crafts was rescued from the physical claims of Thomas Jr. and, instead, forced into a better servitude. She came into the possession of Lucinda Bond Wheeler in 1852, and took up residence, likely, in the Wheeler kitchen dependency, where she began her service to the Wheelers and their many student boarders.[5]

Elbert Bishop, the descendant who shared Newsome's notebook with me, describes Judy's arrangement with Outlaw as "sexual exploitation" and "rape," a practice other descendants of the Outlaw, Bond, Cherry, and Speller families record as a part of their family lineage in Bertie County.[6] If the oral history of Wright Cherry's paternity is true, Cherry's father was Ralph Edward Outlaw (1774–1836), a friend and political ally of neighbor Lewis Bond. According to Bishop, whose account is supported by Newsome's notebook, Ralph Edward Outlaw forced a sexual relationship on Judy Outlaw when she reached sexual maturity early, at the age of twelve. By the time she was seventeen, she had borne five living children before her captor died in 1836. Hannah Jr.'s life looked to be following the pattern of her neighbor Judy Outlaw. Indeed, there was nothing extraordinary in the Indian Woods community about the author's being forced to be her enslaver's forced sexual partner.

"Having been reared in the Great House was a great honor in those days and the slaves that served in the house felt themselves superior to the ones that lived down on the farm," Newsome writes in the composition book where she recorded her family story. She continues: "The house servant and their children served the master, his wife and their children. They did not have to do the tasks on the farm, nor walk in mud to their knees in the ditch, burn brush, take up stumps, or plow." If Newsome passes quickly over her father's paternity, she spends considerable time recording the privileges accorded to Cherry and his mother, Judy, as mixed-race captives connected to their enslavers. "As his mother was the cook at the great house, she would bring a few scraps of food to help out," Newsome explains. She continues: "So Wright became a dependable hand around the home. He was allowed to play with the white boys when not on duty."[7] The notations parallel Crafts's autobiographical portrayal of Hannah, as she sharply distinguishes herself from the "field slaves." Hannah's disdain for labor beyond the household is a defining part of her character in Crafts's novel.

Newsome observes that her father "learned to read and write" from his white half brothers, even though it "was strictly against the law." Wright Cherry's details seem to mirror Hannah Crafts's and the way she depicts her protagonist's journey to literacy in the novel.[8] In Crafts's narrative, Hannah gains the ability to read and write through the agency of a Quaker couple who befriend her. She also gains valuable religious instruction. She writes, "Educated at the north they both felt keenly on the subject of slavery and the degradation and ignorance it imposes on one portion of the human race." She continues: "Yet all their conversation on this point was tempered with the utmost discretion and judgement, and though they could not be reconciled to the system they were disposed to stand still and wait in faith and hope for the salvation of the Lord"

(*TBN* 10). The fact that Crafts's novel attributes Hannah's religious instruction to the influence of Quakers matches the larger social forces that shaped religious practice in the region.

The experiences of Wright Cherry suggest that Hannah Jr.'s literacy would not have been unique for the circumstances of her birth and location. Newsome writes of her father, "One was whipped severely if a book was caught in the house," yet Cherry's literacy was advanced by his half siblings.[9] In *The Bondwoman's Narrative*, the protagonist Hannah is discovered receiving reading and writing lessons, but she ultimately goes unpunished. Clearly, the precedent that Wright Cherry demonstrated in the neighborhood matches a tacit acceptance of some forms of literacy among domestic "servants" in the immediate location where the author Hannah Crafts can be traced.

Cherry, like Hannah Bond (and likely others), seems to have gained in value to his captors due to his acquired literacy, even if the practice was guarded against. "When he became a young man," Newsome notes, "[Cherry] was made an overseer around the plantation." She continues: "It was common to have the slaves brought up on the yard at evening, tied to the whipping post, his shirt tied around his waist, and 9 and 30 lashes put on his naked back, and then salty brine poured on top of that."[10] Cherry's role matches the practice of one of his half nephews, George Outlaw II, the mixed-race child of David Standley Outlaw, Ralph Edward Outlaw's oldest son. When David Standley Outlaw left to represent Bertie County in the U.S. House of Representatives in 1856, he put his mixed-race son George in charge of the plantation where Judy and Wright Cherry formerly served. Hannah Crafts would have known David Standley and George Outlaw while growing up in the household of the adjacent plantation. Her and David's paths converged again in the winter of 1856, when he visited the Wheeler household as he established himself in Washington, D.C.[11]

If Newsome writes in the notebook about the powerful class awareness her father and grandmother held in slavery, the details in the notebook also corroborate the oral tales her siblings shared among the larger

Cherry-Outlaw-Bond-Speller families. Dr. Benjamin Speller, a mixed-race descendant of the Bond family, notes, "If their skin color was white, they could claim that and have more standing in the community." He continues: "The funny thing is, you have to know who is white and who is black. You can't always tell by skin color."[12]

Dr. Speller's grandfather was named William Bond, one of eight children born to Harry and Fannie Bond, Speller's great-grandparents. According to Dr. Speller, Harry and Fannie came to Indian Woods from Maryland, where they first served as captives. Like Hannah Crafts and Wright Cherry, Harry and Fannie Bond's offspring carried mixed bloodlines. Familial ties persisted after slavery. By 1870, Harry Bond had purchased 150 acres from his former captor, Lewis T. Bond, a namesake and nephew of Hannah Crafts's probable father, Lewis Bond. On this property, Dr. Speller's great-grandfather raised his multiracial family. Dr. Speller observes, "The family shows up over the decades on the census records—a mix of white, black and Native American Tuscarora tribe."[13]

Dr. Speller recognizes Harry and Fannie for making the most of their freedom and offering opportunities to their descendants. Harry was known to be good with numbers and successfully farmed his purchased land with one of his sons-in-law as co-manager. Meanwhile, his wife, Fannie, practiced herbal medicine to become a leading health-care provider in the area. "They carried no malice," Dr. Speller observes. "They told their children and grandchildren what happened in slavery without emotion. People do you wrong. Get over it, and go on"[14] (see Figure 22).

Wright Cherry's path was similar. After slavery, Cherry also purchased property from white relatives. The generational wealth that possessing land provided meant lifting whole branches of the Bond and Cherry families out of poverty. Once these families had gained the means to build generational wealth, they flourished. Two generations later, Dr. Speller had risen to become the dean of the School of Library and Information Sciences at North Carolina Central University, and his brother had earned a doctorate in physics. Newsome's nephew Elbert Bishop earned a law degree from Harvard University and another advanced degree from the Massachusetts Institute of Technology. Education and wealth transfer meant these families could rise into the middle class despite the discriminatory practices and entrenched racism that stood in their way.

Such advances were made on the backs of men and women like Wright Cherry and his mother, Judy Outlaw. Like Hannah Crafts's mother, Judy Outlaw was forced to conceive and bear children for her enslaver. And yet, she managed to build family bonds, despite the traumatic circumstances of her family's founding. To develop and maintain ties of love and affection, Outlaw had to draw on perseverance and faith. Just as Hannah Sr. suffered forced separation from her children, Judy Outlaw, too, saw some of her mixed-race children sold away to serve distant white relatives. Crafts describes just such a scene in her novel through the figure of Mr. Cosgrove. His son realizes a purchaser has arrived at the house: "One of the children, a beautiful boy of three or four years run [*sic*] to Mr.

FIGURE 22: Dr. Benjamin F. Speller, a descendant related to Hannah Crafts, pointing out the site of Lewis Bond's Willow Hall plantation near Quitsna, North Carolina

Cosgrove exclaiming 'Why, pa you won't sell, will you? you said that I was your darling and little man.' 'Go to your mother, child' said the cruel father" (*TBN* 177). The boy is sold.

In 1842, in anticipation of her marriage to William Walton, Celia Outlaw, Ralph Outlaw's widow, sold Judy Outlaw and her children Mariah, Esther, Wright, and Harriet to her brother Solomon Cherry Sr. and his wife, Jane Outlaw Cherry. Solomon Sr. also acquired Ralph Outlaw's plantation and more than ten other captives through the Outlaw slave division. Thus, Judy's children acquired the Cherry family surname. The conferral of property to her brother and sister-in-law prepared the way for Celia's move to Greene County, Alabama, where she married William Walton on his large cotton plantation, Strawberry Hill, in 1844.[15]

Wright Cherry was a toddler when Solomon Cherry Sr. acquired him, his mother, and his remaining siblings. Judy Outlaw became the cook and housekeeper on Cherry Sr.'s plantation in the Mitchells community of Bertie County. Because Wright was light-skinned and connected by blood to the new Cherry household, he grew up with the expectation of providing domestic service as a male "servant" and companion to Cherry Sr.'s sons. Eventually, his services included working as an overseer, too, similar to John Thomas Bond earlier.[16]

Wright's service to the Cherry family expanded significantly at the onset of the Civil War. In 1862, when the white adult males left to fight for the Confederacy, Wright took over day-to-day management of Cherry Sr.'s estate. Newsome observes of her father's increased role at this time, "With perfect confidence in Wright, he was left in charge of the home and plantation and he proved himself worthy of the responsibility laid upon him." During these difficult years, as the Confederacy struggled to maintain its grip on the region, Wright reassessed his circumstances and chances of gaining freedom. Newsome quotes her father as saying, "'I have served as a slave long enough.'" Newsome observes, "He wanted to be a free man and to see his mother free as well." "'Live or die,'" she quotes her father in the notebook, "'sink or swim, I'll try.'"[17] He was twenty-seven years old.

Cherry escaped on a horse from his enslaver's stables. "Instead of taking his master's horse to drive over to the plantation and set slaves at work," Newsome recounts, "he turned him down the road and drove 25 miles until he came to the Chowan River." When he reached the banks, Wright unbridled the beast and set it free. Then he "took off his clothes, tied [them] onto his back, and swam across the river and walked three days and nights without food save the buds of trees and sometimes a bit of bread that he found at the house of a slave."[18] Cherry's escape resembles that of Hannah in Crafts's autobiographical novel. Hannah, too, fords rivers and forages for food by gathering fruits and sustenance from the natural world. Crafts writes, "I felt refreshed, but hungry, and while debating with myself how to obtain a breakfast, a cow approached. Her udder was distended with the precious fluid. I thought of Elijah and ravens, and when she came still nearer, and stopped before me with a gentle low as if inviting me to partake, I hesitated no longer, but on her milk and a few simple berries I made a really luxurious meal" (*TBN* 218). She, too, is assisted in her escape by other captives.

Hannah Crafts and her mother grew up direct contemporaries of Judy Outlaw and Wright Cherry, with experiences of concubinage and slavery that seem to have paralleled those of their neighbors. Newsome's document is extraordinary not only for recording details of enslaved life in the immediate world of Hannah Crafts but also for providing examples of the familial bonds and religious faith forged in the crucible of slavery. As Elbert Bishop observes in the prefatory note he shared with family members when he made copies of the notebook, "A strong faith, family pride, deeply instilled values and appreciation for the sacrifices of our ancestors are evident in Maria's notebook. These are some of the qualities which governed the lives of her generation and which sustain our enduring bond."[19]

II

Maria Cherry Newsome's notebook is now in the possession of Dr. Wendel White, another descendant of Wright Cherry. Copies are distributed to family members far and wide. Newsome's request in the final page of her notebook has inspired what is now a biennial reunion of Cherry-Outlaw-Bond-Speller families every other summer. Under the title "My Last Request and Testimony," Newsome writes:

> My Dear Children,
>
> I have given my life that you may have a better chance than I had in this world. I cannot die satisfied without the hope that each of you has accepted the religious principles of Jesus Christ.
>
> It is my last request that you join hands and pledge by the help of God that you stand by and help each other whenever you can, that the principles of Jesus Christ rule in your heart such as love, joy, peace, knowledge, understanding rests with you forever, that you work together as one big family, that you put forth every effort possible to see that no one is lost, that what we have as "the home" be a family shrine and that you work together to develop it, upkeep, and cherish of the treasured spot. That each will have a home here in his lifetime and the children that come after that you remember our forefathers and the sacrifices that have been made for you to be here, that you put forth an effort unless Providence hinders, meet at least once a year and consider these things.[20]

Since its discovery in 2004, Newsome's "Last Request and Testimony" has reinvigorated her family's efforts to honor her memory and to celebrate the courage and fortitude of their forebears. Perhaps it is not surprising that the deep faith and courage Judy Outlaw and Wright Cherry carried into freedom match the qualities that animate Crafts's life story and her autobiographical novel.

CHAPTER 12

RELIGION

I

TO UNDERSTAND HANNAH CRAFTS, WE have to grasp the deep sources of her religious convictions. Although she never embraced militancy, Crafts shared with Nat Turner and James Barefoot a faith rooted in the evangelical ideas circulating among the smaller farms and plantations connecting southeastern Virginia and northeastern North Carolina. Crafts seems to have participated actively in the biracial religious practices of her region. Stretching back to the Great Awakening, prominent church fathers actively incorporated free and enslaved Blacks into worship. The pioneering Baptist leader David Barrow helped establish the practice in the area. Such inclusion found its force, in part, from a strong antislavery Quaker presence that predated the rapid growth of evangelical Christianity along the Virginia–North Carolina border.

Crafts's baptism into religion would be very different from what she observed of the students at Chowan Baptist Female Institute. Indeed, it likely resembled the journey to faith experienced and recorded by Nat Turner. During the 1780s, Protestant evangelists like Barrow converted hundreds of African Americans along the James River and throughout the Tidewater region. These "awakenings" spread south and triggered the establishment of the new Protestant denominations of Baptists and Methodists that became dominant in the borderland between Virginia and

North Carolina, where Barrow himself settled into his ministry in Southampton County, Virginia. Following the influence of local Quakers, Barrow combined a natural-rights argument for the inclusion of Blacks with a religious emphasis on the Golden Rule ("Do unto others as you would have them do unto you"). In this way, he helped establish the tradition of biracial worship into which Turner and Crafts were born.[1]

Worshippers who followed such teachings centered their faith on the belief that Christ died to redeem the sins of all; salvation through Christ became the desired destiny for every worshipper, Black and white, slave and free. Partly as a result of the locally intensive ministry, the period that saw the birth and maturity of Turner and, later, Bond also experienced a dramatic influx of Black men and women joining evangelical churches throughout southeastern Virginia and northeastern North Carolina.[2]

For Crafts, like Turner, evangelical Christianity served as the wellspring of her sense of purpose and mission, as she, too, was caught up in the religious awakenings unique to her locale. Blacks constituted 41 percent of new church members in the lower part of Southampton County between 1788 and 1795. Between 1802 and 1820, the share of Black new members jumped to 60 percent. Such growth was not isolated to areas with dense free and enslaved populations. In the majority-white upper part of the county, membership of Blacks nearly doubled in the 1820s, going from 14 percent before 1795 to 27 percent by the end of the decade.[3]

The story was the same just across the state line in North Carolina, although extant records are sparse. Samuel Jordan Wheeler, one of Crafts's enslavers, wrote a history of the local Meherrin and Murfreesboro Baptist Churches and notes, in the appendixes, that in 1802, of the 185 recorded members, 52 were "colored" (28 percent). By 1846, "more than 200" of 370 recorded members of the Murfreesboro congregation were "colored" (more than 54 percent). He also notes that "the large body of colored people who flock to our convocations" necessitated expanding the meetinghouse in Murfreesboro to accommodate the larger crowds.

Records in nearby Bertie and Northampton Counties tell the same story. In fact, in all the counties where we can trace the best candidates for authorship of *The Bondwoman's Narrative*, participation by Black members flourished. Moreover, these numbers reflect only those who experienced conversion, baptism, and full reception into the Church. Such white-sanctioned acceptance represents only a small portion of Black engagement with evangelical religion. Although church minute books do not record their presence, the number of Black men and women who regularly attended evangelical churches far outpaced the number of registered white and Black parishioners in official membership logs. Because these Black parishioners attended but were never accepted as full members, they remain unrecognized. Still, enlargement of the Murfreesboro meetinghouse to accommodate Black congregants was representative of enslaved and free Black religious enthusiasm.

Rising spirituality led to new forms of worship among Black and white parishioners. Though the planter gentry persecuted the "New Light" ministers engineering these revivals, Virginians and North Carolinians flocked to the gatherings anyway. With the First and Second Great Awakenings, a new sense of religious possibility opened for Black believers as they found a space to pursue and create a faith they could openly proclaim. From zero in 1770 to half a million before Turner's revolt, the number of Methodist parishioners exploded, as did Baptist congregations, which expanded from five hundred to five thousand in the same period.[4] With these new religions, spiritual power devolved downward, away from priestly ceremony and the inscrutable calculations of predestination. Protestant churchmen exiled from New England began to travel through the South telling revival crowds that salvation was at hand. God could come through in an emotional conversion that washed the faithful clean.

White families, like those who enslaved Nat Turner and Hannah Crafts, experienced the transformative power of the new religious spirit. As conversion experiences and churchgoing became social prescription for proper white citizens, many Christian enslavers abandoned the claim that African Americans had no souls to save. "However sable their hue and degraded their condition in life," a group of Baptist ministers reminded their fellow slaveholders, the enslaved "possessed rational and immortal souls."

Evangelical revivals and camp gatherings proved especially successful among African Americans because everyone was welcomed: the poor, the uneducated, the underprivileged, and the enslaved; for a brief time, all joined side by side in the quest for grace. Even though Africans and their children had been enslaved in North America for more than 160 years, few enslaved people had converted to the Anglicanism of the planter elites. But that all changed with the emergence of the informal liturgies and evangelical theology that Methodists and Baptists brought with them. Awakenings swept across the communities that comprised Crafts's world. Free Blacks and captives alike participated in so-called camp meetings along with various other social classes and groups, including immigrants, backcountry farmers, and indentured servants.

Emotional conversion experiences and informal participatory services treated disempowered people as if their souls, too, held value like the souls of the powerful. Critics scoffed: "Some came to be at the camp meeting / And some perhaps to get good eating." In the 1819 pamphlet *Methodist Error, or Friendly Christian Advice to Those Methodists Who Indulge in Extravagant Religious Emotions and Bodily Exercises*, the anonymous author complained that "the *blacks* quarter" of revival camps radiated secular slave songs and extemporaneous verses "sung in the merry chorus-manner of the southern . . . husking-frolic method." The "husking-frolic method" refers to the improvised and passionate songs and stories the enslaved practiced during harvest, when huge piles of corn needed to be shucked for winter storage. Singers stomped rhythms at church revivals just like those at husking time, "the steps of actual negro dancing," the author complained. We cannot "countenance or tolerate such gross perversions of true religion!"[5]

In participating, free and enslaved Black people helped transform the religious landscape. A significant majority of the three generations of forced migrants who populated Virginia and North Carolina still practiced at least some elements of the West African religious traditions they had brought with them. A contemporary of Turner's living nearby, in Nottoway County, Virginia, remembered participating in the "rites and ceremonies practiced by his parents" brought from their homeland in West Africa.[6] The new religions spreading across the countryside held a recognizable appeal. Mass conversions that included fainting, ecstatic dancing, visions, and sometimes unconsciousness resembled and accommodated a spiritual tradition in which it was common for gods to throw people to the ground, to breathe in and through them, to ride worshippers' spirits, and to remake their lives.[7] The dramatic increase in church membership that punctuated evangelical growth was owed in no small part to the cross-pollination of spiritual ideas that formed African American evangelical worship.

II

In *The Bondwoman's Narrative*, faith sustains the protagonist, Hannah, just as it seems to have helped carry Hannah Crafts to freedom. And, so, it is no surprise that religion holds a significant role in Crafts's novel. Her consistent use of Scriptural verses to begin each chapter and her efforts to echo biblical stories are two overt ways that her work is decidedly religious in design. If Stowe could state her Christian design for *Uncle Tom's Cabin* ("There is a ladder to heaven, whose base God has placed in human affections"), it seems fitting that Crafts would be equally explicit in her work. Like Stowe, Crafts shapes her novel as one that both validates the God who presides over the lives of her characters and condemns the institution of slavery. As with Stowe, Crafts's moral universe is grounded in a belief in God's supernatural agency and intervention in human history. But there is a significant difference. Crafts's God, unlike Stowe's, does not see Black skin as a "curse." Rather, the sin of perceiving America as "white" is the true "curse"—to be avenged in her narrative and in the author's own biracial life. Instead of Stowe's tidy stairway to heaven where Black characters are decidedly on the bottom rung, Crafts explicitly frames her design with a question: "Have I succeeded in portraying any of the peculiar features of the institution whose curse rests over the fairest land the sun shines upon? Have I succeeded in showing how it blights the happiness of the white as well as the black race?" (*TBN* 3)

Crafts begins each chapter with a verse of Scripture that renders her text as a literary pulpit as she carries into the pages of her novel the Black evangelical tradition. Each chapter takes a biblical verse as its epigraph, and the successive narrative reflects on the passage. At the deepest level of her narrative, Crafts places the Genesis story of Jacob and Esau. Jacob becomes a symbol of freedom in Crafts's story. It is to the story of Jacob and Esau that Hannah opens her Bible on the eve of her escape from the Wheelers. She writes, "I wished to do right and determined to be guided by the Holy Book of God." Hannah then asks God for direction as she contemplates escape. "I opened it as chance directed but immediately at the place where Jacob fled from his brother Esau." She continues: "The sceptic may smile, but to me it had a deep and peculiar meaning. 'Yes' I mentally exclaimed. 'Trusting in the God that guided and protected him I will abandon this house, and the Mistress who would force me into a crime against nature.'" Hannah's decision to place faith in this sign from God is not taken lightly: "As I have observed before nothing but this would have impelled me to flight. Dear as freedom is to every human being, and bitter as servitude must be to all who experience it. I knew too much of the dangers and difficulties to be apprehended from running away ever to have attempted such a thing through ordinary motives. Shutting my precious Bible and placing it in my bosom I meditated a plan of escape" (*TBN* 213).

And so, when Crafts portrays Hannah's escape, it is probably fitting that an enslaved man named Jacob assists her on her journey north. If Crafts embeds the Genesis story of Jacob and Esau in her novel, her narrative itself embodies, loosely, Jacob's story in Genesis. The scholar Augusta Rohrbach notes as much: "Jacob's presence—in the pages of her Bible and as a character in her novel—facilitates her safe journey to the promised land. . . . His death in the novel, as in Genesis, paves the way to the land of freedom—the North for Crafts, Israel for Jacob, which is the name God gives Jacob."[8]

The connection between slavery and Christianity in the antebellum period makes many readers justifiably uncomfortable with a pious enslaved narrator. Because enslavers co-opted Christian doctrine, many readers today are often disturbed by comments that seem to echo slaveholding rhetoric, such as Hannah's declaration that she "would not even for the blessed boon of freedom change places with [her enslaver], since even freedom without God and religion would be a barren possession" (*TBN* 112). In a climate that often views religion as a means of oppression, we can easily read Hannah's preference for God over freedom as evidence that Crafts was deluded by the ideology of slavery. But the historical context of Crafts's life and writings invites us to take her pious views seriously as part of her courage, strength, and strong opposition to slavery. In this regard, she followed other pioneering radicals in her region, like Nat Turner.

III

Turner's insurrection and *The Bondwoman's Narrative* found fertile ground in the substratum of religious thought and contestation that formed their lived worlds. After Gabriel Prosser's foiled slave rebellion in Richmond, Virginia, in 1800, the Bertie Conspiracy in 1802, and subsequent insurrectionary scares along the Virginia–North Carolina border between 1802 and 1804, church leaders representing the planter class strengthened their grip over regional evangelical associations, especially in the 1820s, when slaveholding became enormously profitable again. They fortified policies that guarded and advanced white supremacy, while also pruning church leadership of perceived radicals.[9] Long gone were leaders like David Barrow, whose hand is still visible in the final set of minutes he recorded for the Virginia Portsmouth Baptist Association shortly before his expulsion: "*[C]ovetousness*, leads Christians, with the people of this country in general, to hold and retain, in abject slavery, a set of our poor fellow creatures, *contrary to the laws of God and nature*." Barrow's strained leadership can be witnessed in his vigorous italicizations and shaky hand and his complaints about enslavers' "*covetousness*." For his criticism, he was relieved of his preceptorship and, shortly thereafter, removed to Kentucky.[10]

Turner and Crafts formed a part of a demographic not commonly depicted in school textbooks: they worshipped in a biracial evangelical tradition. In participating in evangelical churches, Blacks, like whites, subjected themselves to the oversight and discipline of a community of others who had experienced grace, agreeing to "give ourselves to the Lord and to one another by the Will of God."[11] Church members, regardless of race, participated in a common ritual life. They related their experiences of conversion and heard others do so. As Blacks and whites interacted with one another in Baptist and Methodist institutions along the border of Virginia and North Carolina, the rituals of church membership, the vocabulary of divine power and human humility, and the notion of a lived emotional experience of faith provided a language that could, in limited ways, cross the lines of race and slavery. Baptists underwent full-immersion baptism and witnessed the baptism of other new members, while Methodists conducted partial baptism at the baptismal fount, a central ornament and sacramental locus of their shared communion. Mass conversions to Christianity among African Americans were sustained well into the third decade of the nineteenth century.

This may explain why *The Bondwoman's Narrative* is suffused with pious discourses that would also be at home in the white-centered domestic fictions penned by contemporary enslavers. In this immediate context, it is not surprising that Turner's *Confessions* records his enslavers' support for his religious enthusiasm or that Hannah Crafts is "led . . . to the foot of the Cross" by a local Quaker family that also first taught her to read (*TBN* 10). Evangelicals of both races embraced the idea of a direct experience of saving grace as the central dimension of religious experience in keeping with area Quakers.

The resurgence of slavery's profitability and the growing internal slave trade to the expanding frontiers of the Southwest set the stage for the racial fault lines that threatened biracial evangelicalism. For both

Turner and Crafts, a vigorous biracial Christianity helped forge their identities as well as their spiritual and intellectual gifts. In the 1820s and '30s, when the cotton frontier began to remake America, Baptists and Methodists in the region began to separate church functions according to race. Even free Black men, who at one time were listed in church records in the same column as free whites, found themselves enumerated on church rolls with enslaved people. Although baptisms continued to be conducted for both races at the same time, disciplinary hearings conducted in front of church elders began to be held independently. In some congregations, Blacks even began to be ministered to separately from white parishioners, sometimes by a Black religious leader like Turner. During the periods when Turner and, later, Crafts grew to maturity, the strengthening of white supremacy may have, ironically, pushed both into embracing the kind of radical evangelical Christianity that became manifest in their separate rebellions.

Samuel Jordan Wheeler notes the names of enslaved men who preached to the colored congregations at the Meherrin and Murfreesboro Baptist Churches near the site of Turner's rebellion and the author's enslavement. "Robert," "Cyrus," "Joseph," and "Abram" were the exhorters who would have helped form the strongly marked religious views of Milly and Martha Murfree, Eliza Morgan, and Hannah Crafts. "The colored members being numerous [beginning] in 1800, the church appointed" enslaved religious men from the congregation "to attend specially" to fellow Black congregants. Wheeler clearly delineates the place of such "colored members" in his *History of the Baptist Church* for the region, published in 1847, by relegating them to a footnote in the book's Appendix B, where their position as property is duly noted: "Robert, of P. Brown, Cyrus, of Peter Parker, Joseph, of Deberry, and Abram, of C. W. Barnes."[12] These are the only names of Black congregants directly cited in the whole of Wheeler's history. Otherwise, Black participation is summarized as "there are more than 200 colored members besides."[13] Such silence of the majority of the church (53 percent were "colored") gives the lie to the verse Wheeler chose for the cover of the book: "That ye may tell it to the generation following" (Psalm 48). Hannah Crafts and Nat Turner would find other ways to broadcast the story unrecorded in Wheeler's official history.

IV

It is common knowledge that slaveholders used Christianity to buttress the slave system from which they benefited. The antebellum period was rife with biblical justifications for slavery, expressed from pulpits and in pamphlets that maintained that slavery was part of God's plan. In what was considered the best antebellum religious defense of slavery, Thornton Stringfellow argues that God saved Africans both physically and spiritually by bringing them to the United States, where they could be taken care of and hear about Jesus.[14] Moreover, many slaveholders attempted to control their slaves by claiming that God underwrote their ownership and by teaching them Bible verses that enjoined them to obey their masters, such as Ephesians 6:5, Colossians 3:22, and 1 Peter 2:18. Such arguments employed religion as the foundation for a racist economic system.[15]

The most famous antebellum slave narratives, such as those of Harriet Jacobs and Frederick Douglass, frequently cite the hypocrisy of white Christians. In a brilliant parody of the Eucharist, Jacobs writes that her owner, Mrs. Flint, was not "put in a Christian frame of mind" by taking the Lord's Supper. On the contrary, if dinner was served late when Mrs. Flint returned from church, she would spit in the leftovers so the cook would be unable to eat them.[16] Douglass is more explicit in his condemnation of Southern Christianity, calling it "a mere covering for the most horrid crimes,—a justifier of the most appalling barbarity . . . and a dark shelter under which the darkest, foulest, grossest, and most infernal deeds of slaveholders find the strongest protection." In his appendix, however, Douglass differentiates between "slaveholding religion" and "Christianity" proper.[17]

Earlier religious instruction directed at the enslaved conflated enslavers with the Lord delivering the "Good News" of white supremacy: "Let as many servant as are under the yoke count their own masters worthy of all honour, that the name of God and his doctrine be not blasphemed. And they that have believing masters, let them not despise them, because they are brethren; but rather do them service, because they are faithful and beloved, partakers of the benefit. These things teach and exhort."[18]

A contemporary of Hannah Crafts, William Thompson, born sixteen miles outside Richmond, Virginia, remembered how the hypocrisy of "Christian" enslavers had spoiled religion for him, especially as it was mixed with the traffic of humans conducted in plain view: "I went to meeting on Sunday after I had seen the gang chained, but the preaching did me no good."[19] Another contemporary believer, Betsey Madison, found that once she was transported from Virginia to the cotton frontiers of Mississippi, enslavers silenced her from teaching the Gospel of evangelical Christianity. "The great God above has made you for the benefit of the Whiteman, who is your law maker and law giver," one Kentucky enslaver preached to his captives, whom he had assembled in the yard for their Sunday morning sermon.[20]

As a devout Christian, the author of *The Bondwoman's Narrative* anguished over a religious tradition that encouraged nonbelief among Blacks; without religion, she believed, they could only gain the news of a false prophet. In *The Bondwoman's Narrative*, Crafts tells the story of some of these figures, probably drawn directly from her own experience fleeing her enslaver. As "Hannah" makes her escape in the novel, she meets two other fugitive slaves, a brother and sister, who are seeking freedom from enslavement in the Carolinas. But the sister suffers from fever and exposure. Hannah ministers to the gravely ill woman in her last moments because "I could not bear that she should die thus like a brute with no mention of his name, who had died that we might live." She asks, "[D]id you ever pray?" And the dying woman responds: "'I have heard them, when they called it praying, and when it seemed to me they were talking to themselves, or master, or some one else. Ministers used to come among us and pray, but I never minded them. They mostly prayed that we the slaves might be good and obedient, and feel grateful for all our blessings, which I know was fudge. It hardened my heart, I could not bear it.'" Crafts writes,

"How I pitied the poor benighted soul to whom the sweetest influences of religion had become gall and wormwood" (*TBN* 225–26).

The fictional enslaved woman and Crafts herself would have been influenced by white people's interpretation of the story of the "Curse of Ham." In Genesis 9:18–27, Ham views and mocks his naked drunken father, Noah, who, upon waking, curses Ham's son Canaan and condemns him and his descendants to the lowest form of slavery. While the Canaanites were the enemies of the ancient Israelites, there was no mention of skin color in ancient sources. But this did not stop whites from associating the descendants of Ham with dark-skinned people, often through the Canaanite descendant Cush, or Kush. The Kushites occupied the African lands south of Egypt, including Nubia. Nubia runs south of the Aswan Dam to Khartoum, from the Nile's First Cataract. Even though Genesis later notes that "Kush also begot Nimrod," who was the first great king on earth and "was a mighty hunter by the grace of the Lord" (10:8–9), the "Curse of Ham" became the most authoritative justification for "Negro slavery" in the American South. Indeed, the published works of Bond's enslavers John Hill Wheeler and Samuel Jordan Wheeler openly justify slavery by grounding the practice in this false premise.[21]

Hannah Crafts sought to invigorate a radical biblical tradition free of such pro-slavery rhetoric. Formerly, enslavers and overseers presented religion merely as a control mechanism endlessly bound to Colossians 3:22, "Servants, obey in all things your masters according to the flesh; not with eyeservice, as menpleasers; but in singleness of heart, fearing God." To the enslaved and free Blacks, this false Scripture became just another manacle chaining them to the coffle of Ephesians 6:5, "Servants, be obedient to them that are your masters according to the flesh, with fear and trembling, in singleness of your heart."

The author of *The Bondwoman's Narrative* sought to break this chain. Instead of the self-justifying curse of Canaan, the more relevant story of Jesus's identification with the poor and advocacy for the persecuted emerged as the source of Bond's strength. This Bible could brace principles that matched the African American experience. Those who could read or gain access to the stories white enslavers suppressed found contrasting messages of redemption and triumph. They saw themselves as the children of Israel and found parallels between the slavery practiced in their communities and that of ancient Egypt. More radical texts, like the Book of Exodus, came alive and told of a restoration of the Lord's people, the return of the Jews to Jerusalem. In the same manner, Blacks hoped for a return to their homeland, or at least the restoration of their liberty and the God-given right to inhabit the communities they had labored to build. In this common formulation, enslavers were American Pharaohs, and the North, or any place that demarcated freedom, became the Promised Land of Canaan. As we will see, Hannah Crafts found her Canaan in an all-Black community in New Jersey.

CHAPTER 13

THE WHEELERS

I

IN AUGUST 1857, HIDDEN AT Horace Craft's farm, Hannah Crafts wrote the name "Mrs. Wheeler." Then she paged through the manuscript. Where she had once concealed their identities, now she marked them: "Mrs. Wheeler," "Mr. Wheeler," "The Wheelers." Up to this point, Crafts had disguised her story so that she could not be traced. As she knew too well, the Wheelers prosecuted for the return of their escaped captives. But a fresh account of "Mrs. Wh—r" belittling the protagonist's religious fervor called up the same defiant drive that had led Crafts to escape in the first place, even as it fired her imagination (MS 190).

The author refreshed her pen and defended her Christian principles. As Hannah Crafts, she wrote a scene that disclosed the truth for all to see: Mrs. Wheeler was "a bigot in religion"; Mrs. Wheeler's "notions of religion and truth were highly improper for one in her station" (MS 191–92). Crafts even hinted at the deepest wound: "compelled sacrifise [*sic*]" to a "gentleman" and the loss of "virtue, or honor" (MS 192). She put all these words into the mouth of her mistress, Mrs. Wheeler, and she showed her to be a hypocrite.

Hannah's story was not an easy one to tell, especially when the author herself was almost certainly a victim of sexual abuse. Similar to Harriet Jacobs and Harriet Wilson, the other early Black female writers who suffered physical coercion, she sought to share her story within the popular conventions of sentimental and gothic fiction. With the assistance of literary devices that could powerfully dramatize her experiences while providing emotional cover for the pain and outrage of her suffering, Crafts developed her tale. By writing her story as a novel according to the popular conventions of domestic fiction, she hoped to reach the widest possible audience, a course also taken by Harriet Wilson and, later, Harriet Jacobs. In this way, taboo subjects such as sexual subjugation could be packaged in acceptable, generic terms.

Probably still hidden at Horace Craft's farm, the author dipped her pen and constructed a new scene. This time, she told the story of Mrs. Wheeler suffering a bout of constipation. With telling irony, she observed, "I was the attendant of *Mrs. Wheeler*, though it is impossible to say how irksome the duty had become"—and she wrote it boldly: "*Mrs. Wheeler*" (MS 193). This was the kind of insolent power an enslaved servant could possess—power that gained strength, Crafts must have realized, with her willingness to claim it. At the risk of drawing attention to her fugitive status, the author forged ahead. From this point on, the "Wheelers" are named precisely in the manuscript, and their activities in Washington, D.C., and North Carolina are strongly figured.

II

Dorothy Porter Wesley, who purchased the manuscript in 1951, left behind notes identifying John Hill Wheeler as the potential enslaver of the novel's author. When Henry Louis Gates Jr. purchased the manuscript in 2001, he followed up on the lead. "A painstaking search of federal census records for North Carolina and Washington, D.C.," Gates notes, "revealed that only one Wheeler in the entire United States lived in both North Carolina and Washington between 1850 and 1880" (*TBN* lxxvii). Not only did this Wheeler serve in a wide range of governmental positions, but he was also a slaveholder and an ardent and passionate defender of slavery, just as Crafts depicts.[1]

Further pen and ink analysis by Dr. Joe Nickell found that "the novel may be based on actual experiences." Nickell reached his separate conclusion because of the way Crafts handles the names of Mr. and Mrs. Wheeler: "the name 'Wheeler' in the narrative was first written cryptically, for example as 'Mr. Wh—r' and 'Mrs. Wh—r,' but then later was overwritten with the missing 'eele' in each case to complete the name" (*TBN* lxxvi). As Nickell observes, something changed during the development of the work, possibly the author's proximity to or relationship with the Wheelers. This would explain why three quarters of the way into composing the work, the author changes course, returning to expose the name "Wheeler." The alterations suggest an intimate connection between the Wheelers and the author, one central to the author's act of creation preserved in the manuscript.

Gates built on these insights to strongly shape the case that John Hill Wheeler was the enslaver from whom the author fled in the mid- to late 1850s. Important evidence Gates brought to bear came from a careful study of John Hill Wheeler's diaries, housed with his papers in the Library of Congress. Wheeler kept a diary regularly from May 30, 1850, to his death in 1882. The work is generally intact, except for the years 1856 and 1858. The latter half of the 1856 diary is lost after May 23, and the first half of the 1858 diary is illegible because of damage. Circumstantial evidence from these diaries matches details disclosed in Crafts's novel: locations, travel details, even the weather. Policy debates that touch intimately on John Hill Wheeler's life as a government official in Washington, D.C., correspond closely with the concerns and dialogue of "Mr. Wheeler" in the novel. Whoever wrote the novel, Gates argued, seems to have been privy to the Wheeler household in the 1850s. For Gates, there was little doubt: "[T]he person who wrote the novel knew John Hill Wheeler and his wife personally, hated them both for their pro-slavery feelings and their racism, and wanted to leave a record of their hatred for posterity" (*TBN* ci).

Gates and the scholar William L. Andrews made an important additional discovery. For a brief time in 1855, John Hill Wheeler came to national attention as the petitioner in the famous *Case of Passmore Williamson*. The case turned on Wheeler's attempt in 1855 to regain a fugitive captive, Jane Johnson, whom he had purchased one and a half years earlier. In 1855, the case became a cause célèbre, one of the first challenges to the notorious Fugitive Slave Act of 1850. On July 18, 1855, Jane Johnson escaped with two of her children from Wheeler's possession with the assistance of Passmore Williamson and William Still, the prominent African American chairman of the Acting Vigilant Committee of the Philadelphia branch of the Pennsylvania Anti-Slavery Society. The daring flight took place from the deck of the ferryboat *Washington*, which was set to depart Philadelphia for New York City (see Figure 23). For his aid in the escape, Williamson was imprisoned in Moyamensing Prison for more than three months, and William Still and five black dockworkers, who also assisted, were brought to trial for assault and battery for restraining Wheeler.

At a hearing on August 30, Jane made a bold appearance, testifying that she had fled of her own volition, and then hurriedly left the courtroom under the protection of abolitionists and state authorities. A carriage chase ensued through the streets as she and her protectors evaded federal marshals attempting to enforce Wheeler's ownership rights.

FIGURE 23: Engraving from William Still's *The Underground Railroad* (1872)

The author of *The Bondwoman's Narrative* appears to write something of these events into her novel, including Jane Johnson herself. In chapter 12 of the novel, Mrs. Wheeler complains about domestic inconvenience after the escape of an enslaved woman named Jane. While the protagonist is dressing her enslaver's hair, Mrs. Wheeler describes why it appears so tangled:

> "I was too feeble to think of attempting it myself, and since Jane ran off, there has been no one to whom I could think of entrusting my head, till Mrs[.] Henry so warmly recommended you."
>
> "I am much obliged to Mrs[.] Henry I am sure.["]
>
> "Jane was very handy at almost everything" she continued. "You will seldom find a slave so handy, but she grew discontented and dissatisfied with her condition, thought she could do better in a land of freedom, and such like I watched her closely you may depend . . ."

Mrs. Wheeler continues her sour grapes over Jane's escape:

> "Oh dear, this is what I have to endure from losing Jane, but she'll have to suffer more, probably" (*TBN* 153–54).

If Jane Johnson's testimony so discomfited her enslaver that it even changed his physical complexion—"Like a boiled lobster, Mr. Wheeler turned from white to red"—Crafts's novel would extend the same discomfort to Mrs. Wheeler, who, in the signature scene of the novel, comes to find her skin color changed from white to black.[2]

The fact that the author of *The Bondwoman's Narrative* depicts events associated with Jane Johnson in the novel further helps us date its likely production. If forensic evidence placed the composition date between 1853 and 1860, the evidence connecting the manuscript to Jane Johnson's escape and trial suggests a composition window between 1855 and 1860. As we will see, Gates and other scholars provide suggestive reasons that Jane Johnson herself could have been the author.

III

In developing her novel, the author of *The Bondwoman's Narrative* reveals a strong awareness of earlier slave narratives. This should not be surprising. As William L. Andrews, the author of the definitive study of slave narratives, notes, "to tell a free story," one needs to learn how. The first step, of course, is by engaging with the stories of others. The most natural place would be the whispered stories exchanged among the enslaved, those rare moments when white surveillance receded and enslaved men and women could speak their minds, unhindered by a world that otherwise forced their silence. When the enslaved seized this freedom, self-testimony became a kind of personal emancipation. Something of this power is what makes the slave narratives of Frederick Douglass, William Wells Brown, Harriet Jacobs, and Hannah Crafts so compelling.[3]

But it also seems that the author had some access to specific printed narratives then in circulation. Perhaps this should not be surprising, either. The households of the enslavers associated with *The Bondwoman's Narrative* were wealthy and highly literary, and, as noted, they possessed impressive library collections. Further, Milly and Martha Murfree, Eliza Morgan, and Hannah Bond resided, at least for a time, near the library housed in the adjacent Hertford Academy building from the 1830s until 1856, when the library was moved to Chowan's new campus. The fact that two major female colleges were established by the mid-1850s, and two hundred female college students arrived each year to study literature in the town (among other subjects), suggests the richness of the intellectual environment that helped shape Crafts's work.

Approximately fifty American slave narratives had been published in book or pamphlet form by the time Crafts began developing her autobiographical work. As already noted, many influential slave narratives were in the library of John Hill Wheeler, who possessed Crafts from 1856 to 1857. According to Wheeler's 1850 book inventory, by the time Crafts encountered the Wheeler library in Washington, D.C., its holdings also included Frederick Douglass's *Narrative of the Life of Frederick Douglass*

(1845) and William Wells Brown's *Narrative of William W. Brown, a Fugitive Slave* (1847).[4]

To tell her story, Crafts seems to have followed the design of others fugitive authors, especially Douglass and Brown. Specific characteristics made slave narratives successful and attractive to nineteenth-century readers, even those who, like Wheeler, held pro-slavery views, and they must have appealed to Crafts, too. The upward reach of captives seeking a life beyond "the debased state of subservience," the "progress from subhuman conditions" to self-possession, the transition from childhood to adulthood—all these informed Crafts's storytelling, as well.[5] Crafts seems to have drawn on the two most popular and widely circulated slavery memoirs: Douglass's *Narrative* and Brown's *Narrative*.

Crafts's journey shared some similarities that may explain her reliance on Douglass's and Brown's story lines. Like Douglass, Crafts was separated from her mother at an early age, and as with both Douglass and Brown, her enslaver was likely her father. Similar to both, she was light-skinned and served as a domestic servant. If Crafts did not enjoy the oratory and public speaking training that proved so important for Douglass and Brown, she did engage for years with Chowan students practicing their recitation and composition exercises. Obviously, slave narratives served an ideological purpose, including the effort to gain the sympathy of Northern readers while recruiting new supporters for the abolitionist movement. As slave autobiographies gained in popularity, they began to share themes and forms that eventually forged a distinct genre. Crafts seems to have been at least marginally familiar with the emerging type, and her autobiographical novel is in dialogue with the tradition. Her narrative is unique, however, in not having been developed for an abolitionist society or edited under white supervision—unlike Douglass's and Brown's productions, both shaped by William Lloyd Garrison's hand.

Douglass's and Brown's narratives, which have been hailed by scholars as seminal fugitive slave autobiographies, share many parallel themes. Similar experiences may account for some of the thematic coherence both authors helped establish for the genre. Douglass entered the world as a slave. Born in Maryland in 1818, he escaped bondage when he was twenty years old. When he published the first narrative of his life in 1845, the work proved an immediate success. In its first two years, Douglass's *Narrative* went through nine British editions.[6] In Brown's case, his birth is recorded in Kentucky in 1814. He escaped from slavery at the age of nineteen, in 1834. In 1847, following Douglass, Brown published his narrative, which likewise proved a popular success. His *Narrative* reached its ninth American and British edition before 1850.[7] Douglass's and Brown's memoirs found their way into print with the help of William Lloyd Garrison, the president of the American Anti-Slavery Society (AASS), whose Massachusetts Anti-Slavery Office, in Boston, published these works. Douglass's and Brown's extensive experience as orators on the lecture circuit for the AASS paved the way for their books' success. Because Douglass and Brown traveled widely in the United States and Europe on abolitionist circuit tours, their stories were widely known, and their public talks gained a readership for their written narratives. The importance of their oratory training cannot be overstated. Douglass first acquired oratory skills during bondage, when he participated in a secret debating club. Similarly, before lecturing for the AASS, Brown practiced public speaking for years through his work organizing and speaking for a temperance society in Buffalo, New York.[8]

Crafts must have found Douglass's and Brown's struggles in forging their own names and identities both bracing and familiar. Douglass held several names on his path from slavery to freedom. He changed his original name, "Frederick Augustus Washington Bailey," to "Frederick Bailey," and then to "Frederick Johnson." On the day he gained his new freedom, he chose the name "Stanley" before finally settling for "Frederick Douglass." As a child, Brown's mother altered her son's name from "William" to "Sandford," to accommodate her enslaver's white nephew, who was also called "William." Brown fought this change and received several whippings for trying to retain the name his mother had provided him at birth. He recounts in his narrative how he "was not only hunting for [his] liberty, but also hunting for a name."[9]After his escape, Brown reclaimed his original name of "William." He then chose his own adoptive middle and last names, "Wells Brown." These names honored the Quaker who had helped him in his flight.[10] Hannah Jr. seems to have been inspired especially by Brown's model in forging her own name as "Hannah Crafts."

Among the many similarities in all three narratives—Douglass's, Brown's, and Crafts's—we find a lack of information as to the captives' births, an emphasis on the sexual exploitation of enslaved women and girls, and the denunciation of broken family ties. Crafts's story seems to follow the arc established in Douglass and Brown: she develops a narrative that details the difficult daily experiences of enslaved life, explains living arrangements and plantation organization and hierarchy, and demonstrates the limited food and clothing provided for captives. Early pages in each account confront the reader with the physical and emotional abuse of vulnerable bondpeople, especially women and children. Brown describes witnessing his mother being whipped as he is helpless to assist; Douglass recalls his aunt Hester being abused, as noted earlier; and Crafts enlarges upon the death of Rosea and her dog.[11]

With all these similarities, Crafts's experiences would come to match even more closely the narratives of female authors like Harriet Wilson, Harriet Jacobs, Elizabeth Keckley, and Louisa Picquet, who was born in South Carolina. Because she completed *The Bondwoman's Narrative* before these works appeared, she did not have access to them until later in life. Female writers like Crafts captured in their work elements unique to the plight of enslaved women, especially the complex ways sexual harassment and physical assault shaped their lives. There are hints throughout the novel that the author experienced both of these again in Washington, D.C. For reasons that remain a mystery, of all her family's enslavers—including the Pughs and Bonds—the only ones she exposes directly are John Hill Wheeler and Ellen Sully Wheeler. As we will see, by baring the inner lives of Mr. and Mrs. Wheeler so forcibly and openly, Crafts leaves behind the detectable traces of her own life story.

CHAPTER 14

THE NOVEL

In 2004, Henry Louis Gates Jr. and Hollis Robbins edited and published a groundbreaking collection of essays by leading scholars titled *In Search of Hannah Crafts*. Here, Gates and Robbins set out details of the author's intertextual engagement with other writers, especially Charles Dickens. Gates and Robbins draw in more than a dozen leading scholars to build a critical and historical foundation for future work on the novel. The scholars in the volume clarify the minute class and racial elements of the novel, disclose the material contexts of Crafts's work, and position the work in the literary marketplace of its day. In short, they prepare the ground and edifice for understanding important elements of the author's life. What they could not do, however, was mark the specific writer: "Questions of Hannah Crafts's actual identity are put aside in most of the essays that follow," they write.[1]

With Gates and Robbins leading the way, *In Search of Hannah Crafts* brought the novel more fully into view: here was a work "designed to captivate and to provoke." If Crafts claims to present "a record of plain unvarnished facts," the author was also proposing "a literary venture." If she claims that her tale "makes no pretension to romance," she also reaches for high art as she seeks to challenge the institution of slavery. If Crafts states that her narrative has no moral, she also argues that "pious and discerning minds can scarcely fail to recognize the hand of Providence" in the punishments and rewards that accrue to the book's various characters (*TBN* 3). As Gates and Robbins establish, the design is a fascinating mix of fact and fiction in which Crafts claims to tell her own story but also assumes the right to practice the same literary devices that white authors used to gain a popular audience.[2]

Non-scholars rarely realize how collaborative discoveries in history and literature prove to be, but to fully grasp Crafts's novel, it takes much more than proving the identity of the writer. The team of experts Gates and Robbins assembled provided an understanding of the novelist's world even before her life could be known. As Gates and Robbins point out, Crafts alludes to a remarkably impressive range of British and American works found in Wheeler's extensive library.[3] Texts from Wheeler's library reverberate throughout her narrative, but so do works the author was exposed to in Murfreesboro, including Charles Dickens's *Bleak House* and Harriet Beecher Stowe's *Uncle Tom's Cabin*. Another influence appears to be Nathaniel Hawthorne's *The House of the Seven Gables* (1851).[4] Further, there are echoes of Emily and Charlotte Bronte's novels; these, too, circulated at Chowan and were maintained in John Hill Wheeler's library.[5] Also, still much that seems to be literary contrivance is grounded in historical fact.

Physical details directly overlap with the author's experience in locales like Willow Hall in Bertie County; Washington, D.C.; and the Wheeler properties in Murfreesboro, North Carolina, and elsewhere. Travel routes in the novel reflect locations and conveyances familiar to travelers moving in these same circles. Gates and Robbins first noted that Crafts transparently fictionalizes many of her experiences and, like all successful novelists, develops these experiences into a powerful story that transcends mere memoir. A complex cultural milieu and a history of place help write the work just as they helped form the author.

Told in the vein of the genre-defining slave narratives she likely encountered early, especially Frederick Douglass's *Narrative* and William Wells Brown's *Narrative*, Crafts's story depicts the trials and tribulations of the author's real-life experiences; charts her growth from slavery to freedom and from childhood to womanhood; and maps the author's reach for self-actualization or, as she describes it, "deep repose [and] a blest and holy quietude" (*TBN* 244). Indeed, *The Bondwoman's Narrative* is a hybrid work—part autobiographical fiction, part account of sexual abuse, part domestic novel, and part Christian morality tale. The protagonist, Hannah, escapes from Lindendale with her mixed-race mistress, who has wittingly been passing, hoping to free herself from the clutches of Mr. Trappe. Flight and the promise of freedom seem unattainable when Hannah and her mistress find themselves lost.

As the scholar Roselyne M. Jua has noted, the narrative design of Crafts's story is circular: the movement begins at the house called Lindendale, then moves to the woods, back to an unidentified house, and then to slave huts, jail, Mr. Trappe's prison, the Henry estate, and then Wheeler House. Only when the captive Hannah frees herself from the confines of Wheeler House does it become possible for her to assert her independence and agency. And so, according to Jua, "the house is at the center of her narrative, as it is in other 19th-century writing."[6] Freedom depends on the author's relation to the house and her enslaved role there, as Hannah moves within "these circles and cycles of circular spaces, juxtaposing houses and inferring comparisons and thereby insinuating her vision."[7]

Crafts begins her narrative by describing her childhood on Lewis Bond's plantation, Willow Hall. She focuses on Hannah's desire to gain literacy, asserting that she "had from the first an instinctive desire for knowledge and the means of mental improvement" (*TBN* 6). Crafts relates how her protagonist learned to read and write at the instruction of Aunt Hetty and Uncle Siah. Hannah steals away from Lindendale to visit her abettors whenever she can be away from service without being detected. She continues her project of stealth literacy until, one night, she is discovered by the overseer—a character probably based on her mixed-race half brother John Thomas Bond. Although Hannah is not punished, Hetty and Siah are forced from the area.[8]

After the story of Hetty and Siah's removal, Crafts's narrative shifts to the defining events of Hannah's life as a captive. Although there are not precise parallels to what can be recovered of Hannah Bond's life, there are clear autobiographical elements to the narrative. The mystery of the passing mistress becomes a fascinating doppelgänger tale of the author's shadow self, one she may have imagined when she was forced to serve as a sexual victim of Thomas Bond Jr. The events that betoken this "marriage" are unsettled, marked as they are by "supernatural" occurrences on the Bond plantation. Crafts asserts that the passing mistress "seemed haunted by a shadow or phantom apparent only to herself" (*TBN* 27). Crafts also notes that her mistress is suspicious of a man named Mr. Trappe, who lodges at the plantation house as an extended guest of the bridal party.

As the story proceeds, we learn that Hannah's mistress is passing for white. This light-skinned mistress is really the offspring of a slave and the plantation patriarch, but she was switched at birth with a stillborn child of the same patriarch. Further, the narrative discloses that it is Mr. Trappe who "discovered the secret" of the mistress's mixed birth and that he is now using this information as blackmail. Eventually forced to flee from Mr. Trappe, Hannah's mistress runs off from the plantation. Hannah, fearing for the woman's safety, assists with the escape (*TBN* 44–52). The event seems to match what may have been Hannah Bond's temporary escape from Thomas Bond Jr. sometime in the late 1840s, after her sexual subjugation became impossible to manage. In the novel, this escape takes the form of Hannah and her mistress (the shadow self) getting lost in the wilderness and, eventually, being captured by three game hunters. The location of this escape attempt appears to draw on the real-life experience of Sally and Kitty Bell (as we will see in chapter 19). When Mr. Trappe informs the mistress that she is to be sold to a slave trader, she "bursts a blood vessel" and instantly dies (*TBN* 103). The death perhaps represents the shadow self of the author that had been sacrificed in sexual bondage.

In the novel, Hannah is sold to a slave trader, who subsequently moves her to another enslaver, probably reflecting Crafts's real-life enslavement to two of Lewis Bond's daughters, who inherited her in quick succession. Hannah is then injured in a carriage accident and wakes up in the plantation home of a kind woman, Mrs. Henry, who dislikes the institution of slavery but is forced to keep the captives she inherited from her father as part of the terms of his will. As Hannah recovers from her injuries, she becomes very fond of the people and atmosphere of the Henrys' plantation, known as "Forget me not," and seeks for Mrs. Henry to purchase her. Mrs. Henry declines the proposal. Acquiring Hannah would also violate the pledge she made to her father on his deathbed that she would never purchase or sell a human being. Crafts seems to be satirizing the moral sophistry that captors, while professing humanity, frequently conjured to keep their slaves. There is some evidence that the Henry family scenes could be based on Hannah Crafts's stay on the Mulberry Grove holdings of Wheeler relatives Godwin Cotton Moore (1806–1880) and his wife, Julia Munro Wheeler Moore (1814–1887). Mrs. Henry tells Hannah that "a relative . . . wishes to purchase a maid-servant" and that Hannah may suit her needs. Hannah grudgingly agrees because Mrs. Henry describes her relative as "very kind and humane to their slaves" (*TBN* 132).

Mrs. Henry's relative, Mrs. Wheeler, acquires Hannah and takes her to Washington, D.C., where Hannah is forced to serve the household of Mrs. Wheeler and her husband. The exchange, arranged apparently without direct sale, approximates Hannah Jr.'s exchange from Lucinda Bond Wheeler, Hannah Bond's legal owner, to Ellen Sully Wheeler in recognition of debts owed to John Hill Wheeler. Here, the novel starts to track plainly with the real-life experiences of Hannah Crafts.

In the novel, Hannah quickly learns that Mrs. Wheeler is outwardly generous but secretly cruel, observing, "[N]otwithstanding her sociality and freedom of conversation there was something in her manner that I did not like. Her voice was soft and low, but the tone was rather artificial than natural. . . . Then there was a sparkle in her eye, and a tremor in her frame when she became agitated that indicated an effort to keep down strong passion" (*TBN* 156). Additionally, Hannah describes being overworked by Mrs. Wheeler, who requires that she sleep at the foot of her door and who contrives petty assignments at night to prove Hannah's servitude.

Mrs. Wheeler's husband, John Hill Wheeler, the former U.S. minister to Nicaragua, spends his time "haunting the bureau of some department or other" to find a new high-ranking government position, just as the real-life Wheeler did during the years Crafts was in his possession (1856–57) (*TBN* 164). After failing to receive several appointments, Wheeler asks his wife to petition on his behalf. The resulting scene is a masterpiece of imaginative art that turns the tables on the Wheelers and exposes for ridicule the tenets of white supremacy. Hannah's comic exposure of the Wheelers in the novel (explored in detail in chapter 16 of this book) leads to the fictional Wheelers fleeing unwanted fame and embarrassment in Washington, D.C., and returning to Wheeler House in North Carolina. All indications from the historical record suggest that this masterful scene is fictional, but it also tracks with the Wheeler family's return to Murfreesboro, North Carolina, in the spring of 1857.

After a few weeks at the Wheeler family's plantation and at Wheeler House, Hannah is called into Mrs. Wheeler's room and accused of telling the servants about the incident Hannah helped orchestrate in Washington. Crafts's protagonist denies the allegation, arguing that it was Maria, "a dark mulatto slave . . . with snaky black eyes," who informed the servants of the episode. However, Mrs. Wheeler will not accept the narrative and, instead, punishes Hannah by sending her from the house "into the fields to work" (*TBN* 208). She then arranges Hannah's forced marriage to a field slave named Bill. "Doomed to association with the vile, foul, filthy inhabitants of the huts" and "condemned to receive one of them for [her] husband," Hannah, Crafts writes, feels her "soul . . . revolted with horror unspeakable" (*TBN* 211).

In the novel, and probably in real life, Hannah determines that her only option for escaping the punishment to which she has been condemned is to seek freedom. Crafts seems to be writing into her novel a demotion she may have experienced, one in which she was forever banished, like her protagonist, to the family's slave huts in North Carolina. In order to develop an adequate escape plan, Hannah decides to "feign submission" and "place herself under the command of the overseer" (*TBN* 208). Here again, Crafts's narrative appears to track with the author's actual experiences. Crafts, like her protagonist, seems to have made her escape by taking advantage of the distance between Wheeler House and the Liberty Hall plantation outside town, where the overseer confused her absence with her return to Wheeler House. After a few days of agricultural labor, Hannah makes her escape by returning to Wheeler House, where she is assisted in disguising herself and fleeing. Crafts, like Hannah in her novel, eventually reaches New Jersey, where she settles into life as a free woman. At the close of her narrative, Crafts describes Hannah being reunited with her mother, who was sold away from Lindendale. She describes their reunion on the last page of the novel: "[W]e recognized in this the greatest blessing of our lives" (*TBN* 245).

CHAPTER 15

THE LIFE AND TIMES OF ELIZA MORGAN

I

IN SEPTEMBER 1842, THE ENSLAVED Eliza Morgan accompanied John Hill Wheeler and his daughter Elizabeth Brown Wheeler (1832–1921) to the home of his father-in-law, the Rev. Obadiah B. Brown, at 814 E Street NW in the nation's capital. Morgan and her young mistress, Elizabeth, were moving to Washington, D.C., to reside with Brown. Since the early death of Elizabeth's mother, Mary Brown Wheeler, in 1836, Morgan had served as the primary caregiver to the motherless Elizabeth. Now the ten-year-old child was coming north to be raised by her grandparents. If Eliza Morgan is, ultimately, not a convincing candidate for the author of *The Bondwoman's Narrative*, she did end up providing the escape routes of both Jane Johnson and Hannah Bond, as we will see.

Even though Morgan was compelled to go, she was probably excited to join the Brown household. She knew Reverend Brown to possess a "jovial personality," and the house he kept with Mrs. Brown was renowned for "the popularity of its hearth." By 1842, the Browns' three-story mansion was considered a landmark and "one of the finest downtown residences" in Washington (see Figure 24).[1] Morgan had visited the home before, in 1836, but at the time, she was seventeen and caring for a two-year-old. She probably saw little beyond the nursery. Now, as the reverend's carriage brought the Wheeler party into the back courtyard, Morgan saw the slave dwellings clustered near the family's stables. Their presence promised some measure of autonomy and community, and social travel. Just beyond the large kitchen building, the carriage stopped, met by Reverend Brown's manservant John Calvert. Eliza knew him from earlier visits to the property. She also knew the loft of the kitchen building, where she would likely find her lodgings with Sally and Kitty Bell, a mother and daughter who were Mrs. Brown's domestic servants.

Brown and his wife had been devastated when they lost their daughter, the first Mrs. Wheeler, just in the bloom of motherhood. (Mary Brown Wheeler had died of tuberculosis at age twenty-six.) Now the Browns embraced the return of their daughter's spirit through their grandchild,

FIGURE 24: The house of Obadiah Brown at 814 E Street NW, erected in 1821. Here, Eliza Morgan, Sally and Kitty Bell, and John Calvert served the Brown family and the congressmen who lodged with the Browns when Congress was in session.

Elizabeth. From girlhood, Elizabeth's mother, Mary, had shown herself to be a gifted thinker, and Reverend Brown raised her to be "equal in mind to men." Upon her death in 1836, Samuel Jordan Wheeler wrote of his departed sister-in-law, "[T]he whole circle of literature and science she trod with enthusiastic delight. In the Latin and Greek languages, she became more than proficient and could carry on a conversation in the former with classical accuracy and perfect facility."[2] Reverend Brown seemed to cherish the idea of developing the mind of his granddaughter Elizabeth similarly. Eliza Morgan likely knew there would be ample opportunity to learn through proximity to Elizabeth—or, as Crafts put it, "to improve myself by gathering up such crumbs of knowledge as I could" (*TBN* 11).

Contemplating the Browns' urban compound as the party unloaded from the carriage, Morgan may have felt for the first time the full force of her improved prospects. Her new appointment included serving congressional boarders who rented rooms at the Browns' lodgings. Such prominent members of the government frequently kept "servants," and a few of these might prove interesting to the twenty-three-year-old. Moreover, Reverend Brown maintained a successful pastorate at the First Baptist Church, and there was a separate First Colored Baptist Church to which Eliza would now be free to associate on Sundays. The household would be a lively gathering place for statesmen and congregants alike. And there would be a chance at better food.

For Eliza Morgan in 1842, the ghost of Mary Brown portended good things. It had not been so for Ellen Sully Wheeler. That year, Ellen did not make the trip. The second Mrs. John Hill Wheeler had birthed two surviving children of her own, sons, and the younger was still an infant. Further, the Wheeler family had just moved into the plantation house they called Ellangowan, in rural Lincoln County, North Carolina. There also seems to have been bad blood between Ellen Wheeler and her stepdaughter Elizabeth. Evidence suggests a possessiveness in Mrs. Wheeler's character that closed her to children besides those who were blood kin. Indeed, two years after Elizabeth's removal from Ellen Wheeler's circle, John Hill Wheeler's half brother, Junius, would write a letter (noted earlier) disavowing his half sister-in-law ("[The] wife of Col. J. H. Wheeler . . . ought not to bear the name . . . she is as snappish as an old bear cutting his wisdom teeth"). Junius, too, found release from the Wheeler household—in his case, by running away and joining the army.

For the second Mrs. Wheeler, her stepdaughter Elizabeth never really fit into the family. And so, perhaps it is not surprising that Ellen Sully Wheeler commissioned a painting of herself and her biological children *after* the departures of Elizabeth and Junius. On July 3, 1844, Ellen and her boys sat for a portrait in the Philadelphia studio of her famous father, the painter Thomas Sully.[3] The portrait was presented to Mrs. Wheeler the next Christmas, a gift she cherished her whole life. Three years after Elizabeth Brown Wheeler was shunted off to Washington, D.C., and Junius ran off to the Mexican-American War, Thomas Sully's portrait *Mrs. John Hill Wheeler and Her Two Sons* was installed at Ellangowan (see Figure 25). This was the image of herself that Ellen Sully Wheeler contrived to pass down to future generations. Crafts would sketch a very different portrait of "Mrs. John Hill Wheeler" with her pen.

II

In Washington, D.C., urban captives, like Eliza Morgan, Jane Johnson, and, later, Hannah Bond, lived in their enslavers' attics or backyards, usually locations where slaveholders could maintain a degree of surveillance. Reverend Brown's attractive property included a kitchen dependency where Morgan probably resided with Sally and Kitty Bell, the Browns' primary female domestic "servants." The slave quarters in the courtyard housed other domestic captives, like Reverend Brown's manservant John Calvert and the manservants of congressmen lodging at the Browns'. Jane Johnson and Hannah Bond would not be so lucky. Johnson served the Wheelers at their home at 444 H Street. Although the house was large and stately, it was not on par with the Browns' mansion. By the time Hannah Bond became enslaved by Mr. and Mrs. John Hill Wheeler, the Wheelers were renting rooms in the District from Sarah Childress Polk, the widow

FIGURE 25: Thomas Sully, *Mrs. John Hill Wheeler and Her Two Sons* (1844)

of former president James K. Polk. Again, the quarters were sufficiently well appointed, but as enslaved domestics, Johnson and Bond slept on the floor of an adjacent room that also functioned as storage space. The experiences of Johnson and Bond match the practical and uncomfortable arrangements suffered by many other enslaved domestics in the District, even those serving wealthy captors.

Housing for enslaved people "living out," or on the margins of city dwellings, was probably far worse. Hotel guests were disturbed to find that workers had no place to sleep; they simply lay down on the floor of a corridor, without blankets or bedding and, with no access to laundry or bathing facilities, wearing the same clothing they had worn all day. Just before the Civil War, Charles Lyell, the famous Scottish geologist, reported that he found Washington hotels improved: the hallways were now cleared of sleeping captives.[4] The presence of quarters for Reverend Brown's domestic captives may signal why prominent senators and congressmen chose to lodge at his home over the District's hotels.

Despite the poor living conditions for enslaved people, life in Washington was considered far more desirable than servitude on a plantation like Liberty Hall or Ellangowan. An exciting new world beckoned to Eliza Morgan and, later, Jane Johnson and Hannah Bond. In the District, Black domestic workers comprised the majority of the population. Suddenly, these enslaved women found themselves among scores of people just like them. Washington was literally a Black cosmopolitan city. The population was teeming with Black cooks, laundresses, and housekeepers. The expanded opportunity for community within such a dense population figures in Crafts's novel when Hannah encounters acquaintances in the city as she executes chores for Mrs. Wheeler. Whole chapters of the novel relate stories passed among the enslaved in the District, reflecting the importance of such networking.

Black Washingtonians experienced unparalleled opportunities for education and religious community. As early as 1829, members of the American Colonization Society, led by the Rev. Obadiah Brown, formed an African Education Society in the District with the express purpose of educating captives "placed at the society's disposal by their masters on the condition of their emigrating to [*sic*] Africa."[5] With repatriation to Africa mostly unheeded and unfunded, many enslaved people embraced Brown's African Education Society regardless of its colonization principles.

Although sources for gathering a picture of Black life in Washington, D.C., are scattered, the historical record does capture the high priority Blacks placed on education and religion. In 1842, a representative of the Anglican Church's Society for the Propagation of the Gospel in Foreign Parts attended a Sunday school in the District where 320 Black and "coloured" children received oral instruction in reading and spelling as well as the Bible. He observed eager children who showed an "intelligent appearance" and were ready to learn.[6]

Around this time, the same correspondent reported that there were eight schools with "colored" instructors, with as many as five hundred children enrolled; by 1855, there were eight hundred. Although such schools were clearly for those not enslaved, the opportunities of education among African Americans disseminated knowledge through the interconnecting networks of free and enslaved Black Washingtonians. In 1849, the "colored population of the District" created an educational union that included, according to the then-named *Sun of Baltimore*, eight schools, six hundred scholars, and seventy teachers.[7]

Education and religious instruction were inextricably linked for free and captive populations in Washington. District Blacks found companionship and emotional release in the religious experiences that frequently accompanied educational instruction. *The Washington Directory* for 1846 listed four churches: two Methodist, one Presbyterian, and one Baptist (Reverend Brown's congregation).[8] One visitor to D.C., while attending an Episcopal church, saw "richly dressed" women whom he called "Creoles"; their elegant clothing was rare enough to warrant comment. Their "bronze but beautifully regular countenances, formed a strong, contrast to the pink complexions of their fair, white sisters." Observers claimed that, among District Blacks, there were five hundred Roman Catholics and a few Episcopalians, but members of some of those churches had to endure segregated seating—in the case of Catholics, in "side galleries."[9] *The Washington Directory* did not canvass or count the Black churches that separated from their white congregations, but two important such congregations, "not liking their confined quarters in the gallery, and otherwise discontented" with the parent Ebenezer Methodist, were the First Colored Baptist Church, established in 1839, and "Little Ebenezer" Methodist, established "as early as 1820."[10]

Blacks, both captive and free, found diverse opportunities for worship. Sometimes they attended white churches even after a Black congregation had organized for separate service. For instance, Reverend Brown's First Baptist maintained about half its Black free and enslaved parishioners when the First Colored Baptist Church organized its separate church in 1839, now allowing Blacks to serve in leadership roles.[11] Because of racial practice, the parishioners who continued to worship in Brown's First Baptist could attend service only in the balcony seats. For many free and enslaved members, Blacks regarded separate churches as a small but important step toward autonomy. In 1841, District Blacks formed their own Presbyterian church, like the Baptists and Methodists before them, complaining that "the colored members of the Presbyterian and other evangelical churches in good standing do not enjoy, in our white churches, [equal] privileges."[12]

Black Presbyterians were following the lead of Reverend Brown's Black parishioners, becoming the third in the District to organize their own congregation. The First Colored Baptist Church stood just blocks from the home of Mr. and Mrs. John Hill Wheeler, on the site of the former church at Nineteenth and I Streets (see Figure 26), which white church members had abandoned for the new, expanded Tenth Street location that later became Ford's Theatre. The original site became an important and welcomed place for free and Black Washingtonians to congregate outside white control.[13] Here, Eliza Morgan would mix freely with other neighbors, including Jane Johnson and, later, Hannah Bond when they, too, came to serve in the neighborhood.

Again, the infusion of learning and religion in the District came to touch both the free and the enslaved in the city. According to historian David Goldfield, "The interaction [of the free and the enslaved] was greatest in the cities of the Upper South, where skin color, their own recent life as slaves, small numbers, and a harsh prejudice against free blacks combined to push the free into close association with the enslaved."[14]

Like the religious revivals popular in Bertie County, outdoor camp meetings near the District brought together Blacks and whites, enslaved people and free. In 1849, Black Methodists held a revival five miles outside Washington; it was primarily for "colored" Washingtonians, but white people also participated. If Eliza Morgan attended—a rebuke of sorts to Reverend Brown, the leading Baptist in the District—she would have witnessed what an attending clergyman reported as "remarkable spectacles of enthusiasm," with shouts of "Glory" and "Amen" and prolonged hymn singing. "The assembled thousands become wonderfully excited; . . . they scream, jump, roar, clap their hands, and even fall into swoons, convulsions, and death-like trances."[15]

FIGURE 26: Marian Alexander Jones sketch of the First Colored Baptist Church, drawn from photographs in the possession of First Baptist Church of the City of Washington, D.C.

Slaveholders looked on these gatherings skeptically, fearful that such a community gathering could fuel antislavery sentiments. Certainly, this would have been John Hill Wheeler's perspective. Such views sometimes held the authority of the state. For instance, Maryland restricted free Blacks from attending camp meetings, requiring that a white clergyman either be the preacher or provide written permission for Black congregants to attend a service led by a Black preacher. An observer sympathetic to slaveholders felt that District captives neglected their duties and became "troublesome and unmanageable" after attending such gatherings. In despair over religious revivals that welcomed Blacks, a Virginian observed that "it was the greatest misfortune that could happen . . . to have a [N-word] turn Christian."[16] Mr. Saddler, the slave trader, voices as much in Crafts's novel when he says, "I hardly think that religion will do her much good, or make her more subservient. . . . On the whole I should prefer that she wasn't religious because religion is so apt to make people stubborn; it gives them such notions of duty, and that sets them up so, you'll even hear them telling that all mankind are made of one blood, and equal in the sight of God" (*TBN* 108–9).

Methodism in the District proved especially attractive to Black religious seekers, possibly because of its association with the promise of freedom. A fugitive captive living in Canada remembered that his enslaver prohibited him from attending his Methodist church, even though he was a member: "You shan't go to that church—they'll put the devil in you," meaning that "they would put me up to running off."[17] For the Maryland captive John Thompson, Methodism meant a language and "manner so plain" that anyone could comprehend it. Such a gospel "spread from plantation to plantation," where many bondpeople were converted—to the consternation of their owners, who sought to end religious services for their captives. As Thompson experienced religion in slavery: "It brought glad tidings to the poor bondman; it bound up the brokenhearted; it opened the prison doors to them that were bound and let the captive go free."[18]

William Faux, a British citizen who visited a mostly Black Methodist congregation in the District, recorded the "pious prayers" and "sensible, cheerful singing of the poor negroes." Finnish-born writer and reformer Fredrika Bremer visited what must have been Little Ebenezer Methodist in 1853 and observed that the members were well dressed and compassionate. When the preacher announced the pending sale of one of the enslaved congregants, Bremer observed church members instantly taking up an offering seeking to purchase the freedom of the man so that he could remain in Washington. "A pewter plate was set upon a stool in the church," she records, "and one silver piece after another rang joyfully upon it."[19]

For recreation, Blacks did go to the theater, where they were segregated and forced to sit in a balcony set aside for them. Sometimes, if the subject matter was racially sensitive, only whites could attend the performance. For instance, when *The Gladiator* was performed in Washington in 1838, Blacks were banned from the showing because it featured

Spartacus and a Roman slave revolt. Records show that African Americans in the District held balls, which must have been grand affairs, for they were expensive to attend: in one case, a dollar for a couple and fifty cents for a single person. Those holding "an assembly or ball in their homes had . . . to state [the] number of guests expected and the hour at which it would end," and they were subject to the enormous fine of ten dollars if they did not have a permit from the mayor.[20]

Eliza Morgan found a much wider field to flourish in now that she was serving in the Brown household, just as Jane Johnson and, then, Hannah Bond would when they joined her in the District. Still, there is next to no record relating the life and times of Eliza Morgan for the more than twenty years she spent in captivity in Washington, D.C., first in the household of Obadiah Brown, where she served as waiting maid to her mistress Elizabeth Brown Wheeler, and then in the household of George Nancreade Beale, who married Elizabeth Brown Wheeler in 1851. Eliza, at the time, interacted with her former captor John Hill Wheeler when he visited his daughter. For instance, Wheeler notes in his diary visiting Elizabeth Wheeler Beale in D.C. the day of the birth of her third child, John Wheeler Beale. On August 26, 1856, John Hill Wheeler writes, "My daughter presented us with a fine boy at 6 o'clock—to be called John Wheeler."[21] Even though Eliza Morgan mostly raised Elizabeth Brown Wheeler as a surrogate mother and now became a primary caregiver for John Hill Wheeler's new grandson, there is virtually no mention of her in family records. But that does not diminish her life—a life as important, loving, and helpful as any among those whom she served.

The historical record does sketch an important event, however, that touched Reverend Brown's household and Eliza, too. On April 15, 1848, seventy-seven captives attempted to escape Washington, D.C., on a schooner called the *Pearl*. Their plan was to sail south on the Potomac River, then north up the Chesapeake Bay and the Delaware River to New Jersey, where planners could assist in placing the freedom seekers. The distance was nearly 225 miles, and the sheer size of the escape party was designed to strike a blow against policy makers in the nation's capital.

Eliza maintained daily intimacy with one of the planners of the escape, John Calvert, Reverend Brown's manservant. Another frequent visitor to the household was Paul Jennings, who also helped mastermind the attempted escape. Jennings was a well-known Black congregant at Reverend Brown's First Baptist Church. Ultimately, Eliza did not risk an escape, but the personal connections she forged through Calvert, Jennings, and the white abolitionist William L. Chaplin seem to have connected her to the same Underground Railroad network that assisted Jane Johnson and Hannah Crafts when they escaped the Wheelers in 1855 (Johnson) and 1857 (Crafts).

III

Today, the pioneering work of three leaders of the District's Underground Railroad is little known, but Thomas and Elizabeth Smallwood and Charles T. Torrey helped establish the routes that ultimately brought freedom to Johnson and Crafts and hundreds of other D.C.-based captives. They also pioneered the original plans that led to the attempted escape of seventy-seven fugitives on the schooner *Pearl*.

When Charles T. Torrey (1813–1846) arrived in Washington in 1841, he resolved to attend only Black churches as a way to learn about and become a member of the community he felt called to help. In fact, he was infiltrating Black organizations as part of a radical plan to challenge the institution of slavery—first, in the nation's capital, but also as a model for challenging bondage everywhere. Torrey's plan to encourage captives to run away was part of a broader strategy. Because the District of Columbia was both the center of the federal government and the center of the slave trade, and because the federal government had jurisdiction over the District, the District was "the Achilles' heel of the entire institution," Torrey reasoned. The existence of slavery in the nation's capital, he observed, was "a sort of symbol and proof of its control over the government of the country." If large numbers of captives could be induced to run away from Washington and the surrounding regions of Maryland and Virginia, then keeping enslaved people in that region would become increasingly less secure and attractive.[22]

Born in Massachusetts in 1813, the Rev. Charles T. Torrey lost his parents early in life and was raised by his grandmother, who was an abolitionist. Torrey trained in religious studies at Yale University and joined the Anglican ministry, serving in several New England locations before coming south. Once he arrived in Washington, D.C., in 1841, he began assisting fleeing captives from the city, Virginia, and Maryland—particularly nearby Prince George's County, the county with Maryland's largest enslaved population. Tactically, Torrey tapped into the underground efforts of Black Washingtonians who had already forged escape routes around the District and in Maryland. In 1842, he joined his contacts with those already operated by a former Prince George's County captive, Thomas Smallwood (1801–1883), and his wife, Elizabeth (1811–1876).

As an enslaved boy, Smallwood learned to read and write while in the possession of the Rev. John B. Ferguson, who agreed to release him in his twenties if Smallwood purchased his value, placed at five hundred dollars. At the time, Smallwood had been hired out to work at the Washington Navy Yard, and there he gained the necessary funds for his manumission in 1831. While working there, he attended Little Ebenezer Methodist Church, where he met Elizabeth, a free woman of color and an active church member. Here, too, Smallwood engaged many other workers from the shipyard. After buying his freedom, he used his artisan's skills as a successful shoemaker and devoted his free time to assisting others seeking release from slavery. Elizabeth was essential to her husband's activities, bringing to their shared work her connections among free domestic Black women and her leadership among the women of Little Ebenezer Methodist.[23]

Torrey recorded his attendance at Little Ebenezer shortly after his arrival in 1841. As he reported, some members of the congregation were enslaved, others free, "and, when one of the poor women . . . spoke of the 'persecution' she endured, with sobs, I felt my heart filled with new energy to make war upon that hateful institution that so crushes the disciples of the Lord to the earth."[24] Torrey was largely unknown at the time to white authorities, but he was developing a career as an aggressive and politically strategic abolitionist that has only recently come to light, and he is now regarded as "the most successful least known conductor of the Underground Railroad."[25]

The plan Torrey proposed in 1842 was substantially different from the activities of other leading abolitionists and Underground Railroad facilitators. Men like Levi Coffin, Thomas Garrett, and John Rankin did not encourage or incite captives to run away but, rather, served freedom seekers after they had already initiated or planned an escape. Torrey's strategy included both encouraging captives to abscond and then transporting them to freedom. This was key, because men like Torrey helped to connect antislavery financing to the escape networks Blacks had already forged. But his plans could be effective only if they built on the underground activities of Blacks themselves, like the Smallwoods.

Elizabeth Smallwood seems to have become convinced of Torrey's sincerity, and she made the initial contact with him through his landlady, Mrs. Francis Padgett, at whose boardinghouse she sometimes hid escaping captives. The Smallwoods' original operation depended upon collecting fugitives who arrived one, two, or three at a time and then hiding them until there was a considerable number ready to risk transportation to contacts in Pennsylvania. In the 1930s, former captives remembered "churches whose basements served as layovers, and out-of-the-way Georgetown homes that were specially marked for the fugitive."[26] Little Ebenezer and the First Colored Baptist Church were central organizing sites and even stopovers for such activities. Thomas Smallwood's goal was to get fugitives to his contacts in Pennsylvania, a journey he claimed required three nights of hard walking from the District. Smallwood arranged safe places along the way that made it possible for escaping captives to reach freedom. He also relied on the aid of a freedman, Jacob Gibbs, who helped direct the Black underground in Baltimore.

Torrey became valuable because he knew how to raise money in the North, and his white abolitionist contacts could help extend the reach of

Smallwood's and Gibbs's operations into Central New York and all the way to Canada. During the active years of their collaboration, Smallwood and Torrey carried larger and larger parties to freedom, now hiring horses and wagons and carriages to provide transport for women and children, too, who were harder to move without conveyances: the sight of a party of women and children was always more conspicuous than a smaller party of "colored" men. Smallwood and Torrey's first joint fugitive party was a group of fifteen men, women, and children whom they successfully conveyed to Canada. Between 1842 and 1843, Smallwood and Torrey moved an estimated fifty men, women, and children to freedom. Shortly before his death, Torrey maintained that he had been engaged in freeing "nearly 400 slaves," although that number must include many unconnected with his efforts alongside Smallwood.[27]

Still, Smallwood's and Torrey's activities were disruptive enough to become the focus of white enslavers in Washington, D.C., especially the pro-slavery John H. Goddard, who directed the night watch patrol for the District. Goddard's agents bribed and encouraged treachery by some of Smallwood's network, helping to expose part of the group's activities. As a result, in 1843, Torrey relocated to Albany, New York, and the Smallwoods were convinced to move to Canada to escape arrest. By October 1843, the Smallwood family had settled in Toronto when four escaped men whom Smallwood had already assisted approached him seeking a mission to rescue family members back in Washington. In 1844, Torrey and Smallwood reunited for this ill-fated mission, one that led to Torrey's arrest and imprisonment in Maryland and Smallwood's near apprehension by Goddard before he made his way back to Toronto.

Torrey would die of tuberculosis in jail two years later, still serving his sentence for the failed 1844 mission, but the network he and Smallwood had assembled lived on.[28] After his near-fatal capture, Smallwood retired from his underground activities and focused his attention on building a life and a Black community in his adoptive home. The Smallwoods lived the rest of their lives in Toronto, where Thomas and Elizabeth operated a sawmill and became prominent members of the city's Black leadership.

Smallwood died of old age there on May 10, 1883. At the age of eighty-two, he was buried next to his wife, Elizabeth, who predeceased him.[29]

Inspired by Torrey and Smallwood's work, abolitionist William L. Chaplin moved to Washington, D.C., in 1846 to continue their efforts there. Meanwhile, leaders from Little Ebenezer and the First Colored Baptist Church kept the Smallwoods' escape network functioning as they assisted a slow but steady stream of bondmen and -women escaping the District. Known leaders of this next generation include Paul Jennings and John Calvert. By 1848, Jennings, Calvert, and Chaplin were prepared to strike a definitive blow against slavery, one first envisioned by the now-martyred Torrey. Eliza Morgan may have been part of the organizing members centered at the First Colored Baptist Church. Her fellow captives with whom she shared space in the loft of Reverend Brown's kitchen building, Sally and Kitty Bell, may have held a familial tie with another organizer of the plot, Daniel Bell. The *Pearl* disaster would prove particularly catastrophic for the extended Bell family.

IV

For Washington, D.C.–based captives, the threat of being sold south persisted. Church records demonstrate how very real the danger remained, no matter a captive's current circumstances. Take, for instance, Mt. Zion United Methodist Church in Georgetown, whose congregation was largely African American. The registrar book is marked by cases of members bought and sold away. Next to dozens of names in the 1850s are notations such as "lost," "sold to Georgia trader," "sold to the South," "sold and gone," "sold." The power of the threat of sale was a tool slaveowners used frequently, as contemporary letters demonstrate. President James Monroe is one prominent example. In a letter to his overseer, Monroe ordered a male slave to be whipped, calling the targeted man "a worthless scoundrel." Monroe added, "Tell him that you are authorized to sell him to the New Orleans Purchasers, and that you will do it, for the next offense."[30]

Even free Blacks were liable to be kidnapped or sold after false arrest.

In 1843, William Jones petitioned Congress from the Lorton, Virginia, jail, near D.C., claiming that though he was free, he had been apprehended and placed into the prison and advertised for sale. Captives might be sold for any number of reasons: to meet debt obligations, to settle family property arrangements, or for punishment. The District proved to be an active slave market, poised as a clearinghouse for moving a surplus of Upper South captives to the hungry markets of the Lower South. Horace Mann claimed that Washington had become "the Congo of America": "Virginia and Maryland are to the slave trade what the interior of Africa once was. . . . [T]his District is the great Government barracoon [i.e., temporary slave barracks], whence coffles are driven across the country to Alabama or Texas, as slave ships once bore their dreadful cargoes of agony and woe across the Atlantic."[31]

Eliza Morgan would have found more informed captives in the city. They knew that life on a cotton or sugar plantation was much worse than life in Washington. The abolitionist congressman Joshua Giddings maintained that a slave working in cotton fields would survive for seven years; on a sugar plantation, for only five. One visitor observed that the very name "New Orleans" struck "terror into the slave and free Negroes of the Middle States," who did not want to view separation of families as inevitable just because they were in bondage. Coffles regularly passed down Pennsylvania Avenue and other main streets as the District became an important crossroads for America's interstate slave trade.[32]

In her novel, Hannah Crafts makes powerful note of this:

> I was admiring the splendid show made by the President's House and the Capitol; the quantity of Congress men, Senators, navy and Army officers going to and fro; the number of vehicles containing fine Ladies the wives and daughters of foreign Ministers and distinguished strangers. I say I was admiring these no less than wondering at the extraordinary contrast to them presented by some wretches in rags, who appeared to be searching for bones, pins, or other refuse among the rubbish which had accumulated in several places when an incident

> occurred which affected me greatly. A negro designed for sale had broken away from his master and the assistants, and taken refuge beneath the equestrian statue of Jackson, that lover of freedom; and thence he was dragged, though shrieking and praying, and struggling, manacles placed on his limbs, and borne back to the market. (*TBN* 201)

The observation may have been shared by Eliza Morgan—or, perhaps, Crafts witnessed this particular display between 1856 and 1857. Such disturbances were common enough. Slave coffles passing the Capitol Building betrayed the prevalence of the slave trade for members of Congress. Congressman John Van Dyke of New Jersey denounced the "droves of miserable half-naked negroes, bound together," whom he saw "driven along the streets like cattle or swine." Giddings declaimed in Congress, "I have witnessed the chained coffle as they passed by the very walls of the building in which we are now sitting; where the star-spangled banner which floats over us, threw its shadow in bitter irony upon those victims of your barbarous law."[33]

The slave trade flourished in Washington, D.C., because distressed farmers in nearby Maryland and Virginia were looking to sell their human property to the many traders attracted to the region, who assisted in moving captives to the Deep South, where their labor was more valuable. Solomon Northup observed from his own experience, "The voices of patriotic representatives boasting of freedom and equality, and the rattling of the poor slave's chains, almost commingled."[34]

Slavery in the District had been a source of deep antagonism for almost two decades when the *Pearl* arrived in the spring of 1848. A majority of Washingtonians seemed eager to silence opposition to human bondage, choosing, instead, to ignore the trade. A much smaller number fought vigorously to end slavery there. These two views exploded into the open when antislavery activists organized a mass escape plot aboard the *Pearl*. And Eliza Morgan would find herself in immediate proximity to the participants and planners, including Black antislavery leaders John Calvert, Paul Jennings, and Daniel Bell.

V

On April 15, 1848, the schooner *Pearl* moored at the dock of the Seventh Street wharf in Washington, D.C., ready to take on passengers. The wharf was situated in a less traveled area of Southwest D.C. and was selected for its secluded location. It featured a high riverbank, expansive fields, and few buildings, to ensure low foot traffic, providing the *Pearl* crew privacy for her intended cargo. Secrecy was essential for the schooner's passengers.[35]

On the evening of the fifteenth, conveyances arrived at and departed from the obscure wharf as seventy-seven enslaved people silently stepped aboard the schooner. Arriving passengers remained belowdecks, limiting the appearance of activity. By midnight, thirty-eight men, twenty-six women, and thirteen children had packed themselves tightly into the cargo hold, all willing to risk their lives to reach freedom. After midnight in darkness, the *Pearl* lifted anchor and inched along the Potomac River, seeking Chesapeake Bay, where the captain planned to proceed north to Frenchtown, New Jersey. Changing tides and unfavorable winds, however, slowed the vessel.

Black leaders and antislavery activists had planned the escape route months earlier. Free African Americans in D.C. worked with antislavery advocates to establish a plot to secure the freedom of dozens of enslaved friends and family in the District. Free Black men Daniel Bell and Samuel Edmonson are credited with being the primary organizers, along with Paul Jennings and John Calvert.

Jennings had been the captive of James and Dolley Madison. At the White House during the Madison administration, he acted as the president's personal valet and the First Lady's dining room servant. He served in the next administration, of President James K. Polk, while still a captive of Dolley Madison. In 1847, Jennings became the property of Massachusetts senator Daniel Webster, and the two negotiated his manumission once he purchased his freedom by paying Webster his value. By the time the *Pearl* began its journey into the Chesapeake, Jennings had nearly settled this "debt." Indeed, he was risking his own path to freedom by assisting others. Records show that Jennings conspired with Daniel Bell, Samuel Edmonson, and white abolitionist William L. Chaplin to arrange passage on the *Pearl* for nearly eighty captives. The fact that he and John Calvert attended Brown's First Colored Baptist Church, where Eliza Morgan also worshipped, suggests just how closely the plot reached Eliza Morgan's domestic sphere.

On March 25, William L. Chaplin, leader of the Underground Railroad cell in Washington, D.C., alerted Gerrit Smith, the likely financier for the escape venture, that the network of area captives was ready to move. In his letter to Smith, Chaplin explained that "there are not less than 75" enslaved Washingtonians who were ready to escape and that he was "expecting the arrival of a vessel from Philadelphia" that could hold fifty or more captives.[36] On behalf of the African Americans organizing the escape—Daniel Bell, Samuel Edmonson, John Calvert, and Paul Jennings—Chaplin had hired Daniel Drayton, who lived in Philadelphia, Pennsylvania, to procure the vessel to carry out the plan. Drayton had previous experience assisting enslaved people with escape and had helped an enslaved woman and her children seeking transportation out of D.C. during the summer of 1847. He was familiar with the route and agreed to take the job.

Drayton arranged a contract with Edward Sayres to captain the *Pearl* out of the District. The names and numbers of passengers remained obscure to Drayton and Sayers, both to protect the identities of the enslaved and to distance the two white men from culpability in the plot. An additional crew member, Chester English, was employed as a cook, but he was not informed of the nature of the ship's cargo until just before the passengers began to arrive.

The discovery of the plot by slaveholders remains a mystery. Daniel Drayton observes in his memoir that an unnamed "colored hackman" turned informer. According to Drayton, a hired carriage man delivered two of the *Pearl*'s fugitives to the Seventh Street dock and then exchanged information about the escape plot with officials for a financial reward. A separate source named Anthony Blow, a blacksmith who worked alongside Daniel Bell, as the informer, after he was interrogated by police. Other sources identify Judson Diggs, a formerly enslaved man, as the one who betrayed the plot. The different accounts all point to betrayal due to the public nature of the plan.

Among the seventy-seven enslaved people hiding in the hold of the stalled *Pearl* was Ellen Stewart, who was fifteen and one of former First Lady Dolley Madison's enslaved maids. Stewart had been slated to be sold to a slave trader, but had disappeared among the colored population of the District, probably with the assistance of Jennings, who would have known Ellen well from his past service to the former First Lady. Ellen was on the run and successfully evaded capture for five months prior to boarding the *Pearl*; now she prayed with the others for the winds to shift and the ship to move.

At the mouth of the Potomac River, however, adverse winds from the north continued to slow the *Pearl*. Unable to continue, the schooner was forced to anchor in the early morning hours near Point Lookout, Maryland. Meanwhile, forty-one slave owners in Washington, Maryland, and Virginia awoke the next day to discover seventy-seven captives missing. Banding together on the steamer *Salem*, a posse of thirty-five armed white men, representing the justice of the peace, headed out in hot pursuit of the *Pearl*. Winds continued to pour down the Chesapeake on the morning of April 16, while the *Salem*, under steam power, advanced unchecked in pursuit of the *Pearl*. Soon, the *Salem* aligned herself directly alongside the schooner, while members of the posse jumped onto the ship's deck. The *Pearl* and her passengers and crew were apprehended.

If Eliza Morgan and Sally and Kitty Bell had contemplated joining John Calvert and Daniel Bell and his family, their fate must have been particularly painful for the women to witness. Shackled and led through the streets of the District, the fugitives and the schooner's crew became targets for public anger. In his memoir, Drayton describes the danger of the scene: "We met an immense mob of several thousand persons coming down Four-and-a-half street, with the avowed intention of carrying us up before the capitol, and making an exhibition of us there. The noise and confusion was [*sic*] very great. It seemed as if the time for the lynching had come."[37] The *Pearl*'s crew and passengers were placed in a jail outside the city before mob violence could claim them.

Riots ensued for the next three days, with much of the outrage directed at Drayton and Sayres for having participated in assisting the captives to escape. The Lorton, Virginia, jail where Drayton, Sayres, and the captured runaways were imprisoned became a focus for public anger. Angry crowds also gathered at the offices of the *National Era*, an abolitionist newspaper, which the public perceived to be a part of the plot. President Polk was forced to intervene by demanding an increased police presence near the capital and around the Lorton prison. Polk's diary entry for April 20, 1848, observes, "I told Mr. Whittlesey that I would cooperate with the City authorities, if necessary, in any proper steps to preserve the public peace & to cause the laws to be respected."[38] Such executive intervention was necessary to quell public violence as tensions between pro- and antislavery groups continued to escalate near the nation's capital.

To ease the unrest, most of the *Pearl* fugitives were moved to Baltimore slave pens. Baltimore was probably chosen over Alexandria, Virginia, because it was a safer distance from relatives and friends of those freshly recaptured. From Baltimore, many of the fugitives were sold and, later, transported to the Deep South to toil on cotton plantations. One D.C. slave trader, named Hope Slatter, purchased fifty of the enslaved people, including Ellen Stewart, who was prepared to be resold south.[39] Slatter's Baltimore-based operation specialized in purchasing discounted slaves, or captives thought to be escape risks, whom he then "broke" or "improved" to prepare them for the New Orleans market. In the case of Stewart and the *Pearl* fugitives, Slatter moved the captives to Walter L. Campbell's slave pen, a few blocks south in Baltimore. At the time, Campbell was in negotiation to buy Slatter's business.[40]

Antislavery proponents organized fund-raising events to be able to purchase freedom for some of the enslaved prisoners. Baltimore physician and antislavery publisher Dr. Joseph Evans Snodgrass joined forces with William L. Chaplin to purchase Ellen's freedom. With the assistance of antislavery organizers, Daniel Bell was able to purchase his wife, Mary, their son Thomas, and another child. But these efforts could reach only so far. Seven other Bell children were sold south.[41]

And what about Obadiah Brown's manservant John Calvert? He holds the distinction of being the only fugitive from the *Pearl* who is recorded in a ledger of runaway slaves that was discovered in 1991. That year, an employee of the D.C. Department of Corrections found a ledger book propping up another book in an old display case in the abandoned Lorton prison where the captives from the *Pearl* were first taken. The volume, titled *D.C. Department of Corrections Runaway Slave Book*, holds entries beginning in June 1848.[42] That record states that John Calvert was released from the jail to slave trader William Williams on June 22, 1848; he is noted as being committed on April 18, 1848, by order of Justice of the Peace Hampton C. Williams. Earlier ledgers, if they can be found, likely recorded details for the other prisoners from the *Pearl*, most of whom, according to contemporary accounts, were removed from the Lorton prison and transported to Baltimore by train on April 21, 1848. There is no explanation for why Calvert was incarcerated for two months, unlike other captives, and retained near Washington. Perhaps Reverend Brown agreed to allow Calvert a chance to arrange his affairs with family members before his sale south. Whatever Brown permitted, the penalty he enforced was harsh. Calvert entered Williams's notorious Yellow House prison on June 22, where he waited for the slave trader Williams to gather a fresh packet of captives to ship to New Orleans.[43] This was the likely fate that would have befallen Eliza Morgan and Sally and Kitty Bell if they had risked escape on the *Pearl*.

The most graphic, terrifying description of Yellow House comes to us from the kidnapped Solomon Northup, in his memoir, *Twelve Years a Slave* (1853). Northup, a free Black man from the North, was lured to Washington in 1841 by two white men promising him lucrative employment. Once they got him to the capital, the men drugged Northup into unconsciousness, and he awoke in chains in the basement dungeon of Williams's Yellow House. Northup vividly described the scene when his captor, slave trader James H. Birch, arrived and claimed he was a fugitive from Georgia to be sold for Birch's clients. When Northup protested, Birch administered a severe thrashing with a paddle and, when that broke, a rope. Northup, like most who passed through the Yellow House's iron gate, was destined for sale to the Deep South.[44] In the summer of 1848, when John Calvert left Williams's gates, he, too, found himself on a slave ship heading in the opposite direction from the *Pearl*'s bid for freedom. The Rev. Obadiah Brown's "servant" disappears from the historical record at that point.

VI

Eliza Morgan likely stayed connected to Paul Jennings and, potentially, other area Black leaders even after the disastrous *Pearl* incident. Indeed, six months later, Jennings was accepted into full membership at First Baptist. It would seem Reverend Brown did not know of his collaboration with Calvert. On December 8, 1848, Brown records in his own hand in the church's minutes book the executive committee's judgment to receive Jennings as a full member of the congregation: "The Pastor stated that he had written to the Church at Blue Run, Orange County, Virginia, relative to the case of Paul Jennings (colored), and had received a letter of dismission for him; which was read, and Paul received into this church."[45] The "letter of dismission" would have been a careful statement attesting to Jennings's standing and fellowship in his prior faith community and an avowal of his suitability for full release into Brown's church. Ironically, two years earlier, Jennings had been denied acceptance by Brown and the executive committee, with Brown writing, "The outward conduct of Paul is represented as being correct, but the committee are not satisfied that he has yet become thoroughly sensible of the nature and magnitude of his sin, nor experienced true evangelical repentance."[46]

Clearly, word of Jennings's involvement in planning the *Pearl* escape went unnoticed in the time before his full acceptance into the congregation. The fact that the Black organizers from First Baptist kept their role in the *Pearl* confidential shows the shared purpose and trust within the Black community. It also shows the fortitude of Calvert, who never confessed details of the plot in order to receive a lighter sentence from Brown. For Jennings, his baptism into Brown's church must have involved a deeper calling than Brown himself was aware of. The "nature and magnitude" of Brown's own "sin" were apparent in the loss of Jennings's friend John Calvert. Jennings seems to have consecrated himself to effect "true evangelical repentance" by continuing his antislavery activities at Brown's church, one of the most important contact points for Washington's antislavery community. Jennings now set his sights on avenging Calvert's loss by spiriting away other captives to honor his friend's sacrifice.

When Jane Johnson came to live at the Wheelers' H Street house, and Crafts at Mrs. Polk's mansion on I Street nearby, both must have engaged Jennings, who became a leading figure in Brown's church, a man with influence among white parishioners and with access to important escape routes. Likely, Jennings is the contact point that first linked Jane Johnson to William Still in Philadelphia and to the abolitionist William Nell in Boston. Jennings's collaboration with William L. Chaplin during the *Pearl* escape attempt may help explain why Hannah Crafts made her way to Cortland County, New York (Chaplin's home base in 1857), and then to New York Central College (where Chaplin served on the board). Horace Craft's farm was probably part of Jennings's network. Further, Jennings and Chaplin held contacts with Black community members in Burlington, New Jersey, near where the author came to reside after her successful escape.

As for Eliza Morgan, her decision not to flee on the *Pearl* proved a smart one. Instead of capture and sale to the Deep South (as with Calvert), she followed Elizabeth Brown Wheeler into her new home upon Wheeler's 1851 marriage to George Nancreade Beale. For Morgan, her continued servitude to Elizabeth would mean providing child care for the Beales, beginning with the birth of their first child, a daughter, in 1852. The family resided at the Beales' "Bloomington" mansion in the District and also at their Montgomery County "cottage," part of the family's

Indian Spring plantation. The property in Maryland was described in 1854 as "wholly covered with pines large enough to be cut for wood, interspersed with beautiful chestnut trees. The land lies well, and the soil is kind."[47] The Beale family, with Eliza in tow, resorted to its shaded groves and pure spring waters during the summers, a welcome retreat from the heat and humidity of Washington.

From 1854 through 1857, when Jane Johnson and then Hannah Bond served the Wheelers in the District, Eliza, Jane, and Hannah overlapped frequently, as Wheeler's diary entries show. Mr. and Mrs. John Hill Wheeler visited Mrs. Elizabeth Wheeler Beale almost daily when both families were in town. John Hill Wheeler seems to have taken an especially strong interest in his grandson John Wheeler Beale, a lifeline, perhaps, back to his beloved Mary Brown. No letters seem to have been preserved among Morgan, Johnson, and Crafts, but it is not impossible that they existed. The lifelong paths of all three crossed frequently enough that bonds of friendship are not unimaginable.

After the Civil War, Eliza Morgan seems to have taken the name "Eliza Brown," probably from her marriage to a male captive while associated with Reverend Brown's compound in the District. Records are incredibly sparse for Eliza after slavery, as they are for her whole existence, but she appears to have followed her husband in death after suffering a stroke in 1879. She was sixty years old, a widow, and living in the District working as a "washerwoman" at the time.[48] With Hannah Crafts living in Burlington, New Jersey, and surviving into the 1910s, I like to imagine Eliza and Hannah visiting each other after freedom, in the spirit of Crafts's own joyful conclusion to her novel: "Need I describe the little church where we all go to meeting, and the happiness we experience in listening to the words of Gospel truth; and as I could not, if I tried, sufficiently set forth the goodness of those about me . . . I will let the reader picture it all to his imagination" (*TBN* 246).

CHAPTER 16

THE BONDWOMAN'S NARRATIVE AND BLEAK HOUSE

I

PART OF THE CHALLENGE OF reading *The Bondwoman's Narrative* is engaging the work as autobiographical fiction. How does our knowledge of Hannah Crafts's life—and lack of knowledge, too—affect our reading of the work? And what do we make of the author's intertextual play on Charles Dickens's *Bleak House*? For the last twenty years, scholars have grappled with these questions. One of my guiding stars for this research has been the work of Hollis Robbins. We formed a friendship as we researched Hannah Crafts together, swapping new discoveries, trading scholarship, and talking on the phone regularly across the decades. Two primary questions have animated our work: Does Crafts's fiction tell us as much about her life as the historical record? And how do we properly assess the inventiveness of her art?

We both agree: Crafts fashioned the turning point of her novel based on her experiences in Washington, D.C., and on the novel that influenced her most, Dickens's *Bleak House*. Robbins's scholarship sets the arc, and I follow her work closely in this chapter.[1]

Two thirds of the way through *The Bondwoman's Narrative*, Hannah is sent out on a rainy day in the District to procure for her mistress a suddenly fashionable box of facial powder. A "great Italian chemist, a Signor with an unpronounceable name," Crafts writes, "had discovered or rather invented an impalpable powder, fine, highly scented, and luxurious, that applied to the hands and face was said to produce the most marvellous effect" (*TBN* 163). Crafts describes Hannah trekking through sleet, mud, and gloom to the chemist's shop on Pennsylvania Avenue to purchase the very last box for Mrs. Wheeler. Upon her return to the "splendid mansion" the Wheelers occupied, she glimpses a familiar "coat of seedy black." It is the novel's villain, Mr. Trappe. Hannah is distracted and falls on the paving stones. Mr. Trappe helps her up, and Hannah notes that his presence is "ominous of evil," before she rushes home. Delivering the powder to Mrs. Wheeler's apartment, Hannah hears Mr. Wheeler telling his wife that a new government post has opened; the only problem is that he holds a troubled history with the hiring agent. Would Mrs. Wheeler use her feminine charms to assist him in his bid for gaining the office? "I'll go now, this very evening," Mrs. Wheeler decides, eager for the chance to try her beautifying powder (*TBN* 170). At the last minute, she asks for her new bottle of smelling salts.[2]

When Mrs. Wheeler returns later that evening, her face is completely black. "It must have been the powder," Hannah observes. "The powder was white I thought," Mrs. Wheeler responds. Hannah continues:

> The powder certainly is white, and yet it may posses [*sic*] such chemical properties as occasion blackness. Indeed I recently saw in the newspapers some accounts of a chemist who having been jilted by a lady very liberal in the application of powder to her face had invented as a method of revenge a certain kind of smelling bottle of which the fumes would suddenly blacken the whitest skin provided the said cosmetic had been previously applied.

"You wretch!" Mrs. Wheeler cries. "Why didn't you tell me of this before?" (*TBN* 172). Mrs. Wheeler, it seems, had been on her knees asking an agent for a government appointment for her husband while in the guise of a black woman. The Wheelers, mortified, return to North Carolina to avoid disgrace.[3] There, Hannah is punished by being forced into the slave huts of the Wheelers' plantation, and "Bill," a field slave, is set to be her husband. Threatened with this forced marriage, Hannah decides to risk escape.

As Robbins has noted, the incident seems perfectly believable as Crafts portrays it in the novel. The powder appears to include silver nitrate, a substance commonly used by domestic captives like Hannah. The author would have been very familiar with the translucent powdered crystal that, when put into contact with organic substances such as skin, can effect a blackish-purple color. As a house servant, Crafts must have experienced the properties of silver nitrate blackening her fingers and clothes when she was forced to polish silver and service ware for the Bonds and Wheelers.[4] Moreover, mixtures of silver nitrate were commonly used as a hair dye. Indeed, Crafts likely knew that enslavers used the substance to blacken hair to prepare bondpeople for sale, hoping to enhance their market value by making them look younger. Such enhancing arts likely befell the captives of the *Pearl*, as they were a regular practice employed by slave traders like Slatter and Williams.

Some elements of the scene are clearly based on real life. At the time that Crafts served the Wheelers in D.C., the Stabler-Leadbetter Apothecary was a popular cosmetics retailer with a location near the Capitol that served the District's leading families. The scene of fetching the beautifying powder from "a shop on Pennsylvania Avenue, much frequented by the slaves of fashionable Ladies" matches the author's likely experiences (*TBN* 162). There are many other important direct parallels to what can be uncovered about the author's life. Similar to the depiction in the novel, the Wheelers returned to North Carolina with Crafts, to Wheeler House and Liberty Hall, in March 1857. Like Hannah in the novel, the author appears to have been punished while attending Mrs. Wheeler at the

Wheelers' plantation outside Murfreesboro. Quite possibly, just as Hannah is demoted in the novel, Crafts, too, found herself placed in the slave huts at Liberty Hall, where there was an enslaved man named "Bill" fitting the age of the character in the novel.

As elsewhere, fact and fiction converge in the pages of *The Bondwoman's Narrative*. Still, there is a great deal of literary invention at work, too. There is no record of Mrs. Wheeler accidentally presenting herself in blackface to important Washington leaders and their wives. Such an embarrassing gaffe would surely have been preserved by the pen of a contemporary or found its way into the correspondence of Wheeler family members. Although John Hill Wheeler's diary shows him diligently working his contacts in Washington, as he sought a government appointment in the winter of 1856/57, there is no record of Mrs. Wheeler being employed to assist him in this.

If the powder scene initiates a pivot in the plot—it leads to Hannah's demotion—it also holds an identifiable source. As Robbins discovered, Crafts seems to have encountered details about pomades made from silver nitrate in an 1851 article in *Scientific American* that asserted that those made from such a powder will turn the substances they encounter black.[5] The very magazine issue detailing these insights was owned by Crafts's enslaver, John Hill Wheeler, and it also may have been in circulation in the Reading Room at Chowan Baptist Female Institute. What at first seems like pure literary invention proves to have factual basis in what can be recovered of the author's life.[6]

A careful investigation of Crafts's time in Washington only serves to demonstrate further the author's brilliant comedic mind. In addition to the chemical reaction of silver nitrate, Crafts seems to be countering the popularity of blackface minstrelsies by writing against them in her narrative. John Hill Wheeler's diaries show that he and Mrs. Wheeler frequently attended minstrel shows during the same period Crafts served the family. In these shows, white actors performed in blackface caricaturing Southern captives in musical performances and variety acts. The typical program included popular songs like "Dixie" and skits and jokes. Commonly, these shows included "Jim Crow" and "Zip Coon," two popular minstrel figures representing enslaved people. Such shows, which Crafts probably witnessed from the segregated balcony, included farce and physical humor and climaxed with a "walk-around" grand finale in which all the actors in blackface presented their specialty while troupe members clapped to the songs in unison.[7]

Despite the fact that most such performers and many composers had little if any experience with either the South or slavery, minstrelsy centered on a romantic portrayal of life on Southern plantations, and they were rife with ridicule of Black people. Sometimes these performances incorporated popular literature. For instance, John Hill Wheeler seems to have been fond of the performer Frank Bower, who served as a lead in the traveling "Sanford's Minstrels," based in Philadelphia. Wheeler's diaries show him attending Bower's performance in Philadelphia in 1856 and in Washington, D.C., in 1857. Significantly, Bower's specialty was his "Happy Uncle Tom" skit, a song-and-dance routine celebrated in its day. The troupe's director, Frank Sanford, wrote "Happy Uncle Tom" and sold scripts of "Sanford's Southern Version of Uncle Tom" to other minstrel troupes. The surviving scenes and lyrics reveal demeaning images that reduced African Americans to childish figures contented with their enslavement.

"Sanford's Southern Version of Uncle Tom" is lost to us, but one short scene was preserved and published in the *New Orleans Daily Delta* (February 16 and 17, 1854). The setup for the minstrel identifies "Harriet Screecher Blow" as the author and then opens with a "Canadian snow scene" where, "amid old pines bending under waves of snow and glittering ice, the [Negro] fugitives long to get home." In blackface, a group of white people portray fugitives from *Uncle Tom's Cabin*, singing, "Carry me back to Old Virginny, / To Old Virginny's Shore." A more detailed passage is copied in the paper, apparently original to Sanford's script:

> (Scene: Uncle Tom, shivering and forlorn amid the inclemencies of a Canadian winter. A Philanthropist approaches.)

> Phi.: Well, Uncle Tom, you seem to be in trouble. What do you want?
>
> Uncle Tom: Donno, Massa.
>
> Phi.: Do you want a house?
>
> Uncle Tom: No, Massa.
>
> Phi: Do you want clothes?
>
> Uncle Tom: No, Massa.
>
> Phi: Well, what do you want?
>
> (In the distance, the strains of "Old Folks at Home" are indistinctly heard, and Uncle Tom, listening with tears in his eyes, breaks out, saying): "Massa—that's what I want!"[8]

"This point in the drama," the reviewer in the *Daily Delta* commented, "brought tears to the eyes of about every one [*sic*] present, in the same manner as other points produced irresistible laughter." Further, this scene, he said, was "quite melodramatic and also exceedingly correct."[9]

Inspiration for Hannah Crafts's plot device of the blackening powder almost certainly came from her being forced to attend minstrel shows with the Wheelers. Here, Crafts's fiction helps reveal her real-life experiences not otherwise recoverable in the historic record. We even glimpse the author's comedic genius as she develops her art. During those appalling minstrel performances, Crafts surely asked herself what a minstrel show would look like if the satire were reversed and focused, instead, on mocking white people. This is precisely what she developed in her chapter "A Turn of the Wheel." As Hannah in the novel observes after applying the makeup to Mrs. Wheeler, "I had never seen her look better" (*TBN* 170). In the novel, Mrs. Wheeler's blackface performance is a surprise, especially to herself.

> "Hannah bring the mirror."
>
> I complied.
>
> She gazed a moment, and then her mingled emotions of grief, rage, and shame were truly awful. To all Mr[.] Wheeler's inquiries of

> "how did it happen, my dear?["] and ["]how came your face to turn black, my dear?" she only answered that she did not know, had no idea, and then she wept and moaned, and finally went into a fit of strong hysterics. Mr[.] Wheeler and myself quickly flew to her assistance. To tell the truth he was now more concerned about his wife than the office.
>
> "Heaven help me" he said bending over her. "I fear that her beauty has gone forever." (*TBN* 171–72)

Hannah administers soap and water, and, "little by little," Mrs. Wheeler gains "her natural color." Then the latter describes her performance before the hiring agent, beginning with the portrait of a rival:

> "Mrs[.] Piper, how I hate her" ejaculated the lady. ["]How absurd she dresses. False teeth much too large which have the effect of thrusting out her lips; a face on fire with rouge and a ringletty wig. Then she was pinched in and swelled out, and puffed up, and strapped down in a way I never saw. I can't say that she knew me. I can't say that she didn't, but she gave me no sign or token of recognition."
>
> "It's lucky if she didn't," said Mr[.] Wheeler, with a look of extreme mortification.
>
> "At any rate I gave your name as that of my husband, and when Mr. Cattell said [']by courtesy perhaps['] I said [']No, by law['] when they all burst into a titter."
>
> "Then you really asked Cattell for the office?" said Mr[.] Wheeler, hoping to reach indirectly the information he desired.
>
> "Certainly I did."
>
> "And what did he say?"
>
> "That it was not customary to bestow offices on colored people, at which Mrs[.] Piper blustered and said that 'would be very unconstitutionally indeed.['] [']Then you positively refuse this office to my husband['] I said going down on my knees."
>
> ["']Positively, and if either you or him had possessed a particle of common sense, you would not have asked for it.['"] (*TBN* 173–74)

Here, white people's vanity and ambition are the subject of a comic blackface performance. The reader wants the racist Mrs. Wheeler to gain some sympathetic wisdom from Crafts's "A Turn of the Wheel" chapter. Instead, in it, Mrs. Wheeler lashes out at Hannah for failing to warn her that a vengeful chemist had put into circulation a powder that would "blacken the whitest skin" (*TBN* 172).

Crafts may have begun imaging the details of her novel on those many afternoons she spent polishing the Wheelers' silver and service ware under the gaze of *Mrs. John Hill Wheeler and Her Two Sons*. Thomas Sully's portrait of his daughter and grandchildren held pride of place in the Wheelers' parlor wherever they lived, including the Polk mansion the Wheelers rented between 1856 and 1857. One can imagine Crafts's fingers darkening as she polished silver trays in the parlor, even as she conjured the scene of Mrs. Wheeler in blackface. Indeed, Crafts may well have seen the likeness of Mrs. Wheeler reflected back from Sully's portrait in the polished silver she was compelled to clean. For my part, as a biographer, I can see the author's bright smile in that medium, too, reflected back through the surfaces of her art as she turns the minstrel tradition against her captors.

II

If Mrs. Wheeler's startling metamorphosis in the novel is clearly Crafts exacting literary revenge, the author also seems to have found inspiration in the literary model of Charles Dickens's *Bleak House*. In *Bleak House*, the chemical reaction is far more combustible. If Crafts's chemistry blackens Mrs. Wheeler's face for a kind of reverse minstrel show, Dickens detonates an actual character in the novel. In a bizarre but brilliant scene, Krook, the alcoholic rag dealer, dies by means of a fire (spontaneous combustion) that leaves nothing of the old man except an object looking like a "small charred and broken log of wood." Dickens's description of Krook's demise was based closely on that of an Italian aristocrat, Countess Cornelia di Bandi, who was consumed by a fireball in her bedroom. It is possible Crafts imagined just such a fate for the real-life Mrs. Wheeler, but she opted instead for the more telling minstrelsy of her D.C. sojourn.

Significantly, weather plays a crucial role in Crafts's scene, again drawing from Dickens. The unpleasant weather means the government official Mrs. Wheeler wishes to importune will likely be at home and disengaged, and so, she uses the powder before unwittingly initiating her blackface performance. For her chapter, Crafts rescripts and signifies on Dickens, including the famous opening paragraphs of *Bleak House*, a novel that was extraordinarily popular in the United States after 1852, among both Black and white readers. Like the tool of the nitrate pomade, Crafts makes Dickens's novel an instrument of service to her tale. Compare her description of Washington's weather at the beginning of chapter 13 of *The Bondwoman's Narrative*:

> Gloom everywhere Gloom up the Potomac; where it rolls among meadows no longer green, and by splendid country seats Gloom down the Potomac where it washes the sides of huge war-ships Gloom on the marshes, the fields, and heights Gloom settling steadily down over the sumptuous habitations of the rich, and creeping through the cellars of the poor Gloom arresting the steps of chance office-seekers, and bewildering the heads of grave and reverend Senators; for with fog, and drizzle, and a sleety driving mist the night has come at least two hours before its time. (162)

to the second paragraph of *Bleak House*:

> Fog everywhere. Fog up the river, where it flows among green aits and meadows; fog down the river, where it rolls defiled among the tiers of shipping, and the waterside pollutions of a great (and dirty) city. Fog on the Essex marshes, fog on the Kentish heights. Fog creeping into cabooses of collier-brigs; fog lying out on the yards, and hovering in the rigging of great ships; fog drooping on the gunwales of

barges and small boats. Fog in the eyes and throats of ancient Greenwich pensioners. (chap. 1)[10]

This is the most famous and obvious of Crafts's rewriting of Dickens—the paragraph that first leapt out at Hollis Robbins as something new and exciting in the realm of the fiction of the enslaved—and here, it seems clear that Crafts wants us to see that she is reworking Dickens, that she is blackening his landscape just as she did Mrs. Wheeler's face.

Thus, Crafts transforms Dickens's foggy London into the muddy gloom of Washington, D.C.: "Congress men [*sic*] jostling each other at the street crossings, or perhaps losing their foothold, where a negro slave was seen slipping and sliding but a moment before" (*TBN* 161–62). Now "office-seekers" and "grave and reverend Senators" become the focus, along with the question of slavery. The fog of Dickens's Chancery Court is replaced with "mud so deep and dark that you half fancy the waters of deluge have but newly retired from the earth." And at the center is the protagonist, Hannah, who carries the blackening power of Crafts the artist: "Just where the gloom was densest, and the muddy street the muddiest there was I, wrapped in a very thin shawl and carrying a very small box in my hand" (*TBN* 162).

Adapting passages from *Bleak House* to develop a novel about slavery may seem like a surprising choice, but Crafts and Lord Denman (with his collection *"Uncle Tom's Cabin," "Bleak House," Slavery and the Slave Trade*) were not the only people to make the connection. As Hollis Robbins first noted, *Frederick Douglass's Paper* (originally known as the *North Star*) serialized *Bleak House* in its entirety from April 1852 through December 1853. "We wish we could induce everyone to read *Bleak House*," Douglass wrote in the newspaper's June 3, 1853, edition. "Charles Dickens has ever been the faithful friend of the poor—God bless him for that!—and in the portraitures that he, ever and anon, weaves into his books of fiction, we see the touch of a master hand. His delineations are true to the life; and his being able to give them evinces his being intimately acquainted with the dense ignorance, squalid misery, and pressing wants of the London poor. . . . Tis true that 'the story is long,' but time spent upon its perusal is not ill bestowed."[11]

Douglass may not have held such a cheerful assessment of Dickens had he been aware of the English author's private responses to *Narrative of the Life of Frederick Douglass*. Dickens seems to have been repulsed by the frontispiece illustration of Douglass that accompanies the first British edition (see Figure 27). He sent a copy of the Douglass memoir to his friend the actor William Macready, who was leaving for a tour of America, but only after he tore out the engraved portrait. He wrote, "Here is Frederick Douglass." Then he noted in the letter, "There was such a hideous and abominable portrait of him [Douglass] in the book that I have torn it out, fearing it might set you, by anticipation, against the narrative."[12]

Dickens's motivation for tearing out Douglass's portrait remains obscure, but the anecdote suggests the English author's ambivalence: his hatred of slavery did not "necessarily erase racial prejudice."[13] As his biographer Peter Ackroyd notes, "In modern terminology Dickens was a 'racist' of the most egregious kind, a fact that ought to give pause to those who persist in believing that he was necessarily the epitome of all that was decent and benign in the previous century."[14] In *American Notes* (1846), Dickens fiercely condemns the inhumanity of slavery and expresses powerful and dramatic support for abolitionists in America. And yet, his *American Notes* collection includes numerous comic episodes that would be at home in popular Black minstrels, similar to Stowe's use of the character Topsy in *Uncle Tom's Cabin*. Dickens seems to have lost the power of his narrative gifts when he tries to imagine the inner lives of Black people.

Invariably, their dark skin and perceived *otherness* may have stopped him from writing Black characters into his fiction in any meaningful way. "The portraitures that [Dickens], ever and anon, weaves into his books"—as Douglass put it—did not extend to men and women like Douglass. Famously, Dickens kept a large mirror in the room where he composed his novels. Often, he would stand before it and mimic his characters (as an actor would) before going back to write at his desk. In

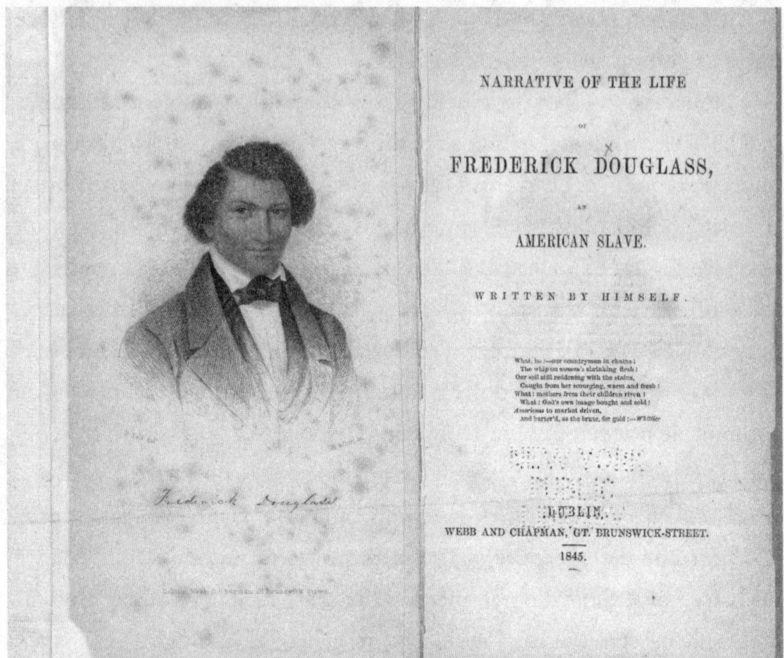

NARRATIVE OF THE LIFE

OF

FREDERICK DOUGLASS,

AN

AMERICAN SLAVE.

WRITTEN BY HIMSELF.

What, ho!—our countrymen in chains!
The whip on woman's shrinking flesh!
Our soil still reddening with the stains,
Caught from her scourging, warm and fresh!
What! mothers from their children riven!
What! God's own image bought and sold!
Americans to market driven,
And barter'd, as the brute, for gold!—*Whittier*

DUBLIN:

WEBB AND CHAPMAN, GT. BRUNSWICK-STREET.

1845.

FIGURE 27: Frontispiece, *Narrative of the Life of Frederick Douglass* (Dublin: Webb and Chapman, 1845)

defacing Douglass's book, he may have been betraying his inability to see himself in Douglass. Perhaps this inability to rise above his own racial bias was reflected in his violent rending of Douglass's image.

The complaint that abolitionists like Lord Denman held for Dickens was the author's inability to engage slavery as more than a monstrous reflection of the British class system. It did not help that, during the mid-century, Dickens was influenced by the strenuous nationalism and racism of his friend Thomas Carlyle. There was Carlyle's essay "The [N-word] Question" (1849; reprinted as a separate pamphlet in 1853). With *Bleak House*, Dickens began to refocus his humanitarian efforts away from international issues like slavery to the "Condition of England" question, following Carlyle. If Carlyle's writings shifted in this period to become xenophobic—even as he focused on addressing poverty in England—the same seems to have happened in Dickens's fiction. The satire of Mrs.

Jellyby in *Bleak House* is a case in point. She is described as a woman living in London who resolutely devotes every waking hour to a project in Africa she refers to as the "Borrioboola-Gha venture." Her goal is the resettlement of impoverished Britons among African natives, all of whom will support themselves through growing and harvesting coffee. Mrs. Jellyby is convinced that no other undertaking in life is so worthwhile or would solve as many social problems. Meanwhile, she ignores, quite literally, problems at home in her own family. In the book's postscript, we learn that the Borrioboola-Gha project failed after the local king sold its volunteers into slavery in order to buy rum.

Dickens's satire is unmistakably brilliant, but it is also a comfortable way for the author to look away from the problem of slavery. Lord Denman notes as much in his volume *"Uncle Tom's Cabin," "Bleak House," Slavery and the Slave Trade* (1853). He writes, "We do not say that [Dickens] defends slavery or the slave-trade; but he takes pains to discourage, by ridicule, the effort now making to put them down." Denman continues: "We believe, indeed, that in general terms he expresses just hatred for [slavery and the slave trade]; but so do all those who profit or wish to profit by them, and who, by that general profession, prevent the detail particulars too atrocious to be endured." Denman asks, "*Who but the slave traders can gain by this course of argument?*"[15]

It would take Hannah Crafts's generous adaptation of *Bleak House* to refocus Dickens's art in the fashion Lord Denman envisioned. Crafts seems to have followed Douglass and his readers in their ready adaptation of *Bleak House*. In *Douglass' Paper*, characters and themes from *Bleak House* served as a rich source of comic and ironic allusion for the work's many antislavery readers, columnists, and letter writers. While some readers complained that serializing Dickens's novel was not an effective use of the pages of an antislavery newspaper, Douglass continued publishing *Bleak House* in installments. He must have seen the positive effect on sales and how his readers responded to the humor and satire. From Dickens's tale championing the underclass, they, like Douglass, drew inferences to the fight against slavery.[16]

If Douglass had no trouble seeing himself in Dickens, neither did Hannah Crafts. The author adapts disparate elements (characters, texts, themes, tropes) from *Bleak House* along with a few other widely recognized sources and combines them all with her own voice such that they are "irrevocably transformed" and powerfully transfigured. Her use of reachable sources can best be described as a kind of literary alchemy. Significantly, Crafts adapts the words of others (primarily Dickens, but there are also riffs on works by Walter Scott and Charlotte Brontë) when she wants to provide embellishment or a rhetorical flourish. In such moments, we see the holographic nature of the narrative: Crafts is developing her art right before our eyes, borrowing and reworking the prose of other authors. In the difficult, hinge moments of her story, she looks to the rhetorical tools that Dickens and others employed. As Hollis Robbins notes, "Typically [the literary borrowing] occurs at the beginnings and ends of chapters, at moments of transition between exposition and apostrophe, or when the genre shifts from candor to craft."[17]

Another way to see Crafts's artistry is to recognize that she is blackening Dickens's text just as Lord Denman had called for in his response to *Bleak House*. Denman noted, "Never had Mr. Dickens a finer opportunity for exercising his unrivalled talent for burlesque than in describing slaveholders."[18] Crafts would deliver, in part, by reshaping Dickens's work. She seems to be wrestling with the same challenges later Black authors faced as they grappled with the larger question of literary tradition and culture. One authoritative response comes from the same literary critic who unearthed Crafts's novel, Henry Louis Gates Jr. In his groundbreaking study *The Signifying Monkey* (1988), Gates provides a powerful theory of African American literature that matches precisely what can be observed on the pages of Crafts's manuscript:

> Our task in developing the [B]lack tradition is not to reinvent our traditions as if they bore no relation to that tradition created and borne, in the main, by white men [and women]. Our writers used that impressive tradition to define themselves, both with and against their

> concept of received order. We must do the same, with or against the Western critical canon. To name our tradition is to rename each of its antecedents, no matter how pale they might seem.[19]

By blackening Dickens's text, Crafts seems to be working out Gates's theory as early as 1856–57. How do you carry forward the "pale" but powerful modes of white writing into a Black-authored text? You do precisely the work that Crafts can be seen performing in her holograph narrative. You build personal experience and narrative into a novel that cultivates the tools and methods of successful authors like Stowe and Dickens. Like Hannah Crafts 150 years before her, Toni Morrison would perform similar acts of literary alchemy—only, she would perform her blackening arts on her more immediate white predecessors, including Virginia Woolf and William Faulkner.

III

Like Frederick Douglass, who so diligently mined his *Columbian Orator* (1797), a collection of political essays, dialogues, and poetry assembled by Caleb Bingham to teach public speaking, Crafts, too, fell in love with the first book she seems to have secretly possessed. To the autodidact, language-loving Crafts, Dickens's *Bleak House* must have seemed like an instruction manual to good writing and storytelling. So, it is probably no surprise, then, that she found solace in interpreting her world by adapting the language and idiom of Dickens. She makes an analogous use of Dickens's character Mr. Tulkinghorn in shaping her villain Mr. Trappe, who is an assembly of the various captors Crafts and her family were associated with: Jacob R. Pope, William Pugh Bond, Lewis Bond, Samuel Jordan Wheeler, and John Hill Wheeler. Trappe resembles Dickens's Tulkinghorn as a stand-in for these real-life models. Trappe and Tulkinghorn are portrayed almost identically; they are described wearing black and stalking their victims by using legal documents as weapons. They meet similar fates. Both are found shot to death in their rooms, facedown on the floor.[20] If their journeys are linked and fictive, they also reflect the story of Jacob R. Pope, the enslaver who murdered Rosea Pope, Crafts's grandmother.

Crafts establishes the parallel between Trappe and Tulkinghorn when she first introduces Trappe in *The Bondwoman's Narrative*. Indeed, Crafts invites the parallel by describing the slave trader in similar language to Dickens's portrait of his villain in *Bleak House*:

> "The old man of the name of Trappe" is "a rusty seedy old-fashioned gentleman . . . great black eyes so keen and piercing that you shrank involuntarily from their gaze." (*TBN* 33, 28)

> The "old man of the name of Tulkinghorn" is "an old-fashioned old gentleman . . . rusty to look at." (*BH* chaps. 33 and 2)

Trappe controls Hannah's mistress with papers documenting her racial mixture just as Tulkinghorn stalks Lady Dedlock (Esther's mother) with proof of her out-of-wedlock daughter:

> [E]ach one watched and suspected the other, that each one was conscious of some great and important secret on the part of the other, and that my mistress in particular would give worlds to know just what the old man knew. (*TBN* 28)

> But whether each evermore watches and suspects the other, evermore mistrustful of some great reservation; whether each is evermore prepared at all points for the other, and never to be taken unawares; what each would give to know how much the other knows—all this is hidden, for the time, in their own hearts. (*BH* chap. 12)

Trappe keeps a room at Lindendale, "a plainly furnished chamber on the second story, old-fashioned like himself and having a quiet impassive air" (*TBN* 32–33), while Tulkinghorn maintains quarters at Chesney

Wold, "a turret chamber of the third order of merit, plainly but comfortably furnished and having an old-fashioned business air" (*BH* chap. 12). Parallels persist throughout the narrative.[21]

The breadth and extent of such adaptations suggest that Crafts had a copy of *Bleak House* (probably in volume form from a student boarder) in front of her while she was writing her narrative. In transforming and transmuting these passages, she seems to be engaged in what Henry Louis Gates Jr. calls "double-voiced discourse" and, especially, the mode he calls "the Speakerly Text." Gates describes a narrative voice characterized by "a hybrid character, a character who is neither the novel's protagonist nor the text's disembodied narrator, but a blend of both, an emergent and merging moment of consciousness."[22] Again, the insight is Gates's. As Robbins notes, "The value of a hybrid or polyvocal character to Crafts is that it complicates the idea of a speaking subject. It is not necessarily Hannah's voice who tells the whole story."[23] Indeed, Crafts's narrator seems to follow a practice that William Wells Brown pioneered in the first known African American novel, *Clotel* (1853).[24] There, Brown adapts a polyvocal voice that speaks the story of multiple characters assumed under the guise of the novel's third-person limited narrator, Currer. *Clotel* is a famously elusive text to trace because it provides an assembly of voices, real and fictive, as Brown tells the story of a young mixed-race captive, Currer, and her two light-skinned daughters fathered by Thomas Jefferson. The real life of Sally Hemings, Jefferson's forced sexual partner, is explored with fictive elements Brown draws from tales he gathered from other captives and written sources he borrowed and reworked.

It is possible Crafts encountered Brown's *Clotel* and used it as a model, as it was in the library of John Hill Wheeler during the years the author was enslaved in Washington, D.C. Crafts's *The Bondwoman's Narrative* holds similarities to *Clotel* in design and execution. Both are fragmented narratives that combine fact, fiction, and external literary sources. Crafts's narrative largely limits its intertextual passages to Dickens's *Bleak House*, while Brown's *Clotel* includes a much larger range of adapted texts and sources. Crafts's novel seems more thoroughly based in her own experiences and the experiences of her fellow captives: Milly and Martha Murfree, Mary Burton, Eliza Morgan, and Jane Johnson.

IV

The blackface scene in chapter 12 of *The Bondwoman's Narrative* is the most dramatic example of Crafts's alchemical arts, but the process of textual transformation is initiated in her novel from the opening page. Crafts's narrator, Hannah, begins by introducing herself modestly: "It may be that I assume too much responsibility in attempting to write these pages. The world will probably say so, and I am aware of my deficiencies. I am neither clever, nor learned, nor talented." Yet, for one in her condition, Hannah maintains surprising optimism: "The life of a slave at best is not a pleasant one, but I had formed a resolution to always look on the bright side of things, to be industrious, cheerful, and true-hearted, to do some good though in an humble way, and win some love if I could" (*TBN* 11). The narrative voice here is compelling, but it is also a different kind of mimicry.[25]

Crafts is drawing here from the words of Esther Summerson, who introduces herself at the beginning of chapter 3 of *Bleak House*: "I have a great deal of difficulty in beginning to write my portion of these pages, for I know I am not clever. I always knew that." Hannah is writing herself out of Esther Summerson's monologue: "I often thought of the resolution I had made on my birthday to try to be industrious, contented, and true-hearted and to do some good to some one and win some love if I could."[26]

If Hannah's fictional being in Crafts's text owes a kind of genealogy to Dickens and Esther Summerson, it is because Crafts responded to and probably admired the temperament and sensibility of Dickens's character Esther. Esther Summerson must have served as a model for Crafts the author, and she passed on those qualities to her protagonist, Hannah. In short, Crafts discovered in the figure of Esther a path for her own autobiographical protagonist. Esther and Hannah's similarities are compelling. Both are orphans; both find their births to be stigmatized by sexual transgressions whose details are withheld from them. Esther's mother, Lady Dedlock, conceives her out of wedlock with a mysterious figure called "Nemo" (Latin for "nobody"). Meanwhile, for the autobiographical Hannah, she is separated from her mother early in life, and her white father is never identified. Likely, Hannah Bond found imaginative fellowship with Dickens's Esther Summerson, so perhaps it is not surprising that she adopted part of Esther's narrative into her story.[27]

As possibly the only book the author possessed while enslaved, *Bleak House* and its heroine, Esther Summerson, became important imaginative companions for Hannah Crafts. Crafts may even have modeled parts of her personal behavior on Summerson's—or, at least, her autobiographical heroine does. Like Esther in Dickens's novel, Crafts's Hannah is deeply religious, and her faith sustains her. Hannah and Esther are fastidious about comportment, modest, and kind to others, even as they struggle to live generously in a world hostile to their presence. Both women are industrious and domestic. Significantly, it is when the author is forced to forge a lie about herself ("penning a libel") that Hannah's path diverges from Esther's.[28]

Until the end of chapter 12, Hannah, like Esther, is presented as sincere and honest. Her rectitude lands her in jail, extends her servitude, and keeps her from aiding Charlotte and William's escape. (Worse, she informs on Charlotte, revealing her plans to Mrs. Henry.[29]) The turning point is when Mrs. Wheeler has Hannah take dictation of a letter. In Hannah's own hand—with the literacy she had to steal—the protagonist is forced to write that she is homely, bigoted in religion, of doubtful ability, and a potential runaway (*TBN* 157)—all so Mrs. Wheeler can negotiate Hannah's transfer at a bargain. The control Mrs. Wheeler tries to wield over the writer's pen is too much. At precisely this moment, Hannah puts aside rectitude and begins to avenge herself against the previously obscure "Mrs. Wh—r." This is when the text begins to blacken the author's final enslavers. Suddenly, Crafts the author changes course, and the novel begins to reveal Mrs. Wheeler's identity by filling in the hidden letters behind "Wh—r" in the manuscript.

Crafts's heroine Hannah now begins to exert more control over the narrative as she parts ways from her more passive and pious literary sister, Esther Summerson. It is as if Stowe's Topsy has arrived and merged with Crafts's Hannah. But Crafts's heroine is no white minstrel figure. Instead, she is a formidable artist ready to blacken even Dickens. Now Crafts exposes Mrs. Wheeler as superstitious, erratic, and mean. Hannah complains that Mrs. Wheeler holds "vanities, and whims, and caprices." In the "dead hours of the night," she forces Hannah to bring her items with well-known herbal powers: "pomegranate for fertility, nutmeg for luck, and citron for wealth" (*TBN* 159). When Mrs. Wheeler requests candy, water, salt, and vinegar—commonly used remedies for constipation—Crafts signals not only her mistress's bad digestion but also her common physicality.[30] It is after this scene that Crafts places her enslaver into the minstrel scene of "A Turn of the Wheel."

After the minstrel scene, Crafts describes Hannah gossiping with her former fellow servant Lizzy. They gossip for two whole chapters as the work's polyvocal voices ventriloquize the story of the new master of Lindendale, Mr. Cosgrove; his wife; and his various enslaved mistresses. Crafts signals some fictional aspect to these tales by borrowing, yet again, from *Bleak House*. Lizzy describes Mrs. Cosgrove's appreciation of another slave, Lilly, in language drawn from *Bleak House*:

> Well our mistress took a great fancy to her at the first sight, I believe, she actually called the girl to her side and caressed and praised her, to the infinite astonishment of the maid who had always been kept at distance. . . . At length Mrs. Cosgrove dismissed her maid. It was a cruel act; for the girl had accompanied her from beyond the seas and had neither friends nor relatives in this country, but who might question her imperious will. (*TBN* 178)

Crafts clearly draws the scene from Dickens's description of Lady Dedlock's choosing Rosa over the French maid Hortense:

> "Come here, Rosa!" Lady Dedlock beckons her, with even an appearance of interest. "Why, do you know how pretty you are, child?" she says, touching her shoulder with her two forefingers. . . . My Lady's maid is a Frenchwoman of two and thirty, from somewhere in the southern country about Avignon and Marseilles. . . . She, Hortense, has been in my Lady's service since five years, and always kept at the distance, and this doll, this puppet, caressed absolutely caressed—by my Lady on the moment of her arriving at the house. (*BH* chap. 12)

Crafts reimagines the scene, of course, but the primary effect is that she protects herself against the charge of identifying specific real-life perpetrators.[31] Events are partially disguised by fiction, as the novel again tries to make legible the history of sexual abuse common to the work's many female characters.

V

In the final chapters of *The Bondwoman's Narrative*, Crafts's signifying on Dickens's novel returns and is more pronounced than before. Crafts's description of the slave huts on the North Carolina plantation is a vivid example:

> There was not that division of families I had been accustomed to see, but they all lived promiscuously anyhow and every how; at least they did not die, which was a wonder. Is it a stretch of imagination to say that by night they contained a swarm of misery, that crowds of foul existence crawled in out of gaps in walls and boards, or coiled themselves to sleep on nauseous heaps of straw fetid with human

> perspiration and where the rain drips in, and the damp airs of midnight fatch [fetch] and carry malignant fevers. (*TBN* 204–5)

Crafts's prose follows Dickens's description of "Tom-All-Alone's," a squalid London alley where the orphaned street-sweeping Jo lives:

> Now, these tumbling tenements contain, by night, a swarm of misery. As, on the ruined human wretch, vermin parasites appear, so, these ruined shelters have bred a crowd of foul existence that crawls in and out of gaps in walls and boards; and coils itself to sleep, in maggot numbers, where the rain drips in; and comes and goes, fetching and carrying fever. (*BH* chap. 16)

The alteration of Dickens's slum to a slave cabin is, once again, thoughtfully rendered by Crafts. "Is it a stretch of imagination?" the author asks.[32] Again, Crafts seems to be following the call of Lord Denman to draw Dickensian portraits of slaveholders. Denman criticized Dickens for heeding his friend Carlyle's xenophobic focus on the "Condition-of-England" question. Here the author of *The Bondwoman's Narrative* crafts Dickens's very language to portray the slave huts Dickens neglects. If *Bleak House* ignores slavery through the satire on the Borrioboola-Gha venture, Crafts redirects Dickens's language to the very real problem of slavery in America.

For her, Dickens's description of an illiterate free British white male is an apt opportunity to remind a different set of readers of the plight of enslaved agricultural workers. Again, perhaps it is not surprising that an autodidact clearly enamored with the one book she likely possessed found in that work parallels to her own world. Thus, her significations propose a kinship of suffering. This affinity is reaffirmed in an additional reworked passage:

> If the huts were bad, the inhabitants it seemed were still worse. Degradation, neglect, and ill treatment had wrought on them its legitimate

> effects. All day they toil beneath the burning sun, scarcely conscious that any link exists between themselves and other portions of the human race. Their mental condition is briefly summed up in the phrase that they know nothing (*TBN* 205–6).

The moment reworks Dickens's language:

> What connexion can there be, between the place in Lincolnshire, the house in town, the Mercury in powder, and the whereabout of Jo the outlaw with his broom, who had the distant ray of light upon him when he swept the churchyard-step? What connexion can there have been between many people in the innumerable histories of this world, who, from opposite sides of great gulfs, have, nevertheless, been very curiously brought together!
>
> Jo sweeps his crossing all day long, unconscious of the link, if any link there be. He sums up his mental condition, when asked a question, by replying that he "don't know nothink." (*BH* chap. 16)[33]

As we have seen, Hannah Bond encountered this very passage as a recitation exercise being memorized among the students she served at Wheeler House (1852–56) while they attended Chowan Baptist Female Institute. Now she transforms it to depict the very slave huts that stood only a few hundred yards from the students practicing their recitations. Crafts's use of Dickens is, once again, a brilliant example of literary alchemy. She is blackening Dickens's text, darkening it, distilling it, and transforming it.[34]

The art first possessed by a student boarder, whether stolen or not, becomes a gift that extends beyond Dickens's xenophobia and racism. In the hands of Hannah Crafts, the work is transformed into a generous mixture of Jo the Sweep; of Esther Summerson; of Douglass and Dickens; and of Milly, Martha, Mary, and Eliza now reflected back in the forming pages of Crafts's narrative. Like her fresh portrait of Mrs. Wheeler, blackened to compete with Thomas Sully's portrait, Crafts is forging new tools for future artists, tools that could be delivered only if she and her manuscript reached freedom.

What changed for the artist to allow her to take a new path with her Hannah in the masterful chapter "A Turn of the Wheel" and those that followed? Forensic analysis of the paper and ink suggests the sourcing of paper was altered for the last third of the novel. Different folio sheets now comprise the manuscript distinct from earlier chapters. Corroborating evidence suggests that there is a pause and a change in compositional circumstances for the writer just as she introduces the "Wh—rs" and then decides to fully identify them as "Mr. Wheeler" and "Mrs. Wheeler." Further, the novel begins to cleave more closely to the traceable life of its author. All evidence points to the same conclusion: the author successfully fled her enslavers during the composition of her work. She must have written "A Turn of the Wheel" and subsequent chapters while in freedom—first, at Horace Craft's farm near McGrawville, New York, and, later, in Burlington, New Jersey. That story, too, is disclosed in the neatly ordered folio sheets that she would later stitch together with needle and thread and leave as an undisclosed gift to future generations.

As Robbins has observed, "If a roomful of witty and well-read literary scholars wanted to concoct a readable text composed of the highlights of nineteenth-century literature they might come up with something like *The Bondwoman's Narrative*."[35] Crafts's work is just such a mixture. It is an extraordinary performance. The author reimagined all that she saw and those whom she knew in slavery and pressed them together between the pages of her novel to preserve "the connexion between the many people" with "innumerable histories," as Dickens had written, "from opposite sides of great gulfs . . . curiously brought together!"

To return to my many debates with Robbins: Does the fiction tell us as much about Crafts as her recoverable history? The answer is a definitive yes. As has always been the case, art discovers life, and life uncovers art. To disclose the life of an artist, especially one obscured from history, requires even more work blending what can be drawn from the artist's work with what is salvageable from the past. Only then can we bring the writer's presence before us. What does Crafts's fictionalizing her experiences tell us about the author and her artistry? Everything that we can know. The only way to recover the life and times of Hannah Crafts is to discover as many facts as possible about her experiences in the world and, then, to creatively engage her art to learn the rest that is knowable. Literary scholarship like that developed by Gates and Robbins is primary.

CHAPTER 17

THE SEARCH CONTINUED

Two difficulties arise in connecting *The Bondwoman's Narrative* directly to the Wheelers: First, John Hill Wheeler was a public figure, especially after the Passmore Williamson case. How do we know that the author of *The Bondwoman's Narrative* did not develop Mr. and Mrs. Wheeler as characters based on press reports? Second, John Hill Wheeler does not appear to have owned a plantation in North Carolina after he was forced to sell his Lincoln County property, Ellangowan, in 1853, because of debts incurred from his backing the unpaid banknotes of his political mentor Richard Mentor Johnson. If the forensic evidence points to the novel's production in the late 1850s, how could the author escape from a plantation Wheeler no longer owned?

Building on the work of Porter, Gates, and Nickell, I decided to establish, as firmly as possible, the precise locations depicted in the novel, so that I could best identify the specific origins of the work. In this way, I hoped to discover the author. I knew that, among the scholarship, there was considerable confusion regarding the location of the novel's "Wheeler plantation." Gates had noted both the Wheeler family property near Murfreesboro, North Carolina, and John Hill Wheeler's plantation at Beatties Ford, near Lincolnton, North Carolina. Most scholars, following Gates, pointed to Ellangowan, John Hill Wheeler's Beatties Ford property, as the site from which Hannah Crafts escaped in 1857.[1]

And so, I began to comb deed and land records in Lincoln and Hertford Counties and court records for the relevant period. As this research suggested, John Hill Wheeler no longer owned a plantation in North Carolina after 1853. The North Carolina Supreme Court had ruled against Wheeler in 1852 at the Morganton August session, requiring him to sell his Beatties Ford property to cover outstanding debts totaling $12,450.53 (roughly half a million dollars in 2023). He sold the 556-acre Ellangowan holding, near Lincolnton on the Catawba River, on June 1, 1853, to Henry W. Connor for $9,000.[2] This is important because Crafts's novel depicts life from within the Wheeler household in Washington, D.C., and North Carolina between 1855 and 1857. If John Hill Wheeler did not possess a plantation in North Carolina after 1853, how could a captive of his write about escaping such a place in 1857?[3]

If an identifiable person were to be found connecting the "Wheeler plantation" to the novel, it was clear that the Wheeler family's property in Eastern North Carolina was the place to search. "In North Carolina," Hannah Crafts writes in chapter 16 of *The Bondwoman's Narrative*, "Mr. Wheeler's fine plantation . . . situated near Wilmington the principal port of the state" (203). This was another signal that the plantation represented in the novel was not Ellangowan, in Lincoln County (220 miles away from Wilmington), but, rather, the "Wheeler plantation" outside Murfreesboro in Hertford County. The author describes the property as

> one of the most beautiful places I had ever seen. . . . [T]here was a luxurious abundance of vines, and fruits, and flowers, and song-birds, and every thing wore such an aspect of maturity and ripeness that I was fairly charmed. The lime-tree walks were like green arcades, the very shadows of orange trees seemed dropping with fruit, the peach trees were so laden that their branches bent nearly to the earth and were supported by stout props, and the purple clusters of grapes hung tempting from the trellis work of I don't know how many arbors. . . . In the distance was a cotton field with the snowy fleece bursting richly from the pod, and sweeping down to the river's edge was a large

> plantation of rice. Of course the labor of many slaves was required to keep such a large estate in thrifty order. The huts of these people were ranged on the back-side of the place, and as far from the habitation of their master as possible. (*TBN* 203–4)

No record of lime, orange, or rice cultivation exists for the Piedmont region of North Carolina, where Ellangowan was located. Not only was the timing of the sale of Wheeler's Beatties Ford plantation inconsistent with the chronological markers presented in Crafts's manuscript, but the description provided in *The Bondwoman's Narrative* does not match the vegetation common to the region. Although the work is fictional and the author, like any novelist, has full license to imagine and create beyond immediate experience, it seems unlikely that Hannah Crafts escaped from Lincoln County.[4] The imaginative depiction of the "Wheeler plantation" in the novel is dissonant with the traceable sources of the Beatties Ford property.

When one accepts that the author is painting a portrait of the Liberty Hall holding near Murfreesboro—and not the Wheeler plantation sold in Lincoln County in 1853—the description in the novel comes to bear a striking resemblance to distinguishable features in the historical record. The fanciful vision of Hannah regarding a property replete with "lime-tree walks," "orange trees," "grape arbors," and cotton and rice fields "sweeping down to the river" fits the accounts of property maintenance and repairs in the reminiscences and diaries of Samuel Jordan Wheeler, the primary proprietor, if not deed holder, of the Wheeler property near Murfreesboro.[5] Records of rice cultivation near Liberty Hall accord with the records of other plantations nearby, especially those in the Perry-town area on the Chowan River. The Wheeler holdings were near Kirby Creek and the Meherrin River, making the land ideal for establishing the drainable low ground necessary for rice cultivation.[6]

But why would this property, in the control of Samuel Jordan Wheeler, be designated the possession of Wheeler's brother in Crafts's novel? Was attribution of Liberty Hall, near Murfreesboro, to John Hill

Wheeler an instance of authorial license? The author clearly regards the plantation depicted in the novel as in the possession of her enslaver. She writes, "Mr. Wheeler had neglected his plantation" (*TBN* 207). And the Mr. and Mrs. Wheeler of the novel consistently refer to owning a plantation in North Carolina. I knew that only by digging deeper into the historical record could I hope to make visible the author's hand. To confirm that the author is indeed describing the Wheeler family plantation near Murfreesboro, I needed to untangle the history of the Wheeler family's property. Upon careful examination of extant property records, wills, and land deeds, I was able to reaffirm unique details provided in the novel.

The Wheeler family property near Murfreesboro passed from John Wheeler to his son John Hill Wheeler upon the death of the father in 1832 and, later, upon the death of John Wheeler Sr.'s third wife, Sarah, in 1833. John Sr.'s will, dated July 13, 1832, reads:

> I also loan her [Sarah] the house in which she now lives for & during the term of her natural life also the lot or lot attached commencing at a point opposite the brick House now belonging I Believe to John A Anderson formerly to Jas Morgan thence down in a north course following the line between Lewis M Cowper & myself until it reaches the river at a point opposite the same place thence down the margin of the river until meet the gully or revine [*sic*] which separates the present lane from the field or land which I now rent to Patrick Brown Esqr. then up the said gully or revine until you come to my land gate on the main street of the town from thence Westwardly until you meet the first point stated from. Together with the stables, corn crib &c which may be on the lot or Tract of Land This I give her in lieu of the dower by which by law she is entitled.
>
> Item 2nd I give and bequeath unto my son John H Wheeler the Land for which I give him a deed for at the period when he arrived at the age of twenty-one situated near Murfreesboro on the Princeton Road bounded by the land of Jas Banks[,] Isaac Pipkin[,] & others containing about 250 acres more or less which profits he has had &

> still retains the possession also the fee simple in the House & Lot now occupied by Mrs[.] Gordon as a Tavern in the town of Murfreesboro also the sum of three hundred dollars to him be paid for such legal services as he may render in managing my Estate to him & his heirs forever.[7]

The property John Hill Wheeler inherited as the "Wheeler plantation" was approximately 267 acres, comprising the 17 acres between the Cowper property on the west, the Meherrin River on the north, the ravine on the east, Broad Street on the south, and the additional 250 acres of property stretching from the Princeton Road to the properties of James Banks and Isaac Pipkin, and the Meherrin River. This substantial holding, considered the "Wheeler plantation" in Crafts's novel, remained intact, as property records show, until after the Civil War.[8]

According to the *Hertford County Record of Accounts*, one of the few old ledger volumes to have survived the burning of the Winton courthouse by Union troops in 1862, John Hill Wheeler, as executor of his father's estate, sold the portion of the property consisting of the family's primary residence in Murfreesboro and the surrounding seventeen acres of land to his brother Samuel Jordan Wheeler in May 1835 for a mere $500. This property was part of the extended Wheeler family holdings valued in court records at over $43,392.36, out of which Samuel Jordan Wheeler had already received $5,322 as his inheritance.[9] The move was likely one of family convenience, as John Hill Wheeler had embarked on a political career that would keep him away from the family's plantation and other holdings in Northampton and Hertford Counties for most of his life.

Historical records demonstrate that despite the title of this portion of the Wheeler family property being transferred to Samuel Jordan Wheeler, the Wheeler property remained in John Hill Wheeler's control, including the Liberty Hall plantation just across the county line in Northampton County.[10] In 1842, when he became financially distressed, Samuel Jordan Wheeler returned his portion of the estate to John Hill

Wheeler, deeding his possessions in trust to him. John Hill Wheeler, in turn, conveyed this property in 1844 to their brother-in-law, Dr. Godwin Cotton Moore, who owned the nearby Mulberry Grove plantation.[11] Dr. Moore was married to John Hill Wheeler's sister Julia Munro Wheeler. Later, in 1851, when John Hill Wheeler faced his own financial emergency, Moore sold the Wheeler family property to Lewis Bond, the author's likely father and Samuel Jordan Wheeler's father-in-law. Through it all, the intent of John Wheeler Sr. was honored. The goal was to keep the ancestral "Wheeler plantation" and property intact, and to do so, John Hill Wheeler moved the deed he controlled in accordance with his father's wishes, including that for the family home and grounds, from his brother Samuel to his sister Julia and her husband. After Samuel Jordan Wheeler's financial troubles in 1842—and with his own in the 1850s—Wheeler shielded the family's holdings to spare the property from creditors.

In his 1857 diary, John Hill Wheeler describes his family's travel from Washington, D.C., back to North Carolina. After visiting at his sister's home, Mulberry Grove, and at his brother's home in Murfreesboro, Wheeler left behind his wife (and presumably Hannah Crafts) at the family household, called Wheeler House, in Murfreesboro. He then traveled to his former Ellangowan plantation, in Lincoln County, across the state, near Charlotte. As I uncovered, Wheeler made this trip to gather money due to him. A mistake I uncovered in Gates's scholarship was that Wheeler was alone on this trip and that his visit to Ellangowan was not, as Gates had thought, to confer with the overseer of his property there but, rather, to collect the money owed to him from its 1853 sale.[12]

These historical facts accord with other important details found in Crafts's novel. In *The Bondwoman's Narrative*, the author describes Hannah's escape as being effected because of confusion over her whereabouts between the plantation's slave huts and the main house. She writes, "I trusted that my escape would be unnoticed probably for some time, as those in the house would naturally conclude that I was living at the huts, and those at the huts might be deceived in the same manner with the expectation of my being at the house" (*TBN* 217–18). At first glance, this seems to be a narrative contrivance—how could a captive's absence go undetected for long? But, as family wills, deeds, and private papers demonstrate, the main property comprising the "Wheeler plantation" was the property also called Liberty Hall, situated four miles outside Murfreesboro. As I previously noted, Hertford County historian E. Frank Stephenson Jr. helped me confirm the property lines. Therefore, a delay in discovery was in fact likely. A considerable distance separated the main living quarters at Wheeler House in Murfreesboro from Liberty Hall's slave huts, situated on the backside of the property outside town. Hannah Crafts's depiction of her escape reflects the geography of the Wheeler family holdings.[13]

While his brother Samuel maintained a busy career as a physician, and Wheeler pursued various federal appointments in Washington, D.C., and abroad, the Liberty Hall plantation was left in the control of an overseer, who occupied the house built by their grandfather Dr. John Wheeler (1747–1814), the patriarch who first established the plantation in 1807. As late as 1906, Liberty Hall still stood "over a mile from any public road. . . . [I]t was on the colonial road leading through Northampton and across the Ramsay Farm to the old town of Princeton on the Meherrin River."[14] The author of *The Bondwoman's Narrative* offers a glimpse into these arrangements: "So the steward only received an injunction to keep the mater's [*sic*] residence in a manner comporting with the family dignity, to see that the vines were properly trained, the flowers tended and especially to look after the figs and pomegranates" (*TBN* 207).[15] Even the injunction to the overseer to "especially" care for the "figs" and "pomegranates" confirms the historical record. As Samuel Jordan Wheeler's account book and medical records reveal, pomegranates and figs were important medicinal sources for the ingredients that made up his dispensary.[16]

A fuller understanding of the history of the real-life "Wheeler plantation" clarifies Ellen Wheeler's possessive comments about the property and Hannah's curious response in chapter 16 of *The Bondwoman's Narrative*. Ellen Wheeler warns Hannah not to discuss the blackening of her face by the facial powder. Crafts writes, "'And mind, too' she continued 'when you get to my place in North Carolina that you don't dare to mention that—that—that—' she hesitated and stammered" (*TBN* 200). Hannah then comments: "[W]e rode down to the boat designed to convey us to Mrs[.] Wheeler's 'place in North Carolina'" (*TBN* 201). The use by Crafts of quotation marks to signify Mrs. Wheeler's possession of the plantation may be an ironic recognition that the ancestral property near Murfreesboro was an oft-cited part of the family's holdings, as Mrs. Wheeler apparently often referred to "my place in North Carolina." In any case, the "Wheeler plantation" left to John Hill Wheeler by his father in 1832, Liberty Hall, was always considered by the extended family as the Wheeler family home. And there is every reason to believe that, as the oldest male heir and its original legatee, John Hill Wheeler considered the ancestral home, as Ellen Wheeler does in *The Bondwoman's Narrative*, "my place in North Carolina."

My work confirming the location of the Wheeler family's properties in North Carolina and their direct connection to Crafts's novel is matched by equally detailed research that I undertook to locate the Wheelers' residence in Washington, D.C., also depicted in the manuscript. Property deeds and Wheeler's diary entries tell this story. On October 1, 1853, Wheeler purchased a home at 444 H Street, a mile east of the White House. The following October, after receiving an appointment as U.S. minister to Nicaragua, he rented this house to George Waldo. On Friday, October 6, 1854, Wheeler notes in his diary that "George Waldo called & we concluded the negotiation about renting House, hiring servants, and purchasing of furniture."[17]

These details are significant because Crafts describes in the novel living with the Wheelers not in their established home at 444 H Street but, instead, in "the splendid mansion they occupied," which was "taken only temporarily" and "could be abandoned at any time" (*TBN* 175). "Mrs. Polk," I discovered in my research, rented this property to the Wheelers for $19.25 a week.[18] This was Sarah Childress Polk, the widow of James K. Polk, the eleventh president of the United States. In this mansion rented from Mrs. Polk, Hannah Crafts served the Wheelers.

Significantly, the Underground operator Paul Jennings had at one time been enslaved in the same household, serving the Polks at the mansion in 1845. By the time Crafts likely encountered Jennings at the First Colored Baptist Church in 1856, he had been free for nearly a decade and was still assisting captives in fleeing slavery.

On March 21, 1857, the Wheeler family left these rented lodgings to return to the Wheeler House and Liberty Hall in North Carolina. Then, when they returned to Washington, D.C., that summer—without Crafts—we find that Wheeler was "unpacking papers & Books" after the family moved back into their permanent home at 444 H Street on June 19, 1857. Significantly, Wheeler notes in his diary entry on the same day, "Mrs. Sarah A[.] McCane and Catherine McCarick—hired as keepers at 6$ [*sic*] per mo." This is the first time there is record of Wheeler paying servants for domestic work (besides the stint in Nicaragua after Johnson's escape), a practice he continues after this point, as reflected in his diaries and account books. As the historical evidence suggests, the author did not return with the family to Washington; rather, she had escaped in May from their plantation outside Murfreesboro after her demotion and removal to the slave huts, just as the protagonist, Hannah, does in her novel. Again, the details and timing presented in Crafts's novel correlate precisely with historical fact.

Establishing the day-to-day facts of the Wheelers in 1856 and 1857 and the specific details of their living arrangements in North Carolina and Washington, D.C., assisted me in narrowing down the field of likely candidates for authorship of the novel. Such research also put me in contact with unexplored source materials. For instance, among property records in Lincoln County I discovered a deed of sale for Wheeler's captive Mary Burton, whom he sold for $450 to a local friend and planter, U.S. congressman James Graham, brother of future North Carolina governor William A. Graham. Among the John Hill Wheeler Papers at the Library of Congress, I also discovered the previously unknown inventory of Wheeler's "servants" scribbled into the pages of his 1832 almanac, as previously discussed. This record included the heretofore unrecorded captives Milly and Martha Murfree and Eliza Morgan.[19] Research among private papers, wills, and local archives of Wheeler family members also disclosed the identity of Hannah Bond, who joined Jane Johnson as a potential author of the manuscript. In this fashion, I assembled my slate of the six likeliest candidates for authorship of the novel: Milly and Martha Murfree, Eliza Morgan, Mary Burton, Hannah Bond, and Jane Johnson. These identifiable Wheeler captives shared motives, means, and opportunities with the author of *The Bondwoman's Narrative*.

CHAPTER 18

THE LIFE AND TIMES OF JANE JOHNSON

I

HISTORIC RECORDS SUGGESTIVELY LINK HANNAH Crafts to Jane Johnson, a Wheeler captive who escaped in 1855 and became the center of a court case that was an international cause célèbre. Gates draws various parallels between details in *The Bondwoman's Narrative* (which does refer to Jane's escape) and details about Jane herself. But he also notes the variances between them that might exclude Jane from further consideration, and he presents other possible theories (*TBN* lxxxi–lxxxvi).

Notable among the negative considerations is this: court documents show Johnson placing her mark ["X"] instead of a signature on each of her 1855 affidavits, meaning her literacy cannot be confirmed, whereas "Hannah Crafts" avers that she learned to read as a child and had become the mistress of a "school for colored children" shortly after her escape. However, efforts to trace details about Johnson's life remained incomplete until Katherine E. Flynn detailed her extensive findings in her 2004 essay, "Jane Johnson, Found! But Is She 'Hannah Crafts'?"[1] Flynn's work is the starting point for this chapter further uncovering the life and times of Jane Johnson.

Jane Johnson's escape from the Wheeler family in 1855 came to light back in 2002, when scholar William L. Andrews noted Johnson's story recorded by William Still. My own work in this chapter will demonstrate that Johnson's escape path was first developed by the early District Underground Railroad conductors Thomas and Elizabeth Smallwood and the martyred Charles T. Torrey. Johnson's escape and experiences, a careful examination shows, foreshadow Hannah Crafts's own path to freedom. By documenting as fully as possible Johnson's identity and her life's journey, we gain a special insight into Crafts's novel—to which Jane Johnson's legacy is intimately tied.

II

In July 1855, John Hill Wheeler arrived in Washington, D.C., to deliver a packet of treaties as U.S. minister to Nicaragua; he then departed via train to Philadelphia. The other details he arranged in the District were personal. He wished to bring back to Nicaragua his enslaved captives Jane Johnson and her two sons, Daniel and Isaiah, to serve as domestic help. Slavery was illegal in Nicaragua, but by this point, Wheeler felt confident there would be no objection among ministerial staff. He had purchased these captives in January 1854, but had left them behind in Washington, hiring them out to George Waldo when Wheeler was dispatched to his post. In the summer of 1855, Wheeler met with President Franklin Pierce at the White House to discuss the urgent matters of his diplomatic mission. Then he arranged with Waldo to release Jane Johnson and Daniel and Isaiah back to his control. The stop in Philadelphia had been scheduled so Wheeler could visit the home of his father-in-law, the celebrated portraitist Thomas Sully. Here, Wheeler intended to stay only as long as necessary to collect a trunk his wife needed. But the party was delayed in Philadelphia, and that meant that Wheeler, Jane Johnson, and her two children missed the early afternoon boat out of Philadelphia that Wheeler had planned to take.[2]

Meanwhile, Johnson had her own plans, probably prearranged from her consultation with Paul Jennings at the First Colored Baptist Church in the District. The stopover in Philadelphia presented an opportunity for escape with the help of Jennings's friend William Still. While Wheeler took dinner at the hotel, Johnson sent a hotel worker for Still, the Black leader of the Pennsylvania spur of the Underground Railroad, who signaled Passmore Williamson, the prominent white abolitionist. Still and Williamson rushed to the hotel, only to find that the Wheeler party had already left for the steamer. Catching up with Wheeler, Johnson, and Johnson's sons on the boat's deck, they informed Wheeler that, under Pennsylvania law, Johnson and her children were free if they chose to exit the boat and forgo Wheeler's custody. There followed a scuffle with Wheeler as Johnson fled with her sons to a waiting carriage.[3]

Wheeler was enraged. He immediately sued Williamson, claiming that his slaves had been taken against their will and demanding their return. Williamson avowed that he did not know the whereabouts of Wheeler's captives. The case went immediately before Wheeler's family contact Judge John Kintzing Kane. Thomas Sully had lived in Philadelphia for more than two decades and kept a close relationship with Judge Kane. Indeed, Kane had served as Sully's lawyer and was a major financial backer for Sully's celebrated trip to England to paint a portrait of the young Queen Victoria. The two grew close when Kane defended Sully's rights to his famous painting of the queen when those rights were contested.[4] Williamson was arrested and imprisoned for assisting in the kidnapping of Jane Johnson and her sons.

From her hideout in New York, Johnson daringly returned to Philadelphia in late August 1855 to serve as a surprise witness at the trial of William Still and the others. As Johnson reported at the trial, "I was the slave of Mr. Wheeler of Washington; he bought me and my two children, about two years ago, of Mr. Cornelius Crew, of Richmond, Va.; my youngest child is between six and seven years old, the other between ten and eleven; I have one other child only, and he is in Richmond; I have not seen him for about two years; never expect to see him again."[5] She proceeded without hesitation to refute Wheeler's earlier account before the court and repeated her claim that she had not been forcibly abducted from Wheeler's possession. Her testimony, an observer noted, "was simply and naturally delivered." "She spoke what was evidently the truth," the journalist for the *Philadelphia Evening Post* reported, "tearing to tatters all the ingeniously devised lies of the prosecution as to her 'forcible abduction.'" Johnson's testimony was "a crusher," recounted Edward Williamson, Passmore's brother.[6]

Indeed, Jane Johnson's testimony was so powerful, and it exposed Wheeler so completely, that Wheeler, unexpectedly, stood and left the courtroom—but not before thoroughly embarrassing himself. As the *Philadelphia Evening Post* reporter noted, "For the first time I pitied that unfortunate man."[7] Some spectators in the gallery thought Wheeler had been surprised by Johnson's appearance at the trial, but they misread his reaction. In fact, Wheeler had fumed because his former captive's compelling testimony had exposed him as a liar. While Johnson testified, Wheeler sat "inside the clerk's desk, where every eye could read his shame." The correspondent for the *National Anti-Slavery Standard* reported that, during Johnson's testimony, "[Wheeler] laughed immoderately and nervously, then became deadly pale, and as the testimony went on, red and pale by turns. At last, he could bear it no longer but picked up his hat and disappeared."[8]

Earlier in the day, Wheeler had sworn out two warrants for Johnson's arrest in the presence of U.S. Supreme Court associate justice Robert Grier. One warrant was for her arrest as a fugitive slave; the second was for larceny, for stealing the apparel she was wearing at the time of her escape, some old garments of Mrs. Wheeler's. Wheeler had contrived for the marshals to enter the courtroom shortly after Johnson's arrival and after the proceedings had commenced. Philadelphia district attorney Robert Mann, sensing that Johnson was in danger at the onset of the trial, quickly summoned a squad of city police officers, who lined the hallway and the corridor of a rear exit.[9]

To many people's surprise, when the verdict came down, Still and three of the five Black dockworkers who had assisted in the escape were acquitted of all charges. In a very public way, Jane Johnson's character had outshone John Hill Wheeler's. The two Black men who were convicted of assault received light sentences, fines of ten dollars apiece and one week in jail. Wheeler's abandonment of the courtroom appears to have weakened his case. It also appears to have weakened the resolve of the deputy marshals ready to arrest Johnson at the trial.

When the city police officers summoned by Mann reversed direction and ushered Johnson through the rear door on the opposite side of the crowded room, U.S. District Attorney James Van Dyke and his marshals allowed them to proceed unhindered into the street and to a carriage prepared for their safe and expeditious removal. In her shorthand, the abolitionist who was assisting Johnson, Lucretia Mott, recorded their escape: "We didn't drive slow coming. Home," she wrote her sister, Martha Coffin Wright. "Miller, an officer—Jane & self—another carriage follow. With 4 officers for protection and all with the knowledge of the states attorney—Miller & the slave passed quickly thro' our house, up Cuthbert St. to the same carriage—wh. Drove around to elude pursuit—I ran to the storeroom & fillg. my arms with crackers & peaches, ran after them & had only time to throw them into the carriage."[10]

A motivating factor for Johnson to make her escape with her children in July 1855 was the fact that they were soon to be carried off for dangerous duty in Wheeler's Nicaraguan household. Likely, Johnson saved her own life and the lives of her children with their flight. Her proxy, Margaret Benn, was not so lucky. After Johnson's exit, Wheeler hired Benn, an Irish servant from the Protestant Servants Association of New York. Benn died from cholera three months after her arrival in Nicaragua.[11] After Johnson fled that surreal Philadelphia courtroom scene in 1855, narrowly escaping reenslavement by Wheeler, where did she go? What happened to her and her two sons, Daniel and Isaiah? And what of her other, unnamed "child in Virginia," whom Wheeler alluded to during the drama on the boat and in court? Flynn's careful genealogical work helps tell much of this story.

III

Testimony in the trial marks essential details about Johnson's life otherwise unrecorded. She was born sometime between 1814 and 1830, in Washington, D.C., and she had at least two children: Daniel, born about 1844; and Isaiah, born about 1848, as she testified. Their birthplaces seem to have been Virginia, and at least one other child was left behind in slavery.[12] Wheeler bought Johnson, Daniel, and Isaiah in Richmond, Virginia, from Cornelius Crew on New Year's Day 1854. Although some contemporary records created by whites call her Jane Wheeler, she consistently called herself Jane Johnson. Two other clues are known from records that came to light during the Passmore Williamson trial: The first is a single line in the records of the October 1855 court proceedings. On Williamson's behalf, Jane filed an affidavit attesting that Williamson did not coerce her to leave Wheeler. To create that affidavit on September 25, Johnson appeared "in person" in the U.S. Court for the District of Massachusetts—a court seated in Boston. The second is a March 1856 letter written by the abolitionist William Cooper Nell to Passmore Williamson reporting that Nell had seen Johnson and her children and that all were well.[13] Flynn's research drew on these grounding facts to help locate Johnson after 1855.

To identify Jane Johnson, Flynn first turned to the 1860 federal census. There are six Jane Johnson entries for Massachusetts—four of them in Boston and surrounding Suffolk County, where we know Johnson was located when she signed the October 1855 affidavit. Census returns for these Jane Johnsons do not match Johnson's profile as disclosed in the 1855 trial. If Johnson was still alive in 1860 and in Boston, she may have married before the census recording, and in that case, her husband would have been considered the head of household, and she would have appeared under his surname. Such a household might be discoverable through the names of Johnson's children, Daniel and Isaiah. They, too, would have appeared in household data recorded for the census. Indeed, a family group in Boston, where Jane Johnson could last be traced, fits the profile of Jane Johnson and her children.

Lawrence Woodfork[?], 40, male, black, cook, born Virginia, literate

Jane 38, female, black, born D.C., literate

Daniel Johnson, 16, male, black, born Virginia, attended school during yr

Isaiah, 12, male, black, born Virginia, attended school during yr

Ellen A[?], 11, female, black, born Virginia, attended school during yr

The 1860 census listing for this household provides other clues. The column for spouses wed within the past twelve months remains unchecked. A total of fourteen individuals, in three family groups, occupied the same dwelling.[14]

All details appear to fit the target profile, including ages, birthplaces, and names. Only "Ellen" stands out. Could she be the daughter of Johnson, even if Johnson had only mentioned leaving a son behind in Virginia during the trial? If so, how did this Ellen, born in 1849, become part of the household? More likely, she was Woodfork's daughter from an earlier marriage. Significantly, by 1860, according to this census record, Jane is listed as able to read and write—although, just five years before, she had affixed her *X* to court documents, denoting her illiteracy.

As Flynn observes, the 1860 census entry presents a research problem. On the original manuscript, the surname for Lawrence and Jane is difficult to decipher. The indexers interpreted it as "Wadford," but Flynn's examination of the enumerator's letter forms showed that "Woodfork" was the correct interpretation. The Boston 1860 directory confirms Jane Johnson and her children now part of the Woodfork family, with Lawrence Woodfork as Johnson's husband and the family living at "3 Revere St. Ct."[15]

IV

In the Boston city index for marriage intents and returns, among several other Jane Johnson intents, there is the following:

Lawrence Woodfor[k], "col'd," of Boston, aged 39 years, a laborer, second marriage.
Born in Essex County, Virginia; son of Thomas.
Jane Johnson, "col'd," of Boston, aged 25 years, second marriage.
Born in Caroline Co., Va.; daughter of John Williams.
Application: 13 August 1856, by "LW" [Lawrence Woodford].

The surnames shown for Jane Johnson and her father, together with the statement that this would be her second marriage, suggest that Jane's husband in slavery likely went by the surname "Johnson." Jane's stated birthplace conflicts with all others that cite Washington, D.C.; yet, even this "contradiction," in data supplied by Woodfork, may suggest another county in which she had lived. The most important details seem to confirm that the escaped Jane Johnson and her children Daniel and Isaiah are traceable to the Woodfork-Johnson marriage application filed on August 13, 1856.[16] Jane Johnson was married a little more than a year after her escape from John Hill Wheeler.

Flynn discovered further details about Jane Johnson and Lawrence Woodfork's life together. Research among city directories from 1855 forward places the couple, with Johnson's sons, Daniel and Isaiah, within a fostering African American community in Boston. And yet the Woodfork household was not stable. City directories show that the family moved often, rarely remaining in the same rented location for more than a year. Their poverty is detailed in the account books of the Boston Vigilance Society, as the family were frequent recipients of support. The treasurer's accounts record on November 10, 1855, the reimbursement of $39 to William Manix, an African American fugitive captive who ran a boardinghouse, for the lodging and meals of Jane Johnson and two children, followed by $4.85 for shoes and other expenses for the same. On November 22, 1855, Robert Wallcut was paid $10 for the furniture he provided Johnson. On February 13, 1856, Wallcut was paid another $10 for expenses for Johnson.[17]

The homes traceable to Johnson and Woodfork appear on the North

Slope of Beacon Hill, where Black residents constituted one of the largest concentrations of free African Americans in the North. Typically, the southern part of Beacon Hill was home to prosperous white families. Commonly, African Americans living in the Black community on the North Slope found domestic work serving their wealthy white neighbors to the south. Others in the community worked in the hotels and restaurants and other service jobs in nearby Boston.[18] It is reasonable to assume Jane Johnson found work as a domestic servant during these years as she, too, worked to support her family.

Jane Johnson's life with Lawrence Woodfork must have included the freedom and joy of living among the vibrant and free African American community of South Beacon Hill. In halls just blocks from her home, Johnson may have heard public programs by such men as John Rock, the first African American attorney to practice before the U.S. Supreme Court. The Woodfork family remained closely associated with antislavery activists and may well have heard abolitionist William Lloyd Garrison and even Abraham Lincoln speak at Faneuil Hall.[19]

Despite their apparent poverty, Johnson and Woodfork lived next door to the leading Black abolitionists Lewis and Harriet Hayden during their first year in Boston (but only that year). Their proximity suggests that perhaps the Haydens provided Johnson and her children with their first shelter. Surely, the Haydens were an inspiration. Lewis, also an escaped captive, had achieved business success and prominently led the Boston Vigilance Society. He and Harriet housed and protected hundreds of fugitive captives seeking safety in Boston or safe passage to Canada.[20] As Flynn's research discovered, Mrs. Jane Johnson Woodfork and her husband, Lawrence, also sheltered fugitives on at least two occasions, December 25, 1857, and April 13, 1859.[21]

V

Instability was common to Johnson's life in Boston, as she struggled to make her way as a free woman. The city directories show Lawrence being absent from the household after mid-1861, and death records help explain why. An entry for Woodfork (indexed as "Wood*falk*") reports that he died on December 9, 1861, age forty-six and a resident of 31 Bridge Street. His parents are given as Thomas and Millea; his birthplace as Essex County, Virginia.[22] Not surprisingly, considering the five moves they had made in the five years of their marriage, Woodfork left no inheritable estate for Johnson and her children.[23]

As the directories demonstrate, the widowed Johnson remarried two and a half years after the death of Woodfork. The Boston marriage register notes:

> William Harris, "col'd" of Boston, aged 37 years, a mariner, second marriage.
> Born in Oldtown [Allegany County], Maryland; son of Samuel and Polly.
> Jane WOODFORK, "col'd," of Boston, aged 26 years, second marriage.
> Born in Washington, D.C.; daughter of John Williams and Jane.
> Married: 20 July 1864, by Peter Ross, M.G. [Bishop, AME Church][24]

Again, the details provided in the historical record show some contradictions, although Johnson's identity is not in doubt. Given that Harris should have been Jane's third husband, not her second, it appears that her slave marriage to Johnson did not hold legal consequence when her marriage to Harris was recorded. At the time of her union to William Harris in 1864, Johnson would have been in her midforties, although the record reduces her age to twenty-six. The marriage with Harris did not last long, as his death is recorded within a year. As city directories show, Jane Johnson was a widow again when the directory was published in December 1865.[25]

Further records from the period show that, in 1863, Johnson's youngest son, Isaiah, who was only fifteen at the time (but claimed to be eighteen), enlisted in the Fifty-fifth Massachusetts Volunteer Infantry, a "colored" unit formed from the overflow of recruits for the famous

Fifty-fourth Massachusetts Regiment. Mustering in as a drummer in Company K in June 1863, he directed that all letters were to go to "Mrs. Jane Woodfork No 2 Revere St Boston Mass (mother)."[26]

Johnson—like many widowed mothers—probably was designated to receive young Isaiah's army pay. The men of Isaiah's unit had been promised pay equal to that of white soldiers—thirteen dollars a month—but when the paymaster allotted wages, the "colored" troops of Isaiah's regiment received only ten dollars. The governor offered to make up the difference from state funds, but units like Isaiah's refused on principle. Not until June 1864 did Congress right this inequity. In the interim of twelve months, Isaiah and his fellow soldiers received nothing, which caused tremendous hardships at home.[27]

Isaiah's unit disbanded on August 29, 1865, in Charleston, South Carolina. The regimental history published in 1868 places Isaiah, along with other men of his unit, back in Boston, although he does not appear in the city directories of 1866–1871.[28] Again, Flynn's intrepid research discovered more. Isaiah's fate after 1872 is obscure but recoverable. A man with a similar name, Isaac Johnson of Xenia, Ohio, posed as the real Isaiah Johnson and began collecting Isaiah's pension benefits. Between 1890 and 1901, the fraud continued until it was finally corrected. The case created an investigation that produced a sizable file. To sort out the real Isaiah Johnson, several depositions were taken from members of the Fifty-fifth in 1901. Here, Ransom Chatman of Company K describes the real Isaiah: "He was a little dark complex'd boy, nothing more than a boy, and enlisted as a drummer. He was the [white] Captains pet."[29] As Flynn observes, repositories hold extant photographs of members of the Fifty-fifth, but none depicts Isaiah Johnson, and federal files of headstone requests for Civil War veterans do not include a record for him.[30]

VI

Johnson and her offspring disappear from traceable records for the five years after the close of the Civil War. But when the compiler of the city directory canvassed Boston for the 1865–66 directory, Jane Johnson, Daniel, and Isaiah were recorded at 22 Vine Street. They seem to have left Massachusetts before the 1865 state census enumerator made his rounds, and they were still elsewhere when the 1870 federal census was compiled. Moreover, they have not been located within the 1870 federal census databases for New Jersey, North Carolina, Virginia, Washington, D.C., or in more specialized census holdings explored by Flynn.[31]

As Flynn notes, whatever Johnson's choices and actions, she reappears in Boston in 1871, settling at 5 Fruit Street. The next year's directory places her and Isaiah again at the same address, shortly before Johnson died of dysentery that summer amid a citywide epidemic.[32]

Dates of death & registration: 2 and 3 August 1872
Name: Jane Harris
M[aiden] N[ame]: Williams
Age: 59 years
Address: 5 Fruit St. Ct.
F[emale] W[idow of]: William
Birthplace: Washington, D.C.
Parents & birthplaces: John [and] Jane Williams; Washington, D.C.
Cause of death & duration: Dysentery, 14 days
Place of Interment: Woodlawn
Informant: L. Jones [Lewis L. Jones, undertaker; 50 LaGrange St.]

No estate records are extant for Johnson, and her death did not draw an obituary or notice in newspapers.[33] Johnson was buried at Woodlawn Cemetery in Everett, Massachusetts, five miles north of Boston. Flynn's research of the records at Woodlawn shows the age and death date in burial records matching the civil registration of Johnson's death. She was interred alone in a double plot. No details are provided about who bought the plot or when it was purchased. Even today, Jane Johnson's grave is identified only by a nameless metal plot marker, similar to many in her section.[34]

VII

Flynn's research turned up two further references in extant letters between William C. Nell and Passmore Williamson that confirm Jane Johnson's identification as Jane (Johnson) Woodfork, wife of Lawrence. The two letters proved to be the source of Flynn's claim that Jane Johnson was the author of *The Bondwoman's Narrative*:

Boston, December 3, 1855

Dear Mr. Williamson,

When I called upon you at Moyamensing prison last October with the committee from the National Convention of Colored Americans I omitted to mention that I met Jane Johnson and her two boys at the Cars in Boston after her escape from Wheeler, in my capacity as a member of the Vigilance Committee, and was subsequently engaged in securing home and employment for her: on each occasion she was full of gratitude to you and the other noble friends who rescued her.

I also intended soliciting your autograph and will feel much obliged if the same be forwarded to the antislavery office Philadelphia or to my address 21 Cornhill Boston.

I remain in the cause of Freedom for all
Fraternally Yours,

William C. Nell

And:

Boston May 26, 1856

Respected Friend,

Accept my thanks for the volume kindly forwarded me.

Jane Johnson called in this morning and expressed much pleasure on hearing from you. She requested my informing you that she now lives No 1 Southack Court—and is quite well. Her boys are progressing finely at school, for all these advantages of freedom she feels heartfelt gratitude for your exertions.

Gratified in the opportunity of communicating as above I remain
Fraternally Yours,

Wm. C. Nell[35]

For Flynn, Nell's second letter, sending Johnson's address to Williamson, is critical for two reasons. First, the address is precisely the same one listed for Lawrence Woodfork in the 1857 directory—establishing beyond a doubt that the Wheeler captive known as Jane Johnson was, indeed, Jane (Williams) Johnson Woodfork Harris. Second, it establishes that Jane Johnson and her family were already on the road to literacy in 1856. Flynn conjectures that Johnson requested that Nell send her address to Williamson because she wished to correspond with him directly.[36] According to Flynn, this opens the door to Johnson's growing literacy and the possibility that she is the author of *The Bondwoman's Narrative*.

VIII

Is "Hannah Crafts" a pseudonym for the Wheeler fugitive Jane Johnson? Gates, for one, proposed this hypothesis, and Flynn used her extensive research to argue the likelihood of Jane Johnson's being the author. In considering this possibility, Gates noted both similarities and differences between the details known for Johnson and the life account given by "Hannah Crafts." However, this hypothesis—one of several Gates proposed to invite further scholarship—faced two serious obstacles: the known illiteracy of Johnson and the failure to track her life as a free woman. Flynn's research engaged both obstacles and, for Flynn, left open the possibility that Jane Johnson was the author of *The Bondwoman's Narrative*.

Because *The Bondwoman's Narrative* is an autobiographical novel, it is hard to know where fiction blends into true events, people, and places.

Although the novel purports to be based on fact, it is difficult to say what is fact and what is fiction. Nonetheless, the genre Crafts used carried certain established conventions. Using a pseudonym was common to protect family members still in bondage. For instance, Harriet Jacobs wrote her *Incidents in the Life of a Slave Girl* (1861) under the name "Linda Brent." While abolitionists encouraged narratives written by escaped authors to "be as . . . exact as possible, to name names and to embrace verisimilitude as a dominant mode of narrative development," many authors had good reason to obscure details of their lives, the identities of their captors, and their paths to freedom (*TBN* lxvi). With the passage of the Fugitive Slave Act in 1850, enslavers could more readily recapture escaped freedom seekers, and retaliation against family members still in bondage was common.

So, we are led to the obvious question: Did one adult domestic captive escape the Wheelers in the 1850s, or did two? Are the details now known for Johnson compatible with evidence the manuscript presents? The author of *The Bondwoman's Narrative* depicts the heroine, Hannah, as being purchased by the Wheelers as a lady's maid to replace "Jane," who had run away (*TBN* 154–55). Gates's scholarship makes the case that the "Jane" in Crafts's novel is the escapee Jane Johnson. This leads Gates to identify the Wheelers as acquiring the real-life "Hannah" after Johnson's escape and to the unsuccessful trial to reclaim her in late 1855. Gates concludes, "Judging from the relevant information contained in Wheeler's diary, Hannah's escape would most likely have occurred between March 21 and May 4, 1857" (*TBN* xci). Flynn contends that perhaps "Hannah" belonged to the Wheelers before 1855.[37]

Here is her argument: Between mid-1853 and mid-1854, the primary Wheeler residence was in Washington, D.C., where John Hill Wheeler served President Franklin Pierce as an assistant secretary. The family departed Washington after Wheeler's August 1854 appointment as resident minister to Nicaragua. Although he briefly returned in the summer of 1855, his family did not. Wheeler was recalled in October 1856, but he had already sent his wife and sons back to the States for their safety in May of that year.[38] Between May 1856 and March 1857, Mrs. Wheeler and her husband resided in Washington, D.C., at the "splendid mansion" Crafts describes that was owned by Sarah Childress Polk (Mrs. James K. Polk), who spent most of her time on her family's "plantation" near Nashville. Flynn's conjectures placing Jane Johnson as Hannah Crafts depend on the Wheelers' living situation being undetermined between 1856 and 1857, but they are documented to be residing in the Polk mansion in Washington.

Flynn reaches for overlaps for the corresponding years of Johnson's service to the Wheelers. She cites the "uncanny" connection of Wheeler's relationship with James Cochran Dobbin. As a North Carolina assemblyman, Wheeler campaigned for Dobbin to win the state's U.S. Senate seat. Dobbin was unsuccessful, but Wheeler's strong advocacy won Dobbin's friendship. When Dobbin was appointed secretary of the Department of the Navy in 1853, he convinced President Pierce to find a more lucrative position for Wheeler; and in August 1854, Pierce appointed Wheeler U.S. minister to Nicaragua. Meanwhile, "Hannah"—early in her Washington chapter—writes of Wheeler's bid for a position in the Department of the Navy. Considering the number of bureaus and departments the manuscript's author could have chosen to weave into her novel, according to Flynn, "it begs disbelief [*sic*] that 'Hannah' accidentally portrayed her Mr. Wheeler as a political suitor of the Navy Department."[39]

Flynn does make substantial contributions by focusing on documented facts and uncovering many new ones. But she also ignores facts, or does not uncover important details related to Wheeler, most notably the family's acquisition of Hannah Bond in May 1856 and their movements and circumstances while Bond served in their household. The circumstantial evidence Flynn develops to try to place Jane Johnson as the author and events from the novel as a match to Johnson are inventive but ultimately unconvincing, especially when one traces the career of Hannah Bond, whose story fits like a glove with the manuscript.

IX

The argument for Jane Johnson stands thus. Records show that Johnson acquired a measure of literacy between 1855 and 1860. After her escape from John Hill Wheeler, she was unable to sign her name to her affidavits and, instead, had to affix her mark. Over the next ten months, William Nell's letters demonstrate that Johnson found employment and that her sons were flourishing at school. By 1860, the first year that a census enumerates Johnson as a free woman, she is recorded as being capable of reading and writing. Could she, in four years, have acquired sufficient literacy to write a novel? According to Flynn in her assessment of the literary quality of *The Bondwoman's Narrative*, Johnson could have composed it. Flynn writes that "Hannah Crafts" naïvely "borrows" from Dickens and others and that both the plot and the style of the novel are more accurately described as "fervent but workmanlike" rather than "fresh and imaginative."[40]

As my discussions in chapters 10 and 16 of this book demonstrate, I hold a much higher opinion of Crafts's literary talent than Flynn does. Still, as Flynn rightly notes, whoever "Hannah" was, she was driven to write her manuscript by powerful emotions. Crafts dwelled extensively on the sexual exploitation of captive women not just by masters and slave traders but also by female captors complicit in forcing bondwomen into sexual unions against their will. Certainly, Jane Johnson had good reason to expose the Wheelers' shallowness and cruel disregard for the lives and feelings of other humans, including her. As Johnson had experienced directly, Wheeler purchased her away from one son and probably away from the husband of her children, too. During that fateful 1855 trip, while passing through Philadelphia, Johnson probably knew Wheeler was transporting her and her remaining sons out of the country. For her, her planned escape before having to set sail for Nicaragua was likely a matter of life and death. Even after she escaped, Wheeler's influence in Democratic circles made him a fearsome adversary to her and her remaining children; in fact, he did everything in his power to recover Johnson and her sons, given that he had a legal claim to them, as his diaries show.[41]

Wheeler held no legal claim to Hannah Bond after her escape and, still, he pursued her, too, on behalf of his brother's family.

Jane Johnson died suddenly in 1872, as Flynn discovered. Building on her work, I have been able to reconstruct the lives of the two sons who escaped with Johnson. Isaiah, the son Johnson lived with at the time of her death, was arrested for assault and battery less than a year after his mother's passing, although he was acquitted.[42] Eventually, the young drummer boy from the Civil War reenlisted and served in the army, rising to corporal in the Ninth Cavalry Buffalo Soldiers.[43] In 1897, at Fort Washakie, Wyoming, where his unit was stationed, Isaiah quarreled with another man in his "colored" unit, Charles Pauley. They fought, then "Johnson picked up his gun and shot Pauley through the body." Pauley "died the following day."[44] Isaiah escaped his first imprisonment, but he was recaptured and later sentenced to "ten years in the penitentiary, a fine of $1000 and cost of the trial."[45] He died fourteen years later, in 1911, in Silver City, New Mexico, after receiving an early release from prison. He appears to have left behind a wife and two sons, from whom he was estranged by at least 1884, possibly much earlier. He was sixty-five years old at the time of his death and likely uninvolved in the lives of his children.[46]

Daniel Johnson, the elder of the two boys who escaped Mr. Wheeler in 1855, lived to the age of eighty-one. He, too, served in the U.S. Army—in his case, for "31 years and six months," as part of the famed all-Black Tenth Cavalry Buffalo Soldiers. Johnson's military service included action in the Spanish-American War (1898), where his unit supported the flank of future president Theodore Roosevelt's "Rough Riders" at the Battle of San Juan Hill in Cuba.[47] Eyewitnesses noted that the Rough Riders would not have prevailed without the Buffalo Soldiers. White and Black soldiers intermingled during the charge to take San Juan Hill. Had he not been imprisoned the year before, Daniel's brother Isaiah would have been in this same battle, with the Ninth Cavalry.

Daniel and his fellow Buffalo Soldiers from the Tenth Cavalry were then assigned to Fort Assiniboine in northern Montana, where Johnson mustered out of the unit upon the fort's closure in 1916. As his Havre,

Montana, obituary notes, Daniel Johnson was married to Margaret Payne for more than fifty-seven years, and the two were the parents of eleven children, six of whom survived Daniel. After his military service, according to his obituary, Johnson "worked as janitor in the Hill County State bank in Havre for years" before his retirement. He was a member of the local Masonic lodge, and he and Margaret were leaders in the small Black community of Havre, a role that included Johnson's service as treasurer to the community's St. Stephen's AME Church.[48] The descendants of Jane Johnson can be traced through Daniel and Margaret all the way down to their great-grandson Thomas Henry Allsup Jr., who died childless in 1982 in Ventura County, California.[49]

For Flynn and others who identify Johnson as the author, Johnson's offspring preserved their mother's manuscript, with Flynn conjecturing that the discovery of the manuscript in New Jersey could be attributed to Johnson's sons or their heirs. But Johnson's children left the Northeast almost immediately after their mother's death, with Daniel and Isaiah both pursuing military careers. There is no record that I can find of a Johnson heir residing in New Jersey to match the work's acquisition there in 1948 by collector Emily Driscoll.

Did Johnson have the means, motive, and opportunity to write *The Bondwoman's Narrative*? Her motivation is beyond question. Most arguments, therefore, revolve around means and opportunity. Johnson arrived in Boston into a community of highly literate African Americans; there, literacy was critical to survival in the competition for employment. Through the Boston Vigilance Society, she had access to the education and support necessary to achieve a degree of literacy. However, if John Hill Wheeler's testimony in the Passmore Williamson case is to be believed, Jane Johnson never served the Wheelers in North Carolina. During the trial, Wheeler is quoted as saying, "These servants were never in North Carolina; they lived with me during the past year in Washington; they were never with me in North Carolina." He explained: "I said they were my slaves under the law of North Carolina because I am a citizen of the State; I got them in Virginia; they were slaves there. I have owned them some three years I believe."[50]

Ultimately, the case for Jane Johnson is circumstantial and fails. Indeed, Johnson's unique legal records and the contemporary accounts by her associates present her as a woman of innate intelligence, with a clear purpose and will to gain freedom for herself and her children—in short, a formidable woman in her era. Her saga is impressive in its own right, as one of the few that have been documented among millions of enslaved lives. As simply Jane Johnson, she represents an important chapter in America's ongoing experiment to realize the ideals to which it aspires. Jane (Williams) Johnson Woodfork Harris lies in a nameless grave, with only a numbered marker to identify her remains, but her story still inspires. Hannah Crafts, however, who overlapped with Jane Johnson while serving among the Wheeler family, likely received knowledge from Johnson that then aided her own escape. Even if Johnson was not the author of Crafts's narrative, her life story clearly inspired important parts of the narrative as Hannah Bond followed a path to freedom that Johnson had already cleared. Johnson helped deliver Crafts's story.

CHAPTER 19

THE LIFE AND TIMES OF HANNAH CRAFTS

I

THE AUTHOR DEVELOPS THE NARRATIVE with poise as she veils her identity. By the time of her escape, Hannah Crafts the author was writing in the voice of Hannah the fugitive narrator, who is passing as a free young white person who is cross-dressed as a male. A handful of sharp epigraphs about life in general, and not just under slavery, address the reader: "Those to whom man teaches little, nature like a wise and prudent mother teaches much" (*TBN* 18)—precisely the kind of writing exercises students boarding at Wheeler House practiced. ("Nature's ample book, so open to all . . . writ by God's own hand.") About slavery, Crafts observes, "But those who think that the greatest evils of slavery are connected with physical suffering possess no just or rational ideas of human nature. The soul, the immortal soul must ever long and yearn for a thousand things inseperable [*sic*] to liberty."[1] Crafts lived with two sets of Wheeler family members in Murfreesboro, North Carolina, and Washington, D.C., between 1852 and 1857.

Her preface is a "mini-masterpiece," as the writer Paul Berman has called it. In the course of five sentences, the author rises from humbly addressing the reader and framing her narrative to invoking an angry God:

> In presenting this record of plain unvarnished facts to a generous public I feel a certain degree of diffidence and self-distrust. I ask myself for the hundredth time How will such a literary venture, coming from a sphere so humble be received? Have I succeeded in portraying any of the peculiar features of that institution whose curse rests over the fairest land the sun shines upon? Have I succeeded in showing how it blights the happiness of the white as well as the black race? Being the truth it makes no pretensions to romance, and relating events as they occurred it has no especial reference to a moral, but to those who regard truth as stranger than fiction it can be no less interesting on the former account, while others of pious and discerning minds can scarcely fail to recognise the hand of Providence in giving to the righteous the reward of their works, and to the wicked the fruit of their doings. (*TBN* 3)

Whom did the author have in mind in addressing "those who regard truth as stranger than fiction"? In fact, Crafts is citing her enslaver John Hill Wheeler and his own claims of presenting compelling history in his life's work, *Historical Sketches*. There, Wheeler uses the epigraph prominently to launch his volume, noting at the center of his title page that "Truth Is Stranger Than Fiction."[2] The phrase was common for slave narratives published in the era, including those Wheeler held in his library.

Wheeler's book would become the standard history of North Carolina until 1879, when his nephew John Wheeler Moore published his equally unbalanced chronicle, *School History of North Carolina, from 1584 to 1879.*[3] (Both narratives would reflect the white supremacy of the college essay "American Aristocracy" penned by the latter's wife, Ann Ward Moore, whom Hannah Jr. served while Ward boarded at Wheeler House.) Together, uncle and nephew determined the standard account of North Carolina history for more than 150 years. Not surprisingly, the Wheelers and Moores excluded Native Americans and African Americans from their narratives, only rarely signaling their presence and always in a subservient role. Like much of the history passed down by other leading white families of the South, the stories preserved and championed by the Wheelers and Moores were self-serving. Lost to these pages are the twenty-eight Wheeler captives—men, women, and children—compelled to march by coffle to Norfolk in 1836 to be sold and shipped to New Orleans. Missing, too, are the nearly million just like them forced to endure other transport along the "Second Middle Passage." In their places are lies about manumissions and paternalistic "masters." Further buried are the Tuscarora and Meherrin Nations, pushed beyond the margins of these pages to make room for the white men who stole their land, the "Distinguished Statesmen, Jurists, Lawyers, Soldiers, Divines, Etc." who are the only legitimate subjects of Wheeler's and Moore's histories.[4]

For Hannah Crafts, there was probably no other book more immediately present and within her reach than Wheeler's *Historical Sketches*. Although, from its publication, Wheeler's book was found to contain "a witch's brew of errors, literary and historical," the first ten-thousand-copy printing sold out, a major publishing success in its day.[5] Multiple copies of *Historical Sketches* were donated to the Reading Room of the original Chowan Baptist Female Institute.[6] Two of Crafts's enslavers, Samuel Jordan Wheeler and John Hill Wheeler, kept copies displayed prominently in their homes. And an additional volume is tallied as checked out by Samuel Jordan Wheeler's son John, from the Enosinian Society at Columbian College in 1856.[7] In short, most everywhere the author turned, she would have been aware of Mr. Wheeler's book.

In his volume, Wheeler opines in another epigraph: "Ill fares it with a State, whose history is written by others than her own sons."[8] As writers, Wheeler and Moore must have seen themselves as the state's chosen "sons." If so, Crafts was an illegitimate daughter.

Surely, with so many copies in her way, Crafts leafed through Wheeler's *Historical Sketches* at some point. Her mother's enslaver William P. Bond is named in Wheeler's book, and so is the author's likely father, Lewis Bond. If Wheeler's narrative is known as "the Democratic Stud Book" for its hagiography of slaveholding party members in North

Carolina, Crafts's *The Bondwoman's Narrative* sketches a very different picture of the people and institutions celebrated by Wheeler and Moore.[9] Its author presents the lives and times of her and her enslaved sisters and others excluded from Wheeler's *Historical Sketches*. In his preface, Wheeler writes, "The time has come when the results of my labors are to be presented to the intelligence and favor of my countrymen. I feel, unaffectedly, how inadequate I am for such a task. My labors, however, may have one effect: they may assist and inspire some abler hand to undertake and complete this work, now so hesitatingly commenced."[10] Crafts would be that "abler hand" ready to tell a more complete story.

Even if not wholly intended, Crafts's preface holds a fascinating dialogue with Wheeler's preface. What at first appears as generic understatement by Crafts may also be a kind of reflection on Wheeler's self-important preface mixing humility with grandiosity. Crafts seems to follow and perhaps satirize Wheeler's mix of bravado and humility. And so, she balances the two with her own interrogatory flourishes (*TBN* 3).

Certainly, Crafts's design for her narrative was the opposite of Wheeler's "Stud Book." Rather, with *The Bondwoman's Narrative*, she seeks to "relat[e] events as they occurred," even by naming the "Wheelers" directly. But she also designs her work to be an autobiographical novel drawing on the popular works of Stowe and Dickens. In her effort to reveal a "truth stranger than fiction," she assures her readers that the work "makes no pretensions to romance," a claim she likely encountered in Dickens's preface to *Bleak House*, where the author stakes out the truth value of his art: "I mention here that everything set forth in these pages . . . is substantially true, and within the truth," even if, as Dickens states, "I have purposely dwelt upon the romantic side of familiar things."[11]

Crafts likely followed Dickens in her faith that the novel form could deliver a more complete "truth" compared with Wheeler's so-called history. Like those who came before her—James Barefoot, Nat Turner, the Smallwoods—she would allow her hand to be guided by the hand of an angry God ("the hand of Providence") to shape her autobiographical novel. Like James Barefoot, Nat Turner, and the Smallwoods, Crafts sought for "the righteous the reward of their works" and brought "to the wicked the fruit of their doings." Her pen would marshal the same forces as James Barefoot's conspiracy, as Turner's revolt, and as the Smallwoods' Underground network. Only, Crafts's conspiracy, revolt, and escape would be effected by her pen, in a story she carried in her sewing box and, later, secreted in a portmanteau that formed a part of her disguise in her bid for freedom.

II

Crafts began her work on paper taken from John Hill Wheeler's supply while she was enslaved by the Wheelers in Washington, D.C., during the 1856–57 period when the family rented the mansion of the widowed Mrs. Sarah Childress Polk. Letters John Hill Wheeler sent to friends in late 1856 and early 1857 match the fiber, cut, and watermarks found in Crafts's early chapters written on the same stationery folded and stitched into folios. Crafts's access to writing materials such as paper, quills, and ink matches Hannah's in the novel, where she is provided these materials by her captor to take dictation for Mrs. Wheeler. In the novel, Mrs. Wheeler commends Hannah for writing "a beautiful letter at her dictation." "Now seal the letter," Mrs. Wheeler commands (*TBN* 158). The moment matches what we know of other Bond and Wheeler captives serving as amanuenses for students at Wheeler House.

Perhaps not coincidentally, sealing wax is used in the actual manuscript where Crafts affixes slips of paper over passages she edits, pressing the repaired passage to the page with her sewing thimble. Quite possibly in real life, Crafts occasionally transcribed Mrs. Wheeler's words for at least some of her correspondence. And she may have sealed those letters, too, with her sewing thimble. I have not been able to track down letters sent by Ellen Sully Wheeler between 1856 and 1857, but my guess is that Crafts's handwriting would match some of those missives and the seal, too—that is, if the letters are preserved and can be discovered again. In fact, locating them would constitute a major historical find.

In May 1856, Ellen Sully Wheeler returned to the United States from Nicaragua with the family's two sons, Sully and Woodbury. At the time, John Hill Wheeler was serving as U.S. minister to Nicaragua, but the political situation was rapidly deteriorating, largely because of his diplomatic mismanagement. One of Ellen's first stops upon her return was at Wheeler House, in Eastern North Carolina. From there, Mrs. Wheeler placed Sully and Woodbury in the Horner School, a military academy in Oxford, North Carolina, where they could finish their secondary education. (The American school at Granada had ceased operating amid rising political violence.) Ellen remained at Wheeler House until late May, before setting off for Washington, D.C.[12] This is when Hannah Bond became her "maidservant." The arrangement parallels Crafts's version of events in the novel. In *The Bondwoman's Narrative*, Hannah becomes the property of "Mrs. Wheeler" after she attends on her during a summer visit to Mrs. Henry at her "Forget me not" plantation. In real life, Ellen hired out Hannah Jr. from her sister-in-law Lucinda Bond Wheeler in May 1856. At the time, Ellen needed domestic help and a traveling companion for her return to Washington. And, so, a private arrangement was made for Hannah Bond to begin service to Mrs. Wheeler and help her reestablish the Wheeler household in the capital, even as they awaited the recall of Minister Wheeler.

As we have seen, Crafts cultivated the skills of authorship mostly through stealth. Her education, likely initiated with the help of a Quaker couple near Indian Woods, continued through her own drive as a gifted autodidact "gathering up such crumbs of knowledge as I could." Essential to her progress were the "lessons" she acquired in the four important years she served boarders at Wheeler House as part of her enslavement to Lucinda Bond Wheeler.

Crafts does not seem to hold Lucinda Bond Wheeler up for scrutiny as she does Ellen Sully Wheeler later in the text. It may be that a blood tie kept her reticent, or that some friendship or warm feeling was maintained between the two. The fact that the early part of her narrative disguises the extended Pugh and Bond families may also relate to the author's captivity. Keep in mind that even after her escape, and until the end of the Civil War, Crafts was still legally the property of Lucinda Pugh Bond Wheeler. Further, the Pughs and Bonds continued to control the lives of the author's surviving family members, including her mother. Crafts's reticence and efforts to obscure the Pughs and Bonds probably reflect her caution over potential reprisals against those she loved still possessed by their families.

Another reason for fictionalizing the Pughs and Bonds may be related to the sexual abuse Crafts experienced. As I have already noted, the author had no outlet for sharing the story of her coercion by Thomas Bond Jr., except by using fiction as a suitable vehicle. Further, there is the taboo of familial rape—as nephew to Lewis Bond, Crafts's likely forced partner, Bond Jr., would have been Crafts's half cousin. Instead, like fellow sexual assault survivor Harriet Jacobs, Crafts turned to the novel form to write about her experiences. This is probably how the sexual relationship between Thomas Bond Jr. and Hannah Crafts became an important plot device, pairing the protagonist, Hannah, with an unnamed passing "mistress." Only when the "mistress" is killed off does the work begin to reach toward resolution and liberty. Writing the novel seems to have helped the author deliver both.

III

Lucinda Bond Wheeler was the most consistent presence in the author's life from the time of Crafts's birth in 1826 to her escape in 1857. Especially important were the four years Crafts lived with Lucinda at Wheeler House as her legal captive. And yet, very little can be gleaned from extant sources about Lucinda, beyond the fact that she was clearly a dedicated mother to her children and a strong helpmate to her husband. Like other Bond-Wheeler family members, Lucinda was a devoted Baptist, and she took seriously her work caring for the boarders who lodged with the family while attending Chowan Baptist Female

Institute. Lucinda also became a financial lifeline for her husband, Dr. Samuel Jordan Wheeler. Her father, Lewis Bond, had purchased the Wheeler property in Murfreesboro in 1851, when Dr. Wheeler and his brother, John Hill Wheeler, were in financial distress. Bond had then gifted the property back to his daughter, Lucinda, stipulating full rights to her and shielding the property from Dr. Wheeler's creditors. These moves helped save Wheeler House and Liberty Hall from foreclosure and ensured that the Wheeler property would remain intact for more than a decade after the Civil War.

There are very few direct records to paint Lucinda's portrait. One sketch is passed down related to her commitment to her husband, although this occurred in 1842, a decade before Hannah Bond became a captive at Wheeler House. As a young man, Bill Harrell, son of an early merchant in the town, wrote a letter describing how he broke his leg in Murfreesboro that summer by "jumping off a high hill down at Mill Pond." The group of other boys he was with "hurried off up town, as fast as possible, to get a doctor to come to my help." Dr. Samuel Jordan Wheeler was among the town's three physicians who raced to the scene. As Harrell observed, "nearly the entire male population of the town" arrived with the physicians, "besides bringing with them a wagon and pillows and bed from home, and they lifted me up in to the wagon, and every move seemed to be tearing my leg from my body." The compound fracture (the skin broken and the bone exposed) must have been severe and in need of immediate treatment. Young Harrell could only agonize as the limb was reset: area physicians had not yet accepted chloroform as an anesthesia.[13]

Dr. Edward Neale appears to have been the one to set Harrell's leg, but when he presented a medical invoice of $150 to Harrell's father in 1843, Dr. Wheeler, who had charged nothing for his own assistance, became incensed. The conflict became so acrimonious that the usually mild-mannered Dr. Wheeler engaged in a public brawl with Dr. Neale. Harrell records the event in this fashion: One day in September 1843, Neale came to Wheeler's store, evidently looking for a fight. "Dr. Wheeler seizing his gun . . . put a load of buck shot into a door post, within two inches of Neale's head, as he stood cursing . . . and as the gun fired, somebody ran down to Mrs. Wheeler and reported that her husband was killed . . . and she (being in two months of her time the birth of her youngest, Julia M. Wheeler), she dropped everything and ran screaming through the streets, and reaching her husband's store fell helpless in the midst of a great crowd." Harrell continues: "She was lifted up placed on a litter and carried as quickly as possible home but it was all over by the time she reached the gate, and the men who helped quietly retired especially as two doctors had arrived."[14] Harrell, like Crafts, seems to have read his Dickens. The scene is described in a fashion reminiscent of the fainting swoons of female Dickens characters like Morleena Kenwigs in the popular *Nicholas Nickleby* (1839).[15]

What was the environment like for Crafts, serving among Chowan Institute students? Records show that there were usually six to eight female boarders living with the Wheelers at any one time during Crafts's tenure with them (1852–56).[16] We have seen how active the early Philomathean literary society was and how boarders participated in the production of its periodical, *The Casket*. The upper age limit for the students Crafts served was around nineteen; the lower, as young as fifteen. There were two sessions to the school year, one beginning in October and the other in March, each lasting about four and a half months. The school year ended with a Commencement Day in mid-July. And it opened with one, too, at the fall launch. The students were given examinations every six weeks, and final examinations were conducted by the president. Any demerits received were recorded in each student's file for misbehavior.[17]

According to letters, diary entries, and school records, the curriculum was rigorous, consisting of English, history, French, Latin, arithmetic, algebra, geometry, trigonometry, logic, mental philosophy, philosophy of natural history, astronomy, botany, chemistry, and religious instruction.[18] For women's colleges like Chowan Baptist Female Institute, safety and shielding female students from male attention were paramount. Anne

Beale Davis, wife of the Rev. Joseph H. Davis, president of nearby Wesleyan Female College, carried this responsibility—as Lucinda Bond Wheeler did for the boarders at Wheeler House. Mrs. Davis's letters are preserved, whereas Mrs. Wheeler's are mostly lost. In those letters, Davis explains how maintaining female propriety was her most difficult responsibility, important not only for ensuring the safety of the school's female boarders but also for safeguarding the reputation of the college.[19] Such care and activity had to have struck Hannah Jr. as the opposite of her own experience, where she was groomed to be sexually assaulted and placed for that purpose in the hands of Lewis Bond's own nephew.

Fellowship and friendship were probably the hallmarks of the college experience, then as now, and it is very likely that Crafts shared in some of these bonds. In just a few sessions of close living, friendships were frequently forged that lasted a lifetime. Preserved letters from the period attest to these experiences, as do records of friendship ceremonies recorded at places like Wesleyan Female College. Anne Davis notes such a friendship declaration ceremony shaped as a marriage rite: "I omitted to say that the girls had three bridal parties among themselves, one couple was Mattie White groom[,] Anna Riddick bride; another Ret Cowper groom[,] Celia Holly bride, and the last I forget who was the groom, but A. Weston was the bride. I believe they jumped over a broom."[20] The broom-jumping followed a practice the young women may have witnessed at slave weddings back home. Quite naturally, these female college students turned to African American rituals to express same-sex bonds not generally sanctioned by their culture.[21]

While attending a female college, the intense scrutiny of sexually controlling men could be forgotten, at least for a while. This extended to boarding arrangements. At Wheeler House, there was only one male beside Dr. Wheeler. That was young John Wheeler, Lucinda's preteen son, who was only twelve years old when Crafts first joined the household. John's adolescent years corresponded with Hannah Jr.'s presence, and a friendship may have developed between the two. Later, John's traceable activities suggest a young man questioning the slaveholding doctrines of his parents and other elders. His letters from college are unique among family correspondence for his always inquiring after the welfare of the family's "servants." John's few remaining personal effects, shared with me by descendants, included the transcript of an abolitionist sermon he attended at the Wells' Meeting House, a Quaker place of worship in Perquimans County, North Carolina, in 1856, about six months before Crafts's escape. This document was interleaved with young John's notebook for a class he was taking at Columbian College at the time. The document, folded into the notebook, appeared to go unnoticed or unremarked upon by family members. When they provided me with John's papers, they were surprised to hear of the transcription.[22] As we will see, it is quite possible that John knowingly provided the "suit of male apparel" in which Crafts, like Hannah, disguised herself to make her escape from Murfreesboro in May 1857.

IV

If Lucinda Bond Wheeler is elusive and difficult to trace in *The Bondwoman's Narrative*, Mrs. Wheeler's boarders and their literary efforts are less so. Crafts must have engaged these students daily and even hourly on some days. And, so, she may have been familiar with Sophia Booth, who, in 1854, composed an essay for *The Casket* detailing her homesickness for her family near Petersburg, Virginia. In the work, Booth, as "S.B.," imagines the "Home Scenes" that go on in her absence. "I will visit my *home* at evening—that season when the most united, and happy families seem more closely drawn together still, as if shunning the darkness in which Nature has wrapt all without." She continues: "They are collected within to rejoice in the light of each other's countenance. They are seated around the bright wood fire in a neat and comfortable parlor of a country house." Booth then shares the scene of an older brother reading from a novel to the assembled family, including her father, Dr. Edwin Booth, "the dignified and agreeable old gentleman seated in the large arm-chair." The scene closes with the father reading from the Bible ("the best of all books") before these "loved and honored ones seek repose."[23]

Such a sentimental vision of family domesticity surely would have struck Crafts as discordant considering what she knew of the Bond slave huts and her own lodging with other domestic captives in the loft of the kitchen dependency at Wheeler House. Further, Crafts may have gathered from Sophia information about the forty-eight captives who worked on the Booth plantation. The impossibility, for these bondpeople, of a similar prospect of domesticity would not have been lost on Crafts. And, yet, she seems to have borrowed an image from Sophia Booth's composition. In the opening of "Home Scenes," S.B. remarks upon the stars as a conduit to reaching her family. She writes, "I love the stars; for the same star I watch here looks down with its bright eyes on those whom I hold dear as life in my own far off Virginia."[24] Crafts seems to engage this image when she describes the escape of Hannah and her mistress from Lindendale.

> It was a starlight night, but the air being soft, and balmy and hazy the stars seemed to look down upon you through a misty veil. They are shining here as they shine over the splendid mansion of my master. And what do they see there? Do they see the house in confusion the servants alarmed, the master distracted. Have the large rooms been overturned, the galleries explored, the chambers searched? Has there been a hurrying to and fro, a racing and chasing around the country, notices posted up, and rewards offered. (*TBN* 63)

The difference is that the stars are shining down on scenes of domestic discord and dysfunction. In Crafts's composition, the stars reflect the escape of Hannah and her mistress from Lindendale, not the comforts of the Booth family's slaveholding circle before the fire near Petersburg.

V

Hannah's first escape, midway through the novel, occurs with her unnamed mistress and seems to reflect the author's sexual abuse at the hands of Thomas Bond Jr. These scenes also appear to be partially based on the real-life experiences of Sally and Kitty Bell when they tried to escape James Roche's plantation in Charles City County, Virginia, before being purchased by Obadiah Brown in 1831.[25] Sally or Kitty Bell could possibly have related the story to Crafts during one of the many visits Hannah Jr. made to the Browns' compound between 1856 and 1857, around the time Crafts began composing her manuscript.

In the novel, Hannah flees with her mistress, but as they attempt to reach freedom, they get lost seeking a steamboat landing near the remote town of Milton, on the James River. Hannah asks of some young boys playing near a riverbank, "We are lost, can you give us the direction to the village of Milton to which the steamboat runs?["] (*TBN* 58). The details seem to match what can be traced of Sally and Kitty's movements upon their initial escape from Roche in 1830. The difference, of course, is Crafts pairs the events with her protagonist and the unnamed "mistress" who is the reason for Hannah's flight in the novel.

Hannah and her mistress become lost and disoriented, only to come upon a farmhouse on the outskirts of a remote village: "It was a happy-looking rural, contented spot, wanting, indeed, in the appearances of wealth and luxury, but evidently the abode of competence and peace." Here, they room for the night and, later, learn that the female proprietor is the sister of Mr. Trappe. When Trappe arrives that night, he parts a curtain to spy on Hannah and her mistress while they prepare to sleep. Crafts writes: "He was then watching us, dogging our footsteps, and would be haunting us everywhere. By a natural instinct I turned towards the bed. Go to bed, to sleep, to rest without fear of being disturbed. How utterly impossible. Would there be rest or quiet anymore for us in this world? Were we ever again to sleep in peace? It seemed not." The details are harrowing, and Hannah and the unnamed mistress flee the house in the dead of night to escape Trappe (*TBN* 60–65).

The scene seems to be a contrivance developed by Crafts to approximate the reach or control of Hannah Jr.'s real-life "Mr. Trappe," Thomas Bond Jr. In Crafts's novel, Hannah's "elopement" occurs when she and her mistress inhabit a remote hunting cabin far from the byways and travel routes of the region. Again, Crafts seems to borrow from Sally and Kitty's story, now placing Hannah and her mistress in a remote area of Charles City County. She writes, "The paths leading to the entrance were choked with weeds, and all appeared forlorn and desolate." Here, Hannah and the unnamed "mistress" reside for many months: "True, a more lonely and desolate place could not well be imagined, but loneliness was what we sought; in that was our security. We could gather our sustenance from the forest, we could quench our thirst at a neighboring spring, and at least we should be free" (*TBN* 67).

Possibly, of course, there were elements here from Sally and Kitty's escape not otherwise recoverable in the historical record. What seems certain is that Sally and Kitty Bell, and Hannah Bond, too, experienced a period of *petit marronnage*—that is, a temporary escape to avoid particularly harsh or cruel treatment, what Crafts calls "elopement." She writes of Hannah, "I have tried elopement. I know what it is. I know what hunger, and thirst and exposure of every kind means. I know what it is to fear the face of man, to seek hiding places in woods, and caverns" (*TBN* 145).

Again, the scenes in the novel match elements of Sally and Kitty Bell's experiences. Sally and Kitty were captured by a group of local hunters who came upon them in a cabin near Milton—just as Crafts describes events for Hannah and her mistress. The Bells were then imprisoned in the Charles City jail and, ultimately, sold by James Roche to the Rev. Obadiah Brown, who may have become aware of the mother and daughter's plight through his friend Gen. John Van Ness, who had purchased Sally's husband, Simon, from Roche only months earlier.[26]

If the story Crafts tells of Hannah's escape and later imprisonment near Milton, Virginia, matches the experiences of Sally and Kitty, it also shows a kind of shared resistance practiced among domestic captives seeking release from sexual bondage. For Sally and Kitty, Reverend Brown's purchase of them meant deliverance from Roche's designs. For Crafts, her escape from Thomas Bond Jr. was the beginning of her release, first, to Lewis Bond's daughter Esther and then, permanently, as the possession of his daughter Lucinda Bond Wheeler. Sally and Kitty's defiance also aided them. They were reunited with Kitty's father, Simon, in Washington, D.C., the family now all part of a shared Black community centered on the First Colored Baptist Church. As she does elsewhere, Crafts seems to knit parts of Sally and Kitty's personal history into her protagonist's journey.

Likely, Crafts had heard the story of the Bell family's saga from Kitty. The Rev. Obadiah Brown and his wife, Elizabeth, both died in 1852, shortly after Eliza Morgan's departure from the property, but the house and Sally and Kitty were passed on to Reverend Brown's son William Van Horne Brown (1812–1862), John Hill Wheeler's college schoolmate, lifelong friend, and former brother-in-law.[27] Kitty appears in William's 1860 slave schedule, while her mother's whereabouts are unclear by that point. Wheeler's diary entries in 1856 and 1857 show Mr. and Mrs. Wheeler frequently dining with and visiting Mr. and Mrs. William Van Horne Brown at the Brown family compound. Crafts likely served alongside Kitty when these families dined together. Dates noted in Wheeler's diaries include February 18, March 3, and March 19, 1857, with March 3 bringing together Kitty Bell, Eliza Morgan, and Hannah Bond.[28]

VI

What Eliza Morgan, Sally and Kitty Bell, Hannah Sr., and Hannah Jr. all shared is what Crafts emphasizes in her autobiographical novel: sexual exploitation and the threat of rape, especially during their most vulnerable years, when they were believed to be strong candidates for bearing children. Their experiences reflected the predatory nature of slavery, where slaveholders placed "value" on the sexual control of women's bodies. The historical record bears out the private trauma that is the primary focus of Crafts's narrative.

When Crafts writes about Hannah being ordered to walk across the room for Mr. Trappe and Mr. Saddler, to show off "what a foot she has, so dainty and delicate, and what an ankle," she is signaling the cruelty of the marketplace in "female flesh," as Crafts observes (*TBN* 106). On the slave block, Crafts knew, men generally cost more than women, skilled laborers more than agricultural workers, and young captives more than those of a more advanced age. Crafts's novel realistically details how the marketplace shaped her life and the lives of her friends. The only real exception to these commercial principles was the trade in "fancy girl[s]" and "good breeding" women, two categories of sexual commodification that were not mutually exclusive, particularly given that many of the female captives targeted for this trade were of mixed race.

Historian Lawrence Kotlikoff conducted a study of slave prices in New Orleans from 1804 to 1862, and the quantifiable data revealed that "light skin color added over 5.3 percent to the female's price; while only 2.29% to the price of enslaved males." If these women proved to be fertile and were impregnated by a white male, the child they bore would be even lighter and, thereby, more valuable monetarily as "slave property" for their owners, particularly if the offspring was female.[29] These were market realities for the Morgans, Bells, and Bonds that helped shape their daily lives and determined how they were managed as property as they reached sexual maturity and beyond.

Systems of *plaçage* (sustained sexual contact between an enslaved woman and her captor) and other forms of concubinage were part of the publicly acknowledged, circum-Caribbean legacy of interracial sex. Although these sexual relations have been documented and studied in large cities of the Lower South, like New Orleans and Charleston, they have not been widely recognized or analyzed outside urban centers. Such practices have been largely neglected for study in rural areas. What descendants in Indian Woods called a "slave-style wife" and what Maria Cherry Newsome carefully recorded in her notebook point to a little-examined practice that is featured at the heart of Crafts's novel.

Basic arithmetic supports records like Newsome's notebook and the focus on enslaved mistresses in Crafts's novel. Federal census enumerators did not typically identify mixed-race bondpeople in their descriptions of the free Black or enslaved populations before 1850. They did so for the first time in the U.S. federal census of 1850, offering substantial evidence of interracial sexual contacts—11 percent of enslaved persons were designated as "mulatto," along with 37 percent of "free blacks."[30] Popular songs from the period demonstrate the sexualized objectification of light-skinned free and enslaved women. Emily Morgan's transformation into a sexualized soldier for slaveholders in "The Yellow Rose of Texas" is only one such example. Throughout the South—as in Kentucky, South Carolina, and Louisiana, for example—enslaved men sang, to the accompaniment of banjo and guitar, the song "Massa Had a Yaller Gal." This version, from South Carolina, suggests the competition between enslaved and slaveholding men for the sexual control of mixed-race women.

> Ol' Mars'er had a pretty yaller gal, he bought her fum de Souf;
> Her hair it curled so berry tight she couldn't shet her mouf.
> Chorus: Way down in Mississippi
> Where de gals dey are so pretty,
> W'at a happy time, way down in ol' Car'line!
> Dis darkey fell in love
> Wid a han'some yaller Dinah.
> Higho—higho—higho![31]

Women like Judy Outlaw, Milly and Martha Murfree, Eliza Morgan, Jane Johnson, and Sally and Kitty Bell would have recognized the beguiling figure of the unnamed, passing "mistress" in Crafts's *The Bondwoman's Narrative*. The violence of what mixed-race captives faced is there in the disturbing line "Her hair it curled so berry tight she couldn't shet her mouf." What appears to be a surprising or "literary" plot device to contemporary readers would have been more readily understood as a designed reflection of sexual practices pervasive in places like Indian Woods and Murfreesboro, North Carolina, and other rural and isolated areas in the early and mid-nineteenth century.

VII

When Crafts moved to Washington, D.C., from Wheeler House in 1856, she experienced a second liberation. Like Eliza Morgan, Jane Johnson, and Sally and Kitty Bell before her, she found herself suddenly in a city abounding with domestic servants and new opportunities for fellowship. Her strong religious faith must have found further support in the welcoming community she encountered at the First Colored Baptist Church, just a short walk from the mansion the Wheelers rented from Mrs. Polk. Here, she could interact with other women whose life experiences she recognized, not simply the college daughters of slaveholders, who probably could not imagine or enter into sympathy with the experiences of the author.

In 1856, as Hannah Crafts first viewed the nation's capital, she witnessed a vast and promising construction site. The Washington Monument, whose cornerstone had been laid on the Fourth of July 1848, had risen to a third of its planned height and then been abandoned due to indecision and lack of funds. Building blocks lay strewn around the aborted obelisk. As for the U.S. Capitol, it was undergoing another enlargement. Two prominent wings—one for the House of Representatives and one for the Senate—were being added by enslaved and free laborers. In May 1856, when Crafts and Mrs. Wheeler returned to Washington, the new House chamber was nearly complete, while construction on the flanking Senate wing was still in process. Former captive Paul Jennings picked up a sample of stone from the site and kept it as a souvenir. (The artifact descended in his family.)[32]

Crafts would immediately have noted the great, yawning space above the Capitol's Rotunda, where a small army of captives and free artisans were laboriously setting the stage for the nearly nine thousand pounds of ironwork envisioned as the new dome by its designer, Thomas U. Walter, the architect behind the House and Senate extensions. A wooden scaffold had been erected on the Rotunda floor, passing through the eye of the temporary roof; the boom and derrick it held would lift the ironwork into place with the power of steam engines fueled by wood salvaged from the old Capitol Dome.[33]

They were making room for *Freedom*. In 1854, Congress commissioned American sculptor Thomas Crawford to design and execute a nearly twenty-foot-tall statue to be called *Freedom* in his studio in Rome, Italy. A bronze casting of the statue was slated to stand at the summit of American democracy, on a pedestal atop the new Capitol Dome. But Crawford died unexpectedly in 1857, just after completing the plaster model. The D.C.-based artist Clark Mills was hired to complete the work. Later, Mills credited his captive Philip Reid with separating Crawford's plaster model into its parts to help recast the work in bronze.[34]

Crafts dramatizes the irony of slavery paired with freedom in the construction of the District's famous monuments. The author tells the story of an enslaved man escaping from a coffle and seeking refuge underneath Clark Mills's equestrian statue of Andrew Jackson ("that lover of freedom"). Crafts writes, "Thence [the slave] was dragged, though shrieking and praying, and struggling, manacles placed on his limbs, and borne back to the market" (*TBN* 201). Crafts's choice of Mills's statue of Jackson, a major slaveholder, is probably no coincidence. The author's D.C. enslaver, John Hill Wheeler, knew Mills (another slaveholder), visited him on three occasions in 1857, and even bought property in Montgomery County, Maryland, from him. It is wholly possible that Crafts met Mills at some point. There is a record of John Hill Wheeler viewing Mills's equestrian statue of George Washington while the plaster model was being designed by Mills between 1856 and 1857.[35] If Mrs. Wheeler attended with her husband on the occasion, it is possible Crafts also viewed the work. (John Hill Wheeler observes in his diary that "Mills' Washington promises to exceed even his Jackson.")

Reid's work on *Freedom* earned Mills his greatest fame and his greatest payout. The team worked on the project for more than eight months, with Mills renting out his foundry to the federal government for $400 a month during production. He also received Reid's daily pay of $1.25, which exceeded the other laborers' $1.00 a day. For his efforts, Reid was allowed to keep the payments he received for his work on Sundays, meaning he worked nearly every day for eight and a half months to clear $41.25. Meanwhile, Mills cleared $3,400 for the use of his foundry and his services, along with pocketing the $247.50 paid directly to him for Reid's efforts.[36] The result was the segmented bronze statue of *Freedom* ready for reassembly atop the Capitol Dome when it was completed.

It is further speculation, but the author may have encountered, at some point, Mr. Mills's captives, possibly Lettie Howard, a direct contemporary of Crafts, and Lettie's daughter, Tilly, and sons, Tom and Ellick. There were also Levi Thomas and his light-skinned wife, Rachel Thomas. And Ann Ross, who is described as "five feet seven inches high, rather slim make, and in good health." Mills particularly notes Philip Reid, whom he purchased in Charleston, South Carolina, for $1,200. Later, as Mills sought reimbursement for his captives, he stated that he had purchased Reid "many years ago when he was quite a youth . . . because of his evident talent for the business in which your petitioner was engaged." Reid is described by Mills as "mulatto color, short in stature, in good health, not prepossessing in appearance, but smart in mind, a good workman in a foundry." He was an important artisan, assisting Mills in casting his famous equestrian statues; Levi Thomas, too, probably helped with these earlier works. At some point, Thomas sustained a debilitating leg injury, likely while casting molten metals for his enslaver. ("[Y]our petitioner is not aware [of] . . . bodily infirmities that impair their value . . . except that mentioned in regard to the stiff leg of Levi Thomas.")[37]

Like Reid and Thomas, Crafts understood the challenges Black artists faced working within the strictures and designs of their white captors: Thomas lost most of the use of one leg to his craft, and Reid's artistry enriched mostly only his captor. Still, the two Black artisans plied their skills and supported their families as best they could in bondage. By the time *Freedom* reached the top of the new Capitol Dome in 1863, Crafts, too, was liberated. In her case, she stole her own freedom before Mills's bronze casting ascended to the peak of American government.

VIII

Women were an active presence in the capital city from its earliest establishment; they were present at all public gatherings, were spectators at Supreme Court hearings, and witnessed most of the District's significant ceremonial occasions. Ellen Sully Wheeler reveled in the drama and excitement. She took advantage of the preferential treatment such as reserved seats in the cushioned front-row gallery of the House of Representatives. She, like the other elite Washington women, read the newspapers, was familiar with political debates, and socialized with the male leadership of the federal government. Crafts captures as much in her depiction of Mrs. Wheeler in her novel. She records Mrs. Wheeler opining on important political matters of the day, which she shares with Hannah. Together, Hannah and Mrs. Wheeler debate "office-seekers" like Mr. Wheeler, who was then unemployed and searching for a federal appointment during the time Crafts was in their service:

> "And what would they do if they had these offices?" I inquired.
>
> ["]To hear their account of it they would do extraordinary things. They would build new ships and hire new steamers, they would go to war and make peace they would take Cuba, or Canada, or Dominica, they would have a rail-road to the Pacific, and a ship Canal across the Isthmus, they would quell the Indians and oust the Mormons, in short their [*sic*] is nothing of possible or impossible that they would not do or try." (*TBN* 202)

Significantly, Mr. Wheeler's diplomatic efforts in Nicaragua collapsed because of his mismanagement of "a ship Canal across the Isthmus." It is doubtful Hannah Crafts knew all the ins and outs of her enslaver's troubles as U.S. minister for Nicaragua (1855–56), but, surely, many of these details filled the conversation she overheard between Mr. and Mrs. Wheeler. Crafts intimates as much, as the "account" by the novel's Mrs. Wheeler of "extraordinary things" details: shipbuilding, seizing land, extending slavery, developing intercontinental commerce, and subduing Native Americans. But Mr. Wheeler's primary aim in the novel is to seek a government appointment.

Crafts depicts these efforts, perhaps aware that her new acquaintance Paul Jennings held a successful appointment in the Pension Department thanks to the recommendation of his final enslaver, Sen. Daniel Webster. Crafts writes of the Wheelers' anger at Mr. Wheeler's being passed over for various appointments. Mr. Wheeler observes, "[T]here's another vacancy. A clerk connected with the Treasury Department after lining his pocket well with the funds has suddenly decamped. If I could only obtain that situation." Crafts records the discussion in her novel, quite possibly transcribing the Wheelers' actual conversation:

> "Why can't you, is there opposition?" inquired the lady.
>
> "Opposition" repeats her husband "why there were two hundred applicants there to[-]day, crowding and jamming each other, and each one intriguing to set forth his claims to the best advantage. There was one, a blacksmith's son from New York, who actually had the insolence to smile when I recommended myself as being the most proper person from my extensive acquaintance with political business."
>
> "A blacksmith's son" repeated the lady, with a sparkle of the eyes and agitation of manner. "A blacksmith's son, indeed; an Abolitionist I dare say, who would reverse the order of nature, and place Negroes at the top instead of at the bottom of society. Really smiled at you, the wretch." (*TBN* 166)

The Wheelers' shared irritation reflects extant letters preserved by family members. Crafts may be reflecting on the response many Southerners felt when free Blacks like Paul Jennings and other antislavery supporters gained employment in the federal government. Indeed, when Paul Jennings first received his government job, the Washington correspondent for the *Georgia Telegraph* filed a story replete with indignant sarcasm. The writer refers to Daniel Webster's procuring a clerkship for Jennings, who is identified only as a "buck negro," displacing "fifty poor white men [who] would have been delighted to receive [the appointment]."[38] In *The Bondwoman's Narrative*, Mrs. Wheeler shares similar envy and prejudice, although her spleen is directed at "a blacksmith's son" who "would reverse the order of nature, and place Negroes at the top instead of the bottom of society" (*TBN* 166).

Even where African Americans performed higher-level roles—copyist or clerk, as with Jennings—they usually retained the lower "laborer" or "messenger" designation and pay. The Virginian memoirist Alfred Chapman, who worked in the same department as Jennings, groused that he held the title of clerk but was charged with only opening the mail, whereas Jennings performed higher-level tasks. "And I have myself seen negroes writing in the passages of the Departments, directing packages, while white men were scrubbing the floors," the writer fumed, concluding, "[I]t is enough to make the blood boil to think of these things."[39] "Emboldened by the success of their brother [N-word]," the writer for the *Georgia Telegraph* noted, "'colored gentlemen' . . . were seeking clerkships!"[40]

We know the details behind Jennings's clerkship only because Alfred Chapman's papers are preserved in the Southern Historical Collection at the University of North Carolina at Chapel Hill. On June 23, 1851, Daniel Webster penned a recommendation letter for Jennings: "Paul Jennings was a servant in our house, for a considerable time. We think him very honest, faithful and sober; and a competent dining room servant. Formerly he was body servant to Mr. Madison." This original document, with its envelope labeled "Paul Jennings," ended up in Alfred Chapman's possession probably because of his work opening mail for the Pension Department. It is even possible that Chapman intercepted the letter, but Jennings still received the appointment.[41]

IX

The key linking Paul Jennings, Jane Johnson, and Hannah Crafts is the community of the First Colored Baptist Church. Jane Johnson was a member while she served the Wheelers in the District between 1854 and 1855. Crafts followed upon her arrival in May 1856. Both captives seemed to have associated with leaders at First Colored Baptist, including Jennings, who held contacts to the network that helped lead both to freedom.

In her biography of Jennings, Elizabeth Dowling Taylor misses completely Jennings's religious life in Washington, D.C., a major misstep in her otherwise definitive work recovering his life. She writes, "Jennings also got to know the Brents through the Methodist Church. John Brent, a prominent African American religious leader, founded the John Wesley A.M.E. Zion Church, the only congregation with which Jennings is known to have associated, and held services in his own home before a church building was secured."[42] But the minute books of the Rev. Obadiah Brown's First Baptist Church in Washington, D.C., show Jennings's active engagement in African American religious life in the District associated with First Colored Baptist. First Colored became Jennings's congregation, his cultural and spiritual home. And it was through First Colored that he likely encountered Jane Johnson, Anna Maria Weems, and Hannah Crafts. For a time, he even served in the very mansion where Crafts was in servitude a year before her escape, while the Wheelers rented from the widowed Mrs. Polk. Fate seems to have brought Jennings and Crafts together.

At First Colored Baptist Church, Crafts probably found fellowship with Jennings's well-educated mixed-race wife, Desdemona Brooks, who married him in 1849 and helped lead the primary outreach of female parishioners in the community. Desdemona, like Paul and Hannah Jr., was the offspring of one Black parent and one white parent, but in her case, it was her mother who was white and free. This meant that Desdemona and her three children from an earlier marriage were also free. Desdemona Brooks was described in the *Alexandria, Virginia, Free Negro Register* of 1835 as a thirty-year-old mulatto woman, five feet four inches tall, with a freckled face and "only one point per tooth." Later census records established her birth date as closer to 1800.[43]

Taylor, in her biography of Jennings, notes that he was characterized by family tradition as a "Jim Dandy" and a "dresser," someone who cared about his appearance and spent income on fine suits and kidskin shoes. "This leads one to suppose that, despite the confounding image of 'only one point per tooth,'" Taylor observes, "Desdemona Jennings, formerly Brooks, was likely an attractive June bride."[44] In 1856–57, while Crafts socialized with the Jenningses, she must have witnessed what a free married household could be. When son Franklin Jennings recalled living with his siblings and their father and Desdemona on L Street, he did not mention any of his stepmother's children living with them, though one or more likely resided there, given that Desdemona's youngest child was just seventeen at this time and that two of her children were living with the joined families by the 1860 census.[45] Engaging with a family made whole despite slavery had to have been inspiring as Crafts contemplated her own future. As she writes of Hannah in her novel, "[M]y strong desire for freedom [had] now become the object of my life" (*TBN* 73–74).

In her novel, Crafts would obscure nearly all the details of her real-life escape, but evidence suggests that she fled to Jennings's D.C. home in May 1857 from North Carolina as she made her way north from the Wheeler plantation. She would have known from Jane Johnson, Eliza Morgan, and others, possibly even Desdemona, the important connections Jennings held for assisting escapees seeking freedom. Because her path took her north to William L. Chaplin, Jennings's old conspirator, and to New York Central College, it seems likely that she sought escape with the assistance of the network within her grasp from her time living in Washington.

Jennings's neighborhood's placement among marsh and cow pastures made the home a safe retreat for Crafts (and others like her), as Jennings continued his Underground Railroad activities, quite possibly sheltering fugitives at the property. The city's finer established residences centered on the area stretching from Capitol Hill to the White House and a small section north and west from there. Though the Jenningses' house was only a few blocks farther northwest, it was beyond white surveillance, as its neighbors were all free Blacks who had only recently acquired property in this new area on the outskirts of the District.[46]

In the years Crafts would have known Jennings, he continued his long-standing association with William L. Chaplin, who now resided in Central New York, where he owned the popular Glen Haven Water-Cure spa, in Cortland County, near New York Central College, where he also served as a board member. Meanwhile, Chaplin continued to receive support from Gerrit Smith, who helped fund New York Central College along with a wide range of other philanthropic concerns. Even as Smith funded these operations, he looked to take a more militant role in undermining slavery through his support of John Brown—including his role as one of the "Secret Six" who covertly funded Brown's ill-fated raid on the armory at Harpers Ferry in 1859 in the hope of starting a slave revolt.

Perhaps Mr. Wheeler's abstraction in seeking a government appointment and Mrs. Wheeler's efforts to reestablish the family among prominent District power brokers afforded Crafts opportunity both to begin developing her novel on paper stashed in her sewing box and to engage more fully in the social opportunities her association with the First Colored Baptist Church provided.

X

The year Crafts spent in the Wheelers' D.C. household featured Mr. Wheeler in his study writing his manuscript "The History of Nicaragua," when he was not seeking employment through his connections. The irony is that Wheeler bought a large stock of paper to use for his Nicaragua history/memoir, and it seems to be partly from this stock that Crafts lifted some of the paper she used to write her novel. Wheeler's racism would have been on full display in both manuscripts. He observed, "The race of Central Americans have conclusively proved to all observant minds, that they are incapable of self-government. Their history, when not enveloped in the mists of savage barbarity, is a continual series of revolutions, convulsions and bloodshed."[47] At the time, the independent country of

Nicaragua controlled the only shipping passage from the eastern United States to California, via the San Juan River and Lake Nicaragua. The California Gold Rush of 1849 had generated a demand for speedier transit from the West Coast to the East Coast, and Nicaragua appeared to offer the fastest passage of all. A thirteen-mile land journey was all that was necessary until a planned canal could be built. One of the wealthiest men in the world at the time, Cornelius Vanderbilt, financed a steamboat transit system to profit from this essential new trade route. Against the direction of Vanderbilt's friend, U.S. Secretary of State William Marcy (1786–1857), Wheeler backed the privateering army of Nashville native William Walker, who sought to annex Nicaragua for the United States. But Vanderbilt had invested heavily in passenger steamboats and commercial rights for passage through the Nicaraguan Isthmus. Wheeler and Walker's disruptive crusade to extend slavery into Central America was bad for business.[48]

Wheeler's views aligned perfectly with Walker's, and he put U.S. influence in the country fully behind Walker's autocratic private army (called "filibusters"). Against instructions from Secretary of State Marcy, Wheeler welcomed Walker's invading private army and allowed them to seize vessels from Vanderbilt's Accessory Transit Company to use as warships. General Walker threw his filibusters into the Nicaraguan civil war, establishing a puppet government supported by Wheeler. He invited emigrants from the United States and additional filibusters to join him in Nicaragua and set about confiscating Nicaraguan properties to distribute to the newcomers. He annulled the existing Nicaraguan agreements with Vanderbilt and decreed the reinstatement of African slavery, which the Nicaraguans had abolished nearly twenty years earlier. Wheeler blithely followed Walker's lead, providing the privateer diplomatic cover. As expected, Walker eventually declared himself Nicaragua's new president.

But Walker, like Wheeler, had gravely miscalculated the Nicaraguan people. The warring red-ribboned Democratic Party army of Nicaragua and the white-ribboned Legitimist Party army united against Walker and U.S. interference. Vanderbilt plowed money into arming forces from

Guatemala, El Salvador, and Costa Rica, and they, too, united to confront Walker and repel his army of five thousand paid volunteers. "Gentlemen, you have undertaken to cheat me. I won't sue you, for the law is too slow. I'll ruin you. Yours truly, Cornelius Vanderbilt."[49] So wrote the tycoon before backing Central American armies arrayed against Walker and Minister Wheeler. General Walker and his filibusters went down to a colossal defeat. Three fifths of the men perished in the struggle (nearly three thousand Americans), and many more Central Americans died, mainly because Walker poisoned the water supply of the city of Rivas with corpses shortly before his army's retreat. The filibuster army also burned down the cities of Masaya and Granada, blackening the United States' reputation in Latin America to this day.[50] And yet, Colonel Wheeler, *el ministro filibustero*, loyally supported "General" Walker, even as Walker died by firing squad years later. In his unpublished "History of Nicaragua," Wheeler wrote the following—while Crafts served in his household: "We cannot stop if we could, and should not if we could. . . . The rifles of the adventurer are first heard, then the axe of the pioneer; then follow school houses, churches and towns with their teeming population. Such is progress—such is 'manifest destiny.'"[51]

XI

Paul Jennings is important to Crafts's story because he was key to the author's escape from slavery and her arrival, first, at Horace Craft's farm in Cortland County, New York, and, then, in what was known as Timbuctoo, New Jersey (near Burlington). Records are sparse, but Jennings is documented helping to organize the *Pearl* escape. His behind-the-scenes management of that important event confirms his long-standing role helping to conduct Underground Railroad activities in Washington, D.C., both while in slavery and after he had purchased his freedom in 1851 and established his own household in the District in 1855. Jennings's contacts within the First Colored Baptist Church community seem to have provided him the local network necessary to run his operations.

By the time of Crafts's arrival in the District, Jennings had maintained friendships with some of the most important antislavery activists of the period: Jacob Bigelow in D.C., William Still in Philadelphia, and William L. Chaplin and Gerrit Smith in Central New York. Together, these men helped keep alive the larger network of safe houses and escape routes first developed by Thomas and Elizabeth Smallwood and expanded by Charles T. Torrey. Specific details and documentation of Crafts's escape do not seem to be fully recoverable, but Crafts's passage north probably relied on the same network used by Jane Johnson, whom Crafts would have known, and also by Anna Maria Weems, who escaped from Washington, D.C., a year and a half before Crafts's bid for freedom. Weems family members attended First Colored Baptist, including Anna Maria's father, John, who had been based in the District for nearly six years while he tried to recover his family from slavery.

Anna Maria Weems's escape is especially relevant because it seems to have drawn on the same sources, locations, and Underground operators that Crafts's journey likely followed. Like Crafts, Weems dressed as a man to make her escape. She hid in Washington, found refuge in Philadelphia, and followed a course through New York City to Central New York and to freedom, a path likely also charted by Crafts before her arrival at New York Central College in August 1857. Anna Maria's movements are known because the Rev. Amos Freeman, pastor of Brooklyn's Siloam Presbyterian Church, published an account of her flight in *Frederick Douglass' Paper* in February 1856. Freeman accompanied Anna Maria on the train ride into Canada. His published account, "The Weems Family," is remarkably detailed, but important facts are obscured to protect Underground operators, including him. Scholars have since backfilled to provide a more complete picture of Anna Maria's daring escape.[52]

On September 23, 1855, Anna Maria Weems ran. She slipped away from the household of Charles M. Price and Catherine Harding Price in Montgomery County, Maryland, and took shelter among the free Black community of Washington, D.C., where her father and mother then resided. Six years earlier, in 1849, Paul Jennings and William L. Chaplin had helped the oldest Weems daughter, Mary Jane, escape. She fled to Geneva, New York, where she was adopted by Henry Highland Garnet, the great abolitionist, minister, educator, and orator. Garnet, a former captive, traveled to England in 1850–51, where among his abolitionist activities he helped organize the Weems Family Ransom Fund. With these monies, abolitionists were able to purchase the freedom of Weems family members, including Anna Maria's mother, Arabella, and one of Anna Maria's sisters. But the Price family refused to sell Anna Maria, and now the youngest Weems child was a fugitive seeking shelter among Black members of the First Colored Baptist Church. At some point, she took refuge with Jacob Bigelow, William L. Chaplin's successor in Washington. Bigelow was a Quaker, and his activities as an agent and conductor of the District's Underground Railroad went mostly unnoticed. With a five-hundred-dollar reward being offered for her capture, Anna Maria hid in Bigelow's attic as Jennings and others tried to arrange a plan to move her north.[53]

In late November, Dr. Ellwood Harvey, the Bigelow family physician, drove his carriage up to the entrance of the White House, the appointed rendezvous spot. There, he was met by Weems, who arrived simultaneously in Dr. Bigelow's carriage. She was disguised in a male driver's uniform that included a jacket, pants, a bow tie, and a cap. Under the assumed name "Mr. Joe Wright," Anna Maria climbed up into the coachman's position of Dr. Harvey's carriage, took over the reins, and proceeded to drive Dr. Harvey up Pennsylvania Avenue. To most observers, Dr. Harvey had just finished doing business at the White House and was now being driven away by his coachman. Crafts may have borrowed from this real-life scene for her character Ellen in the novel, who practices a similar cross-dressing ruse as a coachman—in this case, assisting a character called "Mrs. Wright."

Jennings's familiarity with the White House staff and protocols probably assisted with Weems's successful performance on Pennsylvania Avenue. In costume, then, Anna Maria began her journey to Philadelphia.

On the way, the pair had to lodge at the home of a slaveholder who was a prominent patient of Dr. Harvey's. They improvised. Dr. Harvey claimed a bad headache and the need for "Joe" to attend him in his room. This was to avoid Anna Maria's being placed in the slave quarters, where her disguise might have been discovered. On November 22, 1855, the pair arrived at William Still's home in Philadelphia. Still arranged for a photograph to be taken of Anna Maria in disguise (see Figure 28). A long separation was planned, and the photograph was meant to be a keepsake for her parents, a likeness to keep their daughter close and to celebrate her daring escape, as Anna Maria was destined for Canada.[54] This well-publicized

MARIA WEEMS ESCAPING IN MALE ATTIRE.

FIGURE 28: Anna Maria Weems in male attire, William Still, *The Underground Railroad* (Philadelphia: Porter and Coates, 1872)

ruse was clearly the source of Crafts's account of the use of cross-dressing and possibly inspiration for her own flight.[55]

After Still and Harvey procured her passage, Anna Maria next traveled alone by rail to New York City, still in disguise. There, she took refuge in the household of Brooklyn-based abolitionist Lewis Tappan and his wife, Sarah. The Tappans sheltered Anna Maria for two days and used sixty-three dollars from the Weems Family Ransom Fund to buy her warm clothes to prepare for the Canadian winter.[56] Setting out on November 30, 1855, in the company of Reverend Freeman, Anna Maria traveled from Brooklyn to Cincinnatus, New York. The pair may have stayed near McGrawville, too. In Rochester, Freeman and Weems boarded a train that carried them through Niagara Falls and into Canada, with the pair disembarking at Dresden, Ontario. A carriage completed the journey, bringing them into the Dawn Settlement, where Anna Maria was reunited with her aunt and uncle, who accepted her into their home.[57] Weems remained in Canada for the rest of her life, building a future among other fugitives, including relatives who became leading figures in the settlement.

Parallels abound for what is traceable of Hannah Crafts's escape. Like Weems, Crafts seems to have made her way to Washington, D.C., where she found shelter and assistance for passage north, probably from Jennings and others associated with the First Colored Baptist Church. Likely, Jennings and Bigelow managed movement and shelter for Crafts in the District. Records of her presence at New York Central College and, later, at Horace Craft's farm in August 1857 suggest the same underground network. Although the incomplete accounts of William Still do not identify Crafts, it seems likely she also passed through Philadelphia on her journey, during a period for which Still's records do not survive or do not clearly note her. Because Jane Johnson and Anna Maria Weems appear among Still's preserved papers, their shared circumstances and alliances invite the speculation. The fact that Still continued to collaborate with Jennings and William L. Chaplin in placing D.C.-area fugitives matches Crafts's traceable journey.

Likely, the plan was for Crafts to escape through Rochester and into Canada, just like Weems, but the strategy seems to have changed. It seems that John Hill Wheeler pursued Crafts on behalf of his brother and sister-in-law when he traveled to New York City that August. Most scholars believe the trip was an attempt to repossess Jane Johnson. But, in fact, it seems Wheeler was tipped off about the path Crafts was seeking, quite possibly through Reverend Freeman's published notice of Anna Maria Weems's escape. For this reason, Crafts was carefully removed from New York Central College and placed into the more secure holdings of the little-known rural farmer Horace Craft. Likely, Crafts was just one of "about one hundred and fifty of those weary and travel-worn fugitives" who used Chaplin's network connections in Central New York in 1857.[58]

XII

Some family crisis occurred shortly before the Wheeler family left Washington, D.C., for an extended trip to North Carolina in late March 1857. Wheeler records cryptically in his diary "a Domestic Scene which I hope in the Lord will never never—" Then he notes attending church with his son Woodbury (possibly without Mrs. Wheeler). He observes further in these few lines of his diary that the "Rev. Row Harris preached from Isaiah 53:6:—'And being set low each went their way.'" (The actual verse is "All we like sheep have gone astray; we have turned every one to his own way; and the Lord hath laid on him the iniquity of us all.")[59] In Crafts's novel, of course, the family crisis is depicted as the blackface scene, when Mrs. Wheeler embarrasses herself by begging for a government appointment for her husband while unknowingly disguised as a Black woman. The real nature of what led Mr. Wheeler to recount the difficult "Domestic Scene" remains a mystery.

Crafts journeyed with the family by steamboat, train, and carriage, arriving first at Wheeler House in Murfreesboro at 4 p.m. on March 22. The family seems to have spent most of their time at Maple Lawn, the home of Wheeler's sister Julia Munro Wheeler and her husband, Dr. Godwin Cotton Moore. This would serve as home base for the family for much of the

Wheelers' stay in North Carolina, probably because there was relatively little space to host the family at Wheeler House, where a half dozen female boarders occupied the guest rooms.

The family's movements can be sketched from Wheeler's abbreviated notes in his diary during the stay. The Wheelers moved among relatives and family properties during the two-month visit, including Wheeler House, Liberty Hall, and Maple Lawn. The sojourn lasted from Sunday, March 22, 1857, to Tuesday, May 5, 1857, when Mr. and Mrs. Wheeler returned to Washington. While the family was in North Carolina, John Hill Wheeler traveled to Lincolnton to collect money owed to him from the sale of Ellangowan in 1853. He was absent from the family, attending to these matters from April 9 to April 30. As noted earlier, Crafts did not return with the Wheelers to Washington at the end of their stay in early May. She was left, instead, at the family's Liberty Hall plantation outside Murfreesboro.[60] As John Hill Wheeler's account book shows, upon their return to the District in May 1857, the Wheelers immediately hired two Irish servants to take Crafts's place. The only other time the family hired white servants was following the escape of Jane Johnson in 1855, when they hired the doomed Margaret Benn to join them in Nicaragua in her place.

The nephew John Wheeler, who was now a student at Columbian College in Washington, D.C., had joined the Wheeler party upon their return to Murfreesboro. He, Mrs. Wheeler, and Hannah Crafts visited Willow Hall on Thursday, April 2, perhaps the last time the author ever saw her mother. A week later, the party visited Ann Ward Moore's family in Murfreesboro, and the group toured the new campus of Chowan Baptist Female Institute. John's presence seems important, considering his record of antislavery sympathy. In Crafts's novel, "a suit of male apparel" is acquired by Hannah just before her escape, and it seems possible that John provided this disguise to assist Crafts, if the scene in the novel reflects Crafts's own escape. Significantly, in Wheeler's diary, John had called on his uncle on July 26, 1856, and received an order to purchase clothes at Lahter and Walls, in the District, with Wheeler noting the expense as $5.50. It is conjecture, but this acquisition of "male apparel" by John may have been arranged to purchase clothing with which Hannah Crafts could disguise herself. John's presence in Crafts's life at both Wheeler House (1852–56) and then in Washington, D.C. (1856–57), and upon the Wheeler family's return to Murfreesboro in March–May 1857, just before the author's escape, may signal a relationship or friendship no longer recoverable in the historical record.[61]

Whole days during this period go unrecorded in John Hill Wheeler's diaries, and, of course, there is no record there of the activities of Mrs. Wheeler or Hannah Jr. during the period Wheeler spent traveling to other parts of the state (April 9–30). At some point during the family's two-month stay in North Carolina, Crafts fell out of favor with Ellen Sully Wheeler, and on Sunday, May 3, 1857, the family placed her in the hands of the family's overseer at the Liberty Hall plantation. If events in the novel reflect Crafts's circumstances, the author was now assigned to toil in the fields. Mrs. Wheeler in the novel announces, "You shall depart from the house, and go into the fields to work. Those brutalized creatures in the cabins are fit companions for one so vile. You can herd with them." And then Mrs. Wheeler consigns Hannah to further sexual abuse, now at the hands of a field hand: "Bill, who comes here sometimes has seen and admires you. In fact he asked you of Mr[.] Wheeler for his wife, and his wife you shall be." The idea is so repulsive to Hannah in the novel that she openly rebels:

> "Never" I exclaimed rashly and hastily, and without thought of the consequences. "Never."
>
> "Do you dare to disobey" she almost shrieked. "With all your pretty airs and your white face, you are nothing but a slave after all, and no better than the blackest wench. Your pride shall be broke, your haughty spirit brought down, and now get you gone, and prepare to change your lodgings and employment." (*TBN* 210)

Like Hannah in the novel, these events seem to be the impetus for Crafts's escape. "[C]ondemned to receive one of them for my husband my soul actually revolted with horror unspeakable" (*TBN* 211). Crafts further has Hannah note, "[T]o be driven in to the fields beneath the eye and lash of the brutal overseer, and those miserable huts, with their promiscuous crowds of dirty, obscene and degraded objects, for my home I could not, I would not bear it" (*TBN* 213).

Then, she ran.

CHAPTER 20

THE LIFE AND TIMES OF HANNAH VINCENT

I

IN NOVEMBER 2011, THE FINAL details came into focus. As I stood on the plantation to which I had traced Hannah Crafts's birth, I discovered the author's route to freedom. On that remarkable afternoon, while I paused to watch demolition work on a toppled tree, the last of "the Gospel Oaks," I observed a familiar Dodge van racing up Indian Woods Road. It was my friend and collaborator Gregory Tyler and another local colleague, Joanna Reed, a descendant of Bertie County captives. Joanna waved her cell phone out the window as the two raced to put me in touch with the person on the other end of the line.

That call proved to be the first link in the chain tracing the author of *The Bondwoman's Narrative* to Craft Farm in Cortland County, New York. Writer and lawyer Lee Miller was on the phone, beamed between Bertie County, North Carolina, and Cortland County, New York. Joanna had just been describing to Lee her work assisting me with my Hannah Crafts research. In fact, she had explained that she and Gregory Tyler would be joining me after lunch to search for the grave sites of Bond and Wheeler family members. The names "Crafts" and "Wheeler" struck a chord with Lee. It just so happened that she had recently purchased an old farmhouse in Central New York known as "Craft Farm." In the attic, she had discovered some old papers, including a letter warning of a "Mr. Wheeler" seeking an escaped slave in the region.

The coincidence was so striking that Gregory and Joanna set off from lunch immediately to find me near the old Bond plantation, keeping Lee Miller on the phone. When Lee told me her story, I was speechless. We corresponded for the next few months. The letter she had uncovered established that, in August 1857, John Hill Wheeler traveled to New York to seek a slave who had escaped from the family's North Carolina plantation. Written by a neighboring Quaker farmer, the letter warns Horace Craft that Mr. Wheeler is in the state. It also cautions Craft to carefully shield the person staying with him.[1] The language is vague, as Miller admitted to me, but the facts still illuminate a path I had been tracing for years. Of course, I yearned for more about Horace Craft's abolitionist activities and details about what he may have known of John Hill Wheeler. But there were no other relevant papers among those now in Miller's possession. Still, there was the one letter—and, fortunately, it found me.

For years my research had consisted of uncovering a network of abolitionist operators based in Washington, D.C., who led escaping captives through Philadelphia to Central New York and on to freedom. Indeed, I had recently traced the escape of Jane Johnson, who was likely aided by Paul Jennings via her connection to the First Colored Baptist Church, along this same route. The letter Lee Miller had discovered directed my attention to Cortland County as the conduit for Hannah Bond's escape—similar, it seems, to Jane Johnson's just two years before her.

I was not surprised, then, to find Paul Jennings's longtime collaborator William L. Chaplin living near the Craft property during the 1850s. In 1857, Chaplin operated the spa noted earlier, near McGrawville. As I have observed, he was on the board of nearby New York Central College, and he worked closely with the college's founder, the wealthy abolitionist Gerrit Smith. Local history preserved in the Lamont Memorial Free Library confirms New York Central College as a way station for captives seeking freedom from the time of the college's founding in 1849 until its demise in 1859.[2]

Circumstances also match the recoverable history of the New York Quaker community where Chaplin found practical and financial support for his New York Vigilance Committee activities. Chaplin had long been active organizing among New York Quakers. Indeed, for the better part of two decades, he had solidified and strengthened the Underground Railroad from Washington, D.C., to Central New York and into Canada. During this period, New York Quakers were key allies for Chaplin's activities. It was they who helped raise the funds for Chaplin's release from prison in 1850, even though the monies were forfeited when, by design, he jumped bail. At the time, Chaplin resumed his post as general agent for the New York Anti-Slavery Society, even as he worked to repay the money donated by his Quaker supporters. As general agent of the branch of the society based in Cortland County, it seems likely he recruited Horace Craft to assist with sheltering the author and perhaps others. I felt I could now trace Hannah Crafts's escape route.

The author fled from the Wheeler plantation near Murfreesboro, North Carolina, in May 1857, probably with the help of Wheeler's nephew John, Samuel Jordan, and Lucinda Bond Wheeler's son. John Hill Wheeler's account books and diaries, as well as private papers left behind by the nephew, corroborate this interpretation. Crafts's time in Washington, D.C., in 1856 and 1857 must have brought her into contact with Eliza Morgan, Paul and Desdemona Jennings, and others familiar with the fugitive network organized among parishioners at the First Colored Baptist Church. Like Jane Johnson and Anna Maria Weems before her, Crafts probably enlisted the help of Paul and Desdemona Jennings before being directed to New York Central College. For Hannah Bond, the route to freedom passed through Craft Farm, likely via the agency of Jennings's longtime collaborator William L. Chaplin. The evidence is circumstantial, but again, the recoverable record strongly supports this interpretation.

Crafts's first opportunity to substantially edit her work seems to have occurred only after she found safe shelter with Horace Craft and his family in August 1857. I can only speculate based on the Horace Craft letter, but I can imagine, as I did at the opening of this biography, the author revising the first third of her novel when forensic evidence shows her making substantial revisions to that part of the manuscript. At precisely this point, the author suddenly returns to designate the "Wheelers" as Hannah's captors throughout the text, where they were previously obscured consistently as only "Wh—r." I interpret this as a mark of the author's safety and freedom living with the Craft family.

At the time, the Craft family consisted of Horace (age forty-five), Harriet (forty-two), James (twelve), Mary (eight), and Alice (four). Tax records sketch the modest nature of the Crafts' property. There were twenty acres of farmable land and an additional thirty acres of "unimproved" property. Even the wooded acreage was used. Tax records show the family harvesting substantial quantities of syrup each year from the black and red maple trees on the land. Harriet probably directed these operations with the help of the children. Among this mostly self-sufficient Quaker family, Crafts seems to have found a home as she waited out the efforts of the Wheeler search party.[3]

It remains unclear precisely how long the author stayed at the Crafts' farmhouse, but her time there must have been consequential and meaningful. Her choice to partially assume the Crafts surname suggests an intimacy forged between the author and the family during her stay. It is easy to imagine her contributing to the self-sustaining farm while her life mingled with that of Horace and Harriet Craft. Likely, the author felt some safety on this remote property obscure even to the most intrepid slave catcher. There was little chance that a willing informer would even know about the insular Craft farm miles outside McGrawville. And the handful of faculty, staff, or students who encountered the author at New York Central College could be trusted not to divulge her presence in the area.

Now, secure from the Wheelers, Crafts specifically renounced the paternity and possession of the name "Bond." Instead, like fellow fugitive author William Wells Brown, she adopted the patronym of the family now sheltering her: the "Craft" family. She embraced "Crafts" as her nom de guerre, taking the plural form possibly because she wanted to honor both Horace and Harriet, who risked punishment by shielding her on their modest twenty-acre holding. Then she went farther. Now safe from her captors, the author identified the Wheelers in her novel, returning to the manuscript to fill in their surname. With these changes, Crafts realized and declared her liberty, defying at once the will of her pursuers and the laws of a country that defined her as property.

What little can be recovered about Horace Craft suggests a pious man who lived close to the earth with his family in the manner of New York Quakers. Tax records show the thrift of his family's operation: there was one dairy cow, two working oxen, two sheep, and one pig. The livestock was valued at $150. And yet, with these limited resources, the family successfully farmed their land and sold the surplus, probably to other Quakers. In 1870, when state assessors called to gather tax records, the Craft farm recorded its yield that year: six bushels of peas and beans, twenty-five bushels of potatoes, thirty bushels of buckwheat, five bushels of Indian corn, thirty bushes of oats, eight pounds of wool, ten bales of hay, and an impressive four hundred pounds of maple sugar.[4] Within this working farm, the author appears to have bided her time, probably assisting where possible, while also working on her novel.

By August 31, John Hill Wheeler seemed to have given up his search for Crafts. His diary records that he was ill, and he decided to leave New York City, returning to Washington, D.C., empty-handed.[5] Probably, he was resigned to seeing his extended family lose yet another female "servant." Possibly, slave catchers were still in pursuit with a reward in mind while Crafts remained in hiding with the Craft family. For the sake of safety, she appears to have prolonged her stay with the Crafts from late summer to early fall as she arranged a new destination.

Details are not reflected in Crafts's narrative, probably to protect an operating network aiding hundreds of others escaping bondage. Frederick

Douglass does the same thing in his narrative, disguising and omitting traceable details. Douglass notes:

> First, were I to give a minute statement of all the facts, it is not only possible, but quite probable, that others would thereby be involved in the most embarrassing difficulties. Secondly, such a statement would most undoubtedly induce greater vigilance on the part of slaveholders than has existed heretofore among them; which would, of course, be the means of guarding a door whereby some dear brother bondman might escape his galling chains.[6]

Crafts, too, provides no specifics about her movements by rail or boat, nor identifying markers about those who assisted her. The only intimate detail she reveals is that she dressed as a man to aid her escape, a method already known from Anna Maria Weems's escape along the same network. Like Douglass, Crafts wanted to keep the "door" open for others.

There may be the slightest hint of Harriet Craft in the author's portrait of "Aunt Hetty." When the Quaker woman in the novel points Hannah toward New Jersey, Crafts may be portraying Harriet Craft's role in helping her determine her final escape route. Crafts writes:

> She insisted that I should resume female attire, and travel by public conveyances, as she conceived so much time had elapsed and I was so far from the scene of my escape that I could do so with perfect safety. She said that she never would consent for me to leave her on any other terms. . . . She likewise proposed that I should find refuge among the colored inhabitants of New Jersey, as thereby my journey would be proportionately shortened, and I would escape the extreme cold of Canadian winters. (*TBN* 236)

Whatever the source, I conjecture that Crafts's journey led her first to Timbuctoo and then to Burlington, New Jersey. She provides no specific details beyond the hint that her autobiographical protagonist, Hannah, took "refuge among the colored inhabitants of New Jersey." Like other details in the narrative, Hannah seems to merge with Crafts here. At this point of her journey, Crafts was a fugitive seeking to avoid notice and trying to turn the page on a life stolen by slavery. In many ways, by completing *The Bondwoman's Narrative*, the author was closing the book on her experiences in enslavement. Her life in New Jersey as a free woman would be a fresh start.

How do we know Hannah Crafts left Central New York for New Jersey? She reveals as much in her autobiographical narrative. She seems to offer a glimpse of this new life as she closes out her novel, writing of a new husband for her heroine, Hannah:

> I have yet another companion quite as dear—a fond and affectionate husband. He sits by my side even as I write and sometimes, shakes his head, and sometimes laughs saying "there, there my dear. I fear you grow prosy, you cannot expect the public to take the same interest in me that you do" when I answer "of course not, I should be jealous if it did." He is, and has always been a free man, is a regularly ordained preacher of the Methodist persuasion, and I believe and hope that many through his means, under Providence, have been led into wisdom's ways, which are those of pleasantness. (*TBN* 245–46).

Just like the characters in Crafts's novel, Thomas and Hannah Vincent match Crafts's autobiographical narrative and seem to offer a glimpse into the life of the author after freedom. The two are recorded in Joseph H. Morgan's *Morgan's History of the New Jersey Conference of the A.M.E. Church, from 1872 to 1887* (1887), with Hannah Vincent noted as a "Stewardess" and "Sunday-School Treasurer" and "Teacher," similar to Crafts's Hannah, who "keep[s] a school for colored children" in an unnamed, all-Black town in New Jersey (*TBN* 244).[7] Remarkably, these details match a traceable couple, Thomas Vincent (1822–1883) and Hannah Vincent (1826–1905/10?), also noted in census records, who resided in Timbuctoo, New Jersey, in 1857 and 1858 and then, briefly in 1860, in Philadelphia, Pennsylvania, before returning to live permanently in Burlington, New Jersey.[8]

Gates had first signaled this couple in his original research, but then discounted them because of a different Hannah Vincent who also lived in New Jersey and is traceable to a free family of color from Pennsylvania, outside the origins of Crafts's novel.[9] This second Hannah Vincent became the focus of Gates's scholarship and led critics to give up on the connection. But Gates's original proposal now seems prescient. Years of digging further into the historical record seem to confirm "Hannah Vincent" as the author's married identity. The history of the African Methodist Episcopal Church of Burlington, where Thomas Vincent was a pastor, and its connection to the all-Black community of Timbuctoo invite the conclusion that Hannah Bond left the Crafts' farm and moved to the all-Black community of Timbuctoo in 1857, where she accepted a teaching position at the all-Black African Union School, fitting the same experience of Hannah in the novel. The argument is necessarily speculative, but it strongly fits the historical record.

Recoverable facts fit a picture that pairs Hannah Vincent with the author. The African Union School was unique in New Jersey as the only all-Black institution chartered by the AME Church in the state to teach the children of Black parents. As noted, Crafts writes, "[I] keep a school for colored children." She continues: "It is well attended, and I enjoy myself almost as well in imparting knowledge to others, as I did in obtaining it when a child myself" (*TBN* 244). If the author did escape slavery and become a teacher at an all-Black school in New Jersey, it must have been the African Union School in Timbuctoo, seven miles from Burlington.

There are strong circumstantial forces that would have guided Crafts from Cortland County, New York, to both Timbuctoo and Burlington. Possibly, the idea came from Horace or Harriet Craft, who still maintained contacts with Quaker family members in the area. Or, perhaps the author developed the plan via the underground network that had assisted her. In 1856, William Still's formerly enslaved brother Peter settled near his parents and siblings in Burlington, a companion community to Timbuctoo.[10] Both communities were little known and carefully guarded secrets among Black and white abolitionists. Crafts seems to have set out for Timbuctoo from Cortland County in the late fall of 1857. Her manuscript's discovery by a book scout "in Jersey" in 1948 can be reasonably linked to its possession by Hannah Vincent's stepson, Samuel Vincent, before his death in the 1930s, as we will see.

II

The difficulty in tracing Crafts's life after slavery was by design. In her novel, Crafts's depiction of Hannah's escape is especially opaque, perhaps because Reverend Freeman's publication of Anna Maria Weems's path threatened the very route Crafts herself sought to follow. To portray the escape, Crafts describes the difficulties of her heroine's journey into the wilderness of North Carolina and Virginia. Like Hannah in the narrative, Crafts probably traveled north alone at the outset of her escape from Wheeler House. She describes the fear of capture through her first-person narrator:

> The foxes have holes, and the birds of the air have nests. I stopped not till overcome with fatigue and complete exhaustion. I had traversed fields, leaped fences, and passed for some distance the boundaries of Mr[.] Wheeler's estate, when I was greatly startled by the baying of a dog. There was nothing singular or portentous in the sound. It was just such a bark as you will hear at all times of the night, and probably with unconcern, but mental anxiety and apprehension was one of the greatest miseries of my fugitive condition. In every shadow I beheld, as in every voice I heard a pursuer. Sometimes I paused to listen, when even the ordinary voices of the night filled me [with] indefinite alarm. (*TBN* 217)

She offers this, too, about her autobiographical heroine's escape:

> I cannot describe my journey; the details would be dry, tedious, uninteresting. My course was due North but I made slow progress. Occasionally I found friends, and this my disguise greatly facilitated. The people had no idea of my being a fugitive slave, and they were generally kind and hospitable. I told them I was an orphan who had been left in destitute circumstances, and that I was endeavoring to make my way on foot to join the relatives of my mother who lived at the North. This account, so true and simple, greatly won the sympathies of all especially the women. They would press gifts of food and clothing on me, or condole the cruel fate which deprived me of friends and property at one blow. (*TBN* 218)

As discussed earlier, the fugitives Jacob and his sister join forces with Hannah as they make their way north in the novel. And, yet, only Hannah makes it out safely from the wilderness. Jacob and his sister perish.

In Crafts's narrative, Hannah, too, is nearly killed. When she and Jacob steal a boat for the purpose of crossing a river in Virginia, Jacob is fatally struck by gunfire, while Hannah is thrown from the boat and into the rapids. In the novel, she miraculously washes up on shore hundreds of yards downstream, where she is rescued by "Aunt Hetty," the Quaker woman who taught her to read earlier in Crafts's narrative. This strains credulity as part of the historical record, but such happenstance is common in sentimental fiction, and Crafts follows the model.

The plot device of having "Aunt Hetty" conduct Hannah to freedom is a safe way of shielding Crafts's real-life abettors. Fitting to the sentimental genre, "Aunt Hetty" becomes a kind of guardian angel in Crafts's book, magically emerging from a nearby cottage to resuscitate the author on the banks where she has washed up. An agent of divine Providence, "Aunt Hetty" provides to the heroine food, money, and a path to freedom: "Tears of joy ran down my cheeks, while I revealed my name and circumstances to the venerable dame, and when she learned that I was really the Hannah whom she had taught to read, and instructed in the truths of Christianity at Lindendale, her happiness fully equaled mine" (*TBN* 233).

One challenge for a biographer is to separate the clearly fictional from what seems likely to have actually been experienced and relayed as autobiographical. Crafts helps to distinguish between the two by resorting to received tropes from the sentimental novel and gothic literature. Surely, she did not expect her readers to believe the astonishing coincidence of Hannah's rescue in the novel by "Aunt Hetty" as her own autobiographical experience. And so, Crafts used artistic license to embroider upon her real-life escape story. In doing so, she obscured the efforts of Underground Railroad operatives who assisted her in reaching freedom. Her real "Aunt Hetty" came in the guise not only of the Quaker neighbor who taught her to read but also in the shape of the men and women who became instrumental to her escape.

III

Like her life in bondage, Hannah Crafts's new life as Hannah Vincent is difficult to trace. To continue to mark her requires speculation. Crafts seems to have first settled in the nearby Timbuctoo settlement seven miles to the east of Burlington, also in Burlington County. Located along the Rancocas Creek, Timbuctoo was founded by former captives with the support of local Quakers. A review of extant deeds and other legal documents in the Office of the Burlington County Clerk shows that Black people began buying property in Timbuctoo beginning in September 1826. Over the next three decades, the Black population grew, reaching about 125 by 1860, as Quakers William Hilyard and Samuel Atkinson sold acreage exclusively to Blacks, including to fugitives seeking freedom.

By the time Hannah Crafts likely migrated there, the small community had become one of a handful of all-Black districts known to abolitionists as a safe haven for former captives. The Black community, as well as fugitives who settled in the unincorporated community, could rely on their Quaker neighbors for support. William J. Allinson of Burlington City, Thomas Evans of Evesham, Dr. George Haines of Medford, and William Roberts of Moorestown were active agents on the "Eastern Line" of the Underground Railroad, receiving fugitives from Virginia, Maryland, and Delaware. Together with a growing free Black population, these Quaker agents formed a vigilance committee to protect fugitives who took refuge in the area.[11] Timbuctoo had the African Union School, an AME Zion church, and an established Black cemetery.

Where Crafts writes of Hannah's husband in *The Bondwoman's Narrative* as "a regularly ordained preacher of the Methodist Persuasion," she seems to be describing the Rev. Thomas Vincent, whom she must have first met at either the AME Zion Church in Timbuctoo or in Reverend Vincent's home parish, Bethlehem AME in Burlington. Crafts's autobiographical heroine quickly makes use of her literacy to take a role as a teacher at a community school, almost certainly Timbuctoo's African Union. The 1833 deed for the purchase of the property is preserved in the Office of the Burlington County Clerk and indicates the sellers, buyers, and purpose of the school:

> Whereas, in the Settlement of Timbuctoo . . . and in the vicinity thereof, there are many People of Colour (so called), who seem sensible of the advantages of a suitable school education and are destitute for a house for that purpose. And the said Peter Quire, and Maria, his wife in consideration of the premises, and the affection they bear to the People of Colour, and the desire they have, to promote their true and best interests, are minded to settle, give, grant and convey . . . said premises to the uses and intents hereinafter pointed out and described.[12]

The deed also stipulates that future board members must be "People of Colour" who live within ten miles of the premises. As scholar Guy Weston has noted, this clause is surprising, because it suggests a level of recognition that runs counter to common perceptions about the limitations Black people faced in seeking an education. The document was filed in Burlington during an era known for criminalizing efforts to educate Black people. Despite the many obstacles, the chartered African Union School is a testament to community organizing among Blacks and Quakers in Burlington County.[13]

As a leader at Bethlehem AME, the Rev. Thomas Vincent probably helped oversee the African Union School when Crafts appears to have first settled in Timbuctoo. He may well have had a hand in hiring her in 1857 for the first "job" from which she received wages. I have been unsuccessful in uncovering further records about the school, but federal census records definitively identify Thomas and Hannah together as a married couple by 1860. No marriage record appears in the Burlington County Clerk's Office for this union. Possibly, Crafts's fugitive status meant an extralegal marriage sanctioned only by Bethlehem's AME community. A record of the union may have been made after the Civil War, when the couple could have recorded it, as other former captives did, but I have not been able to find it. It seems reasonable to conclude that, as "Hannah Vincent," Crafts appears in church records alongside her husband, Thomas Vincent, in the late 1860s, '70s, and '80s at the Bethlehem AME Church in Burlington.[14]

The dating of the paper and ink for the closing chapters of Crafts's narrative suggests a completion of the manuscript in 1858, when Crafts bound the work with thread and marked "farewell" on the last page. Pen, ink, and paper forensics match the textual evidence of Crafts's narrative, suggesting that the marriage between Thomas Vincent and Hannah Crafts would have occurred before the work's completion that year, with a wedding before December 1858. If Crafts's intimate glimpse of "another companion quite as dear—a fond and affectionate husband" is based on her union with Thomas—which seems very likely—then circumstantial evidence suggests Crafts completed her novel within a year of her escape in 1857. Her marriage to Thomas Vincent, then, must have taken place in 1858, almost certainly at Bethlehem AME, Reverend Vincent's home parish. As we will see, Bethlehem AME and the close-knit African American community there would come to anchor Thomas and Hannah Vincent for the balance of their lives.

Significantly, according to the federal census of 1860, Thomas and Hannah Vincent resided together in Philadelphia, Pennsylvania, twenty miles southwest of Burlington, just across the Delaware River, in Ward 10 of Philadelphia's East District. Thomas Vincent was a man of relative means by then. He is recorded as holding a thousand dollars in real estate and four hundred dollars in personal property.[15] The real estate value attributed to him suggests that the home they resided in may have been owned by Vincent, making him one of 257 homeowning Blacks in the city that year. At the time, Vincent was working as a "porter," probably serving rail passengers boarding and unloading at the Cohoquinoque Station at Front and Willow Streets, near the Vincents' home in East Philadelphia. Vincent, it would seem, followed the upward mobility of other African Americans, like William Still, who also migrated to Philadelphia from Burlington to seek higher wages. Hannah is recorded as "mulatto" and a "Housekeeper" in the same census. This is the first time she is enumerated as something other than a number and a mark on a federal slave schedule.

Why settle in Philadelphia around 1860 and return to Burlington, New Jersey, soon thereafter? A notice published in April 1858 in the *New Jersey Mirror*, titled "Trouble Among the Darkies," notes (in very racist terms) difficulties in Timbuctoo as a local man is suspected "of giving certain slaveholders information in reference to several runaway slaves in this section."[16] According to the article, a sense of distrust within the Black community had taken hold by that spring, and there was conflict among the families of Timbuctoo. Perhaps fear of possible exposure of Crafts led Thomas and Hannah to resettle briefly in Philadelphia, where Thomas found work as a porter.

But, soon enough, the couple appears to have crossed the Delaware again and returned to Burlington, establishing their longtime residence at 191 Lawrence Street, a mere half mile from Bethlehem AME, where they are recorded in church records as active members from 1862 until their deaths decades later. Perhaps Thomas felt the spiritual call again, and the religious Crafts may also have requested a return to Burlington County. The 1860 federal census record has Thomas and Hannah residing in a mostly white, middle-class Philadelphia enclave. Perhaps the property value listed in the 1860 census is already the house Thomas is shown to possess later in Burlington; or perhaps they sold their property in Philadelphia to return to the vibrant community near Bethlehem AME. Until more records detailing Thomas Vincent's property transactions can be unearthed, interpretation of the records so far recovered remains uncertain.

A son, named Samuel, was born to Thomas and his first wife in 1850, and so, Thomas and Hannah must have taken into account the welfare and educational opportunities open to Samuel when deciding where to settle permanently. The African Union School, where Crafts seems to have begun teaching as early as 1857, was a rare chance for a Black child to receive formal instruction, so it does make sense that the family may have resettled in Burlington with the idea that Crafts would return to teaching and that Samuel, her stepson, would receive his education at the same school.

It seems Thomas and Samuel were darker-skinned than Hannah, as they are enumerated variously as "mulatto" and "black" in census data from 1860 to 1870, whereas Hannah is consistently identified as "mulatto" for these years. In 1860 and 1870, Hannah Vincent's occupation is listed as "Housekeeping," which may throw into doubt her teaching at the African Union School during those years. The occupation for Hannah Vincent is listed as "General work" in the 1890 and 1900 federal census. And in the 1905 New Jersey census, she is listed as "Launderess." Likely, she continued teaching Sunday school at Bethlehem AME for the majority of these years. Whatever the full range of her role at the church in Burlington, she warranted notice in Joseph H. Morgan's *Morgan's History of the New Jersey Conference of the A.M.E. Church, from 1872 to 1887*. Here, Hannah Vincent is recorded holding a wide range of leadership positions: treasurer, stewardess, and teacher.[17] Perhaps it should be no surprise that the deeply religious former captive who wrote *The Bondwoman's Narrative* found in her local church the intimate ties and intellectual community she had craved and pursued while enslaved.

For the era, Crafts's life as Mrs. Thomas Vincent would appear remarkably secure. Unlike Jane Johnson, whose living circumstances changed nearly every year, with multiple husbands and households, Mr. and Mrs. Vincent's marriage was stable, as their lives seemed to center on the active community of Bethlehem AME. They possessed financial security, too. The household is listed in 1870 with a real estate value of eight hundred dollars and personal property valued at one hundred dollars.[18] Industrious and successful, Thomas Vincent purchased the home on Lawrence Street, which he was able to leave mortgage-free at the time of his death in 1883.[19] Hannah Vincent continued to live at this location with Samuel into the 1900s, apparently actively engaged, at least until 1887, in her roles as Sunday school teacher, treasurer, and stewardess.[20]

Crafts, it seems, found an elusive security in freedom rarely recorded by other escaped fugitives who wrote about their experiences. One aspect of her novel that struck early readers upon its discovery and publication in 2002 was the positive way she depicts her life after slavery. Recoverable records of Jane Johnson's experiences belie the difficulty Johnson faced in securing a stable household before dying of dysentery in her sixties. The authors Harriet Wilson and Harriet Jacobs (the other early Black female novelists) note in their novels their hope that publishing their work will improve their financial position in supporting their families. It seems Crafts's optimism at the end of her novel, attributed to Hannah, in fact, foreshadows the long and satisfying life she came to lead as Hannah Vincent. Crafts writes, "There is a hush on my spirit in these days, a deep repose a blest and holy quietude. I found a life of freedom all my fancy had pictured it to be. I found the friends of the slave in the free state just as good as kind and hospitable as I had always heard they were" (*TBN* 244). As African American literary critic William L. Andrews notes, "No slave narrative in the history of African American literature comes to such a marvelously happy, yet curiously hazy, ending."[21]

At the end of *Incidents in the Life of a Slave Girl* (1861), Harriet Jacobs reflects on the freedom she had finally gained after years in the North as a fugitive. If she celebrates her liberty as part of her novel, she also qualifies it. She is "as free from the power of slaveholders as are the white people of the north," but "that, according to my ideas, is not saying a great deal."[22] And Harriet Wilson, the author of *Our Nig* (1859), registers her protagonist Frado's disappointment after her feckless husband abandons her and their son. At the end of the work, Frado and the reader are left contemplating the struggle of caring for an infant in poverty without the support of a partner.

Andrews notes, "Thus, *The Bondwoman's Narrative* raises the implicit question, 'Could a slave woman, practicing virtues typically celebrated in white American 'woman's fiction,' aspire to similar rewards and similar fulfillments as an outcome of her struggles, as was promised to white girls and women?'" The answer Andrews draws from Jacobs and Wilson is a definitive "no." For Andrews and other early critics of *The Bondwoman's Narrative*, the unlikely happy ending for Hannah suggests that the manuscript may not have been written by a formerly enslaved woman.[23]

But, in fact, Hannah Crafts's life in freedom seems to support the happy ending of her narrative. True, the author imagines a reunion for Hannah with her mother in freedom and with former captive friends Charlotte and William—neither of which appears to reflect Crafts's reality. Still, the general optimism and joy of the work's conclusion forecast the author's circumstances when she stitched together the pages of her narrative and closed them between two covers designed to preserve her personal story. In this, Crafts was like author Henry Bibb, whose narrative openly avows his good fortune and attributes the happy ending it provides to, in part, his "superior advantages." Bibb writes, "I do not speak with vanity when I say the contrast was so great between myself and ordinary slaves, from the fact that I had enjoyed superior advantages."[24] His narrative, too, ends with his happy marriage to a freeborn spouse: "My beloved wife is a bosom friend, a help-meet, a loving companion in all the social, moral, and religious relations of life."[25]

As I have noted, writing *The Bondwoman's Narrative* represented a quest for the author to wrest back a life otherwise stolen from her: she was robbed of parents and forced to conceive a child who was also lost to her. The novel itself was a path for Crafts, at once, to control her world, escape it, and then rewrite it with a happy ending. And so, the work is a powerful weave of personal experience, wish fulfillment, and spiritual longing. She chose to record the stories of others she knew in slavery and to mix them with her own. As the novelist Hilary Mantel observed of Crafts, "Hannah as a novelist may be a thing of shreds and patches but so are we all."[26]

Despite her condition in bondage, Crafts wrote her novel for the same reason many people write novels and read them: she yearned to transcend her world by living intimately within a story she could help form. And, in many significant ways, the reimagined journey to freedom she portrays in *The Bondwoman's Narrative* helped her realize the life she came to possess. The Thomas Bond Jr. who forced sex on the young author gave way to a different Thomas—this time, a man who proved worthy as a husband, who recognized and valued Crafts's personhood. The infant she lost in slavery came back to her in the form of a stepson, Samuel, whose education and care she seems to have guided from the age of eight onward. Around the time that Crafts lost her mother to forced migration, she became a mother to a motherless child.

Crafts writes just this kind of reunion into her novel when she observes:

> It had been her incessant prayer by day and by night for many long years, that her child left in slavery might be given to freedom and her arms. She had no means of bringing about this great desire of her heart, but trusted all to the power and mercy of heaven. So strong was her faith that whenever she beheld a stranger she half-expected to behold her child. (*TBN* 245)

Wondrously, the author found her faith rewarded in the same way that she imagined for her characters. The bond Crafts seems to have formed with her stepson, Samuel Vincent, must have been strong. Even after the death of her husband, Thomas, in 1883, Samuel continued to live in the same household with Hannah Vincent. If Hannah Vincent was Hannah Crafts, the author grew old not only with the bond of a seemingly loving husband but also with the support and care of an adoptive son. Bereft for most of her life of family ties, including the infant she lost in slavery, the orphaned author seems to imagine and then forge the loving family she always sought.

One mystery has always been why Crafts never published her work. After all, it is written in an episodic and exciting fashion so well wrought that, even 150 years later, when it was published in 2002, it became a *New York Times* best seller. There are many good reasons for this, but the simplest might be that Crafts felt no need to share her efforts beyond friends and family because she did not need the money. She may well have written the book with an audience in mind when she started it, but by the time she completed the work, she appeared to have felt comfortable keeping it to herself and for those she invited to read it. Indeed, she had little to gain in drawing attention to herself before 1865, and the reception of former captive Elizabeth Keckley's 1868 work, *Behind the Scenes: Or, Thirty Years a Slave, and Four Years in the White House*, was decidedly hostile. Crafts's own exposé of white male predation of Black female captives did not hold promising prospects as a publishing venture in her lifetime. As William L. Andrews has noted, only four narratives by formerly enslaved women appeared in print between 1866 and 1880, and, of these, only Keckley's was written by the author herself. It was roundly criticized in the press as unseemly, and sold poorly.[27]

Still, one can easily imagine Crafts reading her own work to her husband, Thomas. Indeed, she writes such a scene into the novel ("there, there my dear. I fear you grow prosy"). Her beloved stepson, Samuel, also probably read the work, a safe opportunity for Crafts to share her experiences of slavery without the mental trauma of relating her sexual abuse or details about the infant she lost before her new life in New Jersey. Even if she had decided to seek publication as Hannah Vincent, Crafts, as an ordinary woman with no access to the means of production, faced steep odds. The short window that would have been available to her to market her book after the Civil War closed to most Black writers with the rapid rise and fall of Reconstruction, at least for works marketed to both Black and white audiences.

If Hannah Crafts published other works, which is very possible considering her extraordinary talents, the most likely place to search is in the literature of African American periodicals and church publications. As Elizabeth McHenry notes so clearly in *Forgotten Readers: Recovering the Lost History of African American Literary Societies* (2002), "One reason scholars have posited an African American literary tradition as a monolithic entity that begins with the slave narrative is that they have not valued these other literary forms." As she observes further, "[R]ather than bound books, newspapers were the primary sites of publication and sources of literary reading for African Americans."[28] Periodical literature is the most likely avenue for discovering other belletristic works by Crafts, possibly under the married name "Hannah Vincent."

I have not been able to locate the author's death certificate. But it seems she lived a long and full life as Hannah Vincent engaged in the supportive community of the Bethlehem AME Church in Burlington, New Jersey. Census data shows Hannah and Samuel Vincent residing together at the family home at 191 Lawrence Street each year as federal and state census collectors note their presence from 1870 through 1905, when the author would have been seventy-nine years old and her stepson fifty-five. By 1885, after the death of Thomas Vincent two years earlier, Thomas's widowed sister, Sarah Roberts, had joined the household, probably reconnecting with the family at the time of Thomas's illness and death.[29] Hannah Vincent disappears from the historical record more than a decade later, when the author was in her early eighties. When the 1910 federal census taker called at the Vincent household, Hannah was no longer present—which means her death occurred sometime between 1905 and 1910. Samuel inherited the house, free of a mortgage, and worked as a whitewasher, laborer, and plumber, but he appears to have never married. Sarah Roberts, Crafts's sister-in-law, still resided with Samuel when New Jersey census recorders called in April 1910.[30]

Although I have been unable to recover a record of Crafts's last days or much about her life in freedom beyond what appears to be her deep connections to the community of Bethlehem AME, I like to envision her prescient fiction as signaling what this intensely religious woman's last hours were like:

> With our arms clasped around each other, our heads bowed together, and our tears mingling we went down on our knees, and returned thanks to Him, who had watched over us for good, and whose merciful power we recognised in this the greatest blessing of our lives. (*TBN* 245)

In the novel, Crafts is imagining the reunion she sought with the mother who died in slavery. But, in her life, she managed to form a powerful family in freedom. And if her prayer to unite with her mother went unrealized in life, she did have the powerful consolation of a full and loving adoptive family, with her stepson and sister-in-law likely present when she departed this world. One can well imagine the scene as Crafts herself did: "Our heads bowed together, and our tears mingling."

In the pages of the novel she carefully preserved, Crafts provides one of the most powerful imaginative records we have of slavery, unedited and unadulterated by a collaborator, probably because the work went unpublished in her lifetime. The manuscript seems to have been carefully preserved by her stepson after the author's death. Samuel Vincent, like his stepmother, lived into his eighties. At some point, he sold the family's house at 191 Lawrence Street. He appears in census data for Burlington, New Jersey, as late as 1930, still single, living with his employer, Frank Larzelere, who owned and operated a plumbing business.[31] It would seem Samuel worked for years in Larzelere's operation, which opened in the 1900s, on High Street, just blocks from the Vincents' Lawrence Street home.[32]

By the time of Samuel's death, his elderly aunt Sarah Roberts had also departed. Samuel Vincent no longer appears in state or federal census records after 1930—although, again, I have not been able to discover his death certificate. His employer, Frank Larzelere, died in December 1932.[33] What I conjecture happened is that Frank's widow, Claire Larzelere, came into possession of Crafts's manuscript after the death of her husband, Frank, and of their boarder, Samuel, in the early 1930s. Because Samuel appears to have known Claire Larzelere for the many years he worked for her husband's company, Claire may have realized the importance of the manuscript he left among his possessions. My guess is that it was she who passed it on in 1948 to Emily Driscoll's book scout, who was seeking old manuscripts in New Jersey. As Driscoll recounted to Dorothy Porter after selling her the manuscript, "I bought it from a scout in the trade (a man who wanders around with consignment goods from other dealers). Because of my own deep interest in the item as well as the price I paid him I often tried to find out from him where he bought it and all that I could learn was that he came upon it in Jersey!" She continues: "It's my belief that it is based on a substratum of fact, considerably embroidered by a romantic imagination fed by reading those 19th Century novels it so much resembles."[34]

Astonishingly, this first novel written by an African American woman not only survived its author's escape from slavery but also managed to be preserved through three generations before coming into the possession of Henry Louis Gates Jr. My own efforts in these pages owe a debt of gratitude to Gates, Robbins, and all the scholars, like Dorothy Porter Wesley, on whose shoulders this biography stands. My work also owes a debt to the people of Bertie County and Murfreesboro, North Carolina, who attended the many talks I gave in these communities and who invited me into their homes to share their oral histories and family papers. Without the help of all these—or of my departed friends Mack and Clara Bell and the descendants of Wright Cherry, including Dr. Benjamin F. Speller and Dr. Wendell White—the life and times of Hannah Crafts would have remained unknown.

At the close of her life, when Hannah Crafts Vincent (1826–1905/10?) died of old age, at her bedside tending to her and comforting her was not the biological child forced on her by an enslaver but, instead, likely Samuel Vincent, the child of the man she came to love and grow old with. There was also her sister-in-law, Sarah Vincent Roberts. With them, she prayed. Her life had disavowed the alien ties of her white blood relations. Probably, Hannah Crafts had waited on her father, Lewis Bond, in his last hours, where, to the end, he kept her estranged. Now, among the Vincents, she experienced instead the keen sensation of kinship and love. Shortly before her death sometime in the first decade of the twentieth century, perhaps Crafts had the opportunity to open the pages of the manuscript she had stitched together so many years earlier, to reflect on her long life in bondage and beyond. If she did so, she would have encountered her preface, where she writes, "[P]ious and discerning minds can scarcely fail to recognise the hand of Providence in giving to the righteous the reward of their works, and to the wicked the fruit of their doings." As Hannah Crafts surely realized, and as her life made clear, only the inspired love of humans for other human beings can ensure salvation, only by those means can God deliver "to the righteous the reward of their works, and to the wicked the fruit of their doings." Her life and her novel are a testament to this deep faith.

EPILOGUE

On July 31, 2004, a relative of Hannah Crafts's, Calisea Hickerson, married John Maggette at Wheeler House in Murfreesboro, North Carolina. She emerged from one of the preserved slave cabins on the property and walked to the altar arranged before the house from which Crafts had escaped almost 150 years earlier.[1] That same summer, Margaret Worthington, a direct descendant of Samuel Jordan Wheeler, and Isabel Stewart, a descendant of Thomas Bond Jr., met in Chapel Hill, North Carolina, to share the family histories both had been collecting—each knowing full well that Margaret Worthington's ancestors had enslaved Isabel Stewart's family.[2] Such reconciliation and common friendship suggest a picture of racial amity that reflects some of the changes forged from the Emancipation Proclamation through the civil rights struggles to modern-day American race relations. And yet, another picture also emerges in the former plantation communities themselves. Poverty persists. The racial divide carries on as a result of powerful self-interest. The colonizing fictions of global capitalism that first encouraged white people to steal land from the Meherrin and Tuscarora people continue to make a real racial difference. Still, Crafts's life endures through her art, a voice rediscovered, unmasking and challenging the racial bigotry and greed that divide people and nations—then and now. As *The Bondwoman's Narrative* demonstrates, literature can still transcend the divisions of race, gender, and class and, at times, help us imagine and substantiate justice and freedom.

As author Isabel Wilkerson has noted, in 2022, the United States celebrated 246 years as an independent, democratic nation—the same number of years that it had been a slaveholding nation. For the past 246 years, the country has been balanced on the fulcrum of slavery as its defining institution.[3] W. E. B. Du Bois captured the shifting balance. He said, "The most magnificent drama in the last thousand years of human history is the transportation of ten million human beings out of the dark beauty of their mother continent into the newfound Eldorado of the West. They descended into Hell; and in the third century they arose from the dead, in the finest effort to achieve democracy for the working millions which this world had ever seen. It was a tragedy that beggared the Greek; it was an upheaval of humanity like the Reformation and the French Revolution."[4] Hannah Crafts's life and the art she contributed to American letters offer an important chapter to this "most magnificent drama." We would not have Crafts's contribution, however, if not for the efforts of Dorothy Porter Wesley and Henry Louis Gates Jr., who spent their careers and lifetimes preserving and interpreting the "dark beauty" of African American art otherwise lost and discarded by humanity's "upheaval."

In tracing the life and times of Hannah Crafts in these pages, we encountered, as the author did, a wide array of people whom Crafts imagined in small ways and large into her novel. As we have seen, Crafts seemed to take at face value the rhetorical question at the heart of Charles Dickens's *Bleak House*: "What connexion can there have been between many people in the innumerable histories of this world who from opposite sides of great gulfs have, nevertheless, been very curiously brought together!" Dickens's novel, like Crafts's own, is predicated on a series of mysteries. In Crafts's work, the puzzle is the mystery of Hannah's mistress's identity and its relationship to the author. Other mysteries are part of the same network: What is the secret of Hannah's past? How could a father disown his own child and treat her as property? And how could such an abandoned child make a life whole in an alien world?

In writing *The Bondwoman's Narrative*, Crafts faced the same challenges she encountered in pursuing her life: how to express innate gifts of love and intellect in an inhospitable environment; how to counter the moral plague of greed and selfishness when one is considered a mere possession. In Dickens's novel, the thread connecting all the characters and settings is a pandemic disease that originates in Tom-All-Alone's, a London slum. In Crafts's work, that disease is slavery and the racism it breeds. As Du Bois observed, Crafts experienced a "descent into Hell," one where families like hers were torn apart and transported until there was no recognizable family left. The "incessant prayer" that rings through Crafts's pages is a call for kinship, a need to shape community and love in an environment built to deny it (*TBN* 245). Crafts achieves reconciliation by weaving into her story the "many seemingly unconnected people and places" that formed her journey. And so, the Hannah of her novel stands in not only for Crafts herself but also for those she encountered along her journey: James Barefoot, Milly and Martha Murfree, Mary Burton, Eliza Morgan, Jane Johnson, and others.

There was not time to follow some of the important lives beyond their immediate connection to Crafts's narrative in the preceding pages. And yet, these lives, like Crafts's, deserve a fuller treatment. As Du Bois would have noted, they, too, "descended into Hell; and . . . arose from the dead, in the finest effort to achieve democracy for the working millions." In the spirit of Crafts's inclusive art, I offer the following short epilogue to trace further a few of the lives left incomplete in these pages.

James Barefoot (1774–?)

James Barefoot survived his efforts at organizing an insurrection as part of the 1802 Bertie County Conspiracy. He was one of only a handful of accused enslaved people not murdered in retaliation for the threatened unrest (chapter 1). On April 3, 1819, Barefoot joined sixty-two other Pugh captives forcibly marched to Norfolk, Virginia, to sail out on the brig *Calypso* as part of efforts by Austin Pugh and his brother Dr. Whitmell Hill Pugh to establish sugar plantations outside New Orleans.[5] If Barefoot learned of his departure beforehand, surely he would have said goodbye to Rosea Pope (Crafts's maternal grandmother) and to the other Pugh family members with whom he had lived for forty years. Clasped again in a collar and manacles, Barefoot retraced his steps to Port Norfolk, where he began a deeper journey into "Hell."

"A portion of the slaves were shipped from Norfolk to New Orleans, which point they reached after a long and tedious trip," William Hill Pugh wrote, recounting the journey of his father's captives, including Barefoot. "Their suffering was great from their long confinement on board the vessel and great mortality followed their arrival on the Teche."[6] The "Teche" was the first Pugh plantation in Louisiana, established on Bayou Teche, west of New Orleans. Later, when the soil was exhausted from cane harvesting, the Pugh brothers established a second plantation, at Bayou Lafourche. Barefoot's courageous life likely ended in the sugar fields of Bayou Teche or Bayou Lafourche before he reached his sixties. Even a bold fighter like Barefoot could not have lasted into advanced age in a region where most captives did not last a decade. Barefoot is not traceable in further records.

Milly (1797–?), Martha (1826–?), and Tecumseh Murfree (1831–?)

Milly Murfree and her children Martha and Tecumseh served at both Wheeler House and the Liberty Hall plantation just outside Murfreesboro (chapters 3 and 5). When John Hill Wheeler sold twenty-eight family captives in 1836, Milly, Martha, and Tecumseh were spared. Because they were John Hill Wheeler's prized domestic servants, they remained part of Wheeler's household when he moved with his second wife, Ellen Sully Wheeler, to Charlotte, North Carolina, and then, later, to Lincolnton, North Carolina, where Wheeler purchased the plantation he called Ellangowan in 1842.

Like Jane Johnson and Hannah Crafts, Milly, Martha, and Tecumseh must have faced the full spleen and ill temper of Ellen Sully Wheeler. By court order, in 1853, Wheeler was forced to sell Ellangowan. Fortunately, Milly and her children were purchased together with the property. They remained a nuclear family as they passed from the Murfrees to the Cryers (where Martha was born), to the Wheelers (where Tecumseh was born), then to Henry W. Connor.

It is impossible to say with any degree of certainty, but all three appear to match people enumerated in Connor's slave schedule for the 1860 federal census, suggesting they served under Connor's ownership through the Civil War.[7] Perhaps it is unsurprising, but I have not been able to locate Milly Murfree under any likely names ("Murfree," "Wheeler," or "Connor") in the 1870 federal census. She would have been seventy-three years old if she had still been alive then. My best guess is that she likely lived to see emancipation from slavery, but died shortly thereafter.

Her daughter, Martha, is traceable after slavery. In 1870, she married a formerly enslaved man named Pearson Connor, whom she probably knew on the Connor plantation. In 1875, Martha bore a son with Pearson, whom they named Washington Connor. By 1880, the young family is listed in the federal census sharecropping on land near Davidson, North Carolina, twenty miles from the former Connor plantation.[8] Sadly, there is no sign of Tecumseh in these records, which suggests that he perished, possibly in slavery, before reaching his midthirties. It would be a probable outcome for a young enslaved male on a large plantation like Connor's.

By 1891, Pearson Connor was a widower living in Charlotte and working as a laborer.[9] Martha Murfree Connor must have died between 1880 and 1891, somewhere in her late fifties or early sixties, probably during the family's sharecropping days. Their son, Washington Connor, appears to have moved to Charlotte with his father, but he holds a shadowy existence in records there. The death certificate of a woman born in a charity hospital names Washington as her father but lists her birth date as unknown.[10] Poverty and the legacy of slavery, it would seem, were already wounding the next generation. I lose Washington Connor's trail at that point.

Mary Burton (1832–?)

Mary Burton was sold by John Hill Wheeler to the lifelong bachelor and former congressman James Graham for $450 in 1849 (chapter 6). Graham brought Mary to his Earhart plantation, near Rutherfordton, North Carolina, separating her from her parents, Kitt and Cresy. Mary was seventeen years old at the time and had already been the subject of unwanted sexual attention from John Hill Wheeler. Some of James Graham's letters have been preserved, and from these, it is apparent that Graham was largely an absentee landlord at the Earhart plantation. Indeed, in surviving letters, he complains to his brother William A. Graham, then governor of North Carolina, that he cannot maintain talented overseers. They are either too severe and cruel or too sparing of the whip.[11]

When James Graham purchased Mary Burton, he decided to retire from politics and turn his attention to maintaining his plantations at Rutherfordton, Lincolnton, and Gaston. His acquisition of Mary from Wheeler fits a pattern of wealthy men trafficking in "fancy girls." James Graham never mentions Mary in the few letters in which he discusses his captives by name, but his estate papers list Mary and the two children she bore within the first two years she was in his possession.[12] The children's races and sexes are not recorded, but judging from the high number of mixed-race children in James Graham's 1850 slave schedules, chances are high that Mary's two children were fathered by him.[13] In September 1851, James Graham died unexpectedly, leaving all his property to his brother, Governor Graham.

Finding Mary Burton among the records maintained for William A. Graham was complicated by the fact that Governor Graham lived until 1879 and that, by the time his property was probated, there were, of course, no inventories preserved of his former captives. There are dozens of potential candidates for Mary and her children, based on age, proximity, Mary's light skin, and the likely light skin of her children, but here the trail ended for me. No strong matches fit more than just a few criteria.

Mary and her children could well have lived past slavery, but their fuller stories remain obscure.

If I could not further locate Mary Burton, I did discover her father, Kitt, in a newspaper advertisement. On January 18, 1858, the *Charlotte Democrat* features a one-hundred-dollar reward for "a negro Man named Kitt." The ad reads, "He is about 60 years old and is quite bald. He has a wife in the neighborhood of R. McDonald's, where he is believed now to be lurking." Kitt appears to have escaped, seeking to rejoin Mary's mother, Cresy, apparently enslaved on a plantation possessed by "R. McDonald." The advertisement continues, describing Kitt: "He was raised by G. M. R. Burton, and sold to Col. J. Wheeler, and is well acquainted in the neighborhood of Beattie's Ford. I will pay $10 for his apprehension and delivery to me in Charlotte, and $100 for sufficient evidence to convict a responsible white person of harboring him."[14] The piece is signed by R. P. Waring. Despite this rich store of information about Kitt and Cresy, they, like their daughter, Mary, remain mostly unrecoverable to me. The extraordinary lives of the many people Hannah Crafts encountered upon her life journey are best preserved in the literary record Crafts stitched together as a keepsake she called *The Bondwoman's Narrative*, a gift miraculously passed down to us and to future generations.

ACKNOWLEDGMENTS

I have many people to thank for assisting me with the research and writing of this biography. First and foremost are Dr. Henry Louis Gates Jr. and Dr. Hollis Robbins. Dr. Gates and Dr. Robbins kindly engaged this work over the years, assisting with research support and a willingness to read drafts and share their expertise. Dr. Gates's support included a residential fellowship opportunity (2014–15) at the Hutchins Center at Harvard University, where I was able to work on this book and collaborate with an amazing coterie of brilliant writers, including Devyn Spence Benson, Robin Bernstein, David Bindman, Kerry Chance, Kathleen Cleaver, Caroline Elkins, Philippe Girard, Krishna Lewis, Sarah Lewis, Xolela Mangcu, Kate Masur, Steven Nelson, Maria Carla Sanchez, Maria Tatar, and Abby Wolf.

I had the good fortune in 2014 to invite one of my favorite authors, Dr. Jill Lepore, to speak to our fellowship class about her recently published work at the time, *Book of Ages: The Life and Opinions of Jane Franklin* (2013), a biography of Benjamin Franklin's sister. Dr. Lepore's comments inspired me for the many difficult years ahead completing this biography. When one of the fellows asked her about the necessity of honoring the silences and gaps present in the archives for women and "minority" communities, Dr. Lepore was adamant: To "honor" such silences, she explained, was to be complicit in the forces that robbed these groups of their voices. In fact, she passionately argued, we are obligated to keep pushing the boundaries of the archives so such voices can be included in our history. I adopted this as my personal credo as I undertook the research and writing of this work.

I had the additional good fortune to receive a residency fellowship at the National Humanities Center in North Carolina for 2015–16, where I was able to continue collaborating on this project with a new cadre of fellow scholars, including Thomas Brown, Kate Flint, Anthony E. Kaye, Colleen Lye, April Masten, Jane O. Newman, and Brenda E. Stevenson. I also took advantage of this opportunity to establish a friendship with the scholar William L. Andrews, who lives in the area, and whose many conversations and expertise assisted my work throughout the last decade. The same year, I was also supported by a National Endowment for the Humanities Public Scholars fellowship, which allowed me to spend further time away from teaching duties to research and write.

So much of this work was built on collaboration—conversations with scholars over lunch, writing groups assembled with colleagues in various academic settings, travel to small towns where I engaged local historians and community leaders. I will note some here, but not all, because my debt is greater than my memory: Susanna Ashton, Margaret Bauer, Mack and Clara Bell, John Bird, Dr. Elbert Bishop, Casey Cothran, Holly Crocker, Brian Glover, Amanda Hiner, Marydean Jones, Anne Malory, Lee Miller, Marianne Montgomery, Laura Morris, Tommi Powell, Jeanne Provost, Nick Radel, Joanna Reed, Kelly Richardson, David Serxner, Nicole Sidhu, Michele Speitz, Dr. Benjamin F. Speller, E. Frank Stephenson Jr., Joni Tevis, Rhondda Thomas, Gregory Tyler, Dr. Wendell White, and Margaret Worthington. I also want to thank my friend the author Thomas Healy, who helped me first envision this work as a trade book.

Further, I need to thank my close personal friends and brothers who have cheered on this project: Todd Badgley, Robert Beatty, Gary, Paul, and Steven Hecimovich, Gray Kelly, and Keegan Stroup. I also want to signal my gratitude to my literary agent, Paul Lucas, who somehow managed the many missed deadlines as this work took much longer than I ever could have imagined. I owe thanks, too, to the brilliant publisher, editor, and poet Daniel Halpern, who purchased this book for Ecco/

HarperCollins and who believed in it along with multiple other editors who engaged this work during its composition: Norma Barksdale, Sara Birmingham, TJ Calhoun, Denise Oswald, and Hilary Redmon. I am grateful, too, to everyone at Ecco/HarperCollins for their care, patience, and brilliance in seeing this work into the world. There are bound to be errors in this book, and they are mine.

Finally, I want to thank my partner, Christy Geiger, upper-elementary schoolteacher and editor extraordinaire, and my children, Soren and Trey Hecimovich. This book is older than they are; for better or worse, they grew up with Hannah Crafts as a sibling of sorts. All three welcomed Hannah into our shared world these many years, and I am grateful for that. As a family, Christy, Soren, and Trey have approached all my work with the skepticism and grace only a family unit can bring to one of its own. My life and my work are far better for their guidance, love, humor, and generosity.

IMAGE CREDITS

FIGURES 1, 5, 6: Hannah Crafts, *The Bondwoman's Narrative* (Yale Collection of American Literature, Beinecke Rare Book and Manuscript Library, https://collections.library.yale.edu/catalog/2002811).

FIGURE 2: Courtesy of the author (Box 7, John H. Wheeler Papers [1825–1882], https://lccn.loc.gov/mm78045237).

FIGURE 3: Bertie County Slave Records, 1744–1865 (C.R. 010.928.6, Folder: "Slave Papers 1801–1865," North Carolina State Archives, Raleigh).

FIGURE 4: Courtesy of Joe Nickell ("Authentication Report: *The Bondwoman's Narrative*. Prepared for: Laurence J. Kirshbaum, Chairman Time Warner Trade Publishing and Henry Louis Gates Jr. Harvard University. Prepared by: Joe Nickell, Ph.D. June 12, 2001").

FIGURE 7: Courtesy of David F. Allmendinger Jr. and Johns Hopkins University Press (David F. Allmendinger, "Map 1: Southampton County," *Nat Turner and the Rising in Southampton County* [Baltimore: Johns Hopkins University Press, 2014]).

FIGURE 8: Image provided by Dartmouth University, Rauner Rare Books Collection (Rokela, "A Page in History—One of the Tragedies of the Old Slavery Days," *Godey's Ladies Magazine* 136 [March 1898], 128).

FIGURE 9: "Melrose House, 100 East Broad Street, Murfreesboro, Hertford County, North Carolina," July 1840, *Historic American Buildings Survey* (Thomas T. Waterman, Photographer, Library of Congress Digital Collections, http://hdl.loc.gov/loc.pnp/hhh.nc0259/photos.102305p).

FIGURE 10: Courtesy of Dee Akright.

FIGURES 11, 15, 20, 22: Courtesy of the author.

FIGURE 12: Courtesy of the author (Granville County, Estate Records, 1746–1948, C.R. 044.508.033, Folder [#3]: "Burton, Colonel Robert, 1825," North Carolina State Archives, Raleigh).

FIGURE 13: "Burton House/Ellangowan, Beattie's Ford Plantation, Lincoln County, North Carolina," 1938, *Carnegie Survey of the Architecture of the South* (Frances Benjamin Johnston, Photographer, Library of Congress Digital Collections, http://hdl.loc.gov/loc.pnp/hhh.nc0259/photos.102305p).

FIGURE 14: Lincoln County Courthouse, Lincolnton, North Carolina (Sales Receipts in the files of Lincoln County Register of Deeds).

FIGURES 16, 19: Courtesy of E. Frank Stephenson Jr. (Photograph undated.)

FIGURE 17: The National Archives at Fort Worth, Texas ("Slave Manifests, 1817–1861 [36-NO128]," Item 17, Folder 1, Box 33).

FIGURE 18: Courtesy of the author (Bertie County Estate Records, Folder: "Thomas Bond Sr." Box 9, North Carolina State Archives, Raleigh).

FIGURE 21: Courtesy of Dr. Wendel White.

FIGURE 23: Schomburg Center for Research in Black Culture, Manuscripts, Archives and Rare Books Division, the New York Public Library ("Rescue of Jane Johnson and Her Children," New York Public Library Digital Collections, https://digitalcollections.nypl.org/items/510d47df-799c-a3d9-e040-e00a18064a99).

FIGURE 24: Marian Alexander Jones, "House of Obadiah Brown at 814 E Street N.W., Washington D.C. (Sketch)," in the Collection of the Historical Committee of First Baptist Church, Washington, D.C.

FIGURE 25: Courtesy of the Metropolitan Museum of Art (Thomas Sully, *Mrs. John Hill Wheeler and Her Two Sons* [1844]). Image copyright © The Metropolitan Museum of Art. Image source: Art Resource, NY.

FIGURE 26: Marian Alexander Jones, "First Baptist Church, 1802–1834 (Sketch)," in the Collection of the Historical Committee of First Baptist Church, Washington, D.C.

FIGURE 27: Schomburg Center for Research in Black Culture, Manuscripts, Archives and Rare Books Division, the New York Public Library ("Narrative of the life of Frederick Douglass, an American slave [frontispiece and title page]," New York Public Library Digital Collections, https://digitalcollections.nypl.org/items/f2caf3f0-0a87-0130-2bbb-58d385a7b928).

FIGURE 28: Schomburg Center for Research in Black Culture, Manuscripts, Archives and Rare Books Division, the New York Public Library ("Maria Weems Escaping in Male Attire," New York Public Library Digital Collections, https://digitalcollections.nypl.org/items/510d47db-bcce-a3d9-e040-e00a18064a99).

NOTES

Introduction

1 New York Central College Papers, McGraw Historical Society, Lamont Memorial Free Library, McGraw, N.Y. [see folders labeled "Underground Railroad"] (hereafter cited as NYCC Papers MSS). See also "Traces of Old Underground Slave Railroad Still Remain in Central New York Villages," *Syracuse Post Standard*, July 4, 1948; "Excavators Unearth Old Stone Culvert," *Cortland Standard*, October 26, 1955; and "Sewer Work Unveils RR Mystery," *Cortland Standard*, October 16, 1981. Further documentation includes Ellis E. McDowell-Louden, "Report of Archeological Monitoring of the Sewer Related Earthwork," Cortland County, N.Y., January 18, 1981; Karen McCann, "Memorandum: Cultural Resource Review," New York State Department of Environmental Conservation, Project McGraw, October 20, 1981. Additional citations also included in NYCC Papers MSS. When I reviewed these documents in June 2016, I visited the "Farm House" property, which still stands today. Stones from the root cellar where Crafts sought temporary shelter remain visible at the back of the property.

2 Craft Papers, Cortland County Historical Society, Kellogg Memorial Research Center, Cortland, N.Y.; John Hill Wheeler Papers, Library of Congress, Washington, D.C. (hereafter cited as JHW Papers MSS); Map of Taylor Township, *Cortland County Atlas*, Everts, Ensign and Everts,1876, Historical Map Works Rare Historic Maps Collection, https://www.historicmapworks.com/Map/US/15011/. Wheeler's diary entries for August 22 through August 27, 1857 (Box 1, JHW Papers MSS), show him in New York City seeking the return of an enslaved captive while also seeking a publisher for his unpublished manuscript on Nicaragua.

3 Hannah Crafts, Manuscript, "The Bondwoman's Narrative," Yale Collection of American Literature, Beinecke Rare Book and Manuscript Library, Yale University, New Haven, Conn. When citing the manuscript directly is necessary, citations from Crafts's novel will appear in the main text for easy reference, with page numbers drawn from the manuscript (hereafter cited in the text as MS). Most citations of the novel, however, will be provided from the current edition, edited by Henry Louis Gates Jr. (New York: Grand Central Publishing, 2014), hereafter cited in the text as *TBN*.

4 The earliest fictional work of an African American was by Victor Séjour (1817–74), who published the short story "Le Mulâtre" as a free person of color living in France in 1837 (written in French), predating Brown's influential and widely known novel *Clotel* (1853).

5 Dorothy Porter Wesley Papers, James Weldon Johnson Collection in the Yale Collection of American Literature, Beinecke Rare Book and Manuscript Library, Yale University, New Haven, Conn. (hereafter cited as "DPW Papers MSS"). The exchange of letters between Emily Driscoll and Dorothy Porter Wesley appears in Folder 199, Box 22.

6 Julie Bosman, "Professor Says He Has Solved a Mystery over a Slave's Novel," *New York Times*, September 19, 2013, 1, 4.

7 Ezra Greenspan, *William Wells Brown: An African American Life* (New York: W.W. Norton, 2014), 158.

8 Box 7, JHW Papers MSS.

9 Sale receipt of Mary, July 28, 1849, Lincoln County Courthouse, Lincolnton, N.C.

10 Katherine E. Flynn, "Jane Johnson, Found! But Is She 'Hannah Crafts'? The Search for the Author of 'The Bondwoman's Narrative,'" in Henry Louis Gates Jr. and Hollis Robbins, eds., *In Search of Hannah Crafts: Critical Essays on* The Bondwoman's Narrative (New York: Basic Books, 2004), 204, 406–18; Nat Brandt and Yanna Kroyt Brandt, *In the Shadow of the Civil War: Passmore Williamson and the Rescue of Jane Johnson* (Columbia: University of South Carolina Press, 2007); Box 7, JHW Papers MSS.

11 Thomas Pugh, last will and testament, dated August 1806, proved November 1806, North Carolina, Bertie County, Will Book F/26 (CR 5200.10.1346): 16–31; Bertie County Estate Records, Box 9 (Martha Bond, Catherine Turner, and Thomas Bond Sr. folders) and Box 81 (Catherine Bond, Colonel Thomas Bond, and Lewis Bond folders) (CR 010.508), North Carolina State Archives, Raleigh; Pugh Family Genealogical Records, E. W. Pugh Papers, 1855–1899, Private Collection 1631, North Carolina State Archives, Raleigh. This constellation of records is primary in establishing the identity of Hannah Bond and her family members and their ties to the Pughs and Bonds of Indian Woods, North Carolina. I also used family trees and genealogical documents provided to me by Mack and Clara Bell of Windsor, North Carolina.

12 See Nina Baym, "The Case for Hannah Vincent," in Gates and Robbins, eds., *In Search of Hannah Crafts*, 315–31; Richard J. Ellis, "'So Amiable and Good': Hannah Crafts's 'The Bondwoman's Narrative' and Its Lineages," *Mississippi Quarterly: The Journal of Southern Cultures* 62, nos. 1–2 (2009): 137–62; and Thomas C. Parramore, "The Bondwoman and the Bureaucrat," in Gates and Robbins, eds., *In Search of Hannah Crafts*, 354–70.

13 These critics cite the law passed in North Carolina in 1830 making it a crime to teach a slave to read or write ["A Bill to Prevent All Persons from Teaching Slaves to Read or Write, the Use of Figures Excepted" (1830), Legislative Papers, 1830–31 Session of the General Assembly of North Carolina]. Because of the law, some scholars rule out the possibility that Crafts was really an enslaved person connected to the Wheeler family in North Carolina.

14 Baym, "The Case for Hannah Vincent," 321.

15 Correspondence in the Kate Wheeler Cooper Papers housed at East Carolina University helps to demonstrate the point. In a letter dated June 27, 1861, Samuel Jordan Wheeler notes that Moses has received Kate's letter: "I read the letter that you [Kate] wrote to him [Moses], in which you charge him to take good care of his master." Samuel Jordan Wheeler to Catherine Wheeler, June 27, 1861, Folder D, Box 1, Kate Wheeler Cooper Papers, J. Y. Joyner Library, East Carolina University, Greenville, N.C. (hereafter cited as Kate Wheeler Cooper Papers MSS). The fact that the Wheeler children were corresponding by letter with one of their captives suggests an acceptance and encouragement of literacy very different from the legal tradition and conventional wisdom.

16 As Moore studied law and other subjects, he taught these subjects to Harvey. Indeed, after the Civil War, Moore suggested that Harvey move north to try his own career at law, which he did, setting up a successful law practice in Philadelphia. The John Wheeler Moore Papers collected at the Southern Historical Collection at the University of North Carolina–Chapel Hill detail this unique literary friendship. See in particular Folders 1 and

31. Also see Sally Moore Koestler's *Elizabeth Jones of Maple Lawn, Pitch Landing, Hertford Co. North Carolina*, Hertford County Public Library, Winton, N.C., 15.

17 In a letter dated July 20, 1860, a friend of Julia Wheeler observes of Julia's body servant, "By the way, who is that attaché of yours who is so kind as to direct your letters +c? He must be very convenient—I'd like very much to have an amanuensis, particularly if he wrote such a pretty hand as yours does." Fonte Bella Hooper to Julia Wheeler, July 20, 1860, Folder C, Box 1, Kate Wheeler Cooper Papers MSS.

18 Box 1, David Settle Reid Papers, Rockingham County Historical Collections, Gerald B. James Library, Rockingham Community College, Wentworth, N.C.

19 Stationer's embossments—crestlike designs in the upper-left corner of stationery sheets—mark many pages of the manuscript, signaling a specific type of paper and size. I found these same paper types and embossments on letters sent by John Hill Wheeler in 1856 and 1857, including those among the David Settle Reid Papers.

20 In 2004, Gates and Robbins edited and published a collection of essays drawing on the expertise of a range of scholars, literary critics, historians, and genealogists. They note in their introduction (p. xxii) my work tying the novel to the Bond family.

21 Charles L. Perdue Jr., Thomas E. Barden, and Robert K. Phillips, eds., *Weevils in the Wheat: Interviews with Virginia Ex-Slaves* (Charlottesville: University of Virginia Press, 1976), 153.

22 See Kate Clifford Lawson, *Bound for the Promised Land: Harriet Tubman, Portrait of an American Hero* (New York: Ballantine Books., 2003); Melba Joyce Boyd, *Discarded Legacy: Politics and Poetics in the Life of Frances E. W. Harper, 1825–1911* (Detroit: Wayne State University Press, 1994); Harriet E. Wilson, *Our Nig: Or, Sketches from the Life of a Free Black*, ed. Henry Louis Gates Jr. and Richard J. Ellis (New York: Vintage, 2011); Annette Gordon-Reed, *The Hemingses of Monticello: An American Family* (New York: W. W. Norton, 2008); Nell Irvin Painter, *Sojourner Truth: A Life, A Symbol* (New York: W. W. Norton, 1996); and Jean Fagan Yellin, *Harriet Jacobs: A Life* (New York: Basic Books, 2003).

23 Jill Lepore, *These Truths: A History of the United States* (New York: W. W. Norton, 2018), 38.

24 I am inspired in these pages by the historiography practiced by an important slate of contemporary Black female historians: Daina Ramey Berry, Stephanie Camp, Erica Armstrong Dunbar, Marisa Fuentes, Thavolia Glymph, Saidiya Hartman, Tera Hunter, Blair L. M. Kelly, Jennifer L. Morgan, Imani Perry, Annette Gordon-Reed, Stephanie E. Jones-Rogers, Tiya Miles, Christina Sharpe, Brenda E. Stevenson, and Isabel Wilkerson. Each has pioneered new ways to give voice to the Black past. Tiya Miles vividly describes the challenge: "Researchers working in pre-twentieth-century records who care about Black lives are often left with the disparaging theorization of slavery's apologists and the cold notations of plantation diarists. What we might call the blood documents generated by the life of a 'slave'—birth notations, food rations, clothing and blanket distributions, physician bills, bills of sale, death data—routinely confront researchers in Black women's history and the history of slavery." To reach beyond "blood documents," Miles and the others engage material history, memory, and artistic imagining. Like these exemplary scholars, to tell the fuller life of my subjects, I traveled to the locations associated with my figures, gathered oral histories, and engaged communal memory—sources beyond the traditional written archive. In this work, I drew on the inspired practice of Berry, Camp, Dunbar, Fuentes, Glymph, Hartman, Hunter, Kelly, Morgan, Perry, Gordon-Reed, Jones-Rogers, Miles, Sharpe, Stevenson, and Wilkerson.

Chapter 1: Beginnings

1 Will and Estate Papers, Bertie County, 1663–1978 (CR.010.508), Thomas Pugh Sr. folder, Box 81, North Carolina State Archives, Raleigh.

2 My description of the coffle journey draws on Edward E. Baptist's careful reconstruction of the experience in *Half Has Never Been Told* (New York: Basic Books, 2014), 22.

3 Frederick Douglass, *Narrative of the Life of Frederick Douglass, an American Slave, Written by Himself* (Boston: Anti-Slavery Office, 1845), 2.

4 Douglass, *Narrative*, 2.

5 Correspondence between William R. Davie and Benjamin Williams, February 1802, is in the Governor's Letter Book [Benjamin Williams], 542, 552, 560, and 565, North Carolina State Archives, Raleigh, cited in Jeffrey J. Crow, "Slave Rebelliousness and Social Conflict in North Carolina, 1775 to 1802," *William and Mary Quarterly* 37, no. 1 (January 1980): 96.

6 Bertie County Records, Miscellaneous Slave Records, CR.010.928.6 (Folder "Slave Papers 1801–1805") (hereafter cited as Bertie County Slave Records MSS).

7 See William L. Andrews, *Slavery and Class in the American South: A Generation of Slave Narrative Testimony, 1840–1865* (New York: Oxford University Press, 2019), 206–20.

8 Bertie County Slave Records MSS, and Records Received from Other than Official Sources, CRX 396, North Carolina State Archives, Raleigh. Fifteen items originally filed in the folder "Slave Papers 1801–1805" and related to the Bertie County slave uprising in 1802 were illegally removed from the North Carolina State Archives in the early 1970s but later recovered by the State Archives through the cooperation of manuscript dealers in January and November 1999. These materials include depositions surrounding the 1802 Bertie uprising, now stored in Box 396 of the category "Records Received from Other than Official Sources."

9 Bertie County Slave Records MSS.

10 Bertie County Slave Records MSS.

11 Dr. Joe was arrested for conspiring with Tom Copper, a Black fugitive whose camp was hidden in the Great Dismal Swamp near Elizabeth City, North Carolina, along the same trading routes as Windsor and Bertie County. Styling himself the "General to command this county in a plot to kill the white people," Copper staged a daring raid on Elizabeth City's jail in early 1802 with "six stout negroes, mounted on horseback" to liberate the captives held there on a conspiracy charge. Trial of Dr. Joe, May 22, 1802, Pasquotank County Court Minutes, 1799–1802, North Carolina State Archives, Raleigh. Four of Copper's liberators were captured, but two escaped along with Copper. The Pasquotank County court found Dr. Joe innocent of any complicity with Copper, but his enslaver had to post a bond of £200 for Joe's release plus two sureties of £250 each to guarantee his good behavior. Moreover, the court enjoined the preacher not to "Assemble or hold any Meeting, Congregation or other Assembly of Slave or other people of Colour upon or under any pretense Whatsoever."

12 *Raleigh Register*, July 6, 1802, 3; Deposition of Fitt's Fed [*sic*], June 1802, Slave Collection, 1748–1856, North Carolina State Archives, Raleigh. Also cited in Douglas R. Egerton's *Gabriel's Rebellion: The Virginia Slave Conspiracies* (Chapel Hill: University of North Carolina Press, 1993), 143–44.

13 Bertie County Slave Records MSS; *The Times* (London), August 9, 1802, 2.

14 *Raleigh Register*, July 27, 1802, 1, cited in Thomas C. Parramore, "Aborted Takeoff: A Critique of 'Fly Across the River,'" *North Carolina Historical Review* 68, no. 2 (April 1991): 115.

15 Bertie County Slave Records MSS.

16 Bertie County Estate Records, Boxes 9 and 81.

Chapter 2: The Search

1 Revised early portions of the manuscript are inscribed on discarded drafts of material written near the end of the novel. Only after the writer reached freedom does she appear to have conducted final edits, now with the assistance of sealing wax and thimble. Correction slips used in Crafts's manuscript contain revised material that can be dated only after the author identified the Wheelers in her work. That is, these correction slips contain new material written on recycled paper that includes visible evidence only from scenes discarded after the author began identifying the Wheelers (page 187 of the MS). See Crafts, Manuscript, "The Bondwoman's Narrative."

2 Folder 199, Box 22, DPW Papers MSS.

3 Joe Nickell, *Real or Fake: Studies in Authentication* (Lexington, Ky.: 2009), 57.

4 Nickell, *Real or Fake*, 58.

5 The reason holograph manuscripts were maintained for nineteenth-century white authors such as Nathaniel Hawthorne, Herman Melville, Harriet Beecher Stowe, and others is the implicit racism that valued white art and its origins as worthy of future study. No one seems to have valued the belletristic efforts of Black authors, and so, their manuscripts were not preserved or passed down for posterity. The difficult personal circumstances of many of these writers, like Harriet Jacobs, show them fleeing persecution and living a life of financial instability, which limited their ability to save and pass down their manuscripts to future generations. There does also exist the holograph diary of the enslaved craftsman and sailor William B. Gould, published as *Diary of a Contraband* (Stanford, CA: Stanford University Press, 2002). The work was published 140 years after its composition by Gould's great-grandson, William B. Gould IV. The diary begins as an account of Gould's life in freedom. Further, in 2009, a holograph manuscript of a prison diary by Austin Reed emerged. Reed was never enslaved, but he did suffer the injustices of being a Black man incarcerated by the State of New York. The prison memoir was published in 2016 as *The Life and the Adventures of a Haunted Convict* (New York: Random House), edited by Caleb Smith. Finally, Christopher Hager's excellent *Word by Word: Emancipation and the Act of Writing* (Cambridge, Mass.: Harvard University Press, 2012), engages holograph letters from the period, too.

Chapter 3: Nat Turner, the Wheelers, and *The Bondwoman's Narrative*

1 See *Richmond Enquirer*, September 2, 1831. Also [Gray] letter, *Richmond Whig*, September 26, 1831, and *Norfolk American Beacon*, September 30, 1831. I also follow David F. Allmendinger Jr., *Nat Turner and the Rising in Southampton County* (Baltimore: Johns Hopkins University Press, 2014), 102–104. Allmendinger meticulously reconstructs events from original sources.

2 In the communities closest to the rebellion, false reports of slave insurrections were so common every August that fearful people were said to have developed "August madness." The

state of uneasiness persisted for almost a century, to the third and fourth generations. See F. Roy Johnson, *The Nat Turner Slave Insurrection* (Murfreesboro, N.C.: Johnson Publishing, 1966), 214.

3 Thomas R. Gray, *The Confessions of Nat Turner* (Baltimore: Lucas and Deaver, 1831), 12.

4 See Allmendinger, *Nat Turner and the Rising in Southampton County*, 100–104. Allmendinger draws on original sources to reconstruct the route of Turner and his insurgents.

5 Gray, *Confessions*, 11–12; [Gray] letter, *Richmond Whig*, September 26, 1831, and *Norfolk American Beacon*, September 30, 1831. Also see Allmendinger, *Nat Turner and the Rising in Southampton County*, 169.

6 These items were likely carried down and displayed in the parlor—or so they appear in the inventory of sale.

7 The Travis family's house and furnishings can be reconstructed through the following archival materials: Inventory, Joseph Travis, December 20, 1831, Will Book 11:353–54; Account of Sales, Joseph Travis, Will Book 11:338–43, Southampton County Courthouse, Courtland, Va. Details about the house and homestead also appear in letters and newspaper accounts of Turner's insurrection: William C. Parker to *Richmond Compiler*, August 31, 1831, 3; to *Richmond Enquirer*, September 6, 1831; Moses Moore, testimony, trial of Jack Reese, Minute Book, September 3, 1831, Southampton County Court, Courtland, Va., 90. See also Allmendinger, *Nat Turner and the Rising in Southampton County*, 80–82; Gray, *Confessions*, 11–12.

8 Editors of the local newspaper reported that the sun rose in a "light but lively green" that turned to silver white, then pale yellow. At 5 p.m., it appeared "like a globe of silver white through the thick haze," then assumed a "cerulean tint" before passing to light green. "A black spot near the center, was discernible by the naked eye, apparently the size of a walnut, and with a good spy glass two others were distinctly visible." An hour after sunset, the northwest horizon kindled with "ruddy light, bearing a strong resemblance to the red reflection of a large fire," the editors said. "We have heard of no attempt to account for the singular phenomena." Francis A. Rollo Russell, "Previous Analogous Glow Phenomena, and Corresponding Eruptions," in Royal Society (Great Britain), Krakatoa Committee, cited in Allmendinger, *Nat Turner and the Rising in Southampton County*, 22, 312.

9 Allmendinger, *Nat Turner and the Rising in Southampton County*, 171–72, 281.

10 F. M. Capehart to Benajah Nicholls, August 26, 1831, Benajah Nicholls Papers, Collection 252, North Carolina State Archives, Raleigh; John Hill Wheeler, *Reminiscences and Memoirs of North Carolina and Eminent North Carolinians* (Columbus: Columbus Printing, 1884), 210, cited in Thomas C. Parramore, *Murfreesboro, North Carolina, and the Roots of Nat Turner's Revolt, 1820–1831* (Murfreesboro, N.C.: Murfreesboro Historical Association, 2004), 61–62.

11 Gray, *Confessions*, 11.

12 For an authoritative listing of the whites killed, see Allmendinger, *Nat Turner and the Rising in Southampton County*, 286–88.

13 Borland to Governor Stokes, September 18, 1832, Letter Book, 30–32, Governor's Letter Books, 1830–32, North Carolina State Archives, Raleigh; "Carlton" [Colonel D. H. Hardee], *Patron and Gleaner* (Lasker, N.C.), August 29, 1895, quoted in Thomas C. Parramore, *Southampton County, Virginia* (Charlottesville: University Press of Virginia, 1978), 98; also quoted in Drewry, *Southampton Insurrection* (Washington, D.C.: Neale Company, 1900), 80.

14 Box 7, JHW Papers MSS.

15 F. M. Capehart to Benajah Nicholls, August 26, 1831, Benajah Nicholls Papers, cited in Parramore, *Southampton County, Virginia*, 85, 99–100.

16 O. M. Smith, *New Hampshire Post* (Haverhill), September 14, 1831, 3, cited in Parramore, *Murfreesboro, North Carolina, and the Roots of Nat Turner's Revolt*, 63–64.

17 As the scholar Teresa A. Goddu has noted, the gothic genre is not a pathway to escapist fiction but, rather, "a primary means for speaking the unspeakable in American literature." See *Gothic America: Narrative, History, and Nation* (New York: Columbia University Press, 1997).

18 As Nat Turner himself avowed, he adopted for his revolt a mode of "indiscriminate slaughter" to ensure he would "strike terror and alarm" into the hearts of the white community. The reports from the scenes of the revolt as related in the press demonstrate the violence of Turner's actions: "disfigured remains of wives and children," "several children whose brains were knocked out," and, later, "bodies . . . chopped to pieces and tortured to death." Like the crazed prophet of the apocalypse that whites reported him to be, his work left a macabre trail befitting the most extreme gothic novelist. Virginia governor John Floyd summarized, "Our fellow-citizens had fallen victims to the relentless fury of assassins and murderers, even whilst wrapped in profound sleep, and these deeds had been perpetrated in a spirit of cruelty unknown to savage warfare, even in their most revolting form." *Richmond Whig*, September 3, 1831; *Norfolk Beacon*, August 29, 1831; Drewry, *Southampton Insurrection*, 117, 118.

Chapter 4: The Revolt

1 *Western Carolinian* (Salisbury, N.C.), May 28, 1822, 2; and *Hillsborough Recorder* (N.C.), May 22, 1822, 3.

2 Henry Box Brown, *Narrative of Henry Box Brown* (Boston: Brown and Stearns, 1849), 38–40.

3 F. Roy Johnson, *The Nat Turner Story: History of the South's Most Important Slave Revolt, with New Material Provided by Black and White Tradition* (Murfreesboro, N.C.: Johnson Publishing Company, 1970), 182.

4 *Norfolk Herald* (Va.), November 14, 1831, cited in Allmendinger, *Nat Turner and the Rising in Southampton County*, 258.

5 Enumerated as a "Gentleman" in early Colonial records, the original patriarch, William Pope, patented land eight miles southeast of the present Isle of Wight County Courthouse. By 1665, Pope controlled some 950 acres, a sum vast enough for the Crown to authorize the "importation of Negros" to help work Pope's lands. See "Early Landowners of Isle of Wight, VA, and Some of Their Descendants," *Genealogies of Virginia Families from the William and Mary College Quarterly*, vol. 2 (Baltimore: Genealogical Publishing Company, 1981), 292–93.

6 North Carolina, Land Grant Files, 1693–1960 (Jacob Pope, Edgecombe County, Certificate number 222, Book 4, 171) and North Carolina, Land Grant Files (Jacob Pope, Edgecombe County, Grant No. 14, Book 11, 244), North Carolina State Archives, Raleigh.

7 John Miller, *A Twentieth Century History of Erie County, Pennsylvania* (Chicago: Lewis Publishing Company, 1909), 391. Miller traces the prominence of one of Jacob R. Pope's sons, Joseph R. Pope, who became a physician in Erie County, Pennsylvania. In recounting Joseph's life, he writes of Jacob R. Pope's plantation in Halifax County, North Carolina. The

1820 United States Federal Census for Halifax County shows only ten men and women enslaved by Jacob R. Pope, but their number would grow when Jacob inherited the bulk of his father's property upon his older brother's death in 1829. Also see William Allen, *History of Halifax County* (Boston: Cornhill Company, 1918), 10.

8 "Early Landowners of Isle of Wight, VA, and Some of Their Descendants," 296–97; 1800 United States Federal Census, Halifax, North Carolina; the 1820 United States Federal Census, Halifax, North Carolina, Hertford County; and the 1830 United States Federal Census, Second Regiment, Halifax, North Carolina, Halifax County—all from the National Archives and Records Administration, Washington, D.C. (hereafter cited as "NARA").

9 Frederick Douglass, *Narrative of the Life of Frederick Douglass, an American Slave, Written by Himself*, ed. David W. Blight (1845; repr. New York: St. Martin's Press, 1993), 41–42.

10 *Tarboro' Press* (N.C.), September 5, 1834, 2. In Crafts's novel, Mr. Trappe's "man-servant caught a glimpse once or twice of fellows answering their description, who seemed to be lurking, as he thought and as it proved, for evil purposes around the habitation of the former" (241).

Chapter 5: The Candidates

1 Allmendinger, *Nat Turner and the Rising in Southampton County*, 25.

2 Thomas C. Parramore, *Murfreesboro, North Carolina, and the Rise of Higher Education for Women: 1832–1859* (Merry Hill, N.C.: Murfreesboro Historical Association, 2014), 40–41.

3 *Hertford County Record of Accounts, 1830–1840*, Inventories & Sales of Estates, 1830–31 (CR.051.501.01), 17, North Carolina State Archives, Raleigh.

4 Samuel Cryer, last will and testament, dated February 7, 1797, proved March 9, 1800, North Carolina, Northampton County, Wills 1763–1950 (CR 5200.71.352), North Carolina State Archives, Raleigh.

5 More than fifty years later, John Hill Wheeler mentioned Sarah Cryer in his posthumously published *Reminiscences of North Carolina and Eminent North Carolinians*, 215. There, Wheeler extols the pioneering lives of the Murfree family.

6 Russell E. Train, *The Train Family* (Washington, D.C.: Russell E. Train, privately published, 2000), 258–59.

7 Bertie County Estate Records, Box 9 (Martha Bond, Catherine Turner, and Thomas Bond Sr. folders) and Box 81 (Catherine Bond, Colonel Thomas Bond, and Lewis Bond folders).

8 Brown, *Narrative of Henry Box Brown*, 38–40.

9 *Norfolk Herald*, (Va.), August 29, 1831.

10 Solon Borland to Roscius C. Borland, August 31, 1831, in Governors' Papers, Montford Stokes, State Series 62, North Carolina State Archives, Raleigh.

11 E. P. Guion to Thomas Ruffin, August 28, 1831, ed., J. G. de Roulhac Hamilton, *Papers of Thomas Ruffin*, vol. 3 (Raleigh: Edwards and Broughton Printing Company, 1918), 45 (cited in Thomas C. Parramore, *Murfreesboro, North Carolina, and the Roots of Nat Turner's Revolt 1820–1831* [Zebulon, N.C.: Murfreesboro Historical Association, Theo Davis Sons, 2004], 62); Robert S. Parker to Mrs. Rebecca Maney, *Norfolk Herald*, August 29, 1831, John Kimberly Papers, Southern Historical Collection, University of North Carolina, Chapel Hill, and *Halifax Roanoke Advocate*, October 13, 1831.

Chapter 6: Childhood

1 See Alan D. Watson, *Bertie County: A Brief History* (Raleigh: North Carolina Department of Cultural Resources, 1982), 46–48; and Arwin D. Smallwood, *Bertie County: An Eastern Carolina History* (Charleston, S.C.: Arcadia Publishing, 2002), 75–96. Dr. Smallwood's collection of materials that he gathered for his history of Bertie County contains his research materials on Indian Woods, North Carolina, including family memories and invaluable photographs and oral recordings of the area that he obtained in the late 1990s. These appear in the Southern Historical Collection at the University of North Carolina at Chapel Hill as Collection Number 04883: Bart F. Smallwood Papers 1910s–1918, and Collection Number 05316: Arwin D. Smallwood Collection of Indian Woods (N.C.) Photographs, circa 1990s–2005. Along with visiting Indian Woods many times, I found Dr. Smallwood's archived materials a powerful tool for fully immersing myself in this important area so essential to the origins of Hannah Crafts's novel.

2 W. L. Murfree, "Colonel Hardy Murfree of the North Carolina Continental Line," *North Carolina Booklet* 17, no. 3 (January 1918) (Raleigh: North Carolina Society of the Daughters of the American Revolution), 160–64; Wheeler, *Reminiscences of North Carolina and Eminent North Carolinians*, 215–16.

3 *Hertford County Record of Accounts*, North Carolina 1830–40, microfilm C.051.50001, North Carolina State Archives, Raleigh. These early records of Hertford County exist only on microfilm. They have been transcribed and indexed in four volumes by Raymond Parker Founts and David Powell. I make use of Founts and Powell's transcriptions checked against the original microfilm. For transcriptions, see Raymond Founts, *Record of Accounts Inventories & Sales of Estates, Hertford Cunty, North Carolina 1830–31*, vol. 1 (Cocoa, Fla.: GenRec Books, 1988); Raymond Founts, *Record of Accounts Inventories & Sales of Estates, Hertford Cunty, North Carolina 1832–34*, vol. 2 (Cocoa, Fla.: GenRec Books, 1988); Raymond Founts, *Record of Accounts Inventories & Sales of Estates, Hertford County, North Carolina 1832–34*, vol. 3 (Cocoa, Fla.: GenRec Books, 1988); and David Powell, *Record of Accounts & Inventories of Hertford County, North Carolina, 1838–1840* (Winton, N.C.: Liberty Shield Press, 2002). My citations refer to the page numbers of the original documents available both in the microfilm and in the Founts and Powell transcriptions.

4 *Hertford County Record of Accounts*, 17.

5 See Cheryll Ann Cody's "Naming, Kinship, and Estate Dispersal: Notes on Slave Family Life on a South Carolina Plantation, 1786–1833," *William and Mary Quarterly* 39 (1982): 207–9, cited in Deborah Gray White, *Ar'n't I a Woman? Female Slaves in the Plantation South* (New York: W. W. Norton, 1999), 133.

6 Box 81 (Catherine Bond, Colonel Thomas Bond, and Lewis Bond folders), Bertie County Estate Records.

7 Sarah Clifton Wheeler, last will and testament, dated July 11, 1833, proved August 1833, Hertford County, North Carolina, Will Book A, 1830–1856 (CR 5200.51.527), 56–57, North Carolina State Archives, Raleigh.

8 The legend holds that Emily and other Black servants were taken as prisoners and marched with Santa Anna's army. When General Sam Houston's troops feigned retreat, Santa Anna was caught unprepared, encamped, and raped the light-skinned Emily—Bollaert described Emily as "closeted in the tent with G'l Santana." There are plenty of other interpretations of the scant sources behind this legend. But some facts can be estab-

lished connecting Emily Morgan to the legend. On April 16, 1836, while James Morgan was absent in Galveston in command of Fort Travis, Mexican cavalrymen under the command of Colonel Juan N. Almonte arrived in New Washington, Texas, the new home of the Morgan family. They seized Emily and other Black servants at Morgan's warehouse, along with a number of white residents and workmen. According to the legend, Emily's beauty did not go unnoticed, and she came to be in the direct custody of General Santa Anna, who took personal charge of the prisoner. After two days of looting by his troops, Santa Anna ordered Morgan's warehouses to be destroyed by fire. Then he marched his troops to challenge Sam Houston's army, who were outnumbered and encamped ten miles away, on Buffalo Bayou.

9 See James M. Day, *Texas Almanac, 1857–1873: A Compendium of Texas History* (Waco: Texian Press, 1967); W. Eugene Hollon and Ruth L. Butler, eds., *William Bollae't's Texas* (Norman: University of Oklahoma Press, 1956). The Morgan family's connection to General Santa Anna's defeat is explored in detail in Douglas Brode, *The Myth of Emily Morgan* (Jefferson, N.C.: McFarland and Company, 2010), and in Thomas C. Parramore, "Keystone Konquistidors," Wheeler House Folder, Murfreesboro Historical Association, Murfreesboro, N.C., 1987. Further context is explored in Antonio López de Santa Anna et al., *The Mexican Side of the Texan Revolution*, trans. Carlos E. Castañeda (1928; repr. Austin: Graphic Ideas, 1970); Frank X. Tolbert, *The Day of San Jacinto* (1959; repr. Austin: Pemberton Press, 1969); and Martha Anne Turner, *The Yellow Rose of Texas: Her Saga and Her Song* (Austin: Shoal Creek Publishers, 1976). "Passport of Emily West," Texas State Library and Archives Commission, last modified June 19, 2019, https://www.tsl.texas.gov/exhibits/texas175/emilywest.html.

10 See Trudier Harris's "'The Yellow Rose of Texas': A Different Cultural View," in *Juneteenth Texas: Essays in African-American Folklore*, ed. Francis Edward Abernethy et al. (Denton: University of North Texas Press, 1996).

11 "Federal Writers' Project: Slave Narrative Project, Vol. 1, Alabama, Aarons-Young," 376–86, 1936–37, Manuscript/Mixed Material, Library of Congress, Washington, D.C., https://www.loc.gov/item/mesn010/.

12 Frederick Law Olmsted, *A Journey in the Back Country* (New York: Mason Brothers, 1860), 443–45, cited in Stephanie E. Jones-Rogers, *They Were Her Property: White Women as Slave Owners in the American South* (New Haven, Conn.: Yale University Press, 2019), 16.

13 Robert Burton, last will and testament dated 1825, proved 1825, Granville County, North Carolina, Will Book 10/25 (CR 5200.44.221); Granville County Estate Records, CR 044.508.33 (Colonel Robert Burton folders); Robert H. Burton, last will and testament dated 1842, proved 1842, Lincoln County, North Carolina, Will Book 2/132 (CR 5200.60.159); Lincoln County Estate Records, CR.060.508 (Robert H. Burton folders), North Carolina State Archives, Raleigh.

14 1840 United States Federal Census, Lower Regiment and Second Regiment, Lincoln County, North Carolina, NARA.

15 Robert H. Burton, Estate Records 1779–1925, Lincoln County, North Carolina, Box 1 (CR.060.501), North Carolina State Archives, Raleigh.

16 Junius B. Wheeler to Amie Wheeler, April 12, 1845, https://sallysfamilyplace.com/junius-brutus-wheeler/.

Chapter 7: Property

1 Thomas Parramore, "The Burning of Winton in 1862," *North Carolina Historical Review* 39, no. 1 (Winter 1962): 18–31.

2 Box 7, John Hill Wheeler Papers MSS.

3 John Wheeler, last will and testament dated July 13, 1832, proved August 1832, Hertford County, North Carolina, Will Book A (CR 5200.51.526), 50–53; John Wheeler, estate inventory, *Hertford County Record of Accounts, 1830–40*, 90–95, 111–121, North Carolina State Archives, Raleigh; Record of Accounts and Inventory, 353–54, Southampton County Courthouse, Courtland, Va.

4 Johnson, *The Nat Turner Story*, 21–23.

5 Michael Tadman, *Speculators and Slaves: Masters, Traders, and Slaves in the Old South* (Madison: University of Wisconsin Press, 1989), 12, cited in Walter Johnson, *Soul by Soul: Life Inside the Antebellum Slave Market* (Cambridge, Mass.: Harvard University Press, 1999), 5–6.

6 Jacob Stroyer, *My Life in the South* (1885), in Susanna Ashton, ed., *I Belong to South Carolina: South Carolina Slave Narratives* (Columbia: University of South Carolina Press, 2010), 142.

7 Stroyer, *My Life in the South*, 142.

8 Stroyer, *My Life in the South*, 142–44.

9 "Slave Ship Manifests Filed at New Orleans, 1807–1860," *National Archives* (blog), https://www.archives.gov/research/african-americans/slave-ship-manifests.html.

10 Elizabeth Keckley, *Behind the Scenes, or Thirty Years a Slave, and Four Years in the White House* (New York: G. W. Carleton and Company, 1868), 23–24.

Chapter 8: Rosea Pugh and Hannah Sr.

1 Vast quantities of salt were also procured in the Turks before the return voyage.

2 William Tryon, *The Correspondence of William Tryon and Other Selected Papers*, ed. William Stevens Powell, vol. 1 (Raleigh, N.C.: Division of Archives and History, Department of Cultural Resources, 1980), 321–22.

3 The Pughs' strong association with Welsh heritage persists in family records, and in a coat of arms preserved in family papers showing Owen Glendower's personal standard. Thomas Sr.'s great-grandson Dr. E. W. Pugh notes in family papers: "it is implicitly believed by the older members of the family that the name was originally 'ap Hugh' (Welsh), 'son of Hugh,' eventually corrupted into the English name Pugh. The older members also believe that we descended from Sir Owen Glendower through a son of his, Hugh Glendower." E. W. Pugh Family Materials, #1751, Southern Historical Collection, Wilson Library, University of North Carolina at Chapel Hill.

4 Alexis Okeowo (February 27, 2017), "The Provocateur Behind Beyoncé, Rihanna, and Issa Rae," *New Yorker*, February 18, 2017. See also David Cecelski, "The Voyage to Bayou Lafourche," *David Cecelski* (blog), February 10, 2021, https://davidcecelski.com/2021/02/10/the-voyage-to-bayou-lafourche/.

5 Charles Ball, *Fifty Years in Chains or, the Life of an American Slave* (New York: H. Dayton, Publisher, 1859), 63–64.

6 Charles Ball, *Slavery in the United States: A Narrative of the Life and Adventures of Charles Ball* (New York: John S. Taylor, 1837), 212.

7 Adeline, *The American Slave: A Composite Autobiography*, ed. George P. Rawick, vol. 6.1 (Westport, Conn.: Greenwood Press, 1972), 181, cited in Baptist, *Half Has Never Been Told*, 139.

8 See David Cecelski's *The Waterman's Song: Slavery and Freedom in Maritime North Carolina* (Chapel Hill: University of North Carolina Press, 2001), especially chap. 3, "Like Sailors at Sea: Slaves and Free Blacks in the Shad, Rockfish, and Herring Fishery," 83–103. See also David Cecelski's excellent discussion of herring fishing practices, "Portraits of Roanoke River Fisheries, 1870–1910—Bow Nets, Slat Weirs, Fish Wheels, Slides & Seines," *David Cecelski* (blog), February 23, 2019, https://davidcecelski.com/2019/02/23/portraits-of-roanoke-river-fisheries-1870-1910-bow-nets-slat-weirs-fish-wheels-slides-seines/.

9 Watson, *Bertie County: A Brief History*, 58.

10 Thavolia Glymph, *Out of the House of Bondage: The Transformation of the Plantation Household* (New York: Cambridge University Press, 2008), 32–62. See also Emily West, "The Double-Edged Sword of Motherhood Under American Slavery," *Uncommon Sense* (blog), May 7, 2019, https://blog.oieahc.wm.edu/the-double-edged-sword/.

11 "Federal Writers' Project: Slave Narrative Project, Vol. 13, Oklahoma, Adams-Young," 1936, Manuscript/Mixed Material, Library of Congress, Washington, D.C., https://www.loc.gov/item/mesn130/.

Chapter 9: The Early Life of Hannah Crafts

1 See Maria Cherry Newsome, "Some Recollections of the Late Wright Cherry and His Beloved Wife Malinda Gilliam Cherry of Bertie County, North Carolina (notebook), discussed in chapter 11, in the possession of Dr. Wendel White of Stockton, California.

2 On January 10, 1854, a judge in Norfolk, Virginia, sentenced a white woman, Margaret Douglass, to one month in jail for teaching Black children to read. See Zinn Education Project, https://www.zinnedproject.org/news/tdih/woman-jailed-teaching-black-children-to-read/.

3 Will and Estate Papers, Bertie County, 1663–1978 (CR.010.508), Box 09, Lewis Bond folder: North Carolina State Archives, Raleigh.

4 Harriet W. Banks to Samuel Jordan Wheeler, December 24, 1844, Box 2 ("School Records" folder), Kate Wheeler Cooper Papers MSS.

5 Edgar V. McKnight and Oscar Creech, *A History of Chowan College* (Murfreesboro, N.C.: Chowan College, 1964), 45, 53, cited in Parramore, *Murfreesboro, North Carolina, and the Rise of Higher Education for Women*, 45.

6 *Biblical Recorder* (Raleigh, N.C.), May 12, 1849, 2–3, cited in Parramore, *Murfreesboro, North Carolina, and the Rise of Higher Education for Women*, 44–45.

7 William P. Bond to Lucinda Bond Wheeler, April 10, 1857, Box 1, Kate Wheeler Cooper Papers MSS.

8 McKnight and Creech, *A History of Chowan College*, 72.

9 William D. Valentine Diary MS, 1837–1855, Folder 13, October 20, 1853, Southern Historical Collection, University of North Carolina at Chapel Hill.

10 Parramore, Murfreesboro, *North Carolina, and the Rise of Higher Education for Women*, 44.

11 Charles Dickens, *Bleak House*, originally published 1852–53 (London: Penguin Classics, 2011), chaps. 16, 257, 258. (I will include chapter numbers for my citations from *Bleak House* along with page numbers of this most recent scholarly edition.)

12 Box 2 ("School Records" folder), Kate Wheeler Cooper Papers MSS.

13 Enosinian Society Record of Debates, 1822–1831, Folder 2, Box 148, Special Collections Research Center, George Washington University, Washington, D.C.

14 Enosinian Society, Library Record, 1852–1872, Folder 4, Box 148, Special Collections Research Center, George Washington University, Washington, D.C.

15 *Biblical Recorder* (Raleigh, N.C.), September 1, 1849, 2.

16 *Religious Herald* (Richmond, Va.), September 20, 1849, 3.

17 *The Chowan Baptist Female Institute Catalogue* (1851), 27, A. Linda Hassell Archives, Chowan University, Murfreesboro, N.C.

18 *Biblical Recorder* (Raleigh, N.C.), October 18, 1851, 3.

19 McKnight and Creech, *A History of Chowan College*, 141.

20 Horace Mann, *Slavery: Letters and Speeches* (Boston: B. B. Mussey and Company, 1853), 143.

21 James Henry Hammond, "Mudsill Speech" (March 4, 1858), *Slavery Defended: The Views of the Old South*, ed. Erik McKitrick (Englewood Cliffs, N.J.: Prentice-Hall, 1963), 121–23.

22 *Biblical Recorder* (Raleigh, N.C.), September 16, 1853, 2.

23 Thomas Denman, *"Uncle Tom's Cabin," "Bleak House," Slavery and Slave Trade: Seven Articles*, 2nd ed. (London: Longman, Brown, Green, and Longmans, 1853).

24 A. Linda Hassell University Archives.

25 A. Linda Hassell University Archives.

26 Harriet Beecher Stowe to Thomas Denman, January 20, 1853, in Joan D. Hedrick, *Harriet Beecher Stowe: A Life* (New York: Oxford University Press, 1994), 237.

Chapter 10: *The Bondwoman's Narrative* and *Uncle Tom's Cabin*

1 This chapter is inspired by Jean Fagin Yellin's groundbreaking work, "'The Bondwoman's Narrative' and 'Uncle Tom's Cabin,'" which appeared in Gates and Robbins, eds., *In Search of Hannah Crafts*, 106–16. Yellin's scholarship, like Robbins's work (see chapter 16 of this biography), constitutes, for me, the best literary analyses of Crafts's novel. In this chapter, I follow closely Yellin's careful analysis of the influence of Stowe's *Uncle Tom's Cabin*. I embroider over her work new biographical details and interpretations of Hannah Crafts's life and times, but the primary source for this chapter is Yellin's scholarship.

2 Thomas C. Parramore, "The Merchants Foote," *North Carolina Historical Review* 46 (1969): 365–75, http://www.jstor.org/stable/23518278. Also see Meghan Friedmann, "The CT Role in Slavery Was Worse than You Think," *New Haven Register*, February 26, 2019.

3 David S. Reynolds, *Mightier than the Sword:* Uncle Tom's Cabin *and the Battle for America* (New York: W. W. Norton, 2012), xi.

4 Stowe, *The Minister's Wooing* (1859; repr. Boston: Houghton, Mifflin, 1881), 66.

5 Cited in Reynolds, *Mightier than the Sword*, xi.

6 Harriet Beecher Stowe's *Uncle Tom's Cabin* was serialized in the *National Era*, June 3, 1851–

April 2, 1852, and published as a complete volume in 1852. Parenthetical references in the text labeled "UTC" refer to the edition edited by Jean Fagan Yellin and published by Oxford University Press in 1998. For responses to Stowe, see Jean Ashton, *Harriet Beecher Stowe: A Reference Guide* (Boston: G. K. Hall, 1977), 137–38; J. W. Page's *Uncle Robin in His Cabin in Virginia, and Tom Without One in Boston* (Richmond: J. W. Randolph, 1853) and W. L. G. Smith's *Life at the South, or Uncle Tom's Cabin as It Is* (Buffalo: George H. Derby and Company, 1852) are both included in *Catalogue of the Library of John Hill Wheeler* (New York: Bangs and Company, 1882).

7 Cited in Yellin, "'The Bondwoman's Narrative' and 'Uncle Tom's Cabin,'" 106; David Walker, *Appeal, in Four Articles: Together with a Preamble, to the Coloured Citizens of the World, but in particular, and very expressly, to those of The United States of America* (Boston: David Walker, 1829); Herbert Aptheker, *Nat Turner's Slave Rebellion* (New York: Humanities Press, 1966); *The Liberator* (Boston), 1831–1865; Marilyn Richardson, ed., *Maria W. Stewart: America's First Black Woman Political Writer: Essays and Speeches*, 2nd ed. (Bloomington: Indiana University Press, 1987); Douglass, *Narrative*; *Narrative of the Sufferings of Lewis and Milton Clarke* (Boston: Bela Marsh, 1846); Josiah Henson, *The Life of Josiah Henson* (Boston: Arthur D. Phelps, 1849); Henry Bibb, *Narrative of the Life and Adventures of Henry Bibb, an American Slave, Written by Himself* (New York: Henry Bibb, 1849); [Richard Hildreth], *The Slave, or Memoirs of Archy Moore*, 2 vols. (Boston: John H. Eastburn, 1836); Gustave de Beaumont's *Marie, ou L'Esclavage aux Etats-Unis*, first published in France, appeared in an American edition in 1838; Lydia Maria Child, *An Appeal in Favor of That Class of Americans Called Africans* (New York: Allen and Ticknor, 1836); Lydia Maria Child, "The Quadroons," in *The Liberty Bell* (Boston: Anti-Slavery Fair, 1842), republished in Lydia Maria Child, *Fact and Fiction* (New York: C.S. Francis & Company, 1846). Both Douglass's and the Clarkes' narratives are included in the 1882 catalogue of Wheeler's library. See Yellin, "'The Bondwoman's Narrative' and 'Uncle Tom's Cabin,'" 115n2.

8 Yellin, "'The Bondwoman's Narrative' and 'Uncle Tom's Cabin,'" 107.

9 Harriet Beecher Stowe, *A Key to "Uncle Tom's Cabin"* (Boston: John P. Jewett and Company, 1853); A. Woodward, *A Review of Uncle Tom's Cabin* (Cincinnati: Applegate and Company, 1853); Rev. E. J. Stearns, *Notes on "Uncle Tom's Cabin": A Logical Answer to Its Allegations, etc.* (Philadelphia: Lippincott, Grambo and Company, 1853); and Nassau W. Senior, *American Slavery: A Reprint of an Article on "Uncle Tom's Cabin* (London: Longman, Brown, Green, Longmans, and Roberts, 1856).

10 Yellin, "'The Bondwoman's Narrative' and 'Uncle Tom's Cabin,'" 107.

11 Yellin, "'The Bondwoman's Narrative' and 'Uncle Tom's Cabin,'" 107.

12 After her capture Margaret Garner, a Kentucky slave who had escaped to Ohio with her husband and their four children, tried to kill her children to prevent them from being reenslaved; she succeeded in killing one. Garner was sent back to Kentucky and then sold farther south. See "The Garner Fugitive Slave Case," *Mississippi Valley Historical Review* 40 (June 1953): 47–66; Toni Morrison, *Beloved* (New York: Alfred A. Knopf, 1987), cited in Yellin, "'The Bondwoman's Narrative' and 'Uncle Tom's Cabin,'" 108.

13 Yellin, "'The Bondwoman's Narrative' and 'Uncle Tom's Cabin,'" 108.

14 Child, "The Quadroons." For the tragic mulatto figure, see Werner Sollors, *Neither Black nor White Yet Both* (New York: Oxford University Press, 1997), esp. 221–45; for the device of the baby switch, see Sollors, *Neither Black nor White Yet Both*, 436n85; also see Yellin, "'The Bondwoman's Narrative' and 'Uncle Tom's Cabin,'" 108–9.

15 Yellin, "'The Bondwoman's Narrative' and 'Uncle Tom's Cabin,'" 109.

16 Boxes 1 and 7, John Hill Wheeler MSS.

17 Boxes 1 and 7, John Hill Wheeler MSS. Brandt and Brandt make note of Wheeler's sale of three captives from the Rock Creek property in their *In the Shadow of the Civil War*, 59.

18 Yellin, "'The Bondwoman's Narrative' and 'Uncle Tom's Cabin,'" 109.

19 Yellin, "'The Bondwoman's Narrative' and 'Uncle Tom's Cabin,'" 110.

20 Yellin, "'The Bondwoman's Narrative' and 'Uncle Tom's Cabin,'" 111.

21 Nina Baym, *Woman's Fiction: A Guide to Novels by and About Women in America, 1820–70*, 2nd ed. (Champaign-Urbana: University of Illinois Press, 1993), 22.

22 Jane Tompkins, *Sensational Designs: The Cultural Work of American Fiction, 1790–1860* (New York: Oxford University Press, 1985), 125, cited in Yellin, "'The Bondwoman's Narrative' and 'Uncle Tom's Cabin,'" 112.

23 Yellin, "'The Bondwoman's Narrative' and 'Uncle Tom's Cabin,'" 113. Writing of *Uncle Tom's Cabin* in *Frederick Douglass' Paper* of May 20, 1852, the African American professor William G. Allen commented, "[I]f any man had too much piety, Uncle Tom was that man . . . I do not advocate revenge, but simply resistance to tyrants, if it need be, to the death." On, March 26, 1852, William Lloyd Garrison had queried in *The Liberator*, "Is there one law of submission and non-resistance for the black man, and another law of rebellion and conflict for the white man?" (116n12).

Chapter 11: The Notebook

1 Newsome, "Some Recollections."

2 Newsome, "Some Recollections," 11–12.

3 Newsome, "Some Recollections," 1–2.

4 Newsome, "Some Recollections," 2.

5 Box 81 (Catherine Bond, Colonel Thomas Bond, and Lewis Bond folders), Bertie County Estate Records.

6 Elbert Bishop to Gregg Hecimovich, email, May 14, 2022.

7 Newsome, "Some Recollections," 5.

8 Newsome, "Some Recollections," 5.

9 Newsome, "Some Recollections," 5.

10 Newsome, "Some Recollections," 6.

11 Box 1, JHW Papers MSS.

12 Jeff Hampton, "Descendants of Slaves Look Back at Emancipation," June 8, 2015, *Virginian-Pilot* (Norfolk), https://www.pilotonline.com/news/article_ac835b88-4d88-50f9-a22c-2c3a40864b4f.html.

13 Hampton, "Descendants of Slaves Look Back at Emancipation."

14 Hampton, ""Descendants of Slaves Look Back at Emancipation."

15 "Mary Outlaw Letter re Gilliam, Bond and Ward Genealogy, July 14, 1978," email by Elbert Bishop to Gregg Hecimovich, June 10, 2012.

16 Newsome, "Some Recollections," 6.

17 Newsome, "Some Recollections," 6–7.

18 Newsome, "Some Recollections," 8.

19 Bishop, prefatory comment on Newsome, "Some Recollections," in typescript of notebook provided by Elbert Bishop to Gregg Hecimovich, Elbert Bishop, email to author, June 12, 2012.

20 Newsome, "Some Recollections," 11–13.

Chapter 12: Religion

1 Randolph Ferguson Scully, *Religion and the Making of Nat Turner's Virginia: Baptist Community and Conflict, 1740–1840* (Charlottesville: University of Virginia Press), 117–19.

2 Timothy E. Fulop and Albert J. Raboteau, eds., *African-American Religion: Interpretative Essays in History and Culture* (New York: Routledge, 1997), 3.

3 Scully has done extensive work registering demographic data for church membership in southeast Virginia. I draw on his work here, especially pages 150–61.

4 Baptist, *Half Has Never Been Told*, 202.

5 *Methodist Error, or Friendly Christian Advice to Those Methodists Who Indulge in Extravagant Religious Emotions and Bodily Exercises* (Trenton, N.J.: D.E. Fenton, 1819), 30–31; Jane Alexander to Mary Springs, July 24, 1801, Springs Papers, Southern Historical Collection, University of North Carolina at Chapel Hill; R. C. Puryear to Isaac Jarratt, November 16, 1832, Jarratt-Puryear Papers, David M. Rubenstein Rare Books and Manuscripts Library, Duke University, Durham, N.C., cited in Baptist, *Half Has Never Been Told*, 202.

6 William S. White, *The African Preacher: An Authentic Narrative* (Philadelphia: Presbyterian Board of Publication), 59.

7 Baptist, *Half Has Never Been Told*, 200.

8 Augusta Rohrbach, "'A Silent Unobtrusive Way': Hannah Crafts and the Literary Marketplace," in Gates and Robbins, eds., *In Search of Hannah Crafts*, 65–66. Also see Katherine Clay Bassard, *Transforming Scriptures: African American Women Writers and the Bible* (Athens: University of Georgia Press, 2010), 68–69.

9 A long history of support for interracial worship within Baptist and Methodist congregations strengthened Turner's hand.

10 David Barrow, Minutes of the Virginia Portsmouth Baptist Association, 1796, 5, Virginia Baptist Historical Society, University of Richmond, Richmond, Va.

11 2 Corinthians 8:5.

12 Samuel Jordan Wheeler, *History of the Meherrin Baptist Church*, Baptist Historical Papers (Henderson: North Carolina Baptist Historical Society, 1847), 60, 76.

13 Wheeler, *History of the Meherrin Baptist Church*, 76.

14 Thornton Stringfellow, "A Brief Examination of Scripture Testimony on the Institution of Slavery" (1841), in Drew Gilpin Faust, ed., *The Ideology of Slavery: Proslavery Thought in the Antebellum South, 1830–1860* (Baton Rouge: Louisiana State University Press, 1981), 166.

15 Kristin Wilkes, "God and the Novel: Religion and Secularization in Antebellum American Fiction" (PhD dissertation, University of Oregon, December 2014), https://scholars bank.uoregon.edu/xmlui/bitstream/handle/1794/18713/Wilkes_oregon_0171A_11151

.pdf;sequence=1, 158–159. Dr. Wilkes kindly shared her dissertation with me via email on March 4, 2015. What I find so helpful and refreshing in her work is her readiness to take seriously Hannah Crafts's religious faith. I do the same throughout my interpretation of the novel.

16 Harriet Jacobs, *Incidents in the Life of a Slave Girl*, ed. Nell Irvin Painter (1861; repr. New York: Penguin Books, 2000), 14, cited in Wilkes, "God and the Novel," 159.

17 Douglass, *Narrative*, 82, 105, cited in Wilkes, "God and the Novel," 159.

18 1 Timothy 6:1, King James Bible.

19 Benjamin Drew, *A North-Side View of Slavery. The Refugee: Or the Narratives of Fugitive Slaves in Canada* (Boston: John P. Jewett and Company, 1856), 138.

20 Isaac Johnson, *Slavery Days in Old Kentucky* (Ogdensburg, N.Y.: Republican and Journal Print, 1901), 25–26, cited in Baptist, *Half Has Never Been Told*, 204.

21 For an authoritative history of "The Curse of Ham" and its role in the history of white supremacy, see David Brian Davis's *Inhuman Bondage: The Rise and Fall of Slavery in the New World* (New York: Oxford University Press, 2006), 64–76.

Chapter 13: The Wheelers

1 In fact, there was another John Wheeler in Washington, D.C., at the time who served as a government official, John Parson Wheeler. A review of what can be gathered about this Wheeler discounts him as the potential enslaver of the author of *The Bondwoman's Narrative*.

2 "The Wheeler Slave Case," *National Era*, September 6, 1855, 2.

3 See William L. Andrews, *To Tell a Free Story: The First Century of Afro-American Autobiography, 1760–1865* (Champaign: University of Illinois Press, 1986). Andrews's groundbreaking study is still one of the best and most comprehensive discussions of African American autobiography in print.

4 Catalogue of John H. Wheeler Library, June 1850, John H. Wheeler Papers, 1830–1882, Manuscript Collection 765 (Folder 4), Southern Historical Collection, University of North Carolina at Chapel Hill.

5 Lawrence Aje, "Fugitive Slave Narratives and the (Re)presentation of the Self? The Cases of Frederick Douglass and William Brown," *L'Ordinaire des Amériques* [online], November 27, 2014, https://journals.openedition.org/orda/507.

6 Maurice S. Lee, "Introduction" to *The Cambridge Companion to Frederick Douglass*, ed. Maurice S. Lee (Cambridge, UK: Cambridge University Press, 2009), 10, cited in Aje, "Fugitive Slave Narratives," 4.

7 William Wells Brown, *From Fugitive Slave to Free Man: The Autobiographies of William Wells Brown*, ed. and with an introduction by William L. Andrews (Columbia: University of Missouri Press, 2003), 5–6, cited in Aje, "Fugitive Slave Narratives," 4.

8 William E. Farrison, "William Wells Brown, Social Reformer," *Journal of Negro Education* 18, no. 1 (1949): 29, cited in Aje, "Fugitive Slave Narratives," 4.

9 William Wells Brown, *Narrative of William W. Brown, a Fugitive Slave. Written by Himself* (Boston: Anti-Slavery Office, 1847), 97–98.

10 Brown, *Narrative of Henry Box Brown*, 105–6.

11 Aje, "Fugitive Slave Narratives," 11.

Chapter 14: The Novel

1 William L. Andrews's work in the volume clarifies class relations while pointing to the strangeness of the novel's "happy" ending (30–42). Robert S. Levine explores the essentializing traps of racial identity keyed to black and white, both inside and outside the novel (276–94). Lawrence Buell, Ann Fabian, William Gleason, Augusta Rohrbach, Karen Sanchez-Eppler, and Bryan Sinche uncover the work's position in the publishing world of the day (Buell, 16–29; Fabian, 43–52; and Rohrbach, 3–15), its generic conventions (Sanchez-Eppler, 254–75; and Sinche, 175–191), and even its architecture (Gleason, 145–74). See Gates and Robbins, eds., *In Search of Hannah Crafts.*

2 Gates and Robbins, eds., "Hannah Crafts, 'The Bondwoman's Narrative': Introduction to the Critical Essay Collection," 18.

3 Henry Louis Gates Jr., "Borrowing Privileges," *New York Times*, June 2, 2002, Section 7, 18.

4 See Robert S. Levine, *Dislocating Race and Nation: Episodes in Nineteenth-Century American Literary Nationalism* (Chapel Hill: University of North Carolina Press, 2009), 119–78.

5 Catherine Keyser, "Jane Eyre, Bondwoman: Hannah Crafts' [*sic*] Rethinking of Charlotte Bronte," in Gates and Robbins, eds., *In Search of Hannah Crafts*, 87–105.

6 Roselyne M. Jua, "Circles of Freedom and Maturation in Hannah Crafts's 'The Bondwoman's Narrative,'" in *Journal of Black Studies* 40, no. 2 (November 2009): 311.

7 Jua, "Circles of Freedom and Maturation," 311.

8 For my summary of the plot to *The Bondwoman's Narrative*, I am adapting and building on the wonderful summary published by Aushianna Nadri, "The Bondwoman's Narrative, A Summary," *The Bondwoman's Narrative* (blog), November 12, 2009, http://thebondwomansnarrative.blogspot.com/2009/11/bondwomans-narrative-blog-post-one.html.

Chapter 15: The Life and Times of Eliza Morgan

1 Russel E. Train, *The Train Family*, 259.

2 *Biblical Recorder* (Raleigh, N.C.), December 7, 1836, 3.

3 Thomas Sully, register, Dreer Collection, Historical Society of Pennsylvania, Philadelphia, lists the portrait as begun July 3 and finished July 25, 1844. Also see Edward Biddle and Mantle Fielding, *The Life and Works of Thomas Sully* (Philadelphia: Wickersham Press, 1921), 317.

4 Charles Lyell, *A Second Visit to the United States of North America*, 2 vols. (New York: Harper and Brothers, 1859), 1:201, cited in Josephine F. Pacheco, *The Pearl: A Failed Slave Escape on the Potomac* (Chapel Hill: University of North Carolina Press, 2005), 25.

5 Lorenzo D. Johnson, *The Churches and Pastors of Washington, D.C.* (New York: M. W. Dodd, 1857), 133, cited in Pacheco, *The Pearl*, 26.

6 Henry Caswall, *The Western World Revisited* (Oxford: John Henry Parker, 1854), 263–64, cited in Pacheco, *The Pearl*, 26.

7 Janet Duitsman Cornelius, *When I Can Read My Title Clear: Literacy, Slavery, and Religion in the Antebellum South* (Columbia: University of South Carolina Press, 1991), 121–22, cited in Pacheco, *The Pearl*, 26.

8 *The Washington Directory, and National Register for 1846* (Washington, D.C.: Gaither and Addison, 1846), 17, cited in Pacheco, *The Pearl*, 26.

9 Isabella Strange *Trotter, First Impressions of the New World on Two Travellers from the Old in the Autumn of 1858* (London: Longman, Brown, Green, Longmans, and Roberts, 1859), 220; Caswall, *Western World Revisited*, 264, cited in Pacheco, *The Pearl*, 26.

10 John W. Cromwell, "The First Negro Churches in the District of Columbia," *Journal of Negro History* 7, no. 1 (January 1922): 65.

11 Kristopher Roberts, "The First Baptist Church of Washington, D.C.," White House Historical Association, July 19, 2021, https://www.whitehousehistory.org/the-first-baptist-church-of-the-city-of-washington-d-c. See also Robert D. Cochran, *In the House of Philemon: Connections Between First Baptist Church and the African American Community, 1800–1875* (Washington, D.C.: District of Columbia Baptist Convention, 2002).

12 Paul E. Sluby Sr., *Asbury: Our Legacy, Our Faith, 1836–1993*, 2nd ed. (Washington, D.C.: Privately printed, 1996), 17–23, cited in Pacheco, *The Pearl*, 27.

13 Roberts, "The First Baptist Church of Washington, D.C."

14 David R. Goldfield, "Black Life in Old South Cities," in *Before Freedom Came: African-American Life in the Antebellum South*, ed. Edward D. C. Campbell Jr., with Kym S. Rice (Richmond and Charlottesville: Museum of the Confederacy and University Press of Virginia, 1991), 140, cited in Pacheco, *The Pearl*, 27.

15 Journal of Rev. Henry Slicer, May 13, 1850, Lovely Lane Museum of the United Methodist Historical Society of the Baltimore-Washington Conference, Baltimore, Md., August 31, September 2, 1849; Henry Caswall, *America, and the American Church*, 2nd ed. (London: John and Charles Mozley, 1851), 291, cited in Pacheco, *The Pearl*, 29.

16 Alexander Mackay, *The Western World; or, Travel in the United States in 1846–47: Exhibiting Them in Their Latest Development, Social, Political, and Industrial*, 3 vols., 2nd ed. (London: Richard Bentley, 1849), 2:131; Barbara Jeanne Fields, *Slavery and Freedom on the Middle Ground: Maryland During the Nineteenth Century* (New Haven, Conn.: Yale University Press, 1985), 35. Cited in Pacheco, *The Pearl*, 29–30.

17 Drew, *A North-Side View of Slavery*, 111.

18 John Thompson, *The Life of John Thompson, a Fugitive Slave* (1856; repr. New York: Negro Universities Press, 1969), 18–19; Ethan Allen Andrews, *Slavery and the Domestic Slave-Trade in the United States: In a Series of Letters Addressed to the Executive Committee of the American Union for the Relief and Improvement of the Colored Race* (Boston: Light and Stearns, 1836), 121, cited in Pacheco, *The Pearl*, 27–28.

19 William Faux, *Memorable Days in America: Being a Journal of a Tour to the United States, Principally Undertaken to Ascertain, by Positive Evidence, the Condition and Probable Prospects of British Emigrants* (London: W. Simpkin and R. Marshall, 1823), 109; Fredrika Bremer, *The Homes of the New World: Impressions of America*, 2 vols. (1853; repr. New York: Negro Universities Press, 1968), 1:491–92, cited in Pacheco, *The Pearl*, 27.

20 Walter C. Clephane, "The Local Aspect of Slavery in the District of Columbia," *Records of the Columbia Historical Society* 3 (1900): 246–47; Henry S. Robinson, "Some Aspects of the Free Negro Population of Washington, D.C., 1800–1862," *Maryland Historical Magazine* 64 (Spring 1969): 46; Jane M. E. Turnbull and Marion Turnbull, *American Photographs*, 2 vols. in single ed. (London: T. C. Newby, 1859), 2:190, cited in Pacheco, *The Pearl*, 30.

21 John Hill Wheeler Papers MSS, Box 1.

22 Torrey, in *Tocsin of Liberty*, October 27, 1842, quoted in Stanley Harrold, *Subversives: Antislavery Community in Washington, D.C., 1828–1865* (Baton Rouge: Louisiana State University Press, 2003), 5.

23 Thomas Smallwood, *A Narrative of Thomas Smallwood (Coloured Man) Giving an Account of His Birth—The Period He Was Held in Slavery—His Release—and Removal to Canada, etc.: Together with an Account of the Underground Railroad. Written by Himself* (Toronto: James Stephens, 1851), 13 and 18.

24 Joseph C. Lovejoy, *Memoir of Rev. Charles T. Torrey, Who Died in the Penitentiary of Maryland, Where He Was Confined for Showing Mercy to the Poor* (1847; repr. New York: Negro Universities Press, 1969), 89–90.

25 "Charles Torrey—The Most Successful, Least Celebrated Abolitionist," New England Historical Society, updated 2022, https://www.newenglandhistoricalsociety.com/charles-torrey-successful-least-celebrated-abolitionist/.

26 *The WPA Guide to Washington, D.C.: The Federal Writers' Project Guide to 1930s Washington* (New York: Pantheon Books, 1983), 493, cited in Pacheco, *The Pearl*, 44.

27 Lovejoy, *Memoir of Rev. Charles T. Torrey*, 294–96, cited in Pacheco, *The Pearl*, 45.

28 Letter from Charles Torrey to Mary Torrey, September 28, 1845, in Lovejoy, *Memoir of Rev. Charles T. Torrey*, 225, 266–71.

29 Harrold, *Subversives*, 85.

30 Pauline Gaskins Mitchell, "The History of Mt. Zion United Methodist Church and Mt. Zion Cemetery," *Records of the Columbia Historical Society of Washington, D.C.* 51 (1984): 104; Monroe quoted in Brenda E. Stevenson, *Life in Black and White: Family and Community in the Slave South* (New York: Oxford University Press, 1996), 159, cited in Pacheco, *The Pearl*, 30.

31 Mann, *Slavery*, 127–28, cited in Pacheco, *The Pearl*, 30.

32 Joshua R. Giddings, *Speeches in Congress* (Boston: John P. Jewett, 1853), 142–43, cited in Pacheco, *The Pearl*, 32.

33 *Congressional Globe*, Thirty-First Congress, First Session, 19, Appendix 1:323 (March 4, 1850); Giddings, *Speeches*, 349 (February 17, 1849), cited in Pacheco, *The Pearl*, 33.

34 Solomon Northup, *Twelve Years a Slave* (1854; repr. New York: Dover, 1970), 43, cited in Pacheco, *The Pearl*, 39.

35 For my account of the attempted escape on the *Pearl*, I draw heavily on Mia Owens's concise and vivid narrative published for the White House Historical Association: Mia Owens, "'Running from the Temple of Liberty': The Pearl Incident," White House Historical Association, January 26, 2021, https://www.whitehousehistory.org/the-pearl-incident. For the rich contexts, see Pacheco, *The Pearl* (heavily used for this chapter), and Mary Kay Ricks, *Escape on the Pearl: The Heroic Bid for Freedom on the Underground Railroad* (New York: William Morrow, 2007).

36 William L. Chaplin to Gerrit Smith, March 25, 1848, Gerrit Smith Papers, Library of Congress, Washington, D.C., cited in Ricks, *Escape on the Pearl*, 23.

37 Daniel Drayton, *Personal Memoir of Daniel Drayton, for Four Years and Four Months a Prisoner (for Charity's Sake) in Washington Jail, Including a Narrative of the Voyage and Capture of the Schooner Pearl* (1854; repr. New York: Negro Universities Press, 1969), 40.

38 James K. Polk Diary entry, April 20, 1848, James K. Polk Papers: Series 1, Diaries 1845–1849, Library of Congress, Washington, D.C.

39 Harrold, *Subversives*, 132.

40 Ricks, *Escape on the Pearl*, 145.

41 Harrold, *Subversives*, 134.

42 Linda Wheeler, "D.C. Jail Log Unlocks History of Slave Era," *Washington Post*, January 19, 1991, https://www.washingtonpost.com/archive/local/1991/01/10/dc-jail-log-unlocks-history-of-slave-era/c66f68ab-4efe-4675-b279-b5837d4b59ba/.

43 Ricks, *Escape on the Pearl*, 110.

44 Northup, *Twelve Years a Slave*, chapter 3.

45 Church minutes from December 8, 1848, First Baptist Church of the City of Washington, D.C. My thanks to First Baptist historian Janice Osborn and the historian Kristofer Roberts for their assistance in reviewing early records related to the First Baptist Church.

46 Church minutes from December 8, 1848, First Baptist Church of the City of Washington, D.C; Cochran, *In the House of Philemon*, 5.

47 Ken Hawkins, "The Beale Family in Four Corners, 1850–1887," *NFCCA Newsletter*, February 2014, http://www.nfcca.org/news/nn201402j.html.

48 Federal Mortality Census Schedules, 1850–1880, and Related Indexes, 1850–1880 (p. 26), Archive Collection T655, Archive Roll Number 6, Census Year 1879, Census Place "Washington, District of Columbia," NARA.

Chapter 16: *The Bondwoman's Narrative* and *Bleak House*

1 Like chapter 6, this chapter draws heavily on a specific work of scholarship, in this case, Hollis Robbins's groundbreaking essay "Blackening 'Bleak House': Hannah Crafts's 'The Bondwoman's Narrative.'" My chapter traces Robbins's work and builds new interpretations based on her original analysis of Crafts's "borrowings" from Charles Dickens's *Bleak House*. Hollis has been a dear friend since she drew me into this project in 2003, and her scholarship remains as seminal today as it was when she first published it in 2004.

2 Robbins, "Blackening 'Bleak House,'" 71.

3 Robbins, "Blackening 'Bleak House,'" 71–72.

4 Robbins, "Blackening 'Bleak House,'" 72.

5 Robbins, "Blackening 'Bleak House,'" 72–73.

6 Robbins, "Blackening 'Bleak House,'" 72.

7 See William J. Mahar, *Behind the Burnt Cork Mask: Early Blackface Minstrelsy and Antebellum American Popular Culture* (Urbana: University of Illinois Press, 1998).

8 *Daily Delta* (New Orleans), February 15, 1854, 3. See also Joseph P. Roppolo, "Uncle Tom in New Orleans: Three Lost Plays," *New England Quarterly* 27, no. 2 (June 1954): 213–26.

9 *Daily Delta* (New Orleans), February 17, 1854, 5.

10 See Robbins, "Blackening 'Bleak House,'" 83n3.

11 Frederick Douglass, *Frederick Douglass' Paper* (Rochester, N.Y.), 3, cited in Robbins, "Blackening 'Bleak House,'" 73.

12 Julia Sun-Joo Lee, *American Slave Narrative and the Victorian Novel* (London: Oxford University Press, 2010), 3.

13 Lee, *American Slave Narrative*, 8.

14 Peter Ackroyd, *Dickens* (New York: HarperCollins, 1991), 544.

15 Denman, *"Uncle Tom's Cabin," "Bleak House," Slavery and Slave Trade*, 9–10.

16 Robbins, "Blackening 'Bleak House,'" 73–74.

17 Robbins, "Blackening 'Bleak House,'" 74.

18 Denman, *"Uncle Tom's Cabin," "Bleak House," Slavery and Slave Trade*, 27.

19 Henry Louis Gates Jr., *The Signifying Monkey: A Theory of African American Criticism* (London: Oxford University Press, 1988), xxiii, cited in Robbins, "Blackening 'Bleak House,'" 74.

20 Robbins, "Blackening 'Bleak House,'" 78.

21 I continue to follow Hollis Robbins's careful documentation of the many parallels. See Robbins, "Blackening 'Bleak House,'" 85n12.

22 Gates, *Signifying Monkey*, xxv. Robbins brilliantly observes the connection to Henry Louis Gates Jr.'s theory of the "speakerly text" as part of his influential theory of African American literature (Robbins, "Blackening 'Bleak House,'" 78). As Gates puts it, "the principal indices of free indirect discourse direct the reader to the subjective source of the statement, rendered through a fusion of narrator and silent but speaking character" (*Signifying Monkey*, 210).

23 Robbins, "Blackening 'Bleak House,'" 78.

24 This is the case in free indirect discourse in which the narrative voice ventriloquizes the thoughts and words of her characters without marks of ownership.

25 Robbins, "Blackening 'Bleak House,'" 75.

26 Robbins, "Blackening 'Bleak House,'" 75.

27 Robbins, "Blackening 'Bleak House,'" 75–76.

28 Robbins, "Blackening 'Bleak House,'" 76.

29 I follow Robbins, "Blackening 'Bleak House,'" here, too, with this parallel, 76. As she observes in note 9 on page 84, "Hannah claims that 'duty, gratitude, and honor,' prevent her from leaving too. 'And so to a strained sense of honor you willingly sacrifise a prospect of freedom,' William answers. 'Well, you can hug the chain if you please. With me it is liberty or death.' The phrase 'hug the chain' has as its source a short, sardonic poem by Lord Byron called 'Stanzas': 'Could Love for ever / Run like a river, / And Time's endeavor / Be tried in vain—/ No other pleasure / With this could measure; / And like a treasure / We'd hug the chain.'"

30 Robbins, "Blackening 'Bleak House,'" 76.

31 Robbins, "Blackening 'Bleak House,'" 76–77.

32 Robbins, "Blackening 'Bleak House,'" 80–81.

33 Robbins, "Blackening 'Bleak House,'" 81.

34 Robbins, "Blackening 'Bleak House,'" 82.

35 Robbins, "Blackening 'Bleak House,'" 82.

Chapter 17: The Search Continued

1 See the original "Introduction" reproduced in the most recent edition of *The Bondwoman's Narrative*, lxix–lxxii.

2 Letter from Michael Harpold to Gregg Hecimovich, April 25, 2005. Harpold's letter is accompanied by a copy of the handwritten court ruling against Wheeler recorded in Morganton, North Carolina, and by the deed on file in the Lincoln County Courthouse, Lincolnton, North Carolina, in which Wheeler sells his plantation to Connor.

3 A slave no longer in the possession of John Hill Wheeler after 1855 could still have produced the novel, but most evidence points to direct association with the family in 1856 and 1857.

4 I am indebted to the North Carolina historian Thomas C. Parramore for these insights. Parramore's essay "The Bondwoman and the Bureaucrat" stands out for its passionate criticism of Gates's authentication efforts. To Gates and Robbins's credit, they include Parramore's critique in the established literature on the novel. Parramore proved a surprising muse to my research. His article is the source of my point-by-point refutation in "Searching for Hannah Crafts in Eastern North Carolina," *North Carolina Literary Review* 16 (2007): 43–54. Like many passages in *The Bondwoman's Narrative*, the description of the Wheeler plantation holds parallels with characters and themes in Charles Dickens's *Bleak House*.

5 The manuscript diaries of Samuel Jordan Wheeler survive for the years 1865 and 1866, when Wheeler still oversaw the Wheeler plantation in Hertford County. Diaries are also extant for later years when he and his wife, Lucinda Bond Wheeler, had moved to live on the old Bond plantation in Bertie County, near Windsor. These later diaries describe the occasional visits of Wheeler to the old family plantation in Murfreesboro.

> Came on to my dear old home. . . . Walked through field, picked up oranges. Everything looked desolate and dreary, our once beautiful garden a cotton patch, our palings tumbled down, our pleasant walks & lanes overgrown in weeds, our dwelling closed, cold and lonely—our favorite cows Jule and Mayflower looking mournfully through front gate as if begging me to return & take care of them. . . . My heart ached, my soul was sick and faint and I turned aside to find relief in tears.

6 The 1865, 1866, 1867, and 1868 Samuel Jordan Wheeler diaries are located in the Samuel Jordan Wheeler Papers at the Southern Historical Collection at the University of North Carolina, Chapel Hill.

7 Smallwood, *Bertie County: An Eastern Carolina History*, 114.

8 Quoted from *Hertford County Deed Book A* (Winton, N.C.: Hertford County Courthouse), 378.

9 *Hertford County Record of Estates* (p. 221), North Carolina Department of Cultural Resources, Division of Archives and History, Raleigh.

10 *Hertford County Record of Accounts, 1830–36* (492–93) and *Hertford County Record of Accounts, 1836–1840* (98–108), North Carolina Department of Cultural Resources, Division of Archives and History, Raleigh.

11 Indeed, in December 1841, John Hill Wheeler extended the Wheeler plantation property in Northampton County by purchasing land adjacent to the existing 250 acres from James E. Newsom and his wife, Mary Newsom. *Northampton County Deed Book* 30, 11.

12 *Northampton County Deed Book* 30, 11; *Hertford County Deed Book A*, 378.

13 The "Esther, John, and James" whom Wheeler mentions in his April 2, 1857, diary entry

are not slaves, as Gates suggests, but rather, younger cousins of Wheeler's who resided at the Mulberry Grove plantation of Dr. Godwin Cotton Moore: Esther Cotton Moore (b. 1838), John Wheeler Moore (b. 1833), and James Wright Moore (b. 1835).

14 I am indebted to the handwritten notes locating the property written by Samuel Jordan Wheeler's great-grandson Samuel Wheeler Worthington and provided to me by his daughter, Margaret Worthington.

15 *Roanoke-Chowan Times* (Rich Square, N.C.), December 3, 1906.

16 The special cultivation of "pomegranates" and "figs" is fitting with historical records of exotic plants and fruits grown in the antebellum Southeast. See James R. Cothran's *Gardens and Historic Plants of the Antebellum South* (Columbia: University of South Carolina Press, 2003), 188–89, 269.

17 See "Dr. Samuel Jordan Wheeler Notebooks," North Carolina State Archives, Raleigh.

18 Waldo called the next day and provided his "note for furniture $1,500, House $450 a year and hire of servants $102." Box 1, John Hill Wheeler Papers MSS. Jane Johnson was one of these "servants" whom Wheeler hired out before his attempt to retrieve her in July 1855, which led to the famous Passmore Williamson case.

19 February 17 and February 25 entries, Box 1, John Hill Wheeler Papers MSS.

20 Folder 2, Box 7, John Hill Wheeler Papers MSS.

Chapter 18: The Life and Times of Jane Johnson

1 Flynn, "Jane Johnson, Found!," 406–18.

2 Flynn, "Jane Johnson, Found!," 372–73; Box 1, John Hill Wheeler MSS.

3 Flynn, "Jane Johnson, Found!," 373; Box 1, John Hill Wheeler MSS.

4 Flynn, "Jane Johnson, Found!," 373.

5 William Still, *The Underground Railroad* (Philadelphia: Porter & Coates, 1872), 94.

6 *Philadelphia Evening Post*, September 8, 1855; Edward Williamson to "Dear Sir," September 1, 1855, Letters, Passmore Williamson, Chester County Historical Society, cited in Brandt and Brandt, *In the Shadow of the Civil War*, 123.

7 *National Anti-Slavery Standard* (New York), September 8, 1855, cited in Brandt and Brandt, *In the Shadow of the Civil War*, 123; the *Philadelphia Evening Post* is quoted by the *Standard.*

8 *National Anti-Slavery Standard*, September 8, 1855, cited in Brandt and Brandt, *In the Shadow of the Civil War*, 122.

9 Brandt and Brandt, *In the Shadow of the Civil War*, 123–24.

10 Lucretia Mott to Martha Wright, September 4, 1855, Lucretia Mott MSS, Mott Collection, Friends Historical Library, Swarthmore College, cited in Brandt and Brandt, *In the Shadow of the Civil War*, 124.

11 Boxes 1 and 22, John Hill Wheeler MSS.

12 *Narrative of Facts in the Case of Passmore Williamson* (Philadelphia: Pennsylvania Anti-Slavery Society, 1855), 4; Still, *Underground Railroad*, 89, cited in Flynn, "Jane Johnson, Found!," 375 and 400n9.

13 Flynn, "Jane Johnson, Found!," 374.

14 Flynn, "Jane Johnson, Found!," 374–75.

15 Flynn, "Jane Johnson, Found!," 375. Charles Ringold, one of the other family heads who share the dwelling in the 1860 federal census entry, is also listed in the directory at the same address.

16 Flynn, "Jane Johnson, Found!," 376.

17 Francis Jackson, *Account Book of Francis Jackson, Treasurer, the Boston Vigilance Committee* (Boston: Boston Vigilance Society, n.d.), 48, cited in Flynn, "Jane Johnson, Found!," 377.

18 Flynn, "Jane Johnson, Found!," 376.

19 Flynn, "Jane Johnson, Found!," 376.

20 William S. Parsons and Margaret A. Drew, *The African Meeting House: A Sourcebook* (Boston: Museum of Afro-American History, 1990), 39, 78–81, cited in Flynn, "Jane Johnson, Found!," 377.

21 Jackson, *Account Book*, 54, 58, cited in Flynn, "Jane Johnson, Found!," 379.

22 Lawrence Woodfork/Woodfalk entry, Death Records Book 1861, No. 3707, and certified death certificate No. 012592, issued June 11, 2002, by Registry Division, City of Boston, cited in Flynn, "Jane Johnson, Found!," 379.

23 Probate Index, Suffolk County, Massachusetts, 1636–1893, searched by New England Historic and Genealogical Society Research Service, report dated June 5, 2002, cited in Flynn, "Jane Johnson, Found!," 379.

24 Marriage Book 1864, No. 1499, Registry Division, City of Boston, cited in Flynn, "Jane Johnson, Found!," 379.

25 Flynn, "Jane Johnson, Found!," 379.

26 Isaiah Johnson compiled service record (priv., Co. K, Mass. 55th Regt., Col'd.), National Archives and Records Administration M1801, roll 47, cited in Flynn, "Jane Johnson, Found!," 379.

27 Details about Isaiah's unit appear in Charles B. Fox, *Record of Service of the Fifty-Fifth Regiment of Massachusetts Volunteer Infantry* (1868; repr. Freeport, N.Y.: Books for Libraries Press, 1971); Frederick H. Dyer, *A Compendium of the War of Rebellion*, 3 vols. (1908; repr., Dayton, Ohio: Morningside House, 1979), 2:1266; Massachusetts Adjutant's Office, *Massachusetts Soldiers, Sailors, and Marines in the Civil War*, 9 vols. (Norwood, Mass.: Norwood Press, 1931–1937), 4:715–61; Wilbert H. Luck, *Journey to Honey Hill* (Washington, D.C.: Wiluck Press, 1976); James M. McPherson, *The Negro's Civil War* (New York: Ballantine Books, 1991), 240; and Noah Andre Trudeau, ed., *Voices of the 55th: Letters from the 55th Massachusetts Volunteers, 1861–1865* (Dayton, Ohio: Morningside House, 1996), cited in Flynn, "Jane Johnson, Found!," 379–80.

28 Fox, *Record of Service of the Fifty-Fifth Regiment*, 148, cited in Flynn, "Jane Johnson, Found!," 380.

29 Isaac Johnson (drummer/priv., Co. K., 55th Regt., Mass. Vol. Inf.), Civil War invalid pension application 528183, certificate 650621, Record Group 15, Records of Veterans Administration, NARA, Washington, D.C.; see "Deposition E. Ransom Chatman" (July 9, 1901), 34, cited in Flynn, "Jane Johnson, Found!," 380.

30 Flynn, "Jane Johnson, Found!," 380.

31 Flynn, "Jane Johnson, Found!," 380.

32 Jane Harris entry, Death Records, Book 1872, No. 4511, Registry Division, City of Boston, cited in Flynn, "Jane Johnson, Found!," 381.

33 Suffolk County, Massachusetts, Probate Index, 1636–1893, checked by the New England Historic and Genealogical Society Research Service, June 5, 2002, yielded no record for Jane Harris. The Boston Athenaeum Library's obituary index the "Boston Evening Transcript, 1830–1874," by Dorothy Wirth, also omits her; cited in Flynn, "Jane Johnson, Found!," 381.

34 Flynn, "Jane Johnson, Found!," 381.

35 Letters of William C. Nell to Passmore Williamson, December 3, 1855, and May 26, 1856, "Passmore Williamson Visitors Book," MS 76710, Chester County Historical Society, West Chester, Pa., cited in Flynn, "Jane Johnson, Found!," 382. The letters have been digitized: Various, "Passmore Williamson Visitors' Book Part 2: Letters of Support," *Passmore Williamson's Prison Visitors' Book*, https://passmorewilliamson.omeka.net/items/show/8.

36 Flynn, "Jane Johnson, Found!," 382–83.

37 Flynn, "Jane Johnson, Found!," 386.

38 Flynn, "Jane Johnson, Found!," 386.

39 Flynn, "Jane Johnson, Found!," 388–90.

40 Flynn, "Jane Johnson, Found!," 391–92.

41 Flynn, "Jane Johnson, Found!," 394–95.

42 *Boston Globe*, January 20, 1873, 8; *Boston Globe*, February 15, 1873, 8.

43 *United States, Buffalo Soldiers, Returns from Regular Army Cavalry Regiments, 1833–1916*, NARA microfilm publication M744, 16 rolls, Record Group Number 391, Records of U.S. Regular Army Mobile Units, 1821–1942, National Archives and Records Administration, Washington, D.C.

44 *Natrona County Tribute*, August 26, 1897, 4; *Salt Lake Herald*, December 10, 1897, 1.

45 *Salt Lake Herald*, December 15, 1897, 1.

46 Isaiah Johnson, Memory Lane Cemetery, Silver City, Grant County, N.M., https://www.findagrave.com/memorial/92673347/isaiah-johnson. Notice of Isaiah's marriage appears in the *Boston Post*, October 23, 1875, 2. Children born to Isaiah Johnson and Elizabeth Taylor Johnson (1851–1920) appear to have resided with the mother in Newport, Rhode Island, while Isaiah spent the majority of his adulthood in the army, while based on the West Coast, or in prison.

47 Obituary, *Havre Daily News* (Montana), September 21, 1927, 1.

48 *Havre Daily News Promoter* (Montana), December 22, 1925, 4.

49 California Death Index, 1940–1997, Sacramento: State of California Department of Health Services, Center for Health Statistics, Place: Ventura, Date: June 4, 1982, Social Security: 701109604.

50 *New York Tribute*, July 30, 1855, 6.

Chapter 19: The Life and Times of Hannah Crafts

1 I follow the model and language of Paul Berman's opening to his brilliant essay "The True Story of America's First Black Female Slave Novelist," *New Republic*, February 10, 2014,

https://newrepublic.com/article/116329/bondwomans-narrative-hannah-bond-was-first-female-slave-novelist.

2 John Hill Wheeler, *Historical Sketches of North Carolina, from 1584 to 1851* (Philadelphia: Lippincott, Grambo and Company, 1851), title page.

3 John Wheeler Moore, *School History of North Carolina, from 1584 to 1879* (Raleigh, N.C.: Alfred Williams and Company, 1879).

4 Wheeler, *Historical Sketches* (1851), title page.

5 Parramore, "The Bondwoman and the Bureaucrat," 358.

6 A. Linda Hassell University Archives, Chowan University, Murfreesboro, N.C.

7 Enosinian Society, Library Record, 1852–1872, Box 148, Folder 4, Special Collections Research Center, George Washington University, Washington, D.C.

8 Wheeler, *Historical Sketches* (1851), ii.

9 Noble J. Tolbert, ed., *The Papers of John Willis Ellis* (Raleigh, N.C.: State Division of Archive and History, 1964), 96.

10 Wheeler, *Historical Sketches* (1851), xvi.

11 Dickens, *Bleak House*, preface.

12 Box 1, John Hill Wheeler MSS; see diary entries for May 1856.

13 Bill Harrell, "The Road to Carolina," 32, typescript in North Carolina State Archives, Raleigh; *Raleigh Register*, March 4, 1848, cited in Parramore, *Murfreesboro, North Carolina and the Rise of Higher Education for Women*, 14.

14 Harrell, "The Road to Carolina," 33, cited in Parramore, *North Carolina and the Rise of Higher Education in Women*, 15.

15 When the Kenwigs family learns that the inheritance they have been fondly anticipating will never materialize, young Morleena Kenwigs falls "all stiff and rigid, in the baby's chair, as she had seen her mother fall when she fainted away." Morleena, like Lucinda Bond Wheeler, awakens from her swoon quickly, springing up unharmed a page later when she finds that no one has noticed her performance (Charles Dickens, *The Life and Adventures of Nicholas Nickleby* [1838–39; repr. London: Penguin Classics, 2003], 442–42). For Mrs. Wheeler, it is when she is at the gate of Wheeler House that she is revived ("it was all over by the time she reached the gate"). For Bill Harrell, Lucinda's dramatic reaction must have seemed, if comic, also problematic, given that two of the three Murfreesboro doctors joined Mrs. Wheeler to attend to her swoon at Wheeler House, leaving only Dr. Neale to manage the broken bone sticking out of Harrell's skin.

16 "Account Book," Dr. Samuel Jordan Wheeler Notebooks, North Carolina State Archive.

17 *The Chowan Baptist Female Institute Catalogue*, 27.

18 McKnight and Creech, *A History of Chowan College*, 48–51.

19 The Davises faced a potential scandal when a male teacher courted a student in 1856, even though it was with the student's encouragement and, apparently, the support of the student's mother. But then the stepfather intervened and threatened to expose the Davises as not maintaining propriety regarding his stepdaughter. The moment was one of high drama for the budding school and especially for the caretakers, President and Mrs. Davis. As it turned out, the stepfather had designs to marry off the daughter to a male relative. Eventually, peace was restored, but the incident demonstrates the stakes and strict protocols about

male engagement with students, boundaries probably welcomed by the author. See Folders 13–15, Series 1.1, Collection 2572: Beale and Davis Family Papers, Southern Historical Collection, University of North Carolina, Chapel Hill. Also see William E. Stephenson, "The Davises, the Southalls, and the Founding of Wesleyan Female College, 1854–1859," *North Carolina Historical Review* 57, no. 3 (July 1980): 257–79.

20 Anne Davis to John Davis, December 28, 1857, Folder 18, Beale and Davis Family Papers, cited in Stephenson, "The Davises," 264.

21 See Tyler D. Parry, *Jumping the Broom: The Surprising Multicultural Origins of a Black Wedding Ritual* (Chapel Hill: University of North Carolina Press, 2020), 1–13 and 37–67; Eugene D. Genovese, *Roll, Jordan, Roll: The World the Slaves Made* (New York: Pantheon Books, 1974), 478–80; and George P. Rawick, *From Sundown to Sunup: The Making of the Black Community* (Westport, Conn.: Praeger, 1972), 86–87.

22 John Wheeler Papers, in the author's possession, provided to author by the Reverend Joseph Cooper of Windsor, N.C.

23 S.B., "Home Scenes," *The Casket: Periodical of the Chowan Female Collegiate Institute*, ed. Mrs. E. De Lancey Fory (Murfreesboro, N.C.: Office of the Murfreesboro Gazette, 1854), 3–4; A. Linda Hassell University Archives, Chowan University, Murfreesboro, N.C., https://lib.digitalnc.org/record/100555.

24 S.B., "Home Scenes," 4.

25 "James Roche to Obadiah B. Brown, Bill of Sale, January 19, 1829," Charles County Deeds, Book IB, 18:218–19, Charles County Court Land Records. As Kristopher Roberts notes, "By 1830, Brown enslaved four people, including a mother and daughter purchased from James Roche of Charles County, Virginia. According to the bill of sale, Roche sold Sally (age 30) and Kitty Bell (age 3), to Brown. The bill of sale also included specific references to Simon Bell, husband to Sally and father of Kitty, and General John P. Van Ness, Simon's enslaver." Roberts, "First Baptist Church of Washington, D.C."

26 "James Roche to Obadiah B. Brown, Bill of Sale."

27 Register of Wills, District of Columbia, "Will of Obadiah B. Brown," March 20, 1852, Box 19: Wills, Probate Records (District of Columbia) 1801–1930, Washington, D.C.

28 Box 1, John Hill Wheeler MSS.

29 Lawrence Kotlikoff, "The Structure of Slave Prices in New Orleans, 1804 to 1862," *Economic Inquiry* 17 (October 1979): 496–518, cited in Brenda E. Stevenson, "What's Love Got to Do with It? Concubinage and Enslaved Women and Girls in the Antebellum South," *Journal of African American History* 98, no. 1 (Winter 1993): 105.

30 J. D. B. DeBow, *Seventh Census of the United States, 1850: Embracing a Statistical View of Each of the States and Territories, Arranged by Counties, Towns, Etc.* (Washington, D.C.: Robert Armstrong, Public Printer, 1853), see Table LXXII: "Black and Mulatto Population of the United States," 83, cited in Stevenson, "What's Love Got to Do with It?," 101.

31 Henry D. Spalding, *Encyclopedia of Black Folklore and Humor* (1972; rev. ed., Middle Village, N.Y.: Jonathan David Company, 1994), 239–41, cited in Stevenson, "What's Love Got to Do with It?," 101.

32 Elizabeth Dowling Taylor, *A Slave in the White House: Paul Jennings and the Madisons* (New York: St. Martin's Press, 2012), 202.

33 "Capitol Dome," Architect of the Capitol, n.d., https://www.aoc.gov/explore-capitol-campus/buildings-grounds/capitol-building/capitol-dome.

34 "Philip Reid and the Statue of Freedom," Architect of the Capitol, n.d., https://www.aoc.gov/explore-capitol-campus/art/statue-freedom/philip-reid.

35 Box 1, John Hill Wheeler MSS.

36 "Philip Reid and the Statue of Freedom."

37 Washington, D.C., Slave Emancipation Records, 1851–1863, Records of the U.S. District Court for the District of Columbia Relating to Slaves, 1851–1863, Microfilm Serial M433, Microfilm Roll 2, National Archives and Records Administration, Washington, D.C.

38 Alfred Chapman to wife Mary Chapman, December 25, 1850, Alfred Chapman Papers, Southern Historical Collection, University of North Carolina, Chapel Hill.

39 Taylor, *A Slave in the White House*, 183–84.

40 *Georgia Telegraph* (Macon), May 15, 1849, cited in Taylor, *A Slave in the White House*, 183.

41 "Daniel Webster Recommendation Note," June 23, 1851, Folder 3, Alfred Chapman Papers, Southern Historical Collection, University of North Carolina, Chapel Hill.

42 Taylor, *A Slave in the White House*, 166.

43 Taylor, *A Slave in the White House*, 304.

44 Taylor, *A Slave in the White House*, 177.

45 Taylor, *A Slave in the White House*, 200.

46 Taylor, *A Slave in the White House*, 191–92.

47 "History of Nicaragua MS," Box 21, John Hill Wheeler MSS. Also see Parramore, "Keystone Konquistidors," 14.

48 Berman, "The True Story of America's First Black Female Slave Novelist."

49 The venture capitalist Cornelius Vanderbilt wrote these lines in 1856 to his former business partners Cornelius Garrison and Charles Morgan. Garrison and Morgan had made a secret alliance with the "filibustering" general William Walker and with John Hill Wheeler, U.S. minister to Nicaragua (1855–57). Together, they conspired to establish a pro-slavery "Republic of Nicaragua" by appropriating property, transportation, and shipping rights from Vanderbilt and awarding these to Garrison and Morgan while raising capital and diplomatic recognition for Walker's conquering army.

50 Berman, "The True Story of America's First Black Female Slave Novelist."

51 "History of Nicaragua MS," Box 21, John Hill Wheeler MSS. Also see Parramore, "Keystone Konquistidors," 14.

52 Amos Freeman, "The Weems Family," *Frederick Douglass' Newspaper* (Rochester, N.Y.), February 1, 1856, 1.

53 Freeman, "The Weems Family," 1. My account of Weems's escape draws on both contemporary sources and the excellent summary published by Euell A. Nielsen, "Anna Maria Weems (1840–?)," Black Past, March 19, 2016, https://www.blackpast.org/african-american-history/weems-anna-maria-1840/.

54 Freeman, "The Weems Family," 1.

55 Weems's practice of cross-dressing as a man to flee bondage followed other widely noted escapes, like Ellen Craft's escape dressed as her husband's enslaver in 1848. There was also

Clarissa Davis of Virginia, who boarded a New England–bound boat clothed as a man; and Mary Millburn, who stole aboard a ship attired as a man. See Barbara McCaskill's "'Yours Very Truly': Ellen Craft—The Fugitive Text and Artifact," *African American Review* 28 (1994): 509–29. McCaskill's fuller treatment of the lives of William and Ellen Craft appears in her *Love, Liberation, and Escaping Slavery: William and Ellen Craft in Cultural Memory* (Athens: University of Georgia Press, 2015).

56 Nielsen, "Anna Maria Weems (1840–?)."

57 Freeman, "The Weems Family," 1.

58 Rochester Ladies' Anti-Slavery Society Papers, Folder 5, Box 2, Manuscripts Division, William L. Clements Library, University of Michigan, Ann Arbor.

59 Box 1, John Hill Wheeler MSS.

60 Box 1, John Hill Wheeler MSS.

61 Box 1, John Hill Wheeler MSS.

Chapter 20: The Life and Times of Hannah Vincent

1 Lee Miller, phone conversations, November 11, 14, and 16, and December 7, 2011. Letter to Horace Craft, August 27, 1857, in the possession of Lee Miller, Cortland County, N.Y.

2 NYCC Papers MSS.

3 New York State Census 1855, Selected U.S. Federal Census Non-Population Schedules, 1850–1880, Census Year 1860, Taylor, N.Y., Cortland County.

4 Schedule Type: Agriculture, Line 34, p. 5, Roll 21, Archive Collection Number A21, Census Year 1870, Taylor, N.Y., Cortland County.

5 Box 1, John Hill Wheeler MSS.

6 Douglass's escape depended upon his borrowing a "sailor's pass" to portray himself as a freeborn mariner. If not a direct pass from his "master," the document allowed him to take public conveyances, although close scrutiny might have revealed that Douglass did not match the description given on the pass. Good fortune was necessary. In the narrative he shared after his escape, Douglass keeps all the details about the pass and his travel secret. See Douglass, *Narrative*, chap. 11.

7 Joseph H. Morgan, *Morgan's History of the New Jersey Conference of the A.M.E. Church, from 1872 to 1887* (Camden, N.J.: S. Chew, 1887), 65.

8 1860 United States Federal Census, Ward 10 East District, Philadelphia, Pa., NARA; 1870 United States Federal Census, 2nd Ward, Burlington, New Jersey, NARA; *Burlington County Directory for 1876–77 Containing the Names of the Inhabitants of Bordentown, Burlington and Mount Holly, Together with a Business Directory of Burlington County and Much Useful Miscellaneous Information* (Burlington, N.J.: James Shaw, 1876), 141; 1880 United States Federal Census, 2nd Ward, Burlington, New Jersey, NARA; 1885 New Jersey State Census, 2nd Ward, Burlington, New Jersey, New Jersey State Archives, Trenton; 1895 New Jersey State Census 2nd Ward, Burlington, New Jersey, New Jersey State Archives, Trenton; *Boyd's Directory of Burlington County New Jersey, 1905–1906* (Philadelphia: C. E. Howe, 1905), 146.

9 "Hannah Ann Vincent," p. 11b, Roll 443, 1850 United States Federal Census, Burlington, New Jersey, Burlington County; and "Hannah Ann Vincent," New York State Census 1855, various county clerk offices. See Baym, "The Case for Hannah Vincent," 315–31.

10 William C. Kashatus, *William Still: The Underground Railroad and the Angel at Philadelphia* (Notre Dame, Ind.: Notre Dame University Press, 2021), 148.

11 Kashatus, *William Still*, 21. For more information on New Jersey's Underground Railroad history, see William J. Switala, *The Underground Railroad in New York and New Jersey* (Mechanicsburg, Pa.: Stackpole Books, 2006); Dennis Rizzo, *Parallel Communities: The Underground Railroad in South Jersey* (New York: History Press, 2008); James J. Gigantino Jr., *The Ragged Road to Abolition: Slavery and Freedom in New Jersey, 1775–1865* (Philadelphia: University of Pennsylvania Press, 2015); and Giles R. Wright and Edward L. Wonkeryor, "Steal Away, Steal Away . . .": *A Guide to the Underground Railroad in New Jersey* (Trenton: New Jersey Historical Commission, 2002), 4–9.

12 Peter Quire to Edward Giles et al., December 15, 1829, G3:389, Deeds, Burlington County, New Jersey, Burlington County Clerk's Office, Mount Holly, N.J., cited in Guy Weston, "New Jersey: A State Divided on Freedom," *Afro-American Historical and Genealogical Society (AAHGS) Journal* 34 (2017): 3.

13 Weston, "New Jersey: A State Divided on Freedom," 3.

14 Morgan, *Morgan's History of the New Jersey Conference of the A.M.E. Church*, 65.

15 1860 United States Federal Census, Ward 10 East District, Philadelphia, Pa.

16 *New Jersey Mirror* (Burlington), April 15, 1858, 3.

17 Morgan, *Morgan's History of the New Jersey Conference of the A.M.E. Church*, 65.

18 1870 United States Federal Census, 2nd Ward, Burlington, New Jersey.

19 "New Jersey Deaths and Burials, 1720–1971," Index, FamilySearch, Salt Lake City, Utah, 2009, 2010; 1880 United States Federal Census, 2nd Ward Burlington, New Jersey. The 1880 Federal Census shows Hannah Vincent owning the house at 191 Lawrence Street.

20 *Boyd's Directory of Burlington County New Jersey, 1905*, 146.

21 William L. Andrews, "Hannah Crafts's Sense of an Ending," in Gates and Robbins, eds., *In Search of Hannah Crafts*, 36.

22 Jacobs, *Incidents in the Life of a Slave Girl*, 243.

23 Andrews, "Hannah Crafts's Sense of an Ending," 39.

24 Bibb, *Narrative of the Life and Adventures of Henry Bibb*, 105. See William L. Andrews's masterful discussion of Bibb in *Slavery and Class in the American South* (New York: Oxford University Press, 2020).

25 Bibb, *Narrative of the Life and Adventures of Henry Bibb*, 191.

26 Hilary Mantel, "The Shape of Absence," *London Review of Books*, August 8, 2002, reprinted in Gates and Robbins, eds., *In Search of Hannah Crafts*, 429.

27 William L. Andrews, email message to author, September 24, 2022.

28 Elizabeth McHenry, *Forgotten Readers: Recovering the Lost History of African American Literary Societies* (Durham, N.C.: Duke University Press, 2002), 12.

29 1885 New Jersey State Census, 2nd Ward, Burlington, New Jersey.

30 1910 New Jersey State Census, 2nd Ward, Burlington, New Jersey, New Jersey State Archives, Trenton.

31 1930 United States Federal Census, 2nd Ward, Burlington, New Jersey, NARA.

32 1905 New Jersey State Census, 2nd Ward, Burlington, New Jersey, New Jersey State Archives, Trenton.

33 "Frank Lazerele," December 16, 1932, Burlington County, New Jersey, Death Index, 1814–2010. Ancestry.com, Lehi, UT, USA: Ancestry.com Operations, 2011.

34 Emily Driscoll to Dorothy Porter [Wesley], September 27, 1951, Box 22, DPW Papers MSS.

Epilogue

1 "Wheeler–Slave Cabin" folder, Murfreesboro Historical Association Archives, Murfreesboro, North Carolina.

2 Margaret Worthington interview by the author, November 18–19, 2014, Wilmington, N.C.

3 Isabel Wilkerson, *Caste: The Origins of Our Discontent* (New York: Random House, 2020), 46–47.

4 W. E. B. Du Bois, *Black Reconstruction* (New York: Harcourt, Brace and Company, 1935), 727.

5 "Augustine Pugh, Bertie County," *Calypso* departing Norfolk, Virginia, April 3, 1819, Slave Manifests of Coastwise Vessels Filed at New Orleans, Louisiana, 1807–1860, Microfilm Roll 1, Microfilm Serial M1895, NARA microfilm publication M1895, NARA. James Barefoot is listed as "Jacob" in the inventory, a name his enslavers came to use for him, although he seems to have been "James Barefoot" among the other captives.

6 William Hill Pugh, "Pugh Family," in *The Life and Letters of Charles Francis de Ganahl Collected by His Wife for Their Children*, vol. 2 (New York: Richard B. Smith, 1949). See also David Cecelski, "The Voyage to Bayou Lafourche," *David Cecelski* (blog), February10, 2021, https://davidceelski.com/2021/02/10/the-voyage-to-bayou-lafourche/.

7 "Henry W. Connor," 1860 United States Federal Census, Slave Schedule, Lincoln County, North Carolina. Eighty captives are listed on Connor's plantation, including women whose ages match what can be reconstructed for Milly and Martha Murfree.

8 1880 United States Federal Census, Davidson, N.C., Iredell County, NARA.

9 *Turner's Charlotte City Directory, 1891–92* (Charlotte, N.C.: E. F. Turner and Company), 140.

10 "Death Certificate for Lethia McKey," July 19, 1917, Mecklenburg County, Charlotte, North Carolina, North Carolina State Board of Health, Bureau of Vital Statistics, Roll 7, Microfilm S.123, North Carolina Death Certificates, North Carolina State Archives, Raleigh.

11 James Graham to William Alexander Graham, April 21, 1850, *The Papers of William Alexander Graham*, Volume 3: *1845–1850*, ed. J. G. de Roulhac Hamilton (Raleigh: North Carolina State Office of Archives and History, 1960), 320–21.

12 "James Graham," Estate Records, North Carolina, U.S., Wills and Probate Records, 1665–1998, Lincoln, North Carolina, "Goodson, Aaron-Graham, R.C.," 1824–1964; 1772–1964; 1735–1914, North Carolina State Archives, Raleigh.

13 "James Graham," Slave Schedule, 1860 United States Federal Census, Lincoln County, North Carolina.

14 *Charlotte Democrat*, January 19, 1858, 3.

INDEX

Entries in *italics* refer to illustrations.
Enslaved people with no surnames are listed by first name with household in parenthesis.

ABBREVIATIONS:

ESW - Ellen Sully Wheeler
Hannah - protagonist of *The Bondwoman's Narrative*
Hannah Sr. - mother of Hannah Bond Crafts Vincent
HBC - Hannah Bond Crafts (author of *Bondwoman's Narrative*)
JHW - John Hill Wheeler
SJW - Dr. Samuel Jordan Wheeler